GEORDIE PASSION

The Thrills and Spills of
Newcastle United 1969-1996

Mark Hannen

Ken

Very Best Wishes

Mark

(July 1996)

Keepdate Publishing

Published by Keepdate Publishing Ltd,
21 Portland Terrace, Jesmond,
Newcastle upon Tyne NE2 1QQ.

This revised edition published June 1996

ISBN 1 899506 20 9

Designed and typeset by
Keepdate Publishing Ltd, Newcastle upon Tyne.

INTRODUCTION

Geordie Passion is a chronicle of my lifetime devotion to Newcastle United Football Club. From early childhood to present day it is a story encompassing all the emotions a football fan lives through ranging from delirious excitement to anger and sorrow.

It's not just a simple record of Newcastle's games over the years, but a personal diary of all the highs and lows they have brought, together with tales of real life experiences; some humorous, some frightening. It is also a tale of someone totally immersed in football that will appeal not only to the Geordie public but to all football fans, regardless of whom they support.

Geordies are a unique breed and their, and my, love of football is manifested throughout the diary. Geordie Passion is written from the heart and incorporates all of life's emotions as no other sport can do.

THE AUTHOR

Mark Hannen was born in Newcastle upon Tyne on 26th August 1961, the same day Newcastle United beat Preston North End 1-0! After spending his early years in Stanley, Co Durham, the family moved to Ponteland, on the outskirts of Newcastle, in 1967. Educated at Ponteland Middle and High Schools he went on to obtain a degree in Sport Studies from Newcastle Polytechnic before moving to Leeds in December 1983 to commence employment with the English Basketball Association for whom he still works today. The family home remains in Ponteland.

With sincere thanks to Tracey, and my father, for their help, support and assistance, in bringing this publication to fruition.

Dedicated To My Mother

CONTENTS

FOREWORD

I am delighted to write this foreword to *Geordie Passion*, a book that encapsulates the very essence of what being a football supporter is all about – a dedicated passion for the team, a feeling I still retain today.

Hailing from Perth, Scotland, I joined Newcastle United in 1960 when Charlie Mitten was United's manager. I was immediately struck by the warmth of the Tyneside community, and it is no exaggeration to say that its passion for football, and of course Newcastle United, is second to none. Charlie Mitten left the club a year later, and after Norman Smith kept the hot seat warm for one season, Joe Harvey, the single biggest influence on my career, took over the managerial position.

As a player I experienced the highlight of lifting the Inter Cities Fairs Cup back in 1969, and the pleasure of leading the team to Wembley in 1974, and it is fitting that *Geordie Passion* now reflects in the current success of the club in the FA Premiership.

Mark Hannen's *Geordie Passion* begins at approximately the same time as that exiting Fairs Cup evening in Budapest, 27 years ago, and it captures the full spectrum of emotions a football supporter lives through. It is also a captivating story of Mark's life, from his early childhood to the present day, chronicling many of the great matches over the years, the players and managers who have graced St. James' Park, and also his personal thoughts and feelings which I am certain are shared by Geordies all over the world.

I myself can easily relate to the feelings Mark has documented. The book is written from the heart with a passion typical of a genuine Geordie football supporter.

Newcastle United have had more low points than high points in the past three decades, and it is fantastic to see the team now doing so well under the astute guidance of Sir John Hall and Kevin Keegan. Long may it continue.

Enjoy the read, I certainly did so myself.

Bob Moncur.

Bob Moncur
Captain, Newcastle United, 1967-1974.

IN THE BEGINNING

I will never be able to thank my parents enough for the words 'Newcastle upon Tyne' being written on my birth certificate. The fact that both of them are Welsh meant nothing to me and I suppose it was only through the grace of God that my father's Ministerial duties took him firstly away from Swansea, to his training in Cambridge, and then up to the North East of England and Stanley to the Presbyterian Church where he was to be the Minister.

The point about my place of birth (Princess Mary's Maternity Hospital in Jesmond, Newcastle upon Tyne) is that it gave me my true Geordie roots which, apart from the unique footballing tradition, make me both proud and lucky to be a son of Newcastle upon Tyne. You hear of parents (usually fathers) ensuring that their children are born in Newcastle even if they are living away from Tyneside at the time, a practice I certainly approve of. I was also delighted to find out that Newcastle United had won 1-0 at Preston North End on the day I was born (26th August 1961) which undoubtedly gave me the perfect start in life.

Through all my years of watching my beloved Newcastle United I can say without hesitation that there are no other supporters in Britain who can match the Geordies for their loyal, vociferous, passionate and undying support for their team. Football is embedded in the Geordie culture and many say runs in the blood – I can't argue with that and I am truly grateful to have Geordie Passion in my heart.

THE EARLY DAYS

England won the World Cup in 1966 when we were still in Stanley, and to be honest I cannot remember a thing about the greatest day in English Football history, since I was only four at the time. A shame really, but Mum and Dad watched the game on our little black and white television and I'm told I behaved myself fairly well during the match without realising its significance. Brother John was six at the time and he may just have been able to grasp the importance of Kenneth Wolstenhome's commentary – something I came to despair of in future years, but more of that later. Of course I've watched repeats of this match on numerous occasions in more recent years and it still brings a lump to my throat. Had I been older I can imagine how gutted I would have been when Weber scored the equaliser in the last minute, which could have denied England their greatest moment, and I also wonder how Geoff Hurst's life might have turned out if the Swiss referee had stopped play when the pitch was invaded rather than let the West Ham forward run on to complete his hat-trick. Inevitably, there is also the fond memory of the late Bobby Moore hauling himself up the steps of the Royal Box, wiping his dirty hands on his shirt as he approached the Queen, to lift the most treasured trophy in football.

I'm afraid my formative footballing years are rather difficult to recall. I'm told that some sort of a ball was never far away from me, even kicking a balloon around the house would suffice, and having parents who both enjoyed sport and encouraged me must have been a major influence throughout childhood.

Back to ministerial matters and May 1967 saw the family re-located to Darras Hall, Ponteland (where we still live today) where Dad took charge of the Ponteland Presbyterian Church. Strangely enough I can still remember our first day in Ponteland very vividly, if only for the reason that I recall walking towards our neighbour's house by mistake, thinking it was ours – funny how you remember the oddest things. Ponteland is approximately eight miles north-west of Newcastle, a mile or so past Newcastle International Airport, but perhaps more importantly, perfectly situated to easily reach St. James' Park. Anyway, Ponteland was to be the launching pad for football to become the dominant factor in my life, and I wouldn't have had it any other way.

1969/70 – THE FORMATIVE YEARS

August 16th 1969 was a milestone in my life as it marked my first ever visit to St. James' Park. I remember having taken a real interest in the team down the road that played in black and white striped shirts the previous year, when the exploits of Bobby Moncur and Wyn Davies had brought the Inter Cities Fairs Cup back to Newcastle. This itself was a remarkable achievement, since qualification for the tournament was gained by finishing in only 10th position in the First Division at the end of the 1967/68 season; entry had been granted by the then 'one city one club' rule which elevated us above other higher placed clubs whose big city neighbours had already qualified for the competition.

Riding on the wave of this good fortune a somewhat naive but exhilarating Newcastle United, backed by passionate crowds at St. James' Park which reached 60,000 for the semi-final and final ties, incredibly, on their first venture into Europe, defeated six of Europe's best to put themselves on the European roll of Honour – a proud fact indeed. My brother John, who attended Walbottle Grammar School, (situated on the A69 on the outskirts of Newcastle) was later to tell me the story that had become legend and had been passed down to each new year in the school. It centred upon the 2nd leg of the semi-final against Glasgow Rangers at St. James' Park. Thousands of marauding Scots descended on Tyneside and their route from Glasgow took many of them past the school. Well, you can imagine that a number of 'welcoming committees' were organised, as they said at the time, to 'defend our patch' against the Scottish invaders. Needless to say not all the vehicles passing the school that afternoon got past in one piece. For the record Newcastle won 2-0 (which was also the aggregate score) before beating the Hungarians Ujpest Dozsa 6-2 on aggregate in the final.

The start of a new season was eagerly anticipated, especially as there would be a European Trophy to defend. Having a birthday in August was helpful as it meant I could pester Dad to take me (and John) to my first ever football match as a birthday treat. Dad had been to St. James' Park in the past but you could never have described him as a passionate supporter of the club, more of a general football fan and connoisseur of the game. I often wonder what would have become of my life had he 'accidentally' taken me to Roker Park to see Sunderland for my first game – the very idea doesn't bear thinking about!

16/08/69 – NEWCASTLE v MANCHESTER CITY (1-0)

The season had started the previous week with a defeat at West Ham followed by a home midweek fixture with Sheffield Wednesday. Unfortunately evening games were out of the question in those days, even though it was school holidays. So to the Saturday, when Manchester City were due at St. James' Park. I didn't know that much about them, other than Dad telling me that they had won the FA Cup at Wembley three months earlier although the likes of Francis Lee, Mike Summerbee and Colin Bell, such a graceful player, were, even then, household names. I knew I would be going to the match in a few days and each day leading up to the game made me more excited. I didn't have a scarf in those days so quite what I was wearing to my first match was anybody's guess. This was also John's first match; the fact that he'd not been before, I think, said more about the greater inner feeling and love for football that I had, even at such a young age.

We tended to arrive at least an hour before the game for a variety of reasons, not least to ensure a good place on the terrace. In my time of supporting the club my arrival inside the ground has ranged from 90 minutes before the start (in the mid/early 1970s when it was the in-thing to do) to five minutes before kick off which is the fashion these days, especially with season tickets being the order of the day. There is of course the exception to this rule when you got in early to savour the big match atmosphere. In those days children went through the turnstiles with their parents with Dad saying 'one and two halves please' – how times have changed. In the early days we always watched from the Centre Paddock section of the ground which enabled the youngsters like myself to either sit on the barriers, aided by a fatherly arm or, better still, to go right down to the front of the terracing and sit on the wall with your feet on the dirt track surrounding the pitch. In this position you were incredibly close to the action and could see the distinctive topography of the Newcastle pitch which rose as it went to the middle before dropping to a lower level in front of the Popular (now East Stand) side. The strange phenomenon I encountered when watching the game was that when play was on the far side of the pitch you couldn't see the ball or the ankles and feet of the players – most off putting. It was a thrill also to get as close to the tunnel as possible to see the players running out onto the field with the powerful smell of liniment rushing up your nostrils as they passed by. If you couldn't get next to the tunnel then you had to rely on looking across the pitch to the Popular side – when they started cheering you knew Bobby Moncur was leading the team out because they could see right down the tunnel. Also, I always preferred the opposition to come out first so the atmosphere was that little bit more intense to greet the arrival of my heroes, nowadays both teams come out side by side so that little pleasure is denied me!

And so to the game. How enjoyable it was to get a winning start. A Bryan 'Pop' Robson penalty early in the first half was enough to seal the points in front of a massive crowd of 47,000. Quite what I made of it all I can never be really sure – all I can be certain about was that I was as happy as a sand-boy when we left the ground to go home despite the fact that we had got a real soaking midway through the first half after the heavens opened and drenched the shirt-sleeved crowd.

Today was also a significant day in that it marked the first appearance of *Shoot!* magazine, probably the most well known of all the football weeklies that have been on the market in my lifetime. From the first issue I collected every copy and used to have them piled up on my bedroom floor, at one stage the pile was nearly five foot high and in danger of toppling over. The magazine, in its early days, and indeed up until the mid 1980s, was a superb read with many top columnists (Moore, Keegan, Bremner to name but three) contributing to its quality. Sadly, as more magazines began to flood the market, and the youth culture changed, it degenerated into a more glossy publication, with far less quality reading material. As a result I now stick solely to *World Soccer* magazine, the leader in its field.

I can't leave the subject of magazines without mention of *Tiger and Scorcher*, which in fact was a comic. It's not published anymore, but I am sure most football fans are aware of the exploits of Roy of the Rovers (Roy Race of Melchester Rovers) who featured in the comic – a real boyhood hero. There was also Hot Shot Hamish, the story of a Scottish centre forward who, believe or not, packed a dynamic shot in his boots, and finally, my favourite, Billy's Boots. This was the story of a schoolboy who acquired a pair of football boots once used by the legendary Dead Shot Kean, and it enabled

Billy, an ordinary player without this special pair of boots, to become an outstanding player when he wearing the boots. The stories each week were tremendously enjoyable and I used to eagerly look forward to each Saturday morning, when the comic was published, to read the next instalment of Billy's life. Many a time Billy would lose the boots somewhere, find them in the nick of time, and proceed to score a brilliant hat-trick in the local Schools Cup Final. During the summer months, Billy incredibly managed to get hold of a pair of Kean's cricket boots too, which, believe it or not, did the same for him on the cricket field. All in all a brilliant read and next time I see my former school friend Mark Johnson, I must remember to ask him for all the copies of the comic he has as I am certain I would still thoroughly enjoy reading the stories today, some 20 years on from their inception.

30/10/69 – NEWCASTLE v ARSENAL (3-1)

I often wonder, looking back all those years, just how committed a supporter of the club I was at such a tender age. Did I really know what it meant to support Newcastle United? Was I aware of how much winning meant, and did I feel the enormous disappointment of defeat? If I'm truthful I would suspect not, as I was satisfied with the thrill of actually being at a live football match and enjoying each occasion for what it was.

Even in those days you knew all the best players in the country even though the media coverage was not nearly as comprehensive as it is in the 1990s. No satellite television or dedicated sports channel on the radio but, instead, there were football stickers that you could collect in sweet packets and, of course, the renowned Esso Petrol Football Collections – certainly in those days every garage stop had to be at an Esso Station, nothing else was acceptable.

Arsenal were the visitors to St. James' Park for the second match I was privileged to see. Mum had knitted me a marvellous black and white woollen scarf (which I've still got today) and over the years made me numerous bobble hats and rosettes. I was told that the Londoners were a formidable side (who were to go on and complete the prized League and Cup double the following season) but on this day, despite the presence of John Radford and Charlie George spearheading their attack, they were despatched back to London pointless on the wrong end of a 3-1 scoreline.

One thing about Arsenal that bugs me is when people refer to them as 'The' Arsenal, I thought they were just plain Arsenal but maybe that's just me! One of the scorers that day was Alan Foggon who I always remember as a 'right fatso'. I would ask Dad how people like that could ever play football and he'd say 'if they've got the skill to play the game that's really all that counts'. Foggon also scored in the Fairs Cup triumph earlier in the year, so he can't have been that bad! Even today I can't think of many overweight players who have made a good living from the game, although Mick (Sumo) Quinn and John Robertson (formerly of Nottingham Forest) do come to mind!

26/12/69 – NEWCASTLE v LEEDS UNITED (2-1)

My first footballing Christmas soon followed with the present that every football-daft child ever wanted – a complete Newcastle strip, not just the shirt, as people tend to buy these days, but shorts and socks as well. How proud I was to put it on. Wyn Davies, our famous Welsh goal scoring centre forward, was my favourite player then, so naturally enough that's who I was every time I wore the strip. I was also the proud owner of a Newcastle United sports bag with a picture of big Wyn emblazoned on the front. I used it mainly for school and today, the same bag is still lying in the bottom of my cupboard at home, somewhat worse for wear but it will never be disposed of.

Apart from Sunderland, Leeds were our nearest rivals, hence the Boxing Day fixture. I was thrilled to be a part of an incredible 54,000 crowd and even more ecstatic to witness a 2-1 home win against probably the top side in the country at that time. Needless to say Wyn Davies scored one of the goals with 'Pop' Robson scoring the other. The victory moved us up to 12th place in the division which was respectable if nothing more, our minds were on the defence of the Inter Cities Fairs Cup and that really was all that mattered for the remainder of the season.

18/03/70 – NEWCASTLE v ANDERLECHT (3-1)

I wasn't allowed to go to the match against Anderlecht, due to having to go to school the next day, which was a bitter disappointment. It was a second leg quarter-final tie in the Fairs Cup and, having lost the 1st leg 2-0 in Belgium, it was clear that a tough task awaited the team. Incredibly, a 3-0 winning lead was built up until a goal in the last minute by Nordahl for the visitors took them through on the away goals rule. What was this strange rule (which ironically would rear its ugly head again in Bilbao in November 1994) that meant elimination from the competition? I certainly didn't understand it, despite Dad trying to explain to me how two teams could score the same number of goals yet one of them could still lose.

14/04/70 – NEWCASTLE v COVENTRY CITY (4-0)

A sparkling way to round off the season. A week earlier we had smashed five past a shell shocked Manchester United, 'Pop' Robson scoring a hat-trick, and we continued in this rich vein of form against Coventry scoring four without reply. Nearly 33,000 Geordies cheered the team to the hilt and it was a marvellous way to round of the first year of my love affair with the club.

14/06/70 – ENGLAND v WEST GERMANY (2-3)

As I developed an insatiable taste for football I was beginning to learn that Newcastle United weren't the only team that I wanted to win. For instance it would be quite nice for England to succeed again in the World Cup. We didn't have a colour television in those days so the family were very fortunate to be invited round to the Nixons (Church members who obviously were good friends of the family) to watch the match on a large screen colour television. What a thrill. England took a 2-0 lead but then it all went wrong as the Germans pulled it back to 2-2 at full time. It was a match we should have won. Bobby Charlton had been substituted by Alf Ramsey, to 'save his legs' for the semi-final, but possibly, the real reason why we didn't end up winning the game after 90 minutes was, in some people's opinion, the presence of Peter Bonetti in goal rather than the incomparable Gordon Banks who had mysteriously been taken ill before the game. You can never tell but you felt had Banks been playing it would have been a different story – Uwe Seeler's looping back header to give the Germans their equaliser was a bizarre goal and the hapless Bonetti could only look on in horror as the ball hit the back of the net. Worse was to follow in more ways than one because for some reason, and I can't remember why, we inexplicably left the Nixons to go home.

I was devastated! Why, when extra time was about to commence, did we have to leave? I remember leaving the house very reluctantly which of course looking back wasn't the most gracious thing to have done. Unfortunately, England contrived to lose the game in extra time to a Gerd Muller volley and I can't even recall if I managed to watch our demise in black and white.

Earlier in the competition England and Brazil had played out a marvellous match memorable for the contest between Pele and Bobby Moore and of course the breathtaking save Gordon Banks made from Pele's header. Brazil were the team everybody wanted to watch. From Felix in goal, through the likes of Tostao, Jairzinho and Rivelino, they exuded class and played the game in a beautiful free flowing manner that was a joy to behold. It goes without saying that my video collection contains the BBC 'The Boys from Brazil' tape – absolutely brilliant.

1969/70 – Season's Summary

League	P	W	D	L	F	A	Pts.	Pos.
	42	17	13	12	57	35	47	7th

Top Scorers		
Bryan Robson	25
Keith Dyson	12
Wyn Davies	11

1970/71 – ITALIAN GLORY, HUNGARIAN DESPAIR

The summer couldn't pass quickly enough. I wasn't that interested in traditional summer sports such as cricket and golf yet, although that was to change within a couple of years, and so the dawn of a new football season was the one thing to really look forward to.

We were fortunate to have a large field backing on to our house and you would lose count of the number of games we played from morning till dusk in the school holidays, pausing only for the statutory lunch and tea breaks. All our friends from the estate would congregate at our house for the games, and it was always our ball with which we played. Even when John and I weren't actually playing ourselves, for whatever reason, the doorbell would ring and someone would be asking for our ball to play with. The favourite ball of the day was the orange (as opposed to white) Wembley Trophy football which even when it burst was quite easy to repair by using a hot knife and melting the plastic over the hole as I'm sure many other people did. We also had those plastic black and white panelled balls which used to have the names of every First Division team on – sadly they just don't do things like that these days! Other enjoyable playing 'venues' of the day included grassy areas at Pinegarth, Dunsgreen and Whinfell with only Dunsgreen still there today. No-one had any set playing positions and we tended to play all over the pitch; retrieving, defending, passing and best of all, scoring. I also quite fancied myself as a goalkeeper on occasions and used to love diving around the goal mouth, turning shots away at full stretch – getting absolutely covered in layers of mud was half the fun! Goal posts were jumpers or jackets and there would be the inevitable arguments about shots that went over the post as to whether they counted as goals or not. I was always good at keeping the score, and matches tended to be played until the first team scored 20, with 10 being half time and change of ends. I was predominantly right footed but was able to use my left foot as well whereas John was almost all left footed and displayed those characteristics typical of such players. All in all we were very lucky to have a grass field to play on (unlike many children today) without any interruption and so close to home too.

26/08/70 – NEWCASTLE v NOTTINGHAM FOREST (1-1)

Nottingham Forest were the visitors to St. James' Park on my ninth birthday. By now it wasn't just John and I who went to the matches – Dad took our friends as well. Looking back I'm indebted to his kindness in not just looking after me but my footballing friends too. This game was the first evening match I'd been to, and for some reason they had a different and special sort of atmosphere compared to the regular 3.00pm kick offs. Obviously the floodlights play a part in this but there's still that extra little ingredient you can't put your finger on that makes them stand out. A second half goal from our imposing centre back John McNamee gave us a point which, for a birthday present, was obviously better than nothing. It was only our third point of the season, out of a possible eight, and a position of 18th in the division wasn't exactly the start the club would have wished for. I don't think league positions meant that much to me then, as opposed to today when I can study the league tables for a good half an hour or more, more often than not whilst soaking in the bath! I think I also took the fact that we were an established First Division team for granted, after all I had never known anything else, and, looking back, I was lucky to have such an upbringing in the game.

30/09/70 – NEWCASTLE v INTER MILAN (2-0)

Inter Milan (Internazionale to give them their proper name), the world famous Italian side, were on Tyneside for a second leg Fairs Cup First Round match. Their team contained a number of players who had starred for Italy in the Mexico World Cup in the summer, and the likes of Facchetti, an uncompromising defender, and Boninsegna, a fleet footed incisive forward, were household names. In the first leg in Milan we had gained an admirable draw, and so in front of a packed St. James' Park, of which I was one of the lucky 56,000, we started the game as favourites to progress into Round Two. I distinctly remember us playing in red shirts as the Italians wore black and blue stripes and it was the custom in European competitions for the home team to change their kit in the event of a colour clash. Dad told me the Italians had a reputation for being both negative and dirty and he wasn't wrong. They kicked us, pulled shirts and tried every trick in the book to put us off our game. As I hadn't seen that many matches I was outraged by their behaviour and was quick to join in the booing of the Italians with just about everyone else in the ground. The flashpoint in the game came when Wyn Davies challenged their goalkeeper, Vieri, in the penalty box, and in the ensuing melee the keeper ended up punching the referee, knocking him to the ground. We all roared our disapproval and the result was inevitable: Vieri was sent off and Inter were down to 10 men. I remember the police having to come onto the pitch on a few occasions to calm things down, such was the total indiscipline of the Italians. A goal apiece from Davies and Moncur (who always seemed to score on the big occasions) saw us through and the Italians were sent packing back to Milan in disgrace.

I remember how when England played World Cup qualifiers against Italy in the mid to late seventies I hated the Italians, hatchet man Gentile in particular, which I'm sure was caused by my memories of this game. Later in life though I mellowed and came to love the likes of Antognoni, Bettega, Conti and Rossi. Bettega's goal against Argentina in 1978, after playing a neat one-two with Rossi, was a thrilling moment, Rossi's goal scoring exploits in Spain four years later are legendary whilst I will never forget the look of sheer delight on Marco Tardelli's face after he had scored the second goal against the Germans in the Final at Madrid's Bernabeu Stadium. More recently I've come to admire Roberto Baggio, who is my all time favourite foreign player, eclipsing even Pele and Cruyff, but Peter Beardsley will always be my greatest ever hero – an embodiment of everything that football stands for, on and off the field. I'd followed Baggio's career in Italy from his early days at Fiorentina before his transfer to Juventus, and his wonder goal in Italia '90 against Czechoslovakia sent me into raptures so much so that the video tape I keep of that moment must be virtually worn through! The superb solo goal he scored shortly before his departure from Fiorentina, when he picked up the ball just outside his own penalty area and proceeded to beat what seemed like the whole of the Napoli team, before walking the ball into the net, was sheer class and must rank as one of the all time great goals.

Having overcome the might of Inter Milan in Round One, the relative unknowns of Pecsi Dozsa were our second round opponents. We took what looked like a comfortable 2-0 lead to Hungary, but at the end of 90 minutes the scores were level. Thirty minutes of extra time saw no change and so a penalty shoot out was required to find the winner. Unbelievably, Newcastle missed their first three kicks (Robson, Mitchell and Gibb being the guilty men) and with Pecsi scoring all their kicks it must have ranked as one of the quickest penalty shoot outs of all time. The players couldn't get off the pitch quickly enough (a combination of desperate disappointment and shame?) and a couple of players, goalkeeper Willie McFaul and left back Frank Clark, had to be dragged back onto the pitch from the dressing rooms to complete the requisite five penalties. They were the unlikeliest of penalty takers but ironically enough they both scored!

31/10/70 – NEWCASTLE v MANCHESTER UNITED (1-0)

Glamour club Manchester United were the visitors to Tyneside at the end of October. I was young enough at the time to think this until later in life when I came to understand what Manchester United and their followers really stood for. Obviously the fact that they have supporters all over the world dates back to the Munich air disaster in 1958 and the sympathy they rightly received as a result of that harrowing experience – what it doesn't account for is the number of people all over Britain who attach themselves to the club. Why for example is there an Alnwick (a village in Northumberland) branch of the Manchester United supporters club, made up of north eastern people? You can sum up their supporters in a word by simply looking at the 1994 FA Cup Final when, despite having at least 7,000 more supporters in the stadium than Chelsea, they were out-sung by the Londoners, and they won the game 4-0! Just imagine what it would have been like if the Geordies had won 4-0 at Wembley. No doubt you have also heard the record that Manchester United released to mark their end of season successes in the Premier League and FA Cup in May 1994 – how it got to number one in the charts is beyond me – and didn't it just make you cringe when you heard it? Their follow up Wembley song in April 1995, fronted by an appallingly bad local 'rap' artist, was even worse.

Staying on the Manchester United theme reminds me of one of my most galling and embarrassing memories. At Junior School, which incidentally was literally 50 yards from home, we were all classified in house groups. Being a Northumberland School we had four 'houses', each with a name of a Northumbrian Saint;

Aidan, Bede, Cuthbert and Oswald. Each house had their own colour and when I landed up in Cuthbert it meant that red was our colour. You can probably guess the rest; when the inter-house football matches came round we all played for our houses and were forced, yes forced, to wear red shirts and to make it worse someone had produced a few actual Manchester United shirts to wear. Even today I can remember my displeasure at having to do this and can vividly remember losing the final to Aidan in the last few minutes. I can even remember it was my error that cost us the match, some memories never fade away.

Manchester United had a number of world class players in their team in 1970 and to actually be able to see in the flesh the likes of Best, Charlton and Law was fantastic. There are some matches that stand out as 'big' games and certainly Newcastle versus Manchester United is up there with the best of them. Grudgingly, I must admit that, at the moment, they are the biggest and most glamorous club in Britain but their glory-seeking followers, spread all round the country, can never be described as true football supporters.

Much to the joy of everyone on Tyneside, Newcastle won by the only goal of the game, scored by that man Wyn Davies again. It was only our fourth victory of the season (from 15 games) which said a lot about our typically inconsistent form. Little would change throughout the 1970s; brilliant one week and woefully inept the next. Within minutes of arriving home we were straight out to the field to play football reliving all the action we had witnessed earlier in the afternoon. This was to become a ritual after every home match especially as all the excitement of the day was still with us and the goals we had seen (hopefully) were still fresh in our mind. Sadly, building work started in the field in 1973 and life after that was never quite the same as house plots started appearing all over the place until eventually all the lovely green grass disappeared. I remember in particular, round about the time of the FA Cup sixth round replays with Nottingham Forest in March 1974, when there was literally only enough space to play a little game of three or four a-side with house foundations lying all around us. This is a particular bone of contention and I'm sure one that is universally shared – fewer places to play, leading to fewer opportunities for kids to kick a ball around, which ultimately leads to less quality and, possibly even worse, less interest in the game which for the long term health of football could be very damaging. It's sad today to see the youths of the 1990s playing computer games rather than indulging in some outdoor pursuit even if it's not football.

08/05/71 – ARSENAL v LIVERPOOL (2-1)

Arsenal versus Liverpool was the first FA Cup Final I can remember taking a real interest in and needless to say, I've not missed one since. We were again fortunate to be guests at the house of some friends to enable us to see the match in colour. On this occasion the Massinghams were our kind hosts and we managed to stay for the full 120 minutes and see Charlie George sink Liverpool with his famous winner, followed by his even more famous celebratory lie on the pitch.

My life of following Newcastle United in the FA Cup didn't start particularly well – we were supposedly legendary Cup fighters, a legacy of our success in the early 1950s, but in the previous two seasons we had crashed out at the third round stage to Southampton and Ipswich which didn't seem a particularly good effort to put it mildly. I had even wondered who we had beaten in Rounds One and Two to reach the third round until I became better educated! Little did I know that even worse ignominies were to come in the FA Cup the following season.

1970/71 – Season's Summary

League	P	W	D	L	F	A	Pts.	Pos.
	42	14	13	15	44	46	41	12th

Top Scorers		
Bryan Robson		10
Keith Dyson		7
Wyn Davies		6

1971/72 – SUPERMAC

Malcolm Macdonald was a Londoner who signed for Newcastle on 7th May 1971 for £180,000. He was sold by the Luton Town manager, the genial Harry Haslam, to Joe Harvey with the promise that he was buying a unique talent and a player who would go on to represent England. Haslam was of course proved right even from day one when Macdonald arrived at St. James' Park in a black Rolls Royce. The man had style and would go on to take a special place in every Geordie heart.

Macdonald was brought effectively to replace Wyn Davies and hopefully continue the tradition of exciting goal scoring centre forwards at St. James' Park. The first true Geordie hero was I suppose Hughie Gallacher, a Scot who led Newcastle to the Football League Championship in 1927 scoring 36 league goals in the process. In the war years (1939-46) Albert Stubbins was a prolific scorer at the club before the legendary Jackie Milburn arrived on the scene. Being a Geordie lad himself endeared him to the Tyneside public as did his humble and committed attitude, not to mention his goal scoring record at the club. Macdonald though was a little different. He was young, arrogant to the extent of being cocky, and with bow legs, broad sideburns, and a mouth missing numerous teeth, the result of his undoubted bravery in aerial challenges, he would scare the living daylights out of opposing defenders as he bore down on goal. Supermac was to become as big a hero as Keegan and perhaps, for me, as a bright eyed young lad, the biggest football hero I would have until a certain Peter Beardsley arrived on the scene.

14/08/71 – CRYSTAL PALACE v NEWCASTLE (2-0)

Our family holidays in the 1970s consisted of travelling around Britain with a caravan and enjoying the delights or otherwise of each destination we stopped at. The summer of 1971 saw us head off to the south of England and to a caravan site at Burnham Beeches which just happened to be pretty close, well, 30 miles or so, to London. As luck would have it Newcastle's first match of the season was at Crystal Palace, and so it became inevitable that Selhurst Park would be targeted for our day trip on Saturday, much more enjoyable than traipsing around Big Ben, Buckingham Palace and other such dubious attractions as we had been doing earlier in the week. This was my first Newcastle away match but, with a goal in each half condemning us to a 2-0 opening day defeat, it wasn't such a memorable occasion. The whole family went along of course, even Mum who in those days quite enjoyed the spectacle of live football, as she did for a number of seasons when it was her pleasant duty to have to take us to the match (before we were old enough to be allowed to go by ourselves). I don't think she particularly cared for some of the vulgar terrace chants of the 1970s, indeed who would, although I remember her being amused at the rhyme in the 'Brian Clough is a Puff' song which was sung at St. James' Park when Derby were the visitors in 1973. She remained an avid fan, confining her support to listening on the radio or watching on the television, until her death in December 1995.

18/08/71 – TOTTENHAM HOTSPUR v NEWCASTLE (0-0)

Good fortune smiled on the Hannens once again as, amazingly, four days later, Newcastle were scheduled to play at White Hart Lane and so off we all went again. The stadium was the best I'd been in during my brief love affair with the game. Four large stands enclosed the pitch and with the Tottenham cockerel perched high above the main stand it was an arena made for football The match remains memorable for the incident of a missile being thrown on to the pitch by a Spurs supporter which hit Willie McFaul, the Newcastle goalkeeper. It was an incredible situation, McFaul fell to the ground whilst his colleagues immediately surrounded him clearly concerned for his welfare. I couldn't believe what I was seeing, such drama and a situation that I couldn't wait to tell my school friends about. Thankfully McFaul recovered and played a full part in the 0-0 draw we achieved. I felt particularly chuffed after the game, even proud, as my team had managed to overcome such adversity to collect our first point of the season. If this was what supporting Newcastle United was all about then certainly I wanted to be a part of it.

21/08/71 – NEWCASTLE v LIVERPOOL (3-2)

Holidays always have their down sides and today was definitely one of them. I don't recall where we were but the important fact was that I wasn't at St. James' Park to see Malcolm Macdonald make a dream home debut against Liverpool by scoring a hat trick and endearing himself to the supporters for life. After scoring his third he had to leave the pitch with concussion, as a result of a collision with Ray Clemence, and in a way it made him even more of a hero. It was also our first win of the season which is always a welcome boost regardless of whether it comes in the first or 21st game. Supermac became a legend during the five years he spent on Tyneside, and I am privileged to say I watched him at his peak and retain a thousand brilliant memories of him.

During the caravan holidays we also took in matches (not involving Newcastle I'm afraid to say) at such places as The Dell (Southampton v Manchester City), Elm Park (Reading v Manchester United) and Stamford Bridge (Chelsea v Everton), which I can say unquestionably, went a long way to developing my football education and fuelling my passion for the game.

11/09/71 – NEWCASTLE RESERVES v BURNLEY RESERVES

You may wonder why such an obscure match as this appears, but it is included because it was the first time I went to St. James' Park by myself, or rather should I say only with my brother John who was presumably entrusted with the responsibility of looking after me. John is nearly two years older than me (21 months to be exact) and I think it was better to grow up with an older brother rather than a younger one as I could look up to him. Ponteland was served by the No. 5 yellow bus in the 1970s and it was this we caught from outside the school at the end of Broadway to take us all alone into Newcastle, a ride of about nine miles. With the match in question being a Central League fixture, crowds only averaged between 2,000 and 3,000 and so there was obviously no danger of being caught up in a big crowd. We took our places in the Leazes End, my first visit to what was to become my spiritual home in the next few years. I don't remember a thing about the football we saw as I spent most of the afternoon looking around the vast open spaces of the Leazes End and feeling in awe of the surroundings – amazing what concrete steps and orange crash barriers can do to you!

Going to reserve team matches was also the best way of keeping in touch with how the first team were doing as radio commentary was not as comprehensive as it is today. The score was always displayed on a little metal scoreboard and there was always an air of eager anticipation as the operator prepared to update the score with either a goal for Newcastle (hopefully) or, as was more often the case, the opposition. At most games you would keep your eye on the scoreboard for 90 minutes rather than on the reserve team match!

This day also started me off on a trail I was to follow faithfully for the next 17 years – that of collecting match programmes. In those days the club had a programme shop located in the gym opposite the main stand, and it was a visit there before the game that got me hooked. Pocket money was never plentiful but I had enough to buy two old programmes, and from that day on I collected a programme from every home game I went to. Later in the 1970s when I became a little more affluent I began the task of collecting all the away programmes, followed by all the games I hadn't been to, with the target eventually being to complete a collection of every post-war Newcastle United programme. This became a very exciting and enthralling hobby and as the years went by the collection grew and grew until the mid 1980s when I was missing only 15 programmes from the total collection. *Sports Programmes* provided the main source for tracking down old or rare items and I remember every four weeks or so, always on a Thursday, when I would eagerly await their catalogue coming through the letterbox, and then immediately getting on the telephone to them in Coventry to reserve a particular programme I was after. Invariably the line was engaged, but I simply kept on dialling repeatedly until I got through, as I am sure many others were doing also. The joy it gave me when I found out the pro-gramme I was after hadn't been taken by a prior caller was enormous. The collection included many rare items, including the programme from the away leg of the 1969 Inter Cities Fairs Cup Final, but I think the most treasured single item was the 1932 FA Cup Final programme which I paid £80 for – I must have been mad! Then what did I do? Well, I sold them all for £2500 to Roy Calmels of *Sports Programmes*. Why? I'll never know, although if truth be told, it was to help finance the new flat I'd just bought, but more of that later.

05/02/72 – HEREFORD UNITED v NEWCASTLE (2-1)

It was FA Cup time again and we had drawn a team I'd never even heard of – non-league Hereford United who played in the

Southern League. Surely this was going to be our year especially as we had home advantage, but amazingly Hereford managed a 2-2 draw on Tyneside to take the tie back to Edgar Street. Bad weather had delayed the tie until February but with confidence still high John, Patty (David Pattinson) and I headed off that fateful Saturday afternoon to Pod's (Roger Pounder) to play football on his back lawn. Patty and Pod were particularly good friends of John and all three of them attended Walbottle Grammar School. Patty was one of six children and his family ran a thriving market garden business in the estate. I was always fascinated by the enormous greenhouses they had and there was always a very distinctive smell of produce in the air whenever we visited. Pod was a Leeds fan, goodness knows why, but his lawn was just the right size for a game of two a side and it was a pretty good surface too! I remember a very good game ensued and we'd planned to play on while the match was on since a win was confidently anticipated and come 4.40pm we'd go inside and get the final result on *Grandstand*. Well we did, and I can honestly say I've never been so disappointed and heart broken over a result in my life as the Cup winning sensation of many a year was conveyed joyously to the nation. Supermac had opened the scoring but goals by Ronnie Radford (every football fan has surely seen his goal countless times on television followed by the pitch invasion of hundreds of little kids in parka coats which were the 'in fashion' in those days) and Ricky George gave the non-league side a 2-1 victory. They almost shocked West Ham in Round Four I recall, but were defeated after putting up a valiant display. Newcastle meanwhile, in typically unpredictable style, proceeded to win 2-0 at Old Trafford in their next match, moved up to 12th place in the table, and at least made them all believe they actually were good players!

The rest of the day remains a blur in my memory, even at the tender age of 10 this defeat proved a bitter pill to swallow and perhaps went a long way to shaping my outlook on the Magpies for the rest of my life. There would be ups and downs, highs and lows, and inevitably, unless you were a Liverpool fan throughout the 1970s and 1980s, the lows would easily outweigh the highs. But it didn't matter. Newcastle United was in your blood and you were destined to become a supporter for life.

03/04/72 – DERBY COUNTY v NEWCASTLE (0-1)

Every year during the Easter Holidays the family would travel down to Swansea to spend a week with all Mum and Dad's relations. This year was no exception and I will never forget being tuned into *Sport on 2* (which became *Sport on 5* in the 1990s) during the tediously long 10 hour journey and hearing that we had won 1-0 at the Baseball Ground. Tommy Cassidy had scored the only goal of the game and at the time it was a real shock result. Derby were challenging at the top of the league, we were only 11th, and their defeat was a tremendous blow to their title aspirations – fortunately from their point of view they managed to finish the season as League Champions, one point ahead of Leeds United, but only thanks to the Yorkshire outfit surprisingly losing their last match at Wolverhampton. The season before they had also controversially lost the league by a point when they contrived to lose at home to West Bromwich Albion but only thanks to a goal, which was clearly offside, being allowed to stand by the infamous Ray Tinkler. Leeds were an incredibly unpopular side during the early 1970s and most football fans were pleased to see Derby lift the title. There were a number of contributory factors that turned people against them, sure they had some wonderful players, but they could also 'mix' it and the likes of Billy Bremner, Johnny Giles and Allan Clarke could be unsavoury individuals. They also wore little numbered tassels on their socks and, along with Arsenal's Alan Ball and his white boots, they were largely disliked. Having said that I think everyone loved the way they toyed with Southampton at Elland Road on the famous occasion they defeated the Saints 7-0, particularly when Bremner and Giles showed off their party tricks.

1971/72 – Season's Summary

League	P	W	D	L	F	A	Pts.	Pos.
	42	15	11	16	49	52	41	11th

Top Scorers		
Malcolm Macdonald		26
John Tudor		9
Tommy Cassidy		3

1972/73 – THE NEW STAND

By now my own footballing career was beginning to blossom. I was a pretty good all-round player and was proud when I was made captain of the school team, Ponteland Middle School. Our team had all come through the junior school and all in all we were a pretty exceptional year with some very talented players. I played at centre half, sort of in the Bobby Moore role, anticipating situations and generally tidying up and picking up the pieces. All the other lads, Goggs, Ginger, Mini Clark, to name but three, lived nearby so we had a close affinity to each other which I'm sure helped team performances. Goggs, or to give him his full name, Ian Goldsworthy, was probably my closest friend at junior school, possibly because he lived just around the corner, literally 150 yards away. He was one of four children, including three boys, and his younger brother Neil was to become as close a friend as the 1970s unfolded. Apart from the obvious attraction of football I remember both Ian and Neil spent many hours at our house playing with our electric train set, Neil especially seemed to be particularly addicted and I remember he drove the 'shunter' train with great relish. A special friendship was also forged with Mini (Graeme) as we moved into the Middle School. His Dad and brother Ian were keen sportsmen too and many a game of cricket, as well as football, was passionately contested in his back garden.

Matches in those days were always high scoring affairs; 6-4, 7-5 for example and they provide many fond memories. Thanks will always go to Doug Rawlinson, our games master, who encouraged me in particular and whom I still see occasionally at St. James' Park. He is as passionate a supporter of the club as I know and I suppose a true Geordie football fan. We never won anything but were runners-up on numerous occasions to either Chapel House or Cheviot School, our greatest rivals. Nick Stringer, who later went on to play rugby for Wasps and England, was our goal scoring centre forward, but even his goals deserted us in our end of season Cup Final against Chapel House at Claremont School. We lost 2-0 and today it still remains a great disappointment to me especially as the night before I had been dreaming of lifting the Cup on behalf of the school. I suppose there must be thousands like me who have lost Cup Finals but that still doesn't take away the pain of losing. I remember we wore natty blue shirts with white V neck collars and black shorts and always thought it was a tremendous strip despite it not being black and white stripes. Perhaps the success, or rather lack of it, in school football has mirrored itself in the fortunes of Newcastle United – on our day we were good enough to beat anyone and indeed did in an outstanding fashion, but on the other hand never quite good enough when it came to handing out the prizes.

23/09/72 – NEWCASTLE v LEEDS UNITED (3-2)

This was a smashing game. After an indifferent start to the season we had won our last two games, including a magnificent Supermac hat-trick at Coventry the previous weekend, so hopes were high for another exciting and winning performance. Believe me that's what we got, 2-2 at half time and a memorable winner from Supermac in the second half earned both points. The fact that we lost at Everton the following weekend said a lot about the team and the way I felt at the time – good at St. James' Park but never consistent enough to pick up many points away from home.

I was fortunate enough to meet Bobby Moncur towards the end of the 1995/96 season, and he confirmed this point about the inconsistent nature of the team. The Fairs Cup winning team was close to being a great team, if it had been built upon with two or three quality acquisitions, whilst the team of the early 1970s had a number of players who could turn it on every now and again (hence the run to the 1974 FA Cup Final), but would never stand a chance of doing anything noteworthy in the League. Perhaps predictably, at the time, the Board of Directors were either unable, or unwilling, to speculate to accumulate, and a classic example of this concerns the purchase of Jimmy 'Jinky' Smith in July 1969. Newcastle, so Bobby told me, only bought him from Aberdeen for £100,000, because if they hadn't spent the money in question, they would have had to give it back to the tax man – so it seemed sensible to buy a player rather than just give it away! Smith, who also scored in the win over Leeds, was an infuriating talent, brilliant on his day (the nutmeg being his party piece), but also had the habit of drifting out of games and becoming anonymous. Still, he was a marvellous player to watch, and I prefer to remember him for those performances rather than those when he perhaps wasn't in the mood.

03/02/73 – NEWCASTLE v LUTON TOWN (0-2)

Another FA Cup disaster in the shape of a 2-0 defeat but at least there was something 'special' about this match in the shape of the opening of the new East Stand at St. James' Park. The Eastern terrace of the ground had formerly been known as the Popular Side. It was just one long terrace stretching along the length of the pitch and, presumably, got its name by it being a popular place for people to watch the football. From the Centre Paddock on the opposite side of the ground, the most recognisable sight above the Popular Terrace was the old terraced type houses, one of which bore the distinctive yellow neon lighted words 'Score with a Leech House'. I do remember one match in particular which we watched from the Popular Terrace, a 4-2 evening win over West Bromwich Albion in the penultimate match of the 1971/72 season. The game also gave me my first real memory of football songs and chants as I can still picture the Leazes End singing simply 'We are the Newcastle Boys', short and sweet but the catchy little tune is one I've never forgotten.

The New Stand, as it was still remarkably called even throughout the 1980s, (a sad comment on the lack of building progress anywhere else in the ground) was an impressive structure and its opening was intended to be marked by progression into the fifth round of the FA Cup. I don't recall how long it took to construct, but if you've seen Newcastle's match against Arsenal which was featured on *Match of the Day* the previous year, you would have seen the building work progressing in the background. It's now called the East Stand but when it was built it was very much a state of the art structure with its huge cantilever roof filling the Newcastle skyline. On the frequent occasions I come home from Leeds it's always a pleasure to drive over the Tyne Bridge and see St. James' Park in all its majesty – this was particularly so in the summer months of 1993 and 1994 when I would pass the ground to see how the building of the new Leazes and Gallowgate Stands was progressing.

Appearing on *Match of the Day* in the 1970s was a real treat as far as I was concerned. We didn't seem to feature that often but I always felt that as well as giving the Geordies a chance to watch their heroes it gave the whole country an opportunity to see how good we were, at least sometimes anyway. When you talk about *Match of the Day* you also have to talk about *Shoot!* which was Tyne

Tees Television's equivalent of London Weekend's *The Big Match*. Quite frankly *Shoot!* was an appalling production. Its only plus point was that Newcastle were featured fairly regularly because there were only five Football League clubs in the region and, of those, Hartlepool and Darlington only ever appeared once or twice a season at most, probably due to contractual obligations. The minus points were many but the two which annoyed me the most were firstly that, whereas *The Big Match* featured full high-lights from three matches followed by studio discussion and analysis, *Shoot!* spent its whole hour just on the one match. When it could have been showing other action for example, it would irritatingly show the last five minutes plus three minutes of injury time of a game in full when absolutely nothing was happening, I mean how boring, tedious and unimaginative can you get? The second was that between 1974 and 1979 Tyne Tees Television employed Kenneth Wolstenholme as their match commentator! Despite his fame in doing the World Cup Final for the BBC in 1966 his commentaries were drab, uninteresting, unemotional and, worst of all, often factually incorrect. *Shoot!* never really got any better especially when you consider the likes of London-born Arsenal supporter Roger Tames taking over the commentary from Wolstenholme. Can you imagine anything worse? – needless to say Tames' commentaries were never appreciated by the fans. The only other thing *Shoot!* brought to Newcastle United was a rather obvious terrace chant of 'Shoot, Shoot' (with clapping hands) everytime a free kick was awarded to us a reasonable distance from goal or, if you were Mirandinha at Norwich on his debut, 40 yards out.

On the theme of football on television there are a number of interesting points to enlarge on, namely the commentators and the various preview shows that have been on over the years. To commentators first and, putting Wolstenholme on one side, I would say the worst of the lot would have to be Hugh Johns who covered the Central Region for ITV in the 1970s. I've also never been a particular fan of Brian Moore, despite the high regard in which he is held, and it's ironic that the three of them – Wolstenholme and Johns on BBC and ITV respectively and Moore on the radio – were the commentators chosen to broadcast England's greatest moment in 1966. This also explains why we always used to watch the Cup Final on BBC, with the accompanying dramatic commentary of David (1-0!) Coleman, rather than on ITV in the days when both channels used to show the match live. Turning to those I have a lot of time for, two stand out way above the rest: Sky Television's Martin Tyler and the BBC's new recruit from Granada, Clive Tyldesley. Tyler is knowledgeable and knows what to say and, more importantly, when to say it, Tyldesley is blessed with the same qualities but in my view just edges out Tyler for the number one spot due to his ability to capture in descriptive prose the mood of a game absolutely perfectly. For those I haven't mentioned, for example John Motson, Barry Davies and Peter Brackley, I don't have any particular feelings one way or the other although Motson does irritate me slightly when he says 'I think such and such an incident occurred back in 1977' when he knows full well that it did! I even wrote to him about this matter and he was courteous enough to acknowledge my correspondence. I did a similar thing with Jimmy Hill on another occasion and he also was kind enough to reply.

The two main football preview shows in recent years have been the BBC's *Football Focus* and ITV's *Saint and Greavsie*. *Football Focus* is an institution and I remember it fondly going back to the early 1970s when the late Sam Leitch, a chubby cheerful character, hosted the show, to the early 1990s when the ever improving Bob Wilson, often accompanied by the astute Alan Hansen, took centre stage. Now that Bob Wilson has moved over to ITV, surely a backward step given their limited top level football output, we are left with Steve Rider and Gary Lineker to fill the Focus slot. Both do an admirable job even though the programme perhaps isn't quite what it used to be. Going back to ITV and it was a sad day when they took over the televising of League football in the early 1980s and *Football Focus* disappeared from our screens. It did bring with it *Saint and Greavsie*, which I thoroughly enjoyed, mainly because of Jimmy Greaves's humour rather than the somewhat impersonal style of the former Liverpool and Scotland player Ian St John. As ITV have now secured the rights for televising the FA Cup Final, I await their programme presentation with great interest.

A final word on television is to report the sad and petty squabbling that has inevitably taken place between club chairmen up and down the country. Of course it all boils down to one thing, money, the root of all evil in the game. Quite what the effect of the Bosman ruling will have on the financial side of the game remains to be seen.

05/05/73 – SUNDERLAND v LEEDS UNITED (1-0)

All Geordies were brought up to hate Sunderland Football Club (the Mackems) and I was no different. During my formative years as a Newcastle supporter Sunderland were in Division Two and therefore didn't come much to my attention, that is until this fateful day when Ian Porterfield won the Cup for them against all the odds – it must have been something to do with the yellow football that for some reason was used for the match. John and I went to Patty's for the match and I'm sure that the atmosphere created during the game led me to a life of hating the Mackems. Why Mackems you might ask? Well it's because people from Wearside say 'mack' and 'tack' for example instead of 'make' and 'take' – hence Mackem. They'll feature later on in the story, but suffice to say solid foundations had been laid.

TONY GREEN

The 1972/73 season cannot pass without a tribute to Tony Green whose career was tragically ended by a severe knee injury sustained at Crystal Palace on 2nd September after only 33 appearances for the club. Green was only 27 at the time and right in the prime of his career. Nowadays the advances in surgical techniques may have saved his career but in the early 1970s it was regretfully a hopeless cause. I was too young to have appreciated his special talents but I will always remember Doug Rawlinson telling me he was the greatest player he'd ever seen, so quick of thought, marvellously talented and a dream to play alongside. I suppose you could compare him to someone like Gascoigne in today's game, but as much as I love watching Gascoigne play you just sense Green was even better. If ever there was a career unfulfilled in the game then surely this was it – at least he's still involved in football by virtue of his membership of the Pools Panel.

1972/73 – Season's Summary

League	P	W	D	L	F	A	Pts.	Pos.
	42	16	13	13	60	51	45	8th

Top Scorers	
Malcolm Macdonald	19
John Tudor	18
Stewart Barrowclough	7

1973/74 – FA CUP MAGIC

Back in the 1950s Newcastle had won the FA Cup on three occasions: in 1951 against Blackpool, 1952 against Arsenal and 1955 against Manchester City. It was this domination of the competition (we'd also won it three times in pre-war days) that marked us down as renowned cup fighters but in recent seasons this had proved to be something of a fallacy. Non-league Bedford had dumped us out of the competition in 1964, and I've already mentioned the Hereford debacle so the 'success' we were to achieve in 1974 was, to say the least, long overdue.

Harking back to the 1950s, many of the players who donned the black and white shirt went on to become legends on Tyneside. There was the immortal Jackie Milburn (affectionately known as 'Wor Jackie') who played in all three finals, the Robledo brothers, George and Ted, who came to Tyneside from Chile, Frank Brennan, a mountain of a man who upon his retirement ran a successful sports shop in the city, and last, but not least, the late Bobby Cowell, who never really received the credit his performances deserved. Cowell played at right back and, like Milburn, played in all three finals. I was fortunate enough to get to know him because he lived in Ponteland and would regularly watch Ponteland United play whenever Newcastle were not playing at home. As I played in the same position as Bobby he was always on hand to give advice and encouragement which was certainly most appreciated. Later, Terry Hibbitt, who very sadly died from cancer on August 5th 1994 at the age of only 46, moved into the area, and he also took a keen interest in my football career. On the day of Hibbitt's death Newcastle played in a pre-season tournament at Ibrox and the 'Terry Hibbitt on the wing' song was given a full airing – a perfect tribute to a wonderful player.

The other noticeable thing about the 1950s, and our three Wembley visits, is the news-reel coverage of the games and the commentary that accompanied such coverage. It wasn't quite as hilarious as Tom Webster's 'commentary' on the 1934 FA Cup Final which was something else! (if you watched BBC's *Fantasy Football League* in January 1995 you will know what I mean). There was also the marvellous sight of thousands of cloth capped Geordies on the Wembley terraces and the amazing sight of these caps being hurled high into the air to celebrate a goal. If only these pictures were more readily available today, and in colour, they would make compulsive viewing.

01/10/73 – NEWCASTLE v MORTON (1-1)

Morton were the visitors to St. James' Park for a Texaco Cup fixture, a minor competition and comparable to the Anglo Italian Cup in the 1990s. It was an evening fixture and I was allowed to go with John and Patty. Newcastle drew the match 1-1 but won 3-2 on aggregate. However the real excitement centred around an incident involving Patty's older brother, Andrew (Big Patty as I called him), whom we met up with inside the Leazes End. In an era of misbehaviour on the terraces it was evident that many individuals acted rather less than innocently, possibly to establish the credibility among their peers. Anyway at half time Big Patty told us he was going to run across the whole length of the pitch and jump straight in to the Gallowgate End terrace without being caught by the police. To his credit his daredevil stunt came off but, believe you me, it was a risky thing to do. The police attempted to catch him but failed miserably as he quickly disappeared amongst the crowd in the Gallowgate End. Big Patty's mate, John Mew, also tried the same stunt but he wasn't so lucky. He didn't have Patty's speed or elusiveness and ended up in the arms of the law. It was something I never tried to emulate. John Mew went on to fight in the Falklands War in 1982 and I can only surmise that there must be some sort of link between being a football 'hooligan' in your youth and ending up in the Falklands 10 years on.

17/10/73 – ENGLAND v POLAND (1-1)

England's World Cup destiny was dependent upon our beating Poland at Wembley and throughout the day at school little work had been done as the game was so significant as to be on many people's minds. I recall Doug Rawlinson coming to our rescue again by not giving any of our class any maths homework that night in order that we would all be able to watch the match undisturbed – a gesture typical of the man.

Two weeks earlier we had got our first colour television. I'm not sure whether Dad had got it especially for this match, I doubt it somehow, but anyway the timing couldn't have been better. I remember the first colour TV programme I watched on our new set that first night was *Floodlit Rugby League*. This particular sport is actually one I dislike, but the memories of seeing the green grass illuminated by bright floodlights and players in different coloured shirts are still very vivid. As for Poland, the draw they got that night was enough to eliminate England from the competition, something I would become very accustomed to in later years.

The Poles went on to finish third in the 1974 World Cup Finals where the likes of Tomaszewski, Lato, Deyna and Gorgon became household names throughout the world. Tomaszewski was labelled a clown by Brian Clough at Wembley, when he performed miracles to keep the England forwards at bay, whilst it was Norman Hunter's ineffective challenge on the half way line that sent Lato clear to set up Domarski for the crucial Polish goal. I remember Emlyn Hughes's desperate lunge at Domarski's feet as he tried to prevent him shooting but it was to no avail and Hughes was simply left lying in anguish on the turf.

26/12/73 – NEWCASTLE v LEEDS UNITED (0-1)

I was now in a transitional stage of being allowed to go to the match with older friends or still going with Dad. The latter was still the more common occurrence but the former was becoming more exciting as it gave me a greater independence and sense of freedom. By now John had been going himself for a year or two, more often than not with Patty. They were 'Leazes Enders' and to aspire to that status was something I dearly wanted.

I only saw about 25 minutes of this match. The arrangement I had was to go with William Skelchy, who was actually John's age but strangely enough was a closer friend of mine (his garden was another favourite footballing venue of ours), and his older brother who would drive us to St. James' Park. Things started to go wrong when he hadn't arrived to pick us up by 2.30pm, and when he did (from where I don't know) we eventually arrived at the ground at 3.15pm, 15 minutes into the game. The Leazes End was the only place where there was any space, and after entering the ground we found ourselves only able to get as far as the top corner of the terrace, hopelessly crushed against the railings and unable to see anything. The result? – we left five minutes before half time and went home. By the way, Leeds sneaked a 1-0 win, which seemed rather incidental on the day, but made for a pretty miserable Boxing Day.

23/02/74 – NEWCASTLE v LIVERPOOL (0-0)

By now Newcastle had embarked on their marvellous FA Cup run to Wembley which would ultimately result in bitter disappointment but at the same time leave behind some fantastic memories. Non-league Hendon had threatened another Hereford in Round Three before being comfortably disposed of in a replay, Scunthorpe went the same way in Round Four and West Bromwich Albion had been humiliated the previous week in a scintillating United performance at The Hawthorns, captured in all its glory on *Match of the Day*.

Match day in the early 1970s was never complete without buying a pack or two of peanuts from the peanut sellers dotted around the ground. They were all fairly old men and sold these delicious peanuts wrapped up in distinctive cylindrically shaped white paper bags. I can still taste them today and it was a sad day when they disappeared from sale a few years later. I was with Dad, who was never without his half time cup of piping hot Bovril, and I recall it rained non stop throughout the match which may have helped contribute to the 0-0 scoreline. We weren't pulling up any trees in the league but were comfortably placed in ninth position after this game. Three months earlier though we had incredibly been as high as second having taken 19 points from the first 28 on offer (this was in the days of two points for a win) including a con-secutive winning sequence of four games.

One of the rituals that occurred at St. James' Park during the era, and today was no exception, was the sporadic terrace fighting that took place between Newcastle supporters on either the Leazes or Gallowgate End terraces. It tended to occur in the first half and was unmistakable to spot as you would see a section of terrace form itself into a small circle in order to give the two or more pro-tagonists space to attempt to 'kick each other in'. It was difficult for the police to stop as they were more often than not prevented from getting anywhere near the action and in any case the fighting would peter out with the loser usually left with a bloody face. Actually, some fighting was even stage-managed in order to lure the police into the crowd before they were viciously attacked, and the terrace song 'Harry Roberts is our friend' (telling the tale of a infamous villain who had shot a policeman in Epping Forest, London) was very much to the fore at this time.

Terrace rivalry was intense during this period and rival gangs would have their own special place on the Leazes End which they turned into 'no go' areas. I became a regular Leazes Ender the following year and would stand with my mates a little left of centre well away from the nut cases representing the likes of Newbiggin or Kenton 'Bovver' Boys, many of them unmistakable in their 'doctor like' white coats covered in graffiti, skinhead hair cuts and Dr Marten boots. I suppose it was a part of the 1970s terrace culture which also included the chants of 'You're going to get your f****** head kicked in' every time the opposition scored or 'Come and have a go at the Geordie Aggro' to the opposing fans. Newcastle supporters were famous, or is it infamous, for being able to defend their territory (hence the song 'You'll never take the Leazes') and in a funny sort of way it made me proud to feel a part of this even though I was on the outside looking in.

Back to the rain and Liverpool, and the fight in this particular game which sticks in the memory was a man in a yellow waterproof jacket in the Gallowgate End going absolutely crazy and laying in to as many people as he could single-handedly.

09/03/74 – NEWCASTLE v NOTTINGHAM FOREST (4-3)

FA Cup fever was rising rapidly and expectations were enormous. The sixth round draw had proved favourable but it wasn't a match I was able to see. Tickets were like gold dust, all 54,000 of them, and the only way John got his was by queuing overnight outside the ground along with Patty and thousands of others just waiting for the ticket office to open. It was worthwhile as he got his ticket to see one of the most infamous matches in the history of the club whereas I, heartbroken at missing out, had to settle for the radio at home and then *Shoot!* the following day. Newcastle won the match 4-3 after a pitch invasion stopped play when Forest led 3-1, only for play to be resumed some 10 minutes later amid a frenzied atmosphere. Three late goals, including a John Tudor diving header and a Bobby Moncur volley in the last minute, sent the fans into ecstasy. However, Forest's appeal to the FA was upheld and with the match being declared null and void it took two replays at Goodison Park to put Newcastle into the semi-finals.

30/03/74 – NEWCASTLE v BURNLEY (2-0)

FA Cup semi-final day at Hillsborough (the home of Sheffield

Wednesday) and I had to content myself with playing football on the school field. Actually I remember feeling too tense to listen to the match on the radio and so when news of a Newcastle victory filtered through to me I was overjoyed. Both Goldsworthys (Ian and Neil) had gone down with their Dad to the game and I couldn't wait for them to get home so that they could tell me all about it. Of course I watched it on *Shoot!* the next day and how I wished video recorders were common place in those days in order that the highlights could have been taped. Supermac's two goals, which took us to Wembley, were fabulous strikes and just seeing them again makes your body hair stand on end such was the unbelievable thrill of the occasion.

12/04/74 – NEWCASTLE v BURNLEY (2-1)

In the mid 1970s we played in a number of low key competitions including the Anglo Italian Cup (which of course has been resurrected in the 1990s), Anglo-Scottish Cup and Texaco Cup. Back in the 1972/73 season we'd actually won the Anglo Italian Cup by defeating Fiorentina. The competition had dragged on until June and with the Final being played in Italy it wasn't until the morning after that I learned of our success, 2-1, when I woke early and ran across the road to the newsagents to pick up the Newcastle *Journal.* I still remember feeling chuffed walking slowly back home in the warm summer morning air reading the match report as I went.

We'd reached the Texaco Cup Final without too much trouble and it was nice to be meeting Burnley again in the Final as it was only two weeks ago that we'd beaten them 2-0 at Hillsborough. Mum, John and I got seats in the new East Stand for the game as it was a sort of 'special occasion'. Goals from Macdonald and Moncur, scoring once again on the big occasion, carried us to a 2-1 victory and the joy of winning what was frankly a minor competition still proved to be a night to savour. A year later we retained the Texaco Cup, this time beating Southampton in the Final, but if truth be told winning these 'Micky Mouse' competitions was okay but, in the grand scale of footballing achievement, totally insignificant. If we wanted to be a 'big' club then we shouldn't even have been playing in such fare, and I longed to taste real success. Today I'm still waiting, but at least there is genuine hope of ending the drought.

I can't let the Texaco Cup competition pass without mention of Iam (Willie) McFaul our Irish International goalkeeper during this period. Willie was, generally speaking, pretty reliable and went on to become a great servant of the club, eventually inheriting the manager's office, but one clanger he dropped will never be forgotten. I think it was against Aberdeen in the 1974/75 competition when an innocuous shot was heading towards goal and McFaul, thinking he had it covered, nonchalantly moved towards the ball and waved his arms as if to usher it past the post. It was a gross error of judgement as Willie managed only to wave the ball in to the back of the net! If we hadn't been so annoyed at conceding the goal I'm sure the whole ground would have burst out laughing – not quite as famous as Gary Sprake's throw into his own goal at Anfield, but not far behind.

04/05/74 – NEWCASTLE v LIVERPOOL (0-3)

The FA Cup Final and I missed out again on getting a ticket. I was so envious of John, Patty and another mate Popplestone, who had got tickets, when I watched them board the coach, organised by the Gulf garage across the road from our house, at midnight on the Friday night ready to embark for Wembley. At least they deserved their tickets, having been to virtually every home game, and a few away from home too, during the season unlike some of the people who would be attending the game who wouldn't know the difference between a golf ball and a football! I remember Frank Bough, in his preview piece for *Cup Final Grandstand*, commenting on how much he was looking forward to hearing the strains of 'The Blaydon Races' and 'Haway the Lads' echoing around the great stadium and that just served to make things worse for me. I'm sure John's memories of the day are still vivid, mine were made up of watching the build up to the game on television, as usual from 10.00 in the morning, flicking back between the two channels to catch the best of the features followed by total despair during the game itself as we flopped to a humiliating 3-0 defeat without really ever being in the game. Liverpool dominated us on the field for the next 19 years (with the exception of one match in February 1975) and it wouldn't be until 21st November 1993 that revenge was exacted in full.

I didn't go to the homecoming a couple of days later, but by all accounts the welcome home reception accorded to the team was absolutely fabulous. Two years later, after the League Cup Final defeat, I experienced such an occasion, and can honestly say that the Geordie fans never cease to amaze!

11/05/74 – NEWCASTLE v TOTTENHAM HOTSPUR (0-2)

I don't remember why I didn't go to this game (we lost 2-0) but I ended up being at our School Fair instead for some reason. Tottenham were in town and had autographed a football which I managed to claim by winning a penalty shoot out competition at the Fair although I remember missing my last penalty which meant the last person to go (Simon Rowland) could have won the prize if he had scored. Fortunately he missed and I saw him off in the sudden death. I kept the ball on top of a copper plate, which I had proudly made in metalwork classes at school, on our mantelpiece at home, untouched for about a year, and then decided to play with it, burst it, and so that was the end of that.

07/07/74 – HOLLAND v WEST GERMANY (1-2)

I had obviously watched the magical Brazilians defeat Italy in the 1970 World Cup Final in Mexico four years earlier, but this was the first World Cup Final, and indeed tournament, that I had watched incessantly from day one right through to the Final.

England hadn't qualified but the Finals in West Germany were still set to capture my imagination. I would watch every live game and all the highlight programmes, something I've done in every World Cup Tournament since, and I was really in my element. The highlight? The Dutch, of course. I eulogised over Cruyff's 'turn' against Bulgaria and 'take the mickey' goal against Argentina, revelled over Rep and Rensenbrink and thrilled at how Neeskens took Brazil apart in the semi-final. Oddly enough I also loved the Dutch National Anthem and remember before the Final standing to attention pretending I was about to take part in the match (after all I was only 12!). The Dutch got off to a dream start in the Final scoring with a first minute penalty, but much to my disappointment the resilient Germans scored twice before half time and that's the way it stayed.

1973/74 – Season's Summary

League	P	W	D	L	F	A	Pts.	Pos.
	42	13	12	17	49	48	38	15th

Top Scorers		
Malcolm Macdonald	25
John Tudor	9
Terry McDermott	8

1974/75 – LEAZES ENDER

September 1974 was a significant month in that it was my first term at Ponteland High School and a whole new life in comparison to the Middle School, even though the two schools shared the same site. Your first day at a new school is one of those days etched in your memory and I was no different. Stories of older year groups bullying the young newcomers (flushing their heads down the toilet for example) were totally unfounded as far as I was concerned, and perhaps it was my total immersion and aptitude in sport, and football especially, that helped me settle in quickly. The school did have one major problem though in that you could term it as a rugby playing school! The reason for this was clearly that the PE staff were rugby orientated, in stark comparison to the Middle School staff, and it was only through the constant pressure brought upon them by myself and close friends that we succeeded in getting football established in the school. Regretfully a number of our successful Middle School team were converted to rugby, and it is even sadder today to see in the Tyneside Schools Leagues no mention of Ponteland High School within the set-up.

14/09/74 – NEWCASTLE v CARLISLE UNITED (1-0)

Family holidays denied me the pleasure of witnessing mid-August encounters with Coventry and Sheffield United, so table topping Cumbrian upstarts Carlisle were the visitors to St. James' Park for my first match of the season.

My two closest friends in the first years at High School were Nick Ingham and Mini Clark who became my companions at St. James' Park for the next four seasons. Mini you already know a little about, Nick was different in many ways. He was the oldest of four brothers, six days older than me, and the two of us seemed to relate to each other almost telepathically. We lived within half a mile of each other, Nick having recently moved into the estate, and on this warm September afternoon arranged to meet at the bus stop at 12.30pm so we'd arrive at the ground by 1.00pm. Match day dress now consisted of denim jacket, jeans and silk scarf. Mine had 'Leazes Ender' embroided on it (I've still got it at home today) and it was the norm to wear it on your wrist. I also had a large badge collection with my favourite being one with

Harvey's Cream (in recognition of Joe Harvey of course) on it and this too was worn with pride on my jacket. Going to the match on the bus was the 'big' thing to do, although nowadays cars seem a lot more convenient, and we took upstairs seats, as you would expect. Other fans would pile on the bus as it made its way through Woolsington, Kenton Bar and Cowgate and then down Barrack Road to drop us off right outside the ground. Even at this relatively early hour there were hundreds of supporters streaming down the road making their way into St. James' Park, or at least into the confines of the ground instead of going through the turnstiles.

Going to the match a couple of hours before kick off has its advantages. Firstly there was the enjoyment and thrill of just being there; mingling with the crowds all of whom were eagerly anticipating the match to come. There was also the excitement in the front of the car park watching the players arriving in their expensive cars and making their way into the ground while being under siege by enthusiastic autograph hunters which more often than not included myself. Malcolm Macdonald's autograph was a must and his was one I was proud to have in my collection. John also had an autograph book and in fact it's still lying around his bedroom at home. I can't help glancing through it and just seeing the names on each page brings back so many happy memories. The visiting team would arrive at the ground in their coach at about 1.30pm and I always enjoyed looking through the windows and trying to spot all the star players that I knew before they disembarked and were ushered hurriedly into the ground with only a few being courteous enough to stop and sign autographs. Old habits die hard and it brought back many fond memories when I found myself standing outside the main entrance once again on the first day of the 1995/96 season to see Coventry City's arrival. At many away matches I've attended there are always hundreds of Newcastle fans to greet the Newcastle team coach, but you rarely see any away supporters at Newcastle doing the same thing. I think this was partly to do with a number of factors including the fact that Newcastle is so far north that the length of journey put many away fans off travelling (it doesn't stop Newcastle fans travelling away in their thousands though) and the reputation a minority of Newcastle supporters (hooligans) had towards visiting supporters in respect of violent behaviour. You would hear of fans congregating at the Central Station to greet visiting fans and attempting to ambush them on their way to St. James' Park. There was also the sickening indefensible action of one Newcastle supporter who threw a petrol bomb at West Ham supporters, setting one of them alight and leading to an infamous song about the incident. You can never condone such behaviour and it makes me wonder how society had motivated an individual to carry out such an act.

Newcastle had made a reasonable start to the season and victory over Carlisle would consolidate a position in the top half of the table. We would take our places inside the ground by about 2.00pm after having to queue often for 15 minutes or more. The Leazes End must have had at least 10 turnstiles but the queues were always long and windy especially for the Under 16 entrance where I was constantly amazed at how old some people looked! The police weeded out a few obvious 'over age' Under 16s but I'm sure countless managed to get into the ground 'on the cheap'. Once through the turnstiles you would quickly run up the side part of the terracing into the heart of the Leazes End under the roof where the three of us had our favourite barrier which was pretty well back on the terrace and a little left of the goal as we looked on. It is almost impossible to use words to describe the incredible feeling of being part of a terrace crowd, the noise, the surges and unique atmosphere generated by thousands of football loving Geordies. Those of us who were fortunate enough to have been brought up as Leazes Enders have so much for which to be grateful, as it ingrained in us all a passion and feeling for the club second to none.

I remember the match as a pretty tense affair but a single goal by John Tudor late in the game gave us a deserved victory, took us up to eighth in the table, and sent Carlisle back to Cumbria pointless. This was Carlisle's first season in the top flight and incredibly after winning their first three fixtures to top the division, they were to be relegated ignominiously at the end of the season.

Getting home from the match was also an experience in itself. With the final whistle being greeted with resounding cheers you began heading towards the exit carried along in a surge of bodies with the shouts of 'Hey Man, How Man' ringing out as you fought for your position. Contrary to what you might think this was quite an enjoyable experience; well it was for me anyway! Once outside the ground we'd run the 500 yards or so down to the Haymarket

Bus Station, avoiding the inevitable horse dirt that the many police horses had left behind on the ground, where you joined the unfortunate Saturday shoppers in the queues to board the bus back to Ponteland. The buses ran every 15 minutes, so if you missed one, or you couldn't get on because it was too full, you never had long to wait. John and his mates would invariably be on the bus home too and the journey home consisted of reliving the great moments of the game or, if we'd lost, moaning about the deficiencies of some of the players. All in all a wonderful way to spend a Saturday afternoon.

12/02/75 – NEWCASTLE v LIVERPOOL (4-1)

This was our first meeting with Liverpool since that fateful day at the end of the previous season. The players and supporters were desperately keen to turn the tables on the Scousers and it was this belief that led Newcastle to produce an absolutely scintillating display of football to completely overrun the visitors and win 4-1. It was one of the finest games I can remember of the mid 1970s but strangely enough the only goal I can remember is Brian Hall's consolation effort for Liverpool which was a brilliant diving header at the Gallowgate End. I actually met Brian Hall in November 1993 at Anfield (due to the Basketball Association and Liverpool Football Club being involved in a joint promotion with the Carlsberg Brewery) and I reminded him of that day 18 years ago. He certainly remembered his goal and the fact that Newcastle had been absolutely brilliant on the night. Brian was also kind enough to give me a guided tour of Anfield which even for a Geordie was a real thrill.

We were only 11th in the table but who cared when we produced performances like this. Six weeks later Newcastle travelled to Anfield and predictably finished on the wrong end of a 4-0 thrashing. How could the team play so well one day and then be so utterly useless the next? This was to become a question I'd be asking myself many times in the future.

1974/75 – Season's Summary

League	P	W	D	L	F	A	Pts.	Pos.
	42	15	9	18	59	72	39	15th

Top Scorers   Malcolm Macdonald   27
                      John Tudor   15
                      Micky Burns   7

1975/76 – WEMBLEY

The 1975/76 season was to become one of the most exciting in memory. I would see virtually every single home game and have the added joy of a Wembley trip thrown in which, despite ending in defeat, still remains to this day a vivid and lasting experience. Over the years, well from the mid 1980s anyway, I have been very fortunate to visit Wembley virtually every year – alas it has never been to watch Newcastle United again and until this is rectified there will always be a great sadness as each football season passes with dreams of a Wembley trip unfulfilled. That is the true mystique of Wembley Stadium.

As far as I am concerned it is imperative that Wembley remains as our National Stadium. At the end of 1995 various bids were submitted, including one from Wembley, to provide a new arena fit for the next century. Wembley can be the only winner. Tradition must be the overriding factor in reaching the decision, Wembley is Wembley and it's as simple as that.

20/08/75 – NEWCASTLE v MIDDLESBROUGH (1-1)

We had been caravanning as usual in August and in the week leading up to the game had been on the final leg of our trip to Scarborough, memorable only for the plague of ladybirds that descended upon the resort. Anyway, we weren't due back home until the Thursday following the game which as far as I was concerned was madness. I don't recall how I managed to do it but it was agreed Mum and I could go back to Newcastle on the Tuesday with Dad and John following on Thursday as planned. We were despatched off to Darlington from where the two of us caught the train back home and all was set well for the following day.

There is always a fresh sense of optimism and anticipation at the start of a new season and having beaten Ipswich 3-0 at Portman Road on the opening day was a real boost. A new manager was also installed at St. James' Park in the shape of Gordon Lee who had been attracted to the club from Blackburn Rovers. I'd only ever known Joe Harvey as the team manager throughout the 1970s, but he had retired the previous season after a playing and managerial career with the club that was legendary. Harvey was one of the great characters of the game in those days and was up with the likes of Shankly, Clough and Nicholson in this respect. He was a Yorkshire man by birth, blunt and forthright in his manner and never seemed troubled by anything. His team talk at half time of the Fairs Cup Final is legendary – he simply said to the players 'just go out and score and the Hungarians will fall apart' – we did score, Ujpest fell apart, and the rest is history. Lee on the other hand was an unknown character. He was appointed on the basis of the good job he had done at Ewood Park on a relatively tight budget (yes, they did have a tight budget in those days) so I suspect most supporters were willing to give him a fair crack of the whip before pronouncing judgement on him.

Middlesbrough arrived on Tyneside with an opening day defeat at Tottenham behind them but took an interval lead at St. James' Park thanks to a clumsy Alan Gowling own goal. A second half siege on the Middlesbrough goal only brought about a single Malcolm Macdonald strike, but at least our pride remained intact. There was something about Middlesbrough and own goals as later in the season Glen Keeley, Newcastle's gangly raw centre half repeated the act at Ayresome Park in bizarre style which led to us going 3 -1 down before two goals in the last three minutes from full backs Irving Nattress and Alan Kennedy secured an unlikely draw. On the theme of own goals I'll never forget the one Graham Oates (one of Gordon Lee's boys) scored into the Gallowgate End from nigh on 30 yards against Leeds United during the 1975/76 season, but perhaps the best of them all was Willie Donachie's classic for Scotland against Wales at Hampden Park in 1978. For those of you who don't remember, it came as a result of a goal kick played out to Donachie in the left back position which he returned immediately towards the goal. Unfortunately the goalkeeper, Jim Blyth, wasn't awake to the situation and the ball ended up rolling slowly, just inside the post, into an empty net – hilarious to the neutral observer!

23/08/75 – NEWCASTLE v LEICESTER CITY (3-0)

For the lucky 36,084 present at this match it was one they'll never forget. Unlike today, where virtually every match is covered, no television cameras were present in the ground and it was a great shame as they missed a goal in a million by Malcolm Macdonald. Supermac's goal scoring exploits were legendary, particularly the way he used to rampage through the middle of opponents' defences to ram the ball into the net (witness Burnley 1974 FA Cup semi-final), but this effort was something extra special. Scored at the Leazes End it came from a crossfield ball from the right by Irving Nattrass which found its way to Macdonald 30 yards from goal. Without breaking his stride, his left foot shot flew like a rocket into the top left hand corner of the net past the fully airborne visiting goalkeeper Mark Wallington. It was as if time stood still as the fans gasped in total amazement at the goal before celebrating in the normal fashion. For those of us at St. James' Park that day you need only close your eyes and visualise Supermac's majestic strike to bring the memory flooding back. The match finished in a comfortable 3-0 victory, goals from Burns and a second from Macdonald completing the scoring, and after only three matches we were up to second place in the league. Lee had made a marvellous start to his career at St. James' Park and if winning is a method of becoming popular then our new manager was making a pretty good fist of things.

03/12/75 – NEWCASTLE v NOTTS COUNTY (1-0)

The Football League Cup competition, unsponsored throughout the 1970s, was a relatively low key competition in comparison to the FA Cup, but it still offered a Wembley Final and that was enough to inspire any player or supporter. Earlier in the competition Southport, Bristol Rovers and Queen's Park Rangers had fallen to Newcastle, which was something of a minor miracle when looking at the club's record of falling at either the first or second hurdle in the competition in the past 20 years, and the pain and anguish caused by defeats against the likes of Bury, Fulham and Oxford. Notts County, a second division side, were the lambs lined up for slaughter at St. James' Park for the quarter-final, but it was through some dodgy goalkeeping by Eric McManus and his subsequent own goal that we managed to scrape into the semi-finals. The League was looking like it was going to have to take a back seat, we were a respectable 11th (we always seemed to be 11th!) but the thought of Wembley can do the funniest things to you.

21/01/76 – NEWCASTLE v TOTTENHAM HOTSPUR (3-1)

Before the semi-final draw was made I was praying we'd avoid

Manchester City and Middlesbrough and come out against Tottenham, with preferably the first leg being away from home. As luck would have it, that was exactly what we got. I can't remember if the draw was live on the radio, as the FA Cup draws were in those days on Monday lunch times on Radio 2 when it was the norm to huddle round a small transistor radio in the school yard. You always kept your fingers crossed that your team would be drawn out of the bag first and therefore be given a home draw, against whom you didn't really mind, although an inferior team was often preferable. Live television coverage of the draw nowadays isn't quite as exciting, but nevertheless I still sometimes turn the sound down and just watch for the names of the teams to be displayed on the screen!

The first leg of the semi-final had been played at White Hart Lane the previous Wednesday where we had been defeated 1-0, but only thanks to a superb Pat Jennings save from a Tommy Craig thunderbolt. We had also embarked on the FA Cup trail once more and were already in the fourth round, having won a replay at St. James' Park against Queen's Park Rangers earlier in the month. This had been a classic, but tense encounter, with a Tommy Craig penalty clinching victory. You always tend to fear the worst when you're awarded a penalty, but on this occasion Craig emphatically smashed it past Phil Parkes and the evening was capped off marvellously by being able to dash home and watch the highlights on *Sportsnight* with, as was the norm at the time, a bowl of hot tomato soup with bread and butter.

A hugely expectant crowd of 50,000 were packed into St. James' Park for the visit of Tottenham and I'm certain it was the incredible vocal support that night that carried us to our 3-1 (3-2 on aggregate) victory. There's that much more tension towards the closing minutes of a Cup tie than a routine league game, as you hope and pray that the opposition don't sneak an equaliser as they mount a last ditch attack. The relief that the final whistle brings on such occasions is enormous and the unrestrained joy I felt after this game was shared by all of Tyneside.

18/02/76 – NEWCASTLE v BOLTON WANDERERS (0-0)

Football League matches were playing second fiddle to the League and FA Cup matches, even though we had knocked five past Everton and four past Derby in recent weeks. Our cup exploits also meant that league games were being postponed to accommodate the cup matches and it meant falling from 10th to 17th in the league during February as teams not involved in the cup picked up league points and moved above us in the table. The whole of Tyneside's attention was centred on the Cup, and indeed it may have been that the rest of the country was beginning to take an interest too.

This fixture was a fifth round replay which was necessary as a result of a riveting 3-3 draw at Burnden Park, in which Malcolm Macdonald had scored twice including an audacious shot from the corner of the penalty area which had left Barry Siddall, later to become a figure of fun at Roker Park, helpless. I remember a young Peter Reid being outstanding for Bolton, but neither he nor any home player could manage a goal and the replay finished scoreless.

With Wembley looming for the League Cup Final, and the sixth round of the FA Cup due to be played the week after it meant that the second replay against Bolton had to be scheduled for the Monday night of Cup Final week. Not ideal for the team in terms of their preparation, and certainly not ideal for me as I would have loved to have travelled to Elland Road, the neutral venue selected by the FA, for the match. Radio therefore was my only companion for the night, and a joyous night it proved to be as goals from Gowling and Burns earned a 2-1 victory.

Radio commentary, even in those days, was a tortuous experience. Without being able to see any action yourself, you are dependent upon the skill of the commentator to accurately reflect the play. Some of them can make half chances sound like gilt edged open goals, and you can imagine the panic and anguish this causes when you are listening, wondering if your team is about to score or concede a goal. Peter Jones was the doyen of radio football commentators in the 1970s and 1980s, while these days there is no one to match the BBC's Mike Ingham and Alan Green even though the former did blot his copybook by broadcasting to the nation that the Sunderland fans, at Old Trafford for their third round FA Cup tie in January 1996, were singing the 'Blaydon Races'. Local radio commentary is never quite as good, otherwise the presenters would be working for the BBC, however if you do find a good one, for example Radio Newcastle's Mick Lowes (season 1992/93) then the extra passion and excitement they are able to provide is invaluable.

Newcastle's away strip in those days was a little bit like the famous Brazilian strip and had been brought in to replace an all blue or off colour red strip that had been worn on our travels in the early 1970s. I naturally had a replica strip and its funny how by wearing it you felt you could play just like the Brazilians – I wonder if that's what Newcastle thought when they introduced it.

28/02/76 – NEWCASTLE v MANCHESTER CITY (1-2)

Our second Wembley Cup Final in two seasons but the difference between 1974 and 1976 was that this time round I had a ticket. Big match tickets in the 1970s were issued firstly to all the season ticket holders (which of course I wasn't) and then to the general public through the voucher system. Vouchers were contained within all the match day programmes and you had to have virtually a full set to stand any chance of getting a ticket, and even that was no guarantee as I found to my cost. However I was extremely fortunate in that Dad managed to have a word with his brother, Mike, in Swansea and he somehow managed to obtain two tickets for me from Swansea City Football Club. Dad couldn't go so Mini was in the fortunate position of getting the spare one which regretfully meant Nick having to miss out. John and his mates were successful through the voucher system and while they embarked by coach to London once again, Mini and myself went down with his Dad and older brother Ian. We actually left on the Friday afternoon as we were staying the night in Swindon before journeying on to Wembley first thing in the morning. I had a new woollen scarf (but had my Leazes Ender scarf too), bobble cap and flag, and must have really looked the part. My ticket was safely contained within my jacket pocket and I even had a safety pin pinned to the fabric to make doubly sure no one could pinch it – my worst fear. Even during the car journey I couldn't stop feeling the outside of my pocket just to make sure it was still there; ridiculous really, but all part of the excitement.

Swindon came and went in a blur and as we approached northwest London on Saturday morning the excitement was approaching levels never previously reached. As Wembley got nearer and nearer we were all peering out of the car windows trying to spot the world renowned twin towers of Wembley. The stadium has that unique magical atmosphere and when we first caught a glimpse of it over office blocks and through a gap in a row of shops it was one of those once in a lifetime feelings. I don't know if anyone feels quite as I do but for someone like me to whom football was, and still is, the be all and end all of my life, to actually be at Wembley for the first time and see it in all its majesty was simply indescribable. We headed straight for one of the multi-storey car parks and, as our tickets (Mini's and mine) were for a different part of the ground to his Dad and brother, we separated, agreeing to meet back at the car after the game. The two of us immediately ran down the stairs, anxious to get on to the Wembley concourse at the earliest opportunity, and made our way out into the sunshine totally in awe of our surroundings. I cannot emphasise how much it meant to me to be where I was.

Kick-off was still three hours away and the turnstiles were yet to open so it was an obvious opportunity to just mill around the stadium and simply soak up the atmosphere. I got the impression that there were far more Geordies about than Manchester City fans, and certainly the singing and general exuberance of the Tynesiders was clearly evident. The next hour flashed by and we decided it was time to go into the ground. The long steps heading up to the turnstile arch were heaving and as we shuffled closer and closer to the magical entry point I remember looking up at the imposing slate coloured walls and seeing some ticketless supporters risking life and limb by trying to scale the walls and clamber inside the stadium through what seemed to be minute windows. No one fell and those who attempted the dare-devil stunt were successful, although whether they were apprehended once inside the stadium is a different matter.

Carefully unclipping the safety pin I eased my ticket out of my pocket and grasped it in my palm as tightly as I could. No one was going to have a chance of getting their hands on it unlawfully. A few clicks later and my dream was fulfilled, I was inside Wembley to watch my beloved Newcastle United play in a Cup Final. Our tickets were fortunately for the upper tier of the terraces, and as we raced up the access stairs which led to the vast open terraces I wondered just what sort of sight I was about to be greeted with. I was not disappointed. The stadium was everything and more than I had ever imagined. A magnificent arena and undoubtedly better than anything I'd ever seen before in my life – it makes you wonder just what I'd make of the Maracana in Rio.

The steps leading down to the front of our section were huge, perhaps three to four times as deep as anything I'd experienced in the Leazes End. We immediately saw a spot that would provide us with a prime viewing position and, as we were one of the first few into the ground, had no trouble in securing our places just a little off centre of the goal and perched right at the front of the upper tier terrace. I was breathless with excitement and anticipation, and must have had the biggest smile anyone could have had on my face.

As the terraces began to fill so the decibel level generated by thousands of Geordies rose too. It's no exaggeration to say that no other supporters create as much constant noise as the Geordies, and the singing and chanting was incessant and deafening. Standing on the terraces that day made you really proud to be a Geordie. The pre-match ritual of the players coming out to inspect the pitch was imminent as the crowd were entertained by a penalty shoot out on the half way line. Personally I've never really seen the need for pre-match or half-time entertainment at football matches, as the fervour and banter generated by the Geordie public has always been more than sufficient for my liking.

We were housed opposite the Tunnel End, as we had been for the FA Cup Final in 1974 (hopefully not a bad omen I thought) and as the players emerged, a good 150 yards away from us, the sound level was turned up. Naturally the Newcastle players headed down to the far end of the pitch and, looking resplendent in their 'made for the day' suits, acknowledged the cheers of the supporters while waving to friends and family they could spot in the grandstands. If it was a big day for me then, I wondered, what was going through the minds of the players.

And so to the kick off. Newcastle United in their famous black and white striped shirts and Manchester City in sky blue. Tommy Craig had the honour of captaining the Magpies due to regular captain Geoff Nulty having fractured his jaw a week or so earlier – missing out on a Wembley appearance must have been a devastating experience. Nulty was never a total favourite of the St. James' Park crowd, but he was a Lee man and all in all never gave anything less than 100% for the club.

The game could never be described as a classic and, when Peter Barnes opened the scoring for City in the first quarter, the omens did not look good. I couldn't believe City had scored and it was a nightmare moment, but it only prompted the Geordie hordes to even greater support for their team. It was difficult to believe each club had an equal ticket allocation as the City supporters, despite their team having taken the lead, were drowned out. I remember singing virtually every song in our repertoire: 'Blaydon Races' being the favourite followed closely by 'Gordon Lee's Black and White Army' even though Lee never quite won the hearts of the fans, despite this 'successful' season.

Shortly before half-time the moment that I had hoped and prayed for above all else happened. Kennedy to Craig, on to Cassidy, forward to Macdonald and then square to Gowling who poked the ball under the advancing Joe Corrigan. Newcastle United had scored at Wembley and I was there. Unrelenting joy, unbounded emotion and almost certainly the one goal I've celebrated more joyously than any other scored by Newcastle (Cole's at Grimsby in May 1993 would probably come a close second). Pandemonium ensued, and I remember one supporter, with a pot on his broken leg, jumping up and down in joy waving his crutches oblivious to any pain from his injury – that was how much it meant to countless numbers of Geordies. What made it even better was that Gowling had scored at our end of the ground which always adds that little extra something to the celebrations. Half-time arrived and with the scoreline standing at 1-1 it was the Geordie fans who were on a high and confident that another goal in the second half would bring the Cup back to Tyneside.

Mick Mahoney, the Newcastle goalkeeper, received a tremendous reception from the fans as he made his way down the pitch to begin the second half, but alas for both him and the supporters the next five minutes were to prove fateful for United. City attacked early on and when an innocuous looking ball was headed across the penalty area Newcastle-born Dennis Tueart, a Cup winner with Sunderland in 1973, managed to execute a truly magnificent overhead kick which ran agonisingly past the outstretched hands of Mahoney into the corner of the net. It was a goal in a million and despite their bitter disappointment the Geordies were dignified and sporting enough to applaud Tueart's special talent.

A few half chances came and went and as the minutes ticked by the result and the imminent pain of defeat would become a stark reality. Geordie passion was never dimmed though and the unbelievable ovation accorded to the team on the final whistle was better than any winning team could ever have wished for. Unusually the Newcastle team trooped up to the Royal Box first to receive their runners-up medals and, because of the special nature of the occasion and the fact that we couldn't be ignored, there was a lap of 'honour' which certainly was not common practice but was appreciated and thoroughly enjoyed by one and all. City meanwhile had collected the League Cup and made their way to our end first for their lap of honour. I cannot imagine any other winning team being so warmly applauded by the losing supporters as was the case at Wembley that afternoon. I don't know why but even I found myself chanting the words 'City, City' a couple of times as the emotion became overwhelming. Mike Doyle, the City captain that day, later went on record to praise the United supporters' contribution to the Final as the best he had ever witnessed, which was a generous tribute indeed.

And so it was all over. We didn't leave the stadium until it had almost cleared and when we could finally tear ourselves away it was with a feeling of despair at defeat coupled with the pleasure of having been lucky enough to have been part of a day that will live in the memory for ever, despite my not having a video of the game.

01/03/76 – WEMBLEY HOMECOMING

Win or lose it was inevitable that the Tyneside public would give the team a marvellous welcome back to Newcastle. What unfolded was totally beyond belief. Nick, Mini and myself caught the bus to town immediately after school and even then, at least three hours before the team were due back at St. James' Park the crowds were beginning to gather. The choice we had was to either find a good place on the route to the ground or actually go into the ground to see them. Both had their advantages but in the end we decided that a place on the Leazes End was the best option as the atmosphere was likely to be better.

It is unusual these days for returning Cup teams to go back to their grounds, rather they simply go on a tour of the streets and end up outside the City or Town Hall. With Newcastle United having decided to return to the ground no one really knew what to expect or how many people would turn up. In the event 50,000 packed into the ground and this was just to welcome home a team that had lost a Cup Final! Entry to the ground was free and for the thousands unable to gain access they missed an occasion to rank with the best. No goals, no exciting play to applaud, but the passion and enthusiasm generated by the fans when the players humbly appeared from the tunnel sent shivers down my spine. Every player was cheered to the hilt and the whole ground rose in unison to pour adulation upon their heroes. For a losing team the welcoming home 'party' was phenomenal, and could only have taken place at Newcastle United.

03/03/76 – NEWCASTLE v STOKE CITY (0-1)

If ever a match was to prove anti-climactic then this was it. Forty eight hours after such an emotional homecoming 39,000 supporters filed into St. James' Park for the visit of Stoke City. The exertions from the previous Saturday at Wembley, and the thought of an FA Cup Sixth Round tie at Derby in three days time, combined to contribute to a lack-lustre performance which resulted in a 1-0 defeat. There was no booing of the team whatsoever, though such a performance was entitled to be criticised. The Geordies were in no mood to interrupt the party mood and were content to satisfy themselves with a good night out in the town after the match.

This fixture does hold one other memory for me as it featured the home debut, albeit as a substitute, of Ray Hudson. Ray, or 'Rocky' as he was affectionately known, was a true Geordie lad from Dunston and I took an instant liking to him. He was young and immensely talented, a real flair player. Perhaps the management at the club at that time didn't nurture his talent enough as he only went on to make 16 full appearances in the next two seasons before flying off to Fort Lauderdale in Florida to begin a successful career in the North American Soccer League. I thought Hudson was as good as Gascoigne ever was in his early days at Newcastle, and considered it a tragedy that he never fulfilled his undoubted potential on Tyneside.

06/03/76 – DERBY COUNTY v NEWCASTLE (4-2)

Could the lads raise themselves once more and keep what had proved to be such a wonderful season rolling forward? Derby County were more than awkward opposition, especially on their own Baseball Ground pitch which was notorious for being one of the muddiest and heaviest playing surfaces in the Football League throughout the 1970s. It didn't help either that Mick Mahoney was ruled out and Eddie Edgar was thrown in at the deep end to make his United debut. Another of my less than favourite players, Ray 'Bomber' Blackhall was in the side replacing the cultured Irving Nattrass. Blackhall was anything but cultured and, although I suppose he always gave his all, he quite simply wasn't up to it. He did manage two goals in his short Newcastle career, one of which remarkably I can still remember – an outrageous right wing cross against Wrexham in the FA Cup in 1978 which actually ended up being an unintentional shot as it looped over a surprised Dai Davies' head and into the net.

Newcastle were on a hiding to nothing at Derby and in the end the 4-2 scoreline in their favour probably flattered us. I was able to watch the highlights on *Match of the Day* and when you do, knowing that your team is going to lose, it makes for rather uncomfortable and indeed unpleasurable viewing. You still have to watch it though and I was left with the abiding memory of Bruce Rioch smashing a 25 yard thunderbolt past the flailing arms of Edgar as being the end of my 1976 FA Cup dreams. If someone had told me then it would be another 19 years before we would reach the last eight of the FA Cup I would never have believed them. Sad but true.

20/03/76 – NEWCASTLE v MANCHESTER UNITED (3-4)

Manchester United were a resurgent side under the flamboyant Tommy Docherty and came to St. James' Park along with at least five thousand supporters. I hated it when teams brought large numbers of fans to our ground, especially when they scored and got the opportunity to celebrate. Manchester had numerous flair players in their team: Hill, Coppell, Daly and Pearson to name but four and to be honest they were an attractive side. Nevertheless the fact that we scored two own goals (John Bird and Pat Howard) contributed hugely to their 4-3 win and as I left the ground at the end of the game I simply couldn't bring myself to look at the Manchester supporters who were still in a state of animated excitement. Our form around this time was typically up and down, we were hovering between 14th and 15th place in the table, but I suppose based on what we'd seen in the past three months we didn't really have any cause for complaint.

A quick word on John Bird before we move on – a friend of mine from school, Mick Fagan, who was in the next year up, had recently been training at Newcastle during the holidays. He was a defender and had been taken under the wing of Bird who had actually shown him how to commit sly and dirty fouls. It absolutely amazed me that seasoned professionals were teaching impressionable youngsters such conduct. Coincidentally Mick Fagan's career had virtually turned full circle as he was lucky enough to be back playing for Ponteland United in the early 1990s – I just wish I could say the same for myself.

17/04/76 – NEWCASTLE v BURNLEY (0-1)

We weren't to know it at the time but this was to be Malcolm Macdonald's final appearance in a black and white shirt at St. James' Park. Macdonald was worshipped and adored by all of Tyneside and his five seasons at Newcastle were treasured by all who had the privilege of seeing him play. Such highs as his hat-trick against Liverpool on his home debut, his memorable strike against Leicester, five goals in an England shirt against Cyprus in 1975 (upstaging Kevin Keegan, of all people, at the time which delighted us no end, especially as Keegan had dared to criticise Macdonald as being too greedy to play with) and perhaps best of all, his two goals against Burnley in the 1974 FA Cup semi-final at Hillsborough. Macdonald was nothing but a goalscorer and the Geordies loved him almost as much as they had Milburn 20 years earlier. He wore the famous number nine shirt and those players down the years who succeeded in that shirt at St. James' Park were guaranteed to receive a level of adulation they would be unable to find on any other footballing stage. Andy Cole, the man in possession of the shirt from March 1993 until his departure to Manchester United in January 1995, regretfully passed up the opportunity to become the greatest of them all.

It had been apparent during the latter weeks of the season that all was not well at St. James' Park between Gordon Lee and Macdonald. Lee wanted Macdonald to contribute more to the overall team effort and thought he was a lazy type of player only interested in his own personal self glory. Alan Gowling, a far less skilful and exciting player, was Macdonald's striking partner and Lee much preferred him to Macdonald – so much so that he even made public his view that Gowling would outscore Macdonald during the season. I think Lee did this just to spite Macdonald, but he was proved to be correct in his judgement as Gowling knocked in 30 goals to Macdonald's 24. Gowling was one of those players who was never hero worshipped at St. James' Park. He was intellectually very bright and I suppose was not your typical footballer. Nevertheless he did earn the respect of his fellow professionals and, in the end, of the Newcastle public also.

The match itself brings back not a single memory. It is recorded in the record books as a 1-0 away victory for Burnley, but had we known at the time that Supermac would never again grace St. James' Park, things would surely have been very different. Malcolm Macdonald, 228 appearances and 121 goals – thanks for the memories.

During this season we had played close on 60 competitive matches and naturally the clamour to reduce the strain on players had been aired again. It's an argument constantly put forward by many people in the game, most notably Gary Lineker, as to why the England team consistently under-achieves on the world stage, but it's not an argument I agree with. I see no problem with players playing two games a week. Injuries are part and parcel of the game and if players say they can't cope with this, or that they are getting stale, I've no sympathy for them. Players in America's National Basketball Association play nigh on 100 top level games each season and they keep on turning on the style – perhaps the fittest athletes in world sport?, although professional cyclists or elite marathon runners may beg to differ. The other thing of course is that playing a large number of games means that you are having a successful season, and surely no one would object to that.

1975/76 – Season's Summary

League	P	W	D	L	F	A	Pts.	Pos.
	42	15	9	18	71	62	39	15th

Top Scorers		
Alan Gowling	30	
Malcolm Macdonald	24	
Tommy Craig	11	

1976/77 – LEE OUT, DINNIS IN

With Supermac having departed in the summer for £333,000 to Arsenal, many fans wondered quite what the 1976/77 season would bring. I was now in the fifth form at school and that meant 'O' level year. I didn't care too much for school work, as sport was now my only interest in life. Dad did well to guide me through my exams by insisting I did plenty of revision, which proved very boring and frustrating, especially when I could have been outside playing some sort of sport. In the end, without the constant pressure he brought to bear on me, I would never have got any qualifications and for that I will be eternally grateful to him. I'd taken a great liking to such sports as cricket, golf and tennis too, but there was never any doubt that football was, and would always be, the be all and end all of my life, with of course Newcastle United at the forefront of everything.

21/08/76 – NEWCASTLE v DERBY COUNTY (2-2)

The summer of 1976 was of course famous for its long hot August days, and the first day of the football season was certainly a scorcher.

Much to my delight Rocky Hudson was in the starting line up while the post-Macdonald striking line up featured Alan Gowling and Micky Burns. Burns had played in a wide position the previous season but had been moved infield to team up with Gowling for the new season. I liked Micky Burns and you could describe him as a poor man's Peter Beardsley, which doesn't imply any criticism of him only because the genius of Beardsley is incomparable. Stewart Barrowclough, a good but frustratingly inconsistent winger, whom I best remember for dummying a crossfield pass that Supermac put away against Leeds United during the 1972/73 season, made up the forward line. For those of you who never saw Barrowclough, he vaguely reminds me of Everton's Andrei Kanchelskis, although not quite in the same class!

A 36,000 opening day crowd saw four goals shared and, much to my delight, a goal by Rocky Hudson. It was a disappointing beginning although it was the prelude of a season that, in terms of the final league position, proved the most successful in my lifetime of following the club – that is until the 1993/94 season of course.

04/12/76 – ARSENAL v NEWCASTLE (5-3)

The obvious significance of this fixture was that it pitted Malcolm Macdonald against Newcastle United. With us being in third place in the league it was a big game and accordingly the *Match of the Day* cameras were present.

Supermac had of course left United in the summer under something of a cloud. Rumours were that Ernie Clay, the late Fulham Chairman, had had something to do with his transfer but that's another story. The supporters still idolised him but a number of players certainly bore him a grudge and the pre-match atmosphere within the marble halls of Highbury was a little frosty to say the least. The likes of Mick Mahoney though didn't hold such feelings and it was nice to see the two of them laughing and joking together before the game.

Macdonald predictably was anxious to put one over Gordon Lee and the press built up the game as being a vindictive battle between the two. Lee could only prepare his team in the best way he knew how and then sit and watch, whereas Macdonald had much more control over his own fate by actually being on the field of play. And so it proved. Macdonald scored a hat-trick, his third coming very late in the game when he headed past a statuesque Mahoney, raised both arms aloft in triumph and milked the applause from the Arsenal supporters for all it was worth. Lee meanwhile sat grim faced in the dug-out feeling desperately disappointed that the man he had forced out of St. James' Park enjoyed the last laugh. As for me I was pleased in a way that Macdonald had shown his undoubted talent once again but devastated, as I always am, when we lose. There were even occasions, after a defeat, when Mum had to admonish me for being too moody!

27/12/76 – NEWCASTLE v SUNDERLAND (2-0)

Derby day at St. James' Park and for me my first real taste of a fixture against the enemy. Sunderland, despite being only 10 miles away on the coast, exist in an entirely different culture to the Geordies. They are the poor relations of the North East of England and when the rest of the country mistakenly terms them as Geordies it makes my blood boil.

We were lying in a more than creditable fifth position in the league, while Sunderland were anchored to the foot of the table. I was absolutely desperate for a home win, not only because current form demanded it, but because defeat was totally unthinkable. Some defeats are heartbreaking because of the importance of the occasion, for example an FA Cup Final. A defeat against Sunderland would have brought a different type of torture, and the anxiety I felt throughout the match up to the moment Alan Kennedy scored the second and clinching goal in a 2-0 victory, was something I had not experienced before at a match. The Leazes End seemed to be fuller than I had ever known it, and the joyous celebrations on the final whistle at the expense of the Wearsiders (the term Mackem had yet to be introduced in the 1970s) massed behind the Gallowgate goal, went on for what seemed an eternity. Some games stick in your memory more than others and this one for obvious reasons is one of them. I can remember almost exactly where I was standing on the terrace, and even as I write visions of the game flash through my mind in an uncanny sort of way. It's just like being transported back in time, so vivid is the memory, as the ball hits the back of the net at the Leazes End and we all surge uncontrollably forward.

The notion of surging, and the whole issue of terraces, is regretfully something of the past. Despite the magnificently appointed St. James' Park being the archetypal football stadium, and one that I am immensely proud of, the swaying masses of a crowd and the emotions and passions generated by such a gathering are incomparable. The new generation of supporter, who hasn't had the opportunity to experience such terrace life, is one who sadly will probably never appreciate how my generation of supporter was brought up in the game.

Maybe something like the San Mames in Bilbao would have been the answer where the splendid architecture is complemented by small standing areas (maybe holding 4,000) behind each goal. Unfortunately, with Lord Justice Taylor's report being fixed in concrete, this will never realistically be the case. Memories will live forever though.

29/01/77 – NEWCASTLE v MANCHESTER CITY (1-3)

Sheffield United had been beaten in the third round of the FA Cup to set up a mouth watering tie at St. James' Park against Manchester City. The special magic of the Cup had lit up Tyneside again but the game and the hopes of another successful Cup run weren't the only topic of conversation in the week leading up to the game.

Managerial issues were threatening to boil over and all because rumours were rife strongly linking Gordon Lee with a move to Everton, following the sacking of Billy Bingham at Goodison Park. Hardly ideal preparation for the players and the unrest amongst supporters was pretty evident too as the ground began filling up. We'd already been put out of the League Cup earlier in the season by City's neighbours United (I hardly dare mention the 7-2 scoreline which at the time had to be, along with the Hereford result, the most embarrassing defeat I had known) and so a Manchester double was something barely worth contemplating.

With the omens being so bad Newcastle never got out of first gear and an inept performance resulted in a miserable 3-1 defeat. David Craig's bizarre own goal summed up the day, and Alan Gowling's single strike proved meaningless.

Apparently Lee had made up his mind to leave St. James' Park the day before the match, and had told the players as much, but it was only in the wake of our cup exit that his decision to join Everton was confirmed to the supporters. Despite the fact that we were in fifth position in the league some people were pleased to see the back of Lee but it was the manner in which he departed that left a bitter taste in the mouth, a little like the feeling the FA must have felt when Don Revie walked out on the England job for rich pickings in the desert. After a bright start to his time at St. James' Park Lee had caused some resentment among many supporters mainly through the departures of Macdonald and Hibbitt. Had we done anything wrong? I don't think so but that didn't stop him from turning his back on the Geordies and walking out. For the majority of the supporters he never was, and never will be, forgiven for this.

First team coach at the club was the affable and very personable Richard Dinnis. Largely unknown in football circles he had been brought in by Lee and was very popular with the players – so much so that they formed themselves into an 'action group', led by the likes of Nattrass, Kennedy and Cannell, to voice their feelings to the Board of Directors and more or less insist that Richard Dinnis be given the manager's job. After a little procrastination the Board gave in and Dinnis was installed in the St. James' Park hot seat. The Board at this time were, to say the least, not popular – led by the 'pirate' Lord Westwood (he wore a patch over his eye) his fellow board members were, generally speaking, all fairly old men not geared up to running a successful modern day football club and happy to be in a position of power at the club whilst treating the lifeblood of the club, the supporters, with disdain. Nepotism was rife at boardroom level, and when the likes of Malcolm Dix tried to involve himself in boardroom matters (fully supported by nearly all of Tyneside) the board members simply closed ranks, rebuked Dix's challenge, and closed their minds to any progressive action at the club. One little known board member at the time, Gordon McKeag, was to rise to the position of Chairman in the mid 1980s and we'll hear more about him and the turmoil (despite his best intentions) he brought to the club later on. Suffice to say at present that he virtually single-handedly prevented the Sir John Hall era at St. James' Park even starting and that would have been a real footballing tragedy.

08/04/77 – SUNDERLAND v NEWCASTLE (2-2)

Richard Dinnis had proved to be a shrewd appointment as, since the FA Cup defeat, results had picked up and the fine team spirit within the club had helped take us up to fourth position in the league. Sunderland meanwhile had managed to give themselves a fighting chance of avoiding the dreaded spectre of relegation which had seemed a certainty at Christmas. Before our Good Friday clash they had won six out of their last eight matches, risen from bottom to 19th place (they must have been so far adrift at the bottom to have only climbed three places!) and were in a much more confident and buoyant mood as derby day approached.

As for me this was to be my first visit to Roker Park for a match. The voucher system enabled us to obtain tickets for the Roker End of the ground, and as Nick and Mini weren't able to go I'd made plans to travel with some other friends from school, Dave Skipsey and Paul Hughes, mainly because their parents were both going and I'd be able to get a lift. Many thousands descended on Sunderland by bus or train but for me the preferred option was obviously the car. Paul Hughes was a funny character, he was known at school as 'Huggy' or Hug-Hez' due to the fact that on our first day at High School back in 1974 the Geography teacher, when reading out the class register, called Paul 'Hug-Hez' rather than pronouncing Hughes in the normal way. His nickname has stuck ever since – as for me and my brother we were both simply called 'Hanny'; John was 'Big Hanny', because he was older and taller than me, and of course I was 'Little Hanny'.

Sunderland's ground is situated in the Roker/Fulwell area of Sunderland, a little bit outside of the town centre, whereas St. James' Park is located slap bang in the middle of Newcastle. I have always thought the city centre siting of St. James' Park to be a major advantage over many other grounds as it is so much more pleasurable, and convenient on match days to be able to go to town, do whatever you do (pre-match drinking for 99% of Geordies) and then simply roll out of the pub and be able to walk a very short distance to the ground. The atmosphere and identity of a club is much better served with a ground in among the heart of the city rather than at places like say Leeds where it needs a bus ride from the city centre to reach Elland Road. This may appear to be a fairly insignificant point, but I'm convinced it's one of the ingredients that gives the Geordies their unrivalled passion for football.

Roker Park is hidden between countless back to back houses and, not to put too fine a point on it, not in a particularly nice area (apologies to all you Rokerites!). It's quite easy to spot though as you drive along the aptly-named Newcastle Road towards Sunderland as the four floodlight pylons are distinctive landmarks. As we parked I remember Mr. Skipsey being a little uneasy about having to leave his car in a side street for the duration of the afternoon. This is always a problem with football as I was to find out myself in later years. You're always conscious that some of the local yobs may damage your car and so you always try and find a parking space that is safe, provides relatively easy access out to the main road back home, and at the same time isn't too far from the ground. When we went to Derby in April 1992 we parked in an official car park close to the ground, however when we returned to the car after the game we found that some joker, who had obviously arrived late, had left his car blocking the exit. The solution was easy – nine or ten Geordies simply pushed the car out of the way, its wheels scraping along the gravel as it went, and abandoned it on the other side of the road. On another occasion at Leicester we got lost in the numerous side streets near the ground and couldn't remember where we had left the car. When we eventually found it we all breathed a large sigh of relief, especially me, as I was driving!

Away fans, more often than not at football matches, are escorted upon their arrival in a 'foreign' city to the ground. At least that is the intention, and certainly those who arrive in large numbers by coach or rail are easier to contain in this manner. For those like ourselves, and the countless others who arrive independently, there is often no control over our pre-match movements. The ways and means by which Geordies use to travel to away matches never ceases to amaze me. Many a time we have been speeding along the road in a car and have seen mini-buses, transit vans and even 'Luton' vans overflowing with supporters, often with some of them literally hanging out of the back. It goes without saying also that toilet stops on such trips are pretty frequent with passing motorists turning their noses up in disgust as they drive past.

Walking towards Roker Park you could spot the habitual and ritual violence that was prevalent during this era. Rival groups of supporters were roaming the streets and despite the presence of the police you could sense a very uneasy calm. Shouts would be heard at the end of a street and suddenly there would be a mass charge as one or other set of supporters would take off in pursuit of a possible confrontation. I found that while it was a little scary it was relatively easy to stay out of trouble. If you didn't want to get involved you could use your common sense to bypass all the trouble makers and the no-go areas and let the hooligans fight each other! It becomes a little more serious when objects become involved and the throwing of missiles take place. I distinctly remember seeing a photograph of a lad at Liverpool who had been hit in the face by a dart which was actually sticking through his eye. On another occasion at Middlesbrough, while I was walking away from the ground under escort, a full brick came hurtling towards me from the opposite side of the road, fortunately missing me by inches and smashing on to the pavement.

It's only the minority who travel to football intent on being violent – many kids just liked to 'look hard' and would get carried away with the disruptive element without being an integral part of it. You would look and glare suspiciously at the rival gangs lurking on the street corners but shuffle past without anything happening. If you went looking for a fight (and I wonder what mentality a person has to do such a thing) then you would find one, and really it was as simple as that.

We were packed like sardines into the Roker End although not as bad as I was to experience on a couple of occasions in the 1980s. We still had a European place to aim for and the pleasure of putting another nail into the Mackems' relegation coffin was incentive enough. As was the case earlier in the season, defeat would be unthinkable and North East pride was firmly on the line.

In recent weeks Sunderland had smashed six goals past both West Bromwich and West Ham and when Kevin Arnott opened the scoring at the Roker End in the first half our worst fears were brought to the surface. Arnott celebrated his goal at the expense of the Geordies and he naturally received a torrent of abuse. The anger directed towards him was incredible – I don't know how bad I was but the real paranoid hatred of some individuals was frightening.

After a half time interval of trading insults with the Fulwell End, Bob Lee, not the most skilful of centre forwards, put Sunderland 2-0 ahead and the worst defeat imaginable was beginning to look like becoming a reality. If ever you wished your dreams to come true then this was the time for it. Would they? You bet they did as first Paul Cannell and then Tommy Craig, with a stupendous free kick, brought us level and stunned the Mackems into silence. Cannell was never really a regular first teamer but still was something of a cult figure. His most famous goal had probably come at Elland Road earlier in the season when he scored with a remarkable shot from an acute angle, and the fact that his surname also rhymed with a swearing expression beginning with 'F' didn't do him any harm. Not winning was disappointing but to have salvaged a draw at least kept us on course for Europe and the Mackems for relegation. Minor skirmishes outside the ground ensued, but with the volume of Geordies pouring into the streets, safety in numbers saw us clear of the ground and back to the car.

Despite losing four of our last five matches at the end of the season we managed to hold on to fifth place in the league and that was good enough to earn a place in the UEFA Cup (formerly known as the Fairs Cup) for the following season. Sunderland meanwhile continued their battle against relegation and went into their final game of the season at Everton with their fate still in the balance. Stoke City and Tottenham had already been relegated and the final place rested between Sunderland, Bristol City and Coventry, the latter two coincidentally playing each other at Highfield Road on the same night Sunderland were at Goodison Park. There were all sorts of permutations possible and so the

Football League ordered both matches to kick off simultaneously. Despite that directive Coventry City managed to delay their kick off by 15 minutes, purportedly to allow the spectators time to gain access to the ground, and when the Sunderland game ended with them on the wrong end of a 2-0 scoreline the two protagonists at Highfield Road turned the game of football into a farce by making no effort to score again and thus alter the 2-2 scoreline, which both teams knew would keep them up now that Sunderland had lost. You may recall a similar situation occurring in the 1982 World Cup Finals when neighbours West Germany and Austria contrived to play out a 1-0 win for the Germans – a result that would take both teams through to the second phase of the competition at the expense of Algeria who naturally enough were left fuming.

The Football League conducted an enquiry, which predictably came to nothing, and so Sunderland went down. They must have been absolutely livid at what had happened at Coventry, but for all the onlookers on Tyneside it brought nothing but joy and amusement. Although their relegation was greeted with such pleasure, it did mean that the 1977/78 season wouldn't have any derby matches (unless the teams were to be drawn together in the Cup) with all the extra ingredients such clashes produce, and that was rather sad. Their promotion to the Premier League, at the end of the 1995/96 season, at least meant the renewal of Tyne/Wear hostilities – and to think how close they were to footballing oblivion before Peter Reid took over at Roker Park.

1976/77 – Season's Summary

League	P	W	D	L	F	A	Pts.	Pos.
	42	18	13	11	64	49	49	5th

Top Scorers		
Micky Burns	17	
Paul Cannell	13	
Alan Gowling	12	

1977/78 – RELEGATION

Optimism was running high before the start of the season. Our fifth placed finish the previous season augured well as the big kick off approached and, with the added excitement of European football to look forward to once again, life felt pretty good.

This was also the first year that I hadn't gone away on the annual family caravanning holiday as John and I were old enough to be left at home by ourselves. I was about to go into the sixth form at school with eight '0' level passes behind me and I had the dubious pleasure of two years of studying Biology, Chemistry and Geography at 'A' level to look forward to. Why couldn't I have been good enough to have been a professional footballer, I would ask myself, instead of having to endure education in order to earn a living in life?

20/08/77 – NEWCASTLE v LEEDS UNITED (3-2)

The arrival of Leeds United at St. James' Park for the opening day fixture was eagerly anticipated. Being at home meant there would be no difficulty in attending this match and the resulting 3-2 victory, with Micky Burns scoring twice, brought a fine and happy start to another season. Little did anyone know at the time what was going to follow as we inexplicably proceeded to lose our next 10 league matches on the trot (plus defeat at the hands of Millwall in the League Cup) and plummeted to rock bottom of the First Division.

10/09/77 – NEWCASTLE v WEST BROMWICH ALBION (0-3)

I'd forsaken my usual spot on the Leazes End for this game as our newsagent, Graham Wilson, gave me his season ticket for the old West Stand. It was the first time I had been in this part of the ground and I enjoyed the experience immensely. All the seats were wooden and despite the rather archaic condition of the stand there was still something special about it; the way it rose up from the back of the Centre Paddock terrace with its press box famously perched on the arch of the roof. Nowadays it would be considered an eyesore, but in its day it was part of the heritage of Newcastle United.

West Bromwich Albion took us to the cleaners in this match. We were as comprehensively outplayed as I can recall and the 3-0 scoreline could have been a lot worse. The reason for our humiliation was down to two men, namely Cyrille Regis and Laurie Cunningham. Both were youngsters making their way in the game, and both were black players. Nowadays black players are commonplace at virtually every football club but in the 1970s they were a rare species (I remember West Ham's Clyde Best but that was about all) and indeed it wasn't until the following year that Nottingham Forest's Viv Anderson became the first black player to represent England. Regis and Cunningham both played up front for Albion and, in addition to those two wreaking havoc in our defence all afternoon, Brendon Batson, another coloured player, was in the side at right back. The 'three degrees', or 'three black pearls' as they were known, left a lasting impression on me that afternoon and the memory of Cunningham skipping nonchalantly past either David Craig or Alan Kennedy tight on the touch line next to the West Stand remains an abiding memory. There was also the famous occasion in December 1978 when West Bromwich travelled to Old Trafford to defeat Manchester United 5-3 in a memorable display of attacking football inspired by Cunningham and Regis. Cunningham later went on to play in Spain and it was a sad day when I learned of his premature death in a car accident in Madrid.

It is unfortunate to recollect that Newcastle United supporters, or at least a large number of them, have had a notorious reputation in the past 15 years or so in respect of their disgusting behaviour towards coloured players. Nowadays those problems are well behind us and I'm sure the success of Andy Cole and Ruel Fox when they were at Newcastle played a major part in ridding the club of its racist overtones despite rumblings (overplayed by the *Daily Mirror*) of such feelings again surfacing in December 1994. In the days when racism was at its worst, every black player who played against Newcastle was subject to a constant tirade of booing and, worse still, infantile monkey type grunting followed by a barrage of bananas being hurled from the terraces at them. At other grounds even the likes of world class players such as John Barnes were subject to abuse when Liverpool played at Goodison Park.

Newcastle had the occasional black player throughout the 1980s; Howard Gayle (he of the 'He's black, he's broon, he's playing for the Toon' song), Tony Cunningham (of whom a press friend of mine, Peter Ball of *The Times*, said could trap a ball further than most players could kick it! – and that just about summed up his ability or rather lack of it) and of course Mirandinha (who came to the club in a wave of publicity and whilst creating tremendous interest never really left his mark on English football) but the problem of racism was always boiling away under the surface ready to erupt at the first sight of any black player. Racist chanting was never something I condoned and with Andy Cole and Ruel Fox being warmly welcomed and having done so well at St. James' Park throughout 1993 and 1994 it just goes to show how hypocritical many of my fellow Geordies could be.

02/11/77 – NEWCASTLE v BASTIA (1-3)

The French club Bastia were in town tonight for a match all of Tyneside was looking forward to despite our being at the bottom of the table. Bastia were to come to the attention of all of Europe in the late 1980s when a portable stand they had erected for a French League match against Marseilles collapsed, killing many spectators.

In the first round of the competition the Irish side, Bohemians, had been our opponents and after a 0-0 result in Ireland the tie was settled at St. James' Park with a four goal United burst. It wasn't always as convincing as that though as for long periods of the game we led only 1-0 and I couldn't help thinking that if Bohemians had sneaked a goal they would have put us out on the away goals rule. Thankfully our blushes were spared and the goals which eventually followed were a fair reflection of the play.

This was a second round second leg match and we went into the tie trailing 2-1 from the first leg in Corsica. For the first leg, radio commentary was the order of the day and when Paul Cannell put us one up at half-time we were literally hugging our radios with joy. A second-half equaliser from Bastia put a damper on the proceedings and we were all satisfied with what appeared to be an extremely creditable 1-1 draw when, in virtually the last minute, Newcastle naively tried to take a quick throw in – when all they had to do was slow the play down – lost possession and cruelly conceded a second goal. It was one of those nights when you went to bed not believing what had happened, constantly tossing and turning thinking 'if only' and 'why did it have to happen to us'.

Reading the match reports in the paper the following morning didn't do much to cheer you up either, and having to troop off to school just about capped everything.

Bastia had the famous Dutch World Cup star Johnny Rep, he of the famous Cruyff/Neeskens/Rensenbrink master class of 1974, and to see such a player at St. James' Park was a real thrill. I remember the brilliant Portuguese striker Eusebio also turning out at St. James' Park in August 1971 when Benfica came to Newcastle to play a pre season friendly. Perhaps our pre-match optimism was misplaced (how often can you say that) as Bastia established a 2-1 half time lead meaning that we would need three goals in the second half to win the tie on aggregate. For a short while it looked possible as we bombarded the Bastia goal but then, out of the blue, Rep collected the ball just inside our half, strode forward unchallenged and from all of 35 yards unleashed a ferocious dipping right-footed bullet of a shot which flew past Steve Hardwick before he had time to even think about moving. It was a stunning strike and after that both teams knew the tie was as good as over.

31/12/77 – NEWCASTLE v LIVERPOOL (0-2)

What a difference a year makes. As little as 12 months ago we were fifth in the league and a bright future looked assured. Now we had slumped to the bottom of the league with what seemed like a second rate team, a second rate manager and a whole load of discontented and disillusioned supporters.

Richard Dinnis had been sacked in November and this had been about as predictable an event as anyone in football could forecast. Dinnis was not appreciated by the Directors and only found his way into the hot seat through the action of his players. An example of the mistrust that existed was the astonishing situation that had occurred a few weeks into the season when the Directors had bought a player, Ralph Callachan from Hearts, without the knowledge of the manager. An incredible situation and one that was destined never to succeed, despite Callachan being a useful ball player on his day.

In their wisdom the Board appointed the former Wolverhampton Wanderers manager Bill McGarry to replace Dinnis. McGarry was a dour uninspiring character, a strict disciplinarian, and as far as the supporters were concerned, a very unpopular choice. The Board obviously would hope he would come to the club and turn its fortunes around but the fact that they appointed a character like McGarry in the first place spoke volumes about the way they were managing the affairs of the club at the time.

The game against Liverpool was the third of the holiday period and followed defeats against Manchester City (0-4) and Nottingham Forest (0-2). McGarry had brought two new strikers from Scotland, Mark McGhee and Mike Larnach, and the latter made his debut this afternoon. It can't have been easy for either of them (McGhee played his first game at Leeds 48 hours later) as young strikers coming to England to play in what quite frankly was a poor team. Liverpool won 2-0 and Larnach's contribution I recall was one shot that flew high into the Leazes End. Losing was becoming a bad habit and once you were in a slump it was nigh impossible to get out of it. The aforementioned match at Elland Road against Leeds got the New Year off to a good start with a 2-0 victory, but remarkably that was to be our last victory of the season as we went on to collect only a further eight draws from our remaining 19 matches. It was difficult to believe there was a worse team in the division than us, but there was, Leicester, who finished below us albeit on goal difference.

27/02/78 – BLYTH SPARTANS v WREXHAM (1-2)

With Newcastle producing performances of such dire ineptitude Blyth Spartans were to be the season's only bright point. Blyth is a small town in Northumberland situated about 15 miles north of Newcastle, and their football team played in the Northern League. Their exploits in the 1977/78 FA Cup Competition will go down in history, and when you realise how close they were to reaching the sixth round you can only feel terrible sympathy for them.

Our lot in black and white had exited from the competition at the fourth round stage at the hands of Wrexham. After a 2-2 draw at St. James' Park the Welsh side, who were in the Third Division, beat us 4-1, which even in our relegation season was a totally gutless and humiliating defeat. Was I angry? You bet, and it made me think of the comment that Bill Shankly made that football was more important than life or death. The defeat at Wrexham led me to conclude that Shankly was spot on with his assessment. As the first match had been drawn we did feature in the fifth round draw and with Blyth's fourth round tie at Stoke being a victim of the weather, the amazing prospect of Newcastle United at home to Blyth Spartans was thrown up as the draw came out as Wrexham or Newcastle versus Stoke or Blyth. The possibility of this contest was beyond belief but as with many of your footballing dreams they are never fulfilled. Newcastle versus Stoke had been the likely fifth round match but of course it turned out to be Wrexham versus Blyth Spartans.

The whole of the North East, and that's a rare event these days, was behind the Spartans as they travelled to Wales to face Wrexham. It was only a dubious last minute equaliser, due to a corner having to be re-taken because a corner flag had to be put back in place, that cost Blyth a famous victory. St. James' Park was the only venue where the replay could have been staged and a lock out crowd of 42,000, despite there being a ground capacity of 54,000, packed into the ground to cheer the non-leaguers into the sixth round and a dream home tie with mighty Arsenal.

Blyth had a pre-match dressing room ritual of psyching themselves up for the match and you could see their players were all fun loving but down to earth lads who played football in the spirit it was intended. Half an hour before the game the heavens opened and it rained to such an extent that the match could easily have been called off. It wasn't though and on a quagmire of a pitch Wrexham raced in to a two goal lead and held on for victory despite Blyth pulling one back in the second half. Blyth were heroic in defeat and were cheered to the hilt as they left the pitch.

It spoke volumes of Blyth that they, and not Newcastle United, attracted the biggest attendance of the season at St. James' Park.

29/03/78 – NEWCASTLE v MANCHESTER CITY (2-2)

The fact that Manchester City were the visitors to St. James' Park at the end of March wasn't important. The day was significant for every Geordie because the Directors had decreed that the Leazes End would be knocked down after the match in order to prepare it for re-development – funny how it took 15 years to start re-building!

The Leazes End was the spiritual home of every Geordie, and for me in particular I considered it the mecca of world football, and that's no exaggeration. Most grounds in England had their designated home supporters end, The Shed, The Kop, The

Stretford End etc., but for me the Leazes End could never be matched, although grudgingly I did admire Liverpool's Kop for its size and vibrancy. Liverpool and Newcastle probably share the honour of having the two most famous songs in football: 'You'll Never Walk Alone' and 'The Blaydon Races' respectively, and I know exactly how the Koppites felt when their terrace was closed for the last time at the end of the 1993/94 season.

Just to look at the Leazes End left me in awe. Even when walking round the back of the stand the first impression you got was of the large prison-like walls disappearing towards the sky. Even the graffiti adorning the walls was a part of the Leazes End culture with such 'messages' ranging from 'West Ham will die' (illustrating the Geordies' love of Cockneys) to the more general 'NUFC' and the like. Incidentally, while many Geordie fans call all London teams Cockneys, this is in fact not the case since to be a Cockney you need to be born within the sound of Bow Bells in East London. Richard Taylor, a true Cockney, and a good friend of mine by virtue of his basketball journalism, put me right on this point and he would know – he's a West Ham supporter! Anyway, Tottenham, Arsenal, Chelsea and the like therefore aren't strictly speaking Cockneys but we'll always think of them as such!

We had to make the most of the day and, like thousands of others, queued from early in the evening to get into the Leazes in order to be able to savour its unique atmosphere for the last time and for as long as possible. Everyone took up their usual places, even the cluster of old men, probably all over 60 with their overcoats and flat caps, who ritually stood in the same place week after week, fairly near the front but towards the East Stand side of the pitch. The Leazes End was primarily a man's domain but there were always a sprinkling of women to be seen, usually teenagers. Nowadays the proportion of women attending football matches is much higher than in the 1970s, probably as a result of the better facilities and reduced level of violence.

As we were as good as relegated the 2-2 scoreline on the night didn't matter, but after the final whistle virtually no one on the terrace would leave. As well as being a demonstration against the Directors for their indefensible action in closing the Leazes End, it was an act that you simply had to follow. The Leazes End had given us all so much over the years and its passing could almost be seen as a death in the family, although that is probably taking things a little out of perspective.

As the police moved in to clear people out we all left slowly but quietly, each one of us looking round at our surroundings for the last time and taking with us memories that will remain with us for a lifetime.

26/04/78 – NEWCASTLE v NORWICH CITY (2-2)

This was the last home game of the season and, although we weren't to know it at the time, the last match at St. James' Park in the first division for six years. Six years! Yes, that was the length of time we were set to endure in the backwaters of the second division, and had I known it at the time I would have cried – perhaps I did anyway.

I'd been to every single game at St. James' Park during the season but I was destined not to see the final curtain being brought down. The match was scheduled for a Wednesday evening and I had to be away from Newcastle for the whole week on, of all things, a Geography Field Week at Ford Castle in north Northumberland. No one at school could have shared or even appreciated my disappointment at missing the game, as despite it having been a dismal season I still needed to be there for the final act. I made sure I took a portable radio with me and remember missing the evening meal to stay in the dormitory to listen to the match after telling the teachers I wasn't feeling particularly well, was off my food and could I rest instead. A couple of the lads knew the truth but of course they didn't let on. Looking back it seems to be taking your devotion to an incredible degree for such a relatively low key game but it was just something that had to be done.

Attendances at St. James' Park had steadily fallen after Christmas and the turn out for this final fixture was a paltry 7,986 (the season's average was 25,000). It illustrated a total feeling of disillusionment in the supporters that so few turned up. I know that many stayed away purposely to show their dissent at the failings of the club, but I'm sure that those who were in attendance finished the season off in style by backing the team the only way they knew how and rounding proceedings off with a few heartfelt choruses of 'We'll support you evermore'.

Micky Burns and Alan Kennedy, who both would be transferred in the close season, scored Newcastle's goals in a 2-2 draw and all that was left was a visit to Filbert Street, Leicester, the following

Saturday to bring the season to its sad conclusion where a 3-0 defeat proved a pretty apt way of summing up a campaign that had begun with such high hopes but finished with the sorrow of relegation.

An amazing 51 players had been on first team duty throughout the season, which in many ways points to a club in turmoil. I remember when Aston Villa won the Championship in 1981 they only used 14 players – some difference. As you might expect a large proportion of these 51 players were simply not good enough to wear the famous black and white shirt. How on earth the likes of Andy Parkinson, David McLean and Martin Gorry managed to get a game was beyond me, and yet incredibly there was worse to come in the forthcoming seasons.

Another little football anecdote in 1978 concerned an appearance that Ponteland High School made on BBC Radio Newcastle's sports quiz for schools. Our team consisted of Michael Halliday, David Musgrove and myself. Hally will feature a lot more later – David was a statistical dream. He was never much of a performer on the field of play but more than made up for it off it and deservedly captained our team. We did reasonably well but fell at the quarter-final stage of the competition. Our team was organised by the Deputy Headmaster at school, Bob Crosby, who now, having retired does the Newcastle match commentaries for local radio. The following year I took part in Metro Radio's (Newcastle's independent radio station) sports quiz which was an individual test. The presenter, Peter Slater, who has since graduated to BBC Radio 5 Sport, wanted a contestant to answer questions on something other than football for their specialist subject and so he convinced me to tackle golf. I did, and managed nine out of ten which, coupled with the eight correct answers I got in the general round, meant I finished with a very respectable 17 out of 20. I've since lost the tape recording of the programme which Mum did for me, which is a shame as it's the sort of thing I would get a lot of pleasure listening to again.

06/06/78 – ARGENTINA v FRANCE (2-1)

The 1978 World Cup Finals in Argentina brought the fabulous ticker tape welcome from the Buenos Aires fans in the River Plate Stadium on the occasion of Argentina's matches – a wonderful sight – and of course the lament of Scotland manager Ally MacLeod.

Argentina had been out of the limelight in International football since their infamous appearance in the 1966 World Cup Quarter Final at Wembley. Having been given the opportunity by FIFA to stage the world's greatest sporting event, Argentina were ready to show the world they could perform at the highest level. Never mind their 6-0 thrashing of fellow South Americans Peru, the performance that captured my attention was their 2-1 defeat of an emerging French team in a Group One fixture. Platini had equalised for France on the hour but that was just the prelude for Leopoldo Luque, the lesser known of Argentina's striking partnership, to score with a stupendous half volley from the edge of the box. His, and the crowd's celebrations, were phenomenal. Argentina went on to lift the World Cup, and their success prompted Tottenham Hotspur to bring Ardiles and Villa to White Hart Lane, and Birmingham, less successfully, to buy Tarantini. The Mackems also bought an Argentinian a year later, Claudio Marangoni, but he never really adapted to English football and who could blame him – Roker Park not being the ideal environment to show off your footballing skills.

1977/78 – Season's Summary

League	P	W	D	L	F	A	Pts.	Pos.
	42	6	10	26	42	78	22	21st

Top Scorers		
Micky Burns		16
Tommy Craig		6
Alan Gowling		6

1978/79 – DIVISION TWO BLUES

Having been brought up on a diet of top class Division One football since my introduction to the game back in the late 1960s, and having marvelled over the talents of many outstanding players at St. James' Park (and not only those in black and white shirts), the prospect of second rate football was none too appealing. Only a promotion campaign would suffice and a nice little Cup run wouldn't be bad either! When the fixtures came out in the summer the substitution of the likes of Liverpool and Arsenal by Preston North End and Cambridge United, with due respect to the latter two, told its own story.

Somewhat misguidedly, blind passion being the mitigating circumstance, I had high hopes for the new season and along with Simmy (Alistair Sym) bought a season ticket for the Centre Paddock. Simmy lived on a farm three or four miles outside of Ponteland. He was very bright, intellectually, and also very witty. One memory of him stands out which summed up his sharp mind and came oddly enough when we were playing snowballs on the school field. I remember charging through one of the school play ground gates and made an off the cuff remark that we were 'defecting to the East'. Simmy immediately corrected me by saying 'you mean the West' which I don't recall sinking in straight away but of course now I know exactly what he meant! We shared a table in Biology classes at school and it was probably that which contributed to my messing up my Biology 'A' level exam the following summer. We did nothing but talk football (and many other sports too; naming the different Grand Prix drivers and which teams they drove for comes to mind for example) all through the lessons instead of concentrating on such as the symbiotic properties of some insignificant organism.

Peter Withe was our only major signing during the close season and considering that he came from Nottingham Forest it was a good boost to morale that he wanted to play for us. Other stalwarts in the side during the season included old 'favourites' such as Tommy Cassidy, a rotund jolly faced Irishman, Terry Hibbitt, he of the cultured left foot most fondly remembered for supplying ammunition for Supermac to score his goals, and Alan Shoulder, who came to the club in December from Blyth Spartans and would enjoy a good partnership with Withe. One memory of Withe, which demonstrated what a superb professional he was, was on the occasion I went to watch the team training at Close House (Newcastle University's sports ground). After training had finished the players returned to changing rooms that were located at the top of a pretty steep hill – Withe was the only player who sprinted up the hill which impressed me no end and I've always felt the success he went on to achieve at Aston Villa, which included the winning goal in the 1982 European Cup Final against Bayern Munich, was richly deserved.

The fact that I can hardly remember a good thing about the whole season sums up what a dire and forgettable year it was, what a stark contrast to the mid 1990s. After losing the first two matches and slumping to 20th in the league we never recovered. Watford beat us in the first round of the League Cup (yet another early undignified exit) and although we rose to the dizzy heights of sixth place just before Christmas, a five match losing streak quickly destroyed all delusions of grandeur and we hovered round about mid-table for the rest of the season rallying in the closing weeks to finish a mind boggling eighth.

What had become of my beloved Newcastle United? The team were useless, the ground was a mess and the Board lacked any real drive or ambition. It's hard to know how we managed to stomach those days especially with the way things are now and it could only have been our unfailing inbred feeling for the name Newcastle United that kept us going. For supporters who have had to suffer so much abject failure through their lifetime of supporting the club, the success we are reaping now cannot be more deserved by any other football supporters in Britain. It has never ceased to amaze (and annoy) me that 'Mickey Mouse' clubs like Coventry have held their place in Division One since 1967, and the likes of Wimbledon are still in the Premier League (I will greet their relegation with glee), while clubs like Arsenal and Everton have been members of the First Division/Premier League from almost the year dot. Clearly both clubs have experienced their ups and downs but nothing can match the number of disappointments the Geordies have had to endure. Yet through all this we still retain our deep rooted love of the game and demonstrate levels of passion for our team that are unrivalled anywhere.

The mismanagement of the club during this period is, I'm certain, also unique, although I am sure all of those across at Roker Park think that their lot have been equally culpable over the years, especially viewed against the way the two great rivals stand in almost different worlds; Newcastle with their growing wealth, magnificent stadium and top-ranked team, against Sunderland's poverty, ramshackle ageing ground and pathetic team. Even the Mackems wouldn't be able to argue with that and indeed many of them are publicly saying as much. If Peter Reid hadn't saved them from relegation at the end of the 1994/95 season goodness knows what would have become of them – certainly they got rid of the inadequate Mick Buxton just in time or the drop would have been inevitable. Perhaps some members of the Roker Board were wishing for relegation so that they wouldn't have had to implement all the regulations of the Taylor Report!

Back to Newcastle, and the state of St. James' Park in 1978 was an embarrassment. I'm ashamed to admit it but I went to Manchester with Dad just before Christmas and, whilst he was in a meeting, I took the chance to go and have a look at Old Trafford. I managed to get on to the terrace to have a look around and remember thinking how the two grounds were worlds apart. Having got rid of the real Leazes End the majority of supporters took to inhabiting the Gallowgate End with the East Corner being the favoured location. I still have vivid memories of the massive queues, and unique pre-game atmosphere, that used to build up outside the turnstiles, stark contrast to the situation today with terraces a distant memory. For those of you not familiar with St. James' Park the Gallowgate End was an open end and so the hard-core of the club's supporters were effectively made to watch their team in an end without a roof on it which, apart from giving them a soaking every time it rained, obviously detracted from the atmosphere within the ground (I hesitate to call it a stadium). The new Leazes End simply had a small section of terrace with a wall at the back no more than 12 feet high and became the home of the away supporters. All in all a disgraceful situation.

During the season we also suffered the total humiliation of the Mackems coming to St. James' Park and turning us over 4-1 with Gary Rowell notching a hat-trick. I recall that the Mackems, massed behind Leazes End goal, were surprisingly subdued throughout the game and didn't make a great deal of noise, which for a team winning 4-1 at the home of their greatest enemies amazed me. Another of my school friends, Lindsay Graves, who unfortunately grew up as a Sunderland fan, was also at the match and I've never stopped baiting him about this fact. We (I more than anyone else) call him 'Macas' for obvious reasons but to his eternal credit he takes all the stick we give him for being a Mackem really well and unlike the rest of us doesn't hate Newcastle in the way we all hate Sunderland. Macas is one of the rare breed of North Easterners who wants to see all the region's teams doing well, and indeed he often comes to a lot of Newcastle home and away games with the lads and incredibly is as raucous and passionate in his singing as the rest of us – his choruses of the Blaydon Races at Carrow Road on Mirandinha's debut immediately spring to mind. I did though get on the wrong side of Macas's wrath at the end of the 1985/86 season when we'd taken him with us to Leicester on the last day of the season. Newcastle had lost the game 2-0 but it didn't mean anything as we had finished 11th in Division One. Sunderland, on the other hand, were in Division Two and, on the season's final day, on the brink of relegation. I think Macas must have come with us because he couldn't bear the tension of watching Sunderland, anyway as the final whistle went we all wanted to hear how the other results in Division Two had gone hoping above hope that they would be relegated. Rumours spread quickly around the terrace that indeed Sunderland had been relegated and the scenes became joyous. I'd recently broken my foot playing football so I was at the match with a pot on my leg with crutches standing at the back of the terrace so as not to get caught up in any surges (nothing stopped me from going to football!). Like everyone else I began celebrating the news, but with Macas standing next to me it didn't go down too well. In fact he was devastated and looking back in hindsight it was a cruel thing to have done. I think he would have flattened me if I hadn't been incapacitated, but after a few more minutes it became clear that the rumours had been false and had only been spread maliciously. The Mackems had avoided relegation by the skin of their teeth and Macas was able to calm down. I'm pleased to say he's since forgiven me.

05/05/79 – NEWCASTLE v BRIGHTON & HOVE ALBION (1-3)

Brighton brought as many supporters to St. James' Park as any visiting team that I can remember, close on 10,000, for the simple reason that they had come to celebrate their promotion to the First Division. The situation wasn't quite as clear cut as that though, as for the only time I can remember I went to a match hoping we would lose! Incredible you might think but no, a win for Brighton would put a massive dent in Sunderland's promotion aspirations so as we had nothing to play for ourselves we were cheering loudly when Brighton opened up a 3-0 half-time lead. It was brilliant. Sunderland did manage to win 2-1 at Wrexham and it was amusing that their travelling support mistakenly thought that their win had clinched their promotion. Unbeknown to them Brighton's win, 3-1 in the end, coupled with a late Stoke City winner against Notts County, edged them out into fourth place and so we were happy to join in enthusiastically with Brighton's rejoicing.

So what else did the 1978/79 season bring? Apart from an FA Cup fourth round defeat against Wolverhampton in a replay at Molineux, after being so close to winning the tie at St. James' Park before a very late Kenny Hibbitt equaliser dented our hopes, nothing at all, bar that incredible last day of the season fixture against Brighton at St. James' Park. That's a very sad way to remember a season.

1978/79 – Season's Summary

League	P	W	D	L	F	A	Pts.	Pos.
	42	17	8	17	51	55	42	8th

Top Scorers		
Peter Withe	16
Alan Shoulder	11
John Connolly	8

1979/80 – JIM PEARSON

After the agony of witnessing totally crass performances the previous season, the 1979/80 season could only get better. The fact that it did was pretty uplifting but to see it all then fall pitifully away was soul destroying.

05/09/79 – NEWCASTLE v SUNDERLAND (2-2)

In the summer I'd begun training with my local senior football team, Ponteland United, who I had watched many times throughout the 1970s, mainly on the occasions when Newcastle were playing away from home. The team played at Ponteland Sports Centre and the quality of the surface was renowned throughout the north-east as being among the best in non-league football. It was also the biggest pitch in the region and a real pleasure to play on. At the time we were playing in the Tyneside Amateur League and were to progress to the Northern Amateur and the Northern Alliance League during my five seasons with them. I'd also played on and off with Ponteland United Juniors (coached by the excellent Bill Bradley) during the past three seasons and this had given me a good grounding in the game. Matches were more competitive and meaningful than school fixtures especially when you played the likes of Grainger Park Boys' Club. They were located in the Blakelaw district of Newcastle and it's fair to say a few of their players didn't take too kindly to losing – witness the one occasion when after the match we were attacked by some players wielding corner flags as weapons! The club had an affinity of sorts with Newcastle United and it was for that reason that we regularly played pre-season friendlies against them (the Reserves or Juniors) at Ponteland. These matches were of course eagerly looked forward to despite the fact that invariably we ended up on the wrong end of a four or five goal hammering.

You could never beat playing the game, as every manager in the Football League will never tire of telling you, and it was this enjoyment of playing that caused me not to renew my season ticket at the start of the season as I would be concentrating the majority of my Saturday afternoon efforts on playing for Ponteland. A difficult decision really considering my passion for watching Newcastle, but the fact I chose to play didn't for one minute diminish my feelings for Newcastle United. It would mean that generally speaking it would be only the midweek or holiday fixtures I would be able to attend, but it was a sacrifice I was prepared to make. I don't know of course but it may have been the fact that Newcastle were 'messing about' in Division Two at the time that contributed towards my decision. Had we been one of the leading clubs in the first division things may just have been different, I doubt it, but that's something I'll never know.

I reckon that during my early teens I must have played more football than any other kid on our estate. At school for example we would play every morning before nine, break time and then lunchtime. More often than not we'd start with picking teams in the morning and carrying on with the same match for the whole day keeping a running score with the team being ahead at the end of lunchtime the winner. Lunchtime was only 40 minutes but after we'd all stuffed our lunch down in five or ten minutes it was straight out to the yard to resume the game without any thought of our digestion – it didn't seem to affect any of us. Amazingly I can still vividly remember banging in a winner into the top corner of the net (wire fence) and even today, as I quite often go on training runs that take me through the school grounds, I return to the site of this particular goal and the memories come flooding back. The only draw back was going back into school often dripping with sweat and having to concentrate on class work. During matches you prayed the bell wouldn't sound as you were quite simply enjoying yourself so much.

After school and at weekends the Junior School playing field next to home was the best place to play after the demise of our 'own' field at the back of the house, but the problem we often encountered was bring chased off the field by the caretaker, grumpy Godden, who didn't like us playing on his field. Personally I think I must have held the record for being thrown off more times than anyone else. Godden used to go out with his family on Sunday afternoons, so as soon as he went we all began the game and Godden didn't even know we'd been playing! Goggs and I used to play 'keepy-uppy' night after night on the school field and in constantly trying to beat each other I'm sure it made us better players. We also had a portable goal, with net of course, which although only being about four feet high was a perfect companion for our games which always went on long into the night, or at least until darkness prevented us from playing on.

Even when I began playing for Ponteland I was still playing for the school team in the morning but at that age playing two games in one day didn't cause any problems at all. The school team we had in my final year at school was a good one, although we possibly lacked key players in one or two positions. As I'd returned to school to re-sit my 'A' levels (I passed them all I'm pleased to say second time around) the lads I became especially friendly with were the footballing ones whom I'd vaguely known for a couple of years. We were to get much closer, particularly as three or four of them would be joining me on the trail of Newcastle United throughout the 1980s and beyond. Hally, as dedicated a Mag as me, Goggs (Neil), Stuart Rowell, Doc (Nick's younger brother Michael), Macas (Lindsay Graves) and Lowsey (Michael Lowes) all became close allies and these were friendships that would prove lasting. Nick had shared my misfortune of having to return to do an extra year in school and I suppose he, above all the others, had always been the one I was closest to partly I suppose because we had been going to St. James' Park together for a number of years. Mini had gone away to University and, in any case, his devotion to the club had unfortunately declined. Hally, like myself, was also a Subbuteo nut and we spent hours playing at each other's houses, I must admit he tended to have the upper hand – I think he somehow managed to get a little bit more swerve with his players when flicking them! Strangely enough as well as my Newcastle team I also liked the blue of Chelsea and they tended to be my 'second team' whenever there was a colour clash. I also had an England team, all very resplendent in their white kit, and it's interesting to note that in 1994 the manufacturers of Subbuteo include three black players in the 11 man line up which just goes to show how times have changed in respect of the make up of the England football team and of course cultural attitudes too. Speaking of football games I suppose the all time favourite had to be 'Wembley' which I remember getting for Christmas when I was around eight or nine – it went on to give me hours of enjoyment.

Much to my delight we had drawn Sunderland in the League Cup and as it was a midweek competition it meant the chance to see two early season matches. The first leg at Roker Park was an exciting encounter. Sunderland led 1-0 at half time, and when they added a second with only 17 minutes left it was looking bleak to say the least. However, before the Mackems had time to celebrate, Ian Davies put us back in the game a minute later. Thankfully a headed equaliser by the fragile Peter Cartwright, who had come on as substitute, secured a draw and I even remember us almost snatching a winner in the dying moments. A draw seemed a satisfactory result however and the second leg at St. James' Park was set up perfectly. Taking our places on the packed Gallowgate End terraces the atmosphere was just what you would expect on such an occasion. Of course there are numerous other derby matches up and down the country but I think the only one in England that comes close to matching the Tyne – Wear confrontation is the Merseyside derby and even that lacks that little something in comparison. I'm sure the fact that Newcastle and Sunderland are 10 miles apart, rather than being in the same city, creates much more intense rivalry between the supporters, and after all it is they who create the unique atmosphere on derby day. I can't leave this subject without reference to Glasgow and the Celtic/Rangers clashes. I've never been to one but would love to as the passions generated would surely match those on Tyneside. Wadds, one of my mates from Ponteland, is Rangers daft (well, he is Scottish) as well as being a Newcastle fanatic. He's recounted many a tale to me following his trips to Glasgow, and having a foot in both camps is surely in an enviable situation.

Goals from Alan Shoulder and Stuart Boam looked to have clinched a 2-1 win as the game went into its final seconds but it was not to be as Alan Brown, later to join Newcastle on a brief loan period, conjured up an equaliser from nowhere. During all my years of watching Newcastle I have always thought we were the worst team ever at holding on to a one goal lead in the last five minutes of matches. I always felt the opposition would sneak a goal and even when they didn't the near misses would cause palpitations. Panic would set in the back four and we just seemed to go to pieces. Brown's goal on this night was just typical of those feelings.

As a result extra time was played and when it brought no further addition to the scoreline the drama of a penalty shoot out was the scenario about to unfold. The Gallowgate goal was chosen as the end in which the penalties would be taken and Sunderland would take the first kick.

You always fear the worst in these situations, at least I did, and for some reason you have no confidence in your team to win. Well the worst nightmare did come to pass as with Sunderland one kick ahead in sudden death, after both teams had finished level after the regular first five penalty takers had had their turn, Jim Pearson stepped forward and put the ball high into the Gallowgate End. There was a stunned silence all around the ground, bar of course the Mackems in the Leazes End, and it was another one of those occasions when you simply couldn't comprehend what you had seen. Yet it had actually happened and there was nothing you could do about it. Jim Pearson was devastated and I think it affected him so much he was never quite the same player again.

Newcastle's record in penalty shoot outs makes abject reading. Apart from this match losses to Pecsi Dozsa (Fairs Cup 1970/71), Tranmere Rovers (Mercantile Credit Trophy 1989/90) and Bournemouth (FA Cup 1991/92) are balanced only by an insignificant shoot out win over Liverpool at Wembley in 1988 in another of those 'Micky Mouse' competitions. Another thing about penalty shoot outs is that whenever I've watched them as a neutral observer, the team I've wanted to win has more often than not lost – for example Portsmouth versus Liverpool in the 1992 FA Cup semi-final and, most famously, the two World Cup semi-finals in Italia '90 when Italy and England were the unfortunate losers.

More recently there was the shoot out at the end of the 1994 League Cup semi-final between Aston Villa and Tranmere Rovers. In this particular contest fortunes swung first one way and then the other until Tranmere's Liam O'Brien had the opportunity to take his club to Wembley if he could score. As a former Newcastle player he had already missed two crucial penalties during his spell on Tyneside and so, while hoping he would score, I feared the worst. He missed, and when Villa scored with their next kick and Tranmere's Nolan missed his, Rovers were out – one kick away from a dream Wembley final. I truly felt for O'Brien, he must have been really heartbroken and it was even more ironic that in the final minute of normal time he had curled a superb free kick against the inside of the Villa post only to see it bounce away to safety – ironic because it was an almost identical strike to his famous winner at Roker Park in the 1992 Tyne-Wear derby.

01/01/80 – NEWCASTLE v SUNDERLAND (3-1)

The start of a new decade and what better way of welcoming in the New Year than a visit from Sunderland. We were sitting on top of the league, all set for promotion, and had an easy tie against third division Chester to look forward to in the third round of the FA Cup.

The lads had told me we had been playing very well in the period leading up to Christmas and we'd all travelled down to Burnley on Boxing Day full of festive spirit. Burnley were a club with tradition and their Turf Moor ground wasn't a bad little place. We lost the game 3-2 but the lasting memory is returning to the car after the game, and Goggs being set upon verbally by some old woman standing outside her house who accused him of kicking down her door! It was totally unprovoked and while we just ignored her I think it did upset Neil a little.

Sunderland arrived at St. James' Park in fifth position so it was a real top of the table clash. Stan Cummins scored early on to give the Mackems the lead only for Peter Cartwright to equalise before the break. In the second half there was only ever one side going to collect the points as first an Alan Shoulder penalty (and you can imagine the unbearable tension we felt before he tucked it away past Chris Turner) and then a Tommy Cassidy special ensured a 3-1 home win.

Everything was set fair for the remainder of the year, but inexplicably the win over Sunderland was to prove the last highlight of the season. First of all Chester, with a young Ian Rush in their team, came to St. James' Park and dumped us out of the FA Cup (at least we could concentrate on the league we thought!) and then followed a run of 18 matches with only two wins. How could a team that had won 13 matches, up to and including New Year's Day, suddenly lose all semblance of form and confidence and play like a team of strangers incapable of winning a football match? It was beyond me and certainly beyond Bill McGarry who seemed at a loss to turn the tide round.

By the time we went to Roker Park for the return game at Easter we were surprisingly still in with a chance of promotion. Sunderland had edged ahead of us in the table and defeat for either club would probably see an end to the season's promotion hopes. Roker Park was once again packed to the rafters and when Stan Cummins scored what proved to be the only goal of the game, in front of the Fulwell End in the second half, my heart sank and I remember feeling physically sick as the pain of defeat loomed. It was such an important game to lose and I just couldn't take it. Having to look at the Fulwell End during the game was as soul destroying as you could imagine. Think of your worst nightmare, double it, and that gives you an idea of what this day was like.

After we had fallen to an end of season finishing position of ninth, the Mackems were left with an outstanding fixture at Roker Park against West Ham which was scheduled for the Monday after the FA Cup Final in which West Ham had surprisingly managed to defeat Arsenal. Sunderland needed a victory to secure promotion and with the Hammers' minds on other things they seemed to be the ideal opposition for Sunderland. West Ham hardly brought any supporters and so the ground was virtually full of 45,000 Mackems bar me, Hally and Goggs as we'd gone with Macas hoping to see West Ham win, and spoil the Roker Party. We obviously kept our emotions to ourselves inside the ground, but when Sunderland opened up a 2-0 lead late in the game things began to get out of hand, i.e. we were in the middle of a celebrating Roker Park and absolutely hating every minute of it. There was of course only one thing to do and that was to leave. It was obviously a bit tough on Macas who clearly wanted to stay on and enjoy the occasion, but the three of us dragged him out of the ground and off we went home with Macas muttering discontentedly in the car all the way back to Ponteland – we wouldn't even let him listen to it on the radio, well you could hardly blame us could you!

1979/80 – Season's Summary

League	P	W	D	L	F	A	Pts.	Pos.
	42	15	14	13	53	49	44	9th

Top Scorers		
Alan Shoulder	21
Peter Withe	11
Tommy Cassidy	6

1980/81 – SHINTON/CLARKE/RAFFERTY

Possibly the worst season in living memory; nothing to play for in the league after an abysmal start, the hopes of a run into the sixth round of the FA Cup being smashed in totally humiliating fashion at Exeter and, worst of all, the number of absolute no-hopers who were being paraded on the hallowed St. James' Park turf each week masquerading as players. Quite simply the quality of some players at the club, many of whom Bill McGarry had wasted the club's money on, was dreadful. The majority of them lacked skill, commitment and above all a true desire to play for Newcastle United. Players who were at the club simply to pick up a pay packet were an insult to every Geordie. Throughout the whole season we managed to score the measly total of 30 goals (from 42 games) and that fact alone tells you much about the sheer bleakness of the season.

Thankfully McGarry had been sacked in August but it wasn't until a number of weeks later that Arthur Cox was appointed by a Board of Directors who were taking the club in one direction only – downwards. Cox obviously inherited a club with no money to spend on new players and a staff that was woefully lacking in quality, so to a certain extent his hands were tied and it wouldn't be for a couple of years that the dedicated effort he put into the club would bear fruit.

I'd finally left school in the summer and with four 'A' levels had to contemplate my next move which would obviously go a long way to shaping the rest of my life. Academically I wasn't particularly clever, but what I lacked in I.Q. level I made up for in effort and commitment. Mum and Dad were keen for me to do something like Biochemistry but really that wasn't for me. I'd heard that Newcastle Polytechnic had recently started a Sport Studies degree which was a new concept in academic sporting education. I convinced Mum and Dad that this was to be the best course of action for their sports loving son, and I was delighted when they gave me their full backing. I passed an interview to get a place on the course, and so the next three years of my life were mapped out for me. Going back to the interview, there were a few other lads there and one turned out to be an old friend I hadn't seen for about eight years. Paul Elliott was the person in question and we'd first crossed paths when he played centre-forward for Cheviot School in 1971 and, more often than not, I would be marking him for Ponteland Middle School. At that time he was considered to be the best player in our league by a street, and I later had the privilege to play with Paul in the Newcastle Area Select Team at Under 11 and Under 12 level. Paul went on to greater things throughout the 1970s and represented Newcastle Boys, and was even lucky enough to be selected as a ball boy at the Newcastle versus Manchester City League Cup Final, a rare honour indeed. I thought he could have made it as a professional but for whatever reason he didn't quite make the grade. Paul and I went on to be great mates throughout our Poly lives, and I even managed to entice him to Ponteland to play for United where he played alongside me in the back four – I don't think I've told you this yet but we played in black and white striped shirts too and believe me that was a real pleasure.

A young Steve Cram, fresh from the 1500 metres Final at the Moscow Olympics, had also enrolled on the Sport Studies course. I'm sure all of you will know that he is a devout Mackem, so a good few footballing arguments were often the order of the day. I always used to think of myself as being pretty fit but Steve was something else – at least I used to beat him at snooker.

22/10/80 – NEWCASTLE v SHREWSBURY TOWN (1-0)

Due to my playing commitments, Shrewsbury Town's visit to St. James' Park on a bleak October midweek evening was the first league game I saw this season. Earlier in the season I'd seen the Bury game in the League Cup and although we scraped to an embarrassing 3-2 victory we lost the second leg 1-0 at Gigg Lane and went crashing out on the away goals rule. It had been another dire performance and the total despair was shared by all the supporters.

The fact that we were even entertaining teams like Shrewsbury said it all. No team has a divine right to be a successful Division One side, but if tradition and support have anything to do with it, we would be in the top three in the country, permanently.

After defeat at Bolton on the second weekend of the season we had sunk to last place in the league. I vividly remember reading the Football Pink that evening and seeing the name Newcastle United at the bottom of the table. It was both terribly sad and unthinkable. Victory over Shrewsbury by a single goal put us back up to mid-table but the crowd of only 12,000 was an embarrassment to the name of Newcastle United and a clear sign that both on and off the field the club were in a parlous state.

Turning to matters on the field, the team that represented United that night was probably the worst team I have had the misfortune to see. Clearly there have been rank bad players in every era at the club, and you could easily pick a worst ever United team from all of those players, but collectively, and for the number of second rate players all playing together at once, you'd be hard pushed to beat this lot. I will list them for the sake of posterity:

1.	Kevin Carr:	Would only ever be a second division goalkeeper.
2.	Steve Carney:	Came from the Northern League and should have stayed there.
3.	Chris Withe:	Hopelessly out of his depth.
4.	Mick Martin:	A mystery as to how he ever got an Irish International Cap.
5.	Stuart Boam:	Did okay for Middlesbrough but over the hill.
6.	Kenny Mitchell:	A failed centre forward and now a failed centre half.
7.	Bobby Shinton:	Possibly the worst striker ever to wear a black & white shirt.
8.	Kenny Wharton:	I'll let him off for what he did against Luton in 1988.
9.	Chris Waddle:	Making his debut, therefore exonerated from blame.
10.	Billy Rafferty:	See Shinton above.
11.	Terry Hibbitt:	Great servant to the club in the 1970s but past his sell-by date.
12.	Nigel Walker:	A useful player actually but either too nice or too lazy to succeed.
	Manager – Bill McGarry:	Sacked two months earlier but it was still 'his' team.

For those of you who didn't see Shinton or Rafferty in the flesh but have since witnessed the total ineptitude of the likes of Frank Pingel and Rob McDonald then you'll realise exactly what Shinton and Rafferty brought to the club. The 11 listed above were backed up by the likes of Frans Koenan (a poor man's Arnold Muhren), Ray Clarke (almost as fat as Micky Quinn but with none of his goalscoring ability) and last but not least Peter Johnson (so bad I can barely even remember him). Make no mistake about it I still would have been at every single match at St. James' Park had I not been playing but looking back it certainly seemed as if I'd timed my Ponteland United career just right.

The weekend after Shrewsbury saw us travel to Chelsea and finish up on the wrong end of a 6-0 hammering. Was this the season's nadir? The *Match of the Day* cameras were on hand to capture our ignominy in full, and broadcast it to the whole nation for their amusement. With the Mackems in Division One it made things even worse and, to be honest, unbearable. I was at my lowest point, ashamed, dispirited and above all so angry. I wasn't alone either.

26/12/80 – GRIMSBY TOWN v NEWCASTLE (0-0)

A Boxing Day trip to Cleethorpes and Blundell Park. We went, watched, and came back. Nothing to report. We were a totally nondescript 13th in the table, the epitome of mediocrity but in fact it was worse than that. There wasn't a single sign of light at the end of the tunnel – if only we'd known then how different it would be in 13 years time.

14/02/81 – NEWCASTLE v EXETER CITY (1-1)

I'm not sure how we managed it but here we were in the middle of February in the fifth round of the FA Cup. We had landed a plum draw against a lower division side and despite all the turmoil within the club, coupled with our abject league position, it was a marvellous opportunity to reach the last eight of the competition and move to within touching distance of Wembley.

Ponteland's game had kicked off at 2.00pm which meant that I could play and then, after a rapid change, get to St. James' Park soon after 4.00pm for the second half. The only problem was I couldn't get into the ground and so had to content myself with standing outside the Leazes End, which at least afforded me a view of the big scoreboard at the back of the Gallowgate End. Prowling round outside the ground was so frustating, especially when the ground erupted to mark Alan Shoulder's goal. I knew I'd get into the ground at about 4.30pm when the gates would be opened, but before they did Exeter equalised and I felt so bad I almost went straight home. I couldn't though and managed eventually to get into the Leazes End wing Paddock for the final minutes. Predictably no further goals were scored and the prospect of a replay at the other St. James' Park was all that we could look forward to (apart from a visit to White Hart Lane in the sixth round). I didn't get to Exeter but, for those die-hards who did, the 4-0 thrashing we suffered was as close to total humiliation as you could get and worse than anything that had gone before, even Hereford. Watching on *Sportsnight* later in the evening was TV hell. No, it was worse than that and quite how I managed to stomach it all I'll never know.

I saw the midweek games against Blackburn and Grimsby later in the season but they were as dismal as anything that had gone before. The mediocrity of it all left you totally deflated and when the Mackems fluked a 1-0 win at Anfield on the last day of the season to retain their place in Division One, it just about put the final nail in the coffin.

1980/81 – Season's Summary

League	P	W	D	L	F	A	Pts.	Pos.
	42	14	14	14	30	45	42	11th

Top Scorers		
Bobby Shinton	7
Alan Shoulder	6
Mick Harford	4

1981/82 – MID TABLE MEDIOCRITY

This really was a nothing season. After a remarkably similar start to the previous year we had lost our first two matches and found ourselves rooted to the foot of the second division table. It was a sign of the times that the attendance for the opening day fixture at St. James' Park, which traditionally produced a good turn out, was a meagre 19,000.

Life at the Polytechnic was going just fine, in fact I was really enjoying myself. The Sport Studies course I was on was perfect for me, it involved the academic and practical aspects of sport and it even included a skiing field week in Soll, Austria which only cost each of us £40. As you would expect the Newcastle Polytechnic football team was very strong and in two of the three years we played together we won the British Polytechnics Cup. Of particular pleasure was the fact that we came up against the Mackems, sorry, Sunderland Polytechnic, each year in the Preliminary Round. Naturally we won all the games, indeed one season it was by the little matter of 6-1, sheer bliss. Captain of the team was David Irons, who hailed from Dumfries in Scotland, and one of the main reasons for him joining the Sport Studies course was to try and get noticed by an English club side. Newcastle United had a look but nothing more and it was a shame because he's possibly the most talented player I have ever had the pleasure of playing with. On completing his degree Davie returned to Scotland and has played in the Premier League/First Division for the past 12 years. Mick Lindsay, another stalwart of the team, became a firm friend despite being a Mackem! Mick was playing in the Wearside League for Reyrolle at the time and had also been with Sunderland as a junior. Our team was coached by the Newcastle United goalkeeper Steve Hardwick who, despite not having a particularly successful spell at St. James' Park, did a splendid job with us and related to all of the lads really well On the theme of Newcastle United goalkeepers we also had a visit at the Polytechnic from Willie McFaul, who was now on the coaching staff at the club, who lectured us on aspects of football coaching and strategy. We also had a good squad of players at Ponteland so the prospects for a good season ahead were certainly bright. Through it all though Newcastle United were always at the forefront of my thoughts, and their success was the one thing I wanted more than anything else. It is incredible how the fortunes of a football club shape your moods, happiness and indeed your whole life.

23/09/81 – NEWCASTLE v SHREWSBURY TOWN (2-0)

It had to be a coincidence that the visitors to St. James' Park for the first midweek game of the season were Shrewsbury Town. Had the fates conspired against me to keep attracting me to such uninspiring fixtures as this? The name Shrewsbury Town is hardly synomonous with the word football is it? At least it gave me a chance to have a look at our new centre forward Imre Varadi. Arthur Cox had bought him from Everton in August and, although he was to go on and finish the season as the club's leading goalscorer, I never really rated him. Yes he was quick but he lacked a good touch and, perhaps more than anything else, finesse, a quality I've always thought essential in order to be a class player.

Others in the team that night included Chris Waddle who was beginning his first full season in the Football League after his move from non-league Tow Law and a day job of working in a sausage factory. Even in his early days at the club Waddle looked a class player although somewhat naive at times. He ran around with slumped shoulders and looked a bit ungainly at times but his ability to beat his man, often making a total fool of him, and deliver a quality ball into the danger area was second to none. In this most forgettable of seasons at least Waddle shone like a beacon and all credit to Arthur Cox for firstly spotting him, nurturing his talent and cajoling him to a level he never thought possible. What he has achieved since in the game is testament to the upbringing he received under Cox and I'm sure Waddle will be the first to admit that.

I also quite liked 'Special Agent' Dick (David) Barton. He was a Geordie lad playing at centre half and although he was a bit raw around the edges he was a player totally committed to furthering his career with Newcastle United. John Brownlie was a good full back we'd brought in from Scotland, but apart from this handful of players the squad was woefully lacking in real quality and until Cox could do some more wheeling and dealing in the transfer market, even though resources were limited, we were destined to remain as also-rans.

The worst thing about such matches as this was the fact that there was no excitement and nothing to arouse the passions of the Geordies. Even when you were struggling at the bottom of the table you knew (or at least you thought you did) that there was never any real chance of being relegated. On the other hand you knew promotion was about as likely as the Board of Directors releasing money to rebuild the ground, and that's what made our predicament so hard to stomach. I would ask myself what were they in it for? Was it the 'power' such a position provided, the honour, or was it just a 'toy' for them to play with? Whatever it was, we supporters were totally disillusioned and trying to contain our anger proved too much for some, myself included.

24/02/82 – NEWCASTLE v SHEFFIELD WEDNESDAY (1-0)

I hated Sheffield Wednesday. I don't know why really, I just did. Perhaps it was players like Mel Sterland and Gary Megson (I can't believe we actually signed him in 1984) who contributed to my dislike of them. Anyway the 1-0 win we achieved gave me more pleasure than usual.

Bad weather over Christmas and the New Year had brought a postponement to all of Newcastle's holiday fixtures and as this was both a traditional footballing period and a particularly enjoyable time of the year for watching the lads, both home and away, it was doubly disappointing. An away trip on Boxing Day is a festive tradition, even if it is to the likes of places like Grimsby!

Speaking of Grimsby it was defeat at the hands of the Mariners at St. James' Park in late April that finally killed off any misplaced pretensions we had of sneaking into a promotion spot. To be honest though we were living in dreamland to have ever hoped for as much.

28/04/82 – PONTELAND UNITED v DUDLEY WELFARE (3-0)

How could I not tell you about this game? Ponteland United had fought their way to the final of the Northumberland Senior Benevolent Bowl. It had taken three matches to get past West Allotment Celtic (our greatest league rivals) in the semi-final, and we deservedly and proudly took our place at Ashington FC's Portland Park for the Final.

We went into the match as underdogs but the 3-0 winning scoreline we achieved was possibly the finest team performance I had ever played in. Geordie Straughan opened the scoring for us early in the game and then minutes before half time we were awarded a penalty, which yours truly calmly despatched into the corner of the net. Five minutes before the penalty incident I'd been involved in a pretty physical aerial clash which, although I didn't know at the time, resulted in a broken nose as well as mild concussion. There was never any chance of me coming off though, and when Geordie scored his second close to the end, our victory was complete. I must mention Davie Henderson and John Hardy who were magnificent alongside me at the centre of defence and, of course, our managerial team of Kenny Scott and Brian Swan (still playing in the local over 40s League). Scottie in particular was a really nice guy, popular with all the lads and a pleasure to play for. He would often take a good ribbing from the lads and could hit back with his dry sense of humour prevailing but when it came to the serious stuff he did his job superbly. Honesty with his players was another of his virtues and I'm sure this is a characteristic essential in any manager's make up regardless of what level they're working at.

A few weeks earlier I had played my first game under floodlights which was a real thrill. It was something I had dreamed about doing for as long as I had been playing football and I certainly made the most of it. I was selected for a Northern Amateur League 'Select' team to play against a Northern League 'Select' and with the match being played at Whitley Bay's Hillheads ground, it meant my dream would come true. Ponteland obviously didn't have floodlights, and indeed still don't, but I am fortunate that throughout the 1990's, playing under floodlights is now almost a weekly thing, in the winter months at least, as virtually every club in the Northern Counties East League has them.

One of the major regrets I had when leaving Ponteland United to move to Leeds was the fact that I missed out on playing at St. James' Park in the Final of the Northern Alliance Cup when Ponteland reached the final twice in the late 1980s. This is assuming I would have still been in the team of course but I would have given literally everything to have ran out and performed on the hallowed turf and enjoy everything else that the day would have involved – walking into the ground, the changing rooms etc. I guess the closest I'll ever get to that dream now is on one of the clubs' official guided tours of the ground.

Whilst playing at Ponteland I also had the pleasurable task of writing the match reports for the local Ponteland newspaper. I thought I had quite a good style and would tend to write very descriptive reports. Each of the lads took it in turns to receive a particularly good review and, believe it or not, I even managed to sing my own praises on the odd occasion!

05/05/82 – NEWCASTLE v QUEEN'S PARK RANGERS (0-4)

The penultimate match of the season at St. James' Park and what an abject performance I saw. Three down at half-time and a fourth goal for the visitors in the second half resulted in our heaviest defeat of the season. I know end-of-season matches, where there's nothing at stake, often become meaningless contests but was there no pride in the performance of the 11 players who wore the black and white tonight. Regardless of the circumstances the players had a duty, not only to themselves, but to the supporters who could not be expected to tolerate such displays. I can imagine Cox being livid at such a performance but at least he showed his managerial credentials by guiding the team to victories in the final two games of the season which lifted us from our perennial 11th place to ninth. But really what difference did it make in the final analysis. None. It had still been an abysmal season.

I've managed to talk through the season without even mentioning the League and F.A. Cup. When you realise defeats against Fulham and Grimsby (why do they keep cropping up?) respectively brought our Cup hopes to an early and abrupt end you can understand why.

08/07/82 – FRANCE v WEST GERMANY (3-3)

Spain hosted the World Cup in 1982 and it was the brilliance of Zico (apologies to Scottish fans) and the marvellous French team who took my eye. Paolo Rossi's brilliant hat-trick against Brazil is also an abiding memory. The start of the Finals coincided with exams at the Polytechnic, what a nuisance, but it didn't stop me watching Eder and Socrates score two spectacular late goals to defeat Russia in the group stages the night before a sports psychology exam. Talking of spectacular goals the best goal of the year, in my opinion, was the one scored by the Brazilian Cerezo in a pre World Cup warm up match in France. Unfortunately I've never seen it on television again since and as I didn't manage to record it on video it will remain only a blur in the memory banks.

The game of the tournament was the semi final between France and West Germany. No one particularly liked the Germans, they were efficient but arrogant and I was bitterly disappointed when they beat the French on penalties, especially after France had led 3-1 in extra time – who can forget Tresor's fantastic volley or Giresse's marvellous strike in off the post that gave France their two goal lead and indeed the look of absolute joy on his face as he saw the ball nestle in the back of the net.

Before leaving the World Cup I have got to mention the theme tune that the BBC used for the tournament. I absolutely loved it, as I tend to enjoy all the great sporting theme tunes as they come and go. I even went out and bought the record after the competition finished and if you know the tune I'm referring to you will understand why it regularly is played when I get in the 'World Cup' mood and start reminiscing about great deeds of the past.

1981/82 – Season's Summary

League	P	W	D	L	F	A	Pts.	Pos.
	42	18	8	16	52	50	62	9th

Top Scorers		
Imre Varadi		20
Chris Waddle		8
John Trewick		6

1982/83 – KEEGAN MANIA

The title sums it all up. Kevin Keegan, former Liverpool, Hamburg, Southampton and England superstar, was coming to St. James' Park to play for Newcastle United. The way it happened was unbelievable. First the speculation in the *Evening Chronicle* (the best evening football paper I've seen but a little notorious at 'exclusives' turning out to be nothing but damp squibs) and then, as the impossible became a probability, the hastily convened press conference at the Gosforth Park Hotel to announce Keegan's arrival at the club. Even the marvellous ITV Television programme *Auf Wiedersehen Pet* covered Keegan's signing when Dennis, Neville and Oz were discussing it on the boat back to England. After four seasons in Division Two the signing of Keegan was a master stroke by Cox and Stan Seymour, and the much derided Board of Directors deserve due credit for masterminding what in effect was a sensational move that took the whole football world by surprise. You can imagine how it also fired the imagination of the Geordies, and the opening day fixture against Queen's Park Rangers at St. James' Park just couldn't come quickly enough.

28/08/82 – NEWCASTLE v QUEEN'S PARK RANGERS (1-0)

A pre-season training injury at Ponteland kept me from playing until September. Being sidelined is the worst possible thing from a playing point of view, and the frustration of not being able to join in with the rest of the lads is, to me, soul destroying. Anyway, as every cloud supposedly has a silver lining the fact that I was able to get a ticket for Keegan's debut at St. James' Park was fantastic.

Going to the ground with plenty of time before kick off was just like the old days. There was a buzz in the air again which had been so sadly lacking over the past few years and it was a real joy to share in the anticipation and excitement of all my fellow Geordies.

The reception accorded to Keegan by the capacity crowd when he led the lads out at five to three was brilliant. I'm not sure what he had expected and, although he had experienced the fervour of the Scousers in his days at Liverpool, what he was sampling today must have taken even his breath away.

A nervy and tense first half followed and the scoreline was blank at the interval but early in the second half the inevitable happened. Queen's Park Rangers were always going to be on a hiding to nothing at having to undertake this fixture, and so it proved. Johnny Craggs and Imre Varadi combined on the near side touch line (I was in the Centre Paddock) and set Keegan free with only Peter Hucker standing between him and the back of the net at the Gallowgate End. What would he do? Well we needn't have worried as the little man strode forward and in typical fashion stroked the ball past Hucker. When I say the whole ground erupted I'm making a gross understatement. The scenes were absolutely sensational and it left you shaking with excitement. Queen's Park Rangers threatened to ruin Keegan's day late on but when they had failed to breach United's rearguard by the time the final whistle sounded, the celebrations that ensued were to last all weekend.

01/09/82 – BLACKBURN ROVERS v NEWCASTLE (1-2)

A midweek trip to Ewood Park was just what the doctor ordered, and with 6,000 plus Geordies thinking likewise the small Lancashire town was turned into a mini Tyneside for the day.

Keegan fever was rising by the day, and when he and Mick Martin put us two up at the interval we were in seventh heaven. Although the home side pulled one back in the second half, victory was ours and so was top spot in the division.

I thought we were destined to remain in top spot for the remainder of the season but I was getting carried away. The 3-1 defeat at Bolton the following weekend, Keegan scoring for the third successive game, brought us crashing back to earth. In reality the team we had was much the same as that which had struggled so pathetically over the last two seasons, and to expect such a turn around in fortunes through the presence of one man alone was, looking back, naive to say the least. We took a point from Middlesbrough at St. James' Park the following midweek, with a goal from Mick Channon on his debut. Channon only played another three games before being sent packing, I suppose his face just didn't quite fit into the St. James' Park set up. Although he was a decent enough player I wasn't sad to see him go. Anyway the 'rot' had set in and consecutive defeats against Shrewsbury Town and Barnsley consigned us to a mid-table position once more. Rot is probably too strong a word to have used here, but as expectations were so high then the disappointments were much greater.

29/09/82 – GLASGOW RANGERS v BORUSSIA DORTMUND (2-0)

It was a blank midweek footballwise for us in England so a trip to Ibrox looked a very inviting prospect. Alan Frame, one of the Scottish lads in Ponteland, aside from Wadds, was a fervent Rangers fan and so Hally, Goggs, Stu and myself joined him for the trip to Glasgow eager to witness the 'new' Ibrox Stadium for the first time and to see what the Rangers supporters were all about. Ibrox didn't disappoint and it will be even better when they eventually fill in the corner sections in 1995 with a view to staging a future European Cup Final. Alan had family in Glasgow and so the plan was to make an early start, and stop off briefly for a few ritual pleasantries with the Frame family before moving on to Ibrox. We'd taken two cars up and just as well we did as one of them broke down on the dual carriageway on the outskirts of Glasgow. Using the other car we found a friendly garage nearby, and some two hours later we were on our way again. Something a little out of the ordinary always seems to crop up on away trips and today proved no exception. Still it was all part of the enjoyment and no-one really seemed to mind at all.

It wasn't quite a capacity crowd, near enough 42,000, so we were fortunate enough to get good seats in the middle of the core of Rangers' fans behind the goal. It proved to be a unique experience. Having been brought up on standing terraces, the thought of watching from a seated area left me sceptical as I imagined the atmosphere to be less intense. How wrong I was as the Rangers fans proceeded to generate an incredible night of passion and we ended up playing a full part in their celebrations when Derek Johnstone and Davie Cooper (his death in 1995 was a tragic loss to the game) scored the goals which gave the Scots a 2-0 victory. The religious element of the chanting fans was a new experience for me and also an enlightening one. Rangers are of course a Protestant club, and this was clearly reflected in the nature of the terrace songs which I'm sure went beyond acceptable limits to many people.

All in all a thoroughly enjoyable day trip to Glasgow, and it was nice for Newcastle to play there in Ally McCoist's testimonial in August 1993 and in the Ibrox International Challenge Trophy a year later, where we proved beyond any doubt to the Rangers fans who the number one supporters in Britain were. It's ironic really that I ended up 'supporting' Rangers that night, as I'd always been

more Celtic than Rangers before, and indeed still am. Most football supporters up and down the country would favour one of the
two and, for some reason that I can't pinpoint, Celtic were my
team. Naturally therefore, in all the Old-Firm clashes down the
years, I've hoped for Celtic to come out on top. The fact that they
haven't done so much in recent years hasn't really bothered me
though. While we adopted a liking for either Celtic or Rangers we
never did the same thing with the other two-club cities, for
example Liverpool, where both Everton and Liverpool played,
were accorded equal contempt. I suppose it was partly because
they played in a different country, and the fact that the Geordies
respected the passion the Glaswegians had for their teams. In the
days of the old Leazes End a match wouldn't pass without the
'Rangers/Celtic' chant being heard with the side you followed
being shouted out louder than the other. People even wore
bobble hats which were divided into one half for Newcastle and
the other half for either the green of Celtic or blue of Rangers.

A British League, with Newcastle United regularly playing the
likes of Celtic and Rangers, would undoubtedly be some occasion
but it may be some time before this comes about – indeed it may
never happen.

06/10/82 – LEEDS UNITED v NEWCASTLE (1-0)

The previous weekend we had demolished Rotherham United 5-1
on their own patch. Hally, Goggs, Macas and Stu had all gone
down and with Terry McDermott making his debut, having
rejoined the club from Liverpool (who will ever forget his
marvellous goal in September 1978 when Liverpool demolished
Tottenham 7-0 or his immaculate finish to a flowing move when
he scored the first of Liverpool's three goals in the 1977 European
Cup Final in Rome), the performance, including a sparkling four
goal haul for Keegan, was out of this world. The *Match of the Day*
cameras were there to see it and for a change it was a pleasure to
watch as we toyed with the Rotherham defence all game. Keegan,
smashing the ball past Mountford in the home goal behind which
the Newcastle supporters were going absolutely loopy, is a treasured memory.

I was back playing by now and of course back at the Poly. I went
to Leeds for this game, a first leg match in the League Cup, on the
Supporters Club bus with David Holding, another good mate from

Poly. David was actually a Manchester City fan but during his time on Tyneside became an adopted Geordie and even adapted his accent accordingly. He was full of fun, managed to integrate into the Tyneside culture very easily, and made good friends with many devoted Geordies on his travels. 'Mighty' Leeds United had been relegated at the end of the 1981/82 season and I remember being in the Diamond Inn in Ponteland on the night they lost to West Bromwich Albion in May which condemned them to the drop – needless to say it put a large smile on the face of everyone in the pub when the news filtered through.

You always get a warm welcome at Leeds and as we stepped off the bus in the big car park that adjoins Elland Road, the anti Geordie feeling we witnessed was rife. On the vast majority of away trips you never really feel threatened but there were a few places, Leeds being one of them, where you wouldn't think of taking your mother!

A single goal from Imre Varadi was enough to win the game but the match would be remembered for an incident involving Kevin Keegan who was struck in the face by a coin thrown at him from the Leeds Kop. An unsavoury incident of course, but with Keegan being such a superstar figure he naturally became the target of hate and abuse from the Leeds hooligan element.

A large police presence saw us back on to our buses for the journey home and an escort to see us clear of the ground was also necessary if you wanted to avoid a brick or two smashing through the windows; such pleasant memories these away trips!

Three weeks later in the second leg at St. James' Park, Leeds exacted their revenge in full with a conclusive 4-1 victory. Arthur Graham in particular tore us apart on the flanks, and yet another League Cup campaign was over at the first hurdle. On the terraces a handful of Leeds supporters had managed to find their way into the Gallowgate End. Whether this had been planned or whether inadvertent they were quickly identified, and I distinctly remember seeing them being thrown out over the wall at the back of the terrace with the obligatory kicking to help send them on their way. The drop over the wall must have been at least 10 feet, and the fate that befell them was seen, by those who were involved, as retribution for what we had suffered at Elland Road.

12/01/83 – NEWCASTLE v BRIGHTON & HOVE ALBION (0-1)

Christmas and the New Year had come and gone but I'd had the misfortune of missing out on my favourite away trip of the season! Yes you've guessed it, Grimsby's Blundell Park! I'd picked up a stomach bug which apart from ruining my Christmas Day lunch saw me vomiting all night before we were due to leave for Grimsby in the morning.

I'd still wanted to go though but Mum would have none of it and of course she was right. A quick phone call to Stu got rid of my ticket and off he went with Hally and Goggs leaving me to recuperate at home. We got a draw, but had we won I would have felt even worse as it wasn't that often we had the pleasure of seeing Newcastle win away from home. We were too far adrift in the promotion hunt to draw any genuine hope for the second half of the season, even though a run of six wins in the last eight matches took us up to fifth place, so I suppose we would have to find some inspiration from a good run in the FA Cup.

The game against Brighton was a third round replay and normally, after gaining an away draw, you expect to win through at home. I'd convinced four of my Poly mates that this was a match not to be missed so I took them onto the Gallowgate terraces promising them a night of football to remember. We got one, but for all the wrong reasons and that was down solely to one man – referee Trelford Mills of Barnsley.

Brighton went ahead early in the second half but there was still plenty of time left in the game to at least force an equaliser, and as we were literally camped in the Brighton half it seemed only a matter of time before we scored. Mills had other ideas though as he constantly pulled up Newcastle's attacks with decisions of such ineptitude that the wrath and scorn of all of Tyneside was heaped upon him. A goal we all thought to be legitimate was ruled out for handball by Varadi but Mills was saving his best until the end. A crossfield ball was headed on to the unmarked Keegan just outside the six yard box and when he buried the chance in the back of the net relief swept around the ground, but wait, what was this? Mills had blown his whistle and disallowed the goal for what remains a mystery even to this day (the *Sportsnight* cameras couldn't spot the infringement either although it was later claimed to have been a push by Carney as he set up Keegan) and I have never seen a referee be subjected to as much vilification as Mills. I've always thought referees do a good job and have been loathe to criticise them, but even I lost control of my emotions that night and gave him a torrent of abuse. To make matters worse Neil (Spotty) McDonald proceeded to lash a 20 yard screamer against the cross-bar and when the final whistle sounded Brighton left the field as the luckiest team in the country to still be left in the Cup. Remarkably their luck held throughout the competition as they went on to reach the final against Manchester United, running out only in the final minutes at Wembley when Gordon Smith missed the sort of gilt edged chance your Grannie could have tucked away that would have won them the Cup. I think it's very amusing that Brighton's fanzine is entitled 'And Smith must Score' – at least it shows they've got a sense of humour.

As for Mills he must have feared for his safety as he left the field of play and I'm sure he felt a strange sense of pleasure in having denied Newcastle their place in the competition. Amazingly the Football League appointed him for a fixture at St James' Park only five weeks later (against Oldham) but fortunately have had the sense to only send him back to Newcastle on five occasions since. We all thought it was a truly awful display of officiating which you would think could not be matched. This was certainly the case until a certain Brian Coddington appeared on the scene at Derby in April 1992.

As we're on the subject of referees there are a few worth a men-tion. Back in the early seventies I remember the likes of Norman Burtenshaw (who once famously sent off George Best at Chelsea), Gordon Hill and Jack Taylor, who reached the pinnacle of refereeing achievement when he was selected to take charge of the 1974 World Cup Final. Later in the seventies we saw Clive 'The Book' Thomas who is best remembered for disallowing a Brazilian goal in the 1978 World Cup Finals as it was scored literally seconds after he had blown for full time following a corner kick. He may well have been right in his judgement of time having expired, but I'm sure he regretted the decision in hindsight (BBC's *Fantasy Football League* programme covered the incident supremely well in their 'Phoenix from the Flames' feature). Everton fans will no doubt also remember him for disallowing Brian Hamilton's goal against Liverpool in the closing stages of the 1977 FA Cup Semi Final at Maine Road, a goal that would have taken the Goodison outfit to Wembley. He rarely appeared at St. James' Park, mainly due to the fact he lived so far away (South Wales), but nevertheless he was a highly respected figure. On the other hand Colin Seel, from nearby Carlisle, was a regular at Newcastle, and although he quite often got a bit of stick I didn't think he was such a bad sort. Other prominent officials in this era and in the early 1980s were Neil Midgley and local officials Pat Partridge and George Courtney, with the latter never particularly endearing himself to the Geordies. Another high ranking official, Sheffield's Keith Hackett, is another who is subject to abuse when he visits Tyneside, which I think is rather sad. Turning to the modern day officials, my favourites are David Elleray (who described himself as a neo-fascist before the 1994 FA Cup Final!), Roger Milford, Joe Worrall and, in particular, Keith Cooper, from Pontypridd, who goes about his job in a friendly, unassuming, but firm manner with the interests of the players uppermost in his mind – unlike some of the 'robots' who seem to take a perverse pleasure from brandishing their yellow and red cards. Finally, to return to the World Cup, and USA '94 in particular, the performances of two officials, Mexican Arturo Brizio Carter and Syrian Jamal Al-Sherif, left an awful lot to be desired. The second phase matches that they took control of, Italy v Nigeria and Bulgaria v Mexico respectively, and the ludicrous red cards they showed, made a mockery of the game and I really felt for the three players who were dismissed particularly the Italian player Gianfranco Zola.

Football League referees in the 1994/95 season were also subject to a fair bit of criticism but in my opinion only some of it was justified. The 1994 World Cup led to a new approach being adopted as the new season kicked off in England. There was an inevitable spurt of red and yellow cards in the early weeks of the season as players and managers struggled to come to grips with the new interpretations which, after all, were intended to clean up the game, get rid of the 'thugs' in football and encourage creative talent to flourish. There were some mistakes made by the men in the middle but so what, players make mistakes too and if they expect referees to be 100 per cent spot on every time then they're living in cloud cuckoo land.

It's a shame too that so few former players become referees when they retire from the game. They would bring an obvious 'understanding of the game' to the role, but I suspect it's because it would take an absurd number of years for them to become qualified that makes them feel it isn't worth the effort. Sports such as cricket are packed full of umpires who were formerly first class cricketers, and it's about time football followed suit. Maybe Nigel Clough, who recently attended a Football Association Referees Course, will become the first high profile player to do so. Goodness knows how David Speedie would fare if he took to the whistle also, as it was rumoured towards the end of the 1995/96 season. I couldn't believe he was serious when I heard the story, but you never know, it would be a real Jekyll and Hyde case! I refereed one of Ponteland United's Northern Alliance fixtures once, when I had an arm injury and couldn't play. The referee hadn't turned up and both teams were happy to have me as the 'man in the middle'. As it turned out I thought I did a pretty good job!

04/05/83 – BARNSLEY v NEWCASTLE (0-5)

Final examinations were looming at the Poly and I suppose I shouldn't have really gone to this game but Dave Holding and I made the trip probably because we'd done enough work during the week and this was the reward – at least that's what we told ourselves.

The season had had its high points but even with the arrival of Keegan we had flattered to deceive and the final analysis had still shown a team capable only of inconsistency even though our final league position of fifth was 'respectable'. Barnsley proved a classic example of what might have been as they were destroyed by five goals without reply. However it was too little too late as far as we were concerned despite the fact that the promotion equation wasn't finally settled until the last game of the season. At least we could genuinely look forward to next season as there was something to build on; between the two of them Cox and Keegan were getting it right, even if it would take more than one season to achieve.

1982/83 – Season's Summary

League	P	W	D	L	F	A	Pts.	Pos.
	42	18	13	11	75	53	67	5th

Top Scorers		
Imre Varadi	22	
Kevin Keegan	21	
Terry McDermott	7	

1983/84 – BEARDSLEY AND PROMOTION

I began the season in limbo. I was delighted to have achieved a degree with commendation in Sport Studies from Newcastle Polytechnic but since completing the course in June had failed to find employment and so was naturally a little concerned, although always hopeful that something would appear soon – it did, but not until December. At least the break afforded me more time to myself (spent mainly on the golf course) and of course to devote to Newcastle United.

06/09/83 – MIDDLESBROUGH v NEWCASTLE (3-2)

We'd made an 'iffy' start to the season, winning 1-0 at Elland Road on the opening Saturday despite Chris Waddle having to take over in goal from the injured Kevin Carr (there was of course the inevitable post-match incident when Goggs and I had to take evasive action to avoid being 'laid into' on the way back to where his car was parked). But this mighty performance was followed by promptly losing at home to Shrewsbury Town of all people 48 hours later. Talk about building up the hopes of the St. James' Park crowd only to promptly let them down amid abject disappointment (something Newcastle have made quite a habit of doing actually). We'd got back to winning ways against Oldham before the visit to Middlesbrough came round. We filled the car with the usual mob from Ponteland before setting off down the A19 to Teesside, a trip of some 30 miles, which for an away fixture was something of a luxury for us. People often overlook the enormous distances the Geordies have to travel in support of their team in comparison to other fans, and it is testament to their love of the club that it proves to be no obstacle. It just means the long trip home after a defeat is that much more miserable.

Ayresome Park was a dump (at least the new Riverside Stadium is a slight improvement, even though it looks like it has been built from meccano) and Teesside not that much better. The skyline is dominated by ICI chimneys and quite frankly is a depressing sight. Their nickname of the 'smog monsters' seems pretty apt. Middlesbrough are also the poor relations of the North East in comparison to Newcastle and Sunderland. Much as their supporters hate having to admit it, they lack the tradition and support of their rivals further up the coast, and that really hurts them although Bryan Robson is doing his best to swap places with the Mackems as the Rokermen slide into obscurity. Sunderland call themselves the 'caring club' but it seems to me they don't appear to care that much about their own supporters given their current plight. To the game itself and after fighting back on two occasions to equalise, through David Mills, a former Boro' favourite, and Keegan, it seemed a point beckoned. Alas a late Boro' goal stopped us in our tracks and dropped us to sixth in the table. This goal was a real sickener and the celebratory mood of the home players as they greeted the goal made my blood boil, I daren't repeat what I, and I'm sure countless others, were screaming at them.

21/09/83 – ENGLAND v DENMARK (0-1)

The fact that I just happened to go to this match was incidental to the real reason I was down in London – well Watford anyway. Although I'd completed my degree at the Polytechnic our Course Leader, George Wilkinson, was still keen to utilise my expertise, along with Paul Elliott, to continue a project he was undertaking for the Watford manager Graham Taylor. Wilkinson was a disciple of the Wing Commander Reep school of football, which in layman's terms means the long ball game and taking as few passes as possible to get the ball into the opposing penalty area. The fact that he also conversed with his namesake Howard at Sheffield Wednesday says a lot about that particular manager also.

George had been specifically engaged by Watford Football Club to carry out physiological and psychological testing on their players, and Paul and myself were required by George to undertake all the various tests. We travelled down to Watford early on the Wednesday morning in the Sport Studies mini bus, packed full of masses of testing equipment, arriving at Vicarage Road at lunch time. We were met by Graham Taylor, at the time one of the brightest up and coming managers in the League, and it was fast becoming a thrilling experience. We set up camp in the home team dressing room and started first on the physical fitness testing which we did on the pitch. That was followed by all the cardio-respiratory and muscular tests which we undertook in the dressing rooms, and by the time we'd completed all of those it was almost 6.00pm. We obviously knew England were playing at Wembley later in the evening but when Graham Taylor invited the three of us along to the match as his guests we were flabbergasted. Needless to say we went on to enjoy a thoroughly enjoyable evening despite England losing the game 1-0, Allan Simonsen scoring from the penalty spot for the Danes.

Believe it or not we actually spent the night in the Watford ground as well, sleeping on the physio tables in the dressing rooms. You might have expected us to have stayed in a local hotel but funnily enough I preferred the option of the ground – it just seemed more of an adventure. The following day we did a bit more testing on the pitch before rounding off the day with the psychological tests which were nothing more than detailed questionnaires. In between times, I should add, we were treated to lunch in the Boardroom with the club President, a certain Bertie Mee, the former manager of the Arsenal 'Double' winning side of 1971 – things just kept getting better.

John Barnes was with Watford at the time and was just beginning to make a real mark in the game. I remember him as a very boyish but confident individual and his level of skill, even when just messing about on the pitch, was exceptional. Some of the senior professionals were a little sceptical of what we were doing, whilst youngster Nigel Callaghan struck me as being somewhat arrogant, but on the whole we were shown every courtesy and all in all it was a fabulous and unforgettable two days.

The weekend after we had done our work, Watford hosted Tottenham at Vicarage Road and in the game Glenn Hoddle, as you may recall, scored one of the all time great goals. Upon receiving the ball on the corner of the penalty box, he flicked it in-between his legs and virtually in the same instant lifted a delicate chip over Steve Sherwood in the Watford goal. Because I had been standing on that same pitch only a few days earlier, this goal has always had a special significance for me.

26/10/83 – OXFORD UNITED v NEWCASTLE (2-1)

A midweek League Cup game and a first for me, as the method of travel involved hitch-hiking. I went with David Holding who, after finishing at the Poly, remained on Tyneside rather than returning home. His brother was in Oxford so we'd arranged to go down on Tuesday, stay a couple of nights in Oxford, and come back to Newcastle on Thursday. As we were both unemployed money was tight and so with nothing better to do, it seemed like a good way to spend a few days away. I met up with him at Eldon Square (the main Shopping Centre in Newcastle) and we began our trek down towards the Tyne Bridge with thumbs of course hanging out. Fortunately we only had to walk a mile or so through Gateshead before a big wagon stopped and drove us all the way to Coventry. Not quite where we'd intended to finish up but we had plenty of time on our hands. From Coventry we managed two car rides to Banbury, and then on to Oxford and we'd made it. The following morning we just hung about the town and were a little surprised at how many Newcastle supporters were already milling around before lunchtime. Oxford's supporters thought they had a reputation of being 'hard cases' but they seemed to respond well to having so many Geordies about the place. The Manor Ground was a couple of miles outside the centre of town in the Headington district, so we decided to walk up there in good time and take refuge in a very large public house virtually next to the ground. Needless to say it soon filled up with Geordies and a smashing time was had by one and all. Getting into the ground is a tale in itself as you have to walk round the back of a row of houses, through a narrow wooded area before eventually arriving at the away terrace. Needless to say the ground was appalling and, regretfully, so was Newcastle's performance which resulted in a 2-1 defeat and the obligatory early round Cup exit. It seemed strange having nowhere to go after the game, and when we finally left Oxford the following morning the journey home took us through the delights of Milton Keynes and Watford Gap Services before getting a ride all the way back to Tyneside, via Leeds, in a big juggernaut. Home at about 8.00pm and an experience if nothing else.

29/10/83 – NEWCASTLE v MANCHESTER CITY (5-0)

A day of mixed emotions really. Firstly, my last game for Ponteland United, I'd scored in our 3-1 victory but had to leave the field with a bad knee injury which would keep me inactive for the next six weeks. Meanwhile at St. James' Park the gates had been locked soon after 2.00pm, with Goggs among those locked out. To the delight of the vast majority of the lucky 33,000 inside the ground we hammered City 5-0 and it was the first time the Keegan/Waddle/Beardsley show had come to the nation's attention. We were up to second position in the table, which was an automatic promotion spot, and passions among the supporters were rising at a rapid rate. Beardsley had been signed a month earlier by Cox and, after failing at Manchester United (or was it that he didn't get a chance) and having gone on to play in the NASL for Vancouver Whitecaps, he had returned to his home town club something of an unknown quantity. Beardsley was built up by Cox as a potential superstar and this he undoubtedly was – along with Waddle the two were to become truly world class players.

19/11/83 – SHEFFIELD WEDNESDAY v NEWCASTLE (4-2)

Alan Clarke, one of the technicians at the Poly who worked in the Sports Department (as opposed to the former Leeds player) gave me a lift to Hillsborough for this match. Aside from the 4-2 defeat we suffered, which dropped us down to fourth, the game will always remain in my memory for the awful crush on the terraces. Everyone knows about the tragedy involving the Liverpool fans on the Leppings Lane terrace during the 1989 FA Cup semi-final, but many Newcastle fans would tell you it was almost pre-empted six years earlier. Thousands of Geordies had travelled to South Yorkshire and the queues outside Hillsborough were massive. It took almost until kick-off time to get into the ground and even then we were stuck in the tunnel leading out to the terraces unable to move with the force of people both behind and in front of you making things decidedly unpleasant. I don't know how but we eventually got onto the terraces where the crush intensified, and people were clambering up to the seats above to escape the panic. It was an obvious case of mismanagement by the home club, and it wasn't until well into the first half, when an additional part of the ground was made available to the Newcastle contingent, that matters became a little more bearable. I enjoy big crowds, packed terraces, surges and the like, but this was taking things a little too far and it could have proved fatal. It goes without saying that when I heard of the tragedy in 1989 my mind immediately flashed back to this day.

A week later on and I'd be back in Yorkshire, Leeds of all places, for a job interview with the English Basketball Association, and what a significant day in my life it was to be. I was offered the job and reluctant as I was to leave Newcastle it would have been foolish of me to have turned it down, so I packed my bags and began contemplating life as a Geordie exile in Leeds. That evening I'd returned to Newcastle by train from Leeds and caught the bus back to Ponteland. As I stepped off the bus to walk the hundred yards or so home the first two people I saw amazingly happened to be Nick and Lowesy and as I was wearing my suit they gave me a whole load of stick – none of us ever wore suits in those days and it was an embarrassing situation to have been caught in, even if they were my best mates!

Today I'm still in Leeds, and remain in the world of basketball, despite the desire to try and find work in the football industry. Although having taken root (regretfully) in Leeds I miss Newcastle so much, not just the football club of course but the city, its people and the unique Geordie culture. For those of you fortunate enough to live and work in Tyneside you'll never realise how lucky you are. Even little things like reading John Gibson or Alan Oliver in the Chronicle every night (what fantastic jobs they have – being paid to watch and report on the club every day), or tuning in to Charles Harrison's sports round up on Metro Radio are sorely missed. Talking of Charles Harrison, I will never forget the laugh his namesake, Alistair, gave me when he reported from a Newcastle match in the late 1970s, that one of the Newcastle players had 'limped off the pitch with a cut head'! Alistair Harrison, who incidentally denied making the comment when I asked him about it shortly afterwards, even though it was broadcast on television, had the job of media liaison for the European Championship matches at St. James' Park in June 1996. I'm proud to say I've never resorted to once buying the *Yorkshire Post* or *Evening Post* in 12 years as it would simply be out of the question. I get the *Pink* and *Journal/Chronicle* match reports posted down from home each week and the envelope dropping though the letterbox each Tuesday morning is one of the highlights of the week. Even little things, like watching the new Leazes and Gallowgate End stands growing up day by day, from metal frameworks to the finished article, is something I have really missed – you need to be a Geordie to understand this last comment. Still it's only 100 miles from door to door and over the years I've come to know the A1 like the back of my hand.

The week after I moved to Leeds, and into my pokey little Headingley bedsit, *Auf Wiedersehen Pet* began on ITV and apart from being an absolutely superb series it made you really proud to be a Geordie. Jimmy Nail, who played Oz in the series, later went on to star in *Spender* in the early 1990s and this programme too had a similar effect on me – if anything it made me long even more to be home.

27/12/83 – CARLISLE UNITED v NEWCASTLE (3-1)

I was home for Christmas and it was nice to have a relatively short trip to undertake the day after Boxing Day's draw with Blackburn at St. James' Park. On the way across the A69 we noticed an unusually large number of cars that had broken down, and even some that had left the road. One had finished up half way through a hedge and it made you wonder exactly what some of the drivers had 'been on' over the last couple of days. Brunton Park is another of those grounds in dire need of a face lift – the away end was so open and exposed it was akin to standing on a non-league terrace. How the Cumbrians enjoyed putting one over the Geordies though, as we turned in a shamefully poor performance not in keeping with our recent fine form. We had slipped back down to fourth, behind Chelsea, Manchester City and Sheffield Wednesday, and it was clear it would be a straight battle between the four of us to claim the three promotion spots available. I just hoped that as we entered the New Year the same ugly fate that befell us back in the 1979/80 season wouldn't strike again.

06/01/84 – LIVERPOOL v NEWCASTLE (4-0)

Liverpool were clearly a tough draw in the third round of the FA Cup and, as the game was being billed as Keegan's return to Anfield, the BBC moved it from its normal Saturday slot to Friday night for the benefit of live television.

The Geordies like nothing better than converging on clubs such as Liverpool and Manchester United with thousands of supporters and, to all intents and purposes, taking over the ground and singing themselves hoarse for a couple of hours or more. I remember this particular night's exercising of the vocal chords beginning at least an hour before kick off and not letting up until well after the final whistle.

I managed to leave work mid afternoon and journeyed to Liverpool by train. I wasn't the only Geordie on board and upon arrival at Lime Street a number of us jumped in a taxi for a ride to the ground. Hally meanwhile had moved to Liverpool Poly to further his studies, whilst Goggs and Alan had come down from

Newcastle that afternoon. Meeting up inside the ground was a great feeling and although we ended up losing 4-0 it was one of those nights you'll never forget, simply because of the unique atmosphere generated by the Geordies. It made you feel so proud to be a Geordie and you can't say any better than that.

The game also made up Keegan's mind to retire at the end of the season. During the match he had been up against the classy Mark Lawrenson and barely got a kick. Realising that he couldn't do himself justice again at the top level his decision to call it a day come May was a brave and logical decision.

12/05/84 – NEWCASTLE v BRIGHTON & HOVE ALBION (3-1)

This match was the climax to the season but it was the five preceding matches that will always remain memorable as promotion kept on getting closer and closer, until finally it was achieved on an emotional afternoon in Huddersfield.

My work commitments earlier in the year meant that as well as having to temporarily suspend my playing career I couldn't even get away to watch Newcastle. This was a total disaster, however as the season's end approached so did the end of the basketball season and it meant being able to go to all five of those crucial and, as it turned out, hugely memorable games.

It started at Ewood Park, Blackburn, on Good Friday and I teamed up again with the regular crew: Hally, Goggs and Macas (despite being a Mackem he seemed to be a pretty regular away follower!) for the trip to Lancashire. I'd just bought my first car (my Dad's old Ford Cortina) and so it fell to me to do the driving. Blackburn is renowned for three things: the relatively friendly nature of the home supporters, the number of pubs close to the ground from which to choose and, from our point of view, the length of time it takes to drive out of town after the game – one single windy uphill road doesn't do too much to assist traffic flow!

A trip to play Blackburn is never an easy task and with the Geordies descending on Ewood Park in their thousands the home team, who were pretty handily placed in the league themselves, were naturally going to rise to the occasion. That they did and it was a great relief when John Trewick, a player who never quite cracked it at St. James' Park, scored the equaliser at our end which sparked off tumultuous celebrations.

So we were still on course for Division One, safe enough in

third position, and with a home game to come on Easter Monday against Carlisle our fate was very much in our own hands. I don't need to tell you that St. James' Park was filled once again to the rafters and the 5-1 victory that we saw left us with one foot in Division One. This victory was eventually as conclusive as the scoreline suggested but the game turned on a remarkable incident early in the second half. Kevin Carr saved Malcolm Poskett's penalty and from the resulting clearance Newcastle went straight up the other end of the field and scored through a Keegan header. We were delirious and when Beardsley smashed in his second from point blank range, after another flowing move and marvellous dummy from Keegan, we were left gasping – brilliant football, an unbelievable atmosphere and promotion virtually wrapped up – what more could you ask for in life?

Cambridge United were next in line the following Saturday. I drove again and Alan had joined the happy travelling band. Macas meanwhile had returned to Nottingham where he was studying so we had to pick him up en route. Cambridge are another of these teams who, with all due respect, shouldn't really be in the same division as us. The fact that they were was testament to the shrewd management of their limited resources and of course the bad management that had led to us being in Division Two.

The Abbey Stadium is nowhere near the centre of Cambridge, which is perhaps just as well as I'm sure the 'peaceful' people of Cambridge wouldn't have known what had hit them if the Geordies had been let loose on their University haven. Instead we eventually located it on the ring road on the outskirts of the city and even then you weren't sure if you had come to the right place because the ground was so small. We parked in a nearby field (yes a field!) and had to walk past a herd of cows to reach the ground. We all had tickets, Goggs, Macas and myself for the seats and Hally and Alan for the terraces but what we found once we'd got in to the ground was a farce. Naturally our seat tickets had been more expensive but we'd seen Hally and Alan on the terrace on the other side and they found they were able to walk round the perimeter of the ground and find a standing place right next to our seats. All that divided us was a wall about three feet high! Although you were annoyed at being ripped off you had to laugh at the situation. In a ground holding no more than 8,000 the Geordies must have had at least three quarters of it. Regretfully though there was little cheer about as we turned in an inexplicably poor display to lose by the only goal of the game. It wouldn't matter as it turned out but it was still desperately disappointing at the time. With the car not wanting to start for about half an hour after the match it just about made our day.

On the way home Macas and Alan fancied a night out so we ended up stopping at some quaint little Nottingham village called Bottesford. A good meal was the first priority and after finding a suitable place we all ordered massive platefuls of steak, chips and the works, that is with the exception of Macas! Macas, being a student still, was always claiming poverty so while the rest of us were tucking in he ordered a measly sandwich. We couldn't stop laughing at Macas afterwards when it turned out that the restaurateurs didn't produce a bill for us so we ended up with a free meal which Macas missed out on. What an irony, especially if you knew what a huge appetite he usually has. Later on Alan proceeded to fail miserably in his attempts to charm the local talent and so we just gave up after a while and headed back north to civilisation but not before Alan had taken out his frustration on some vehicles left in the car park – I've always thought Scots were mad!

Derby County arrived at St. James' Park the following Saturday and, putting the Cambridge result down as a 'blip', Newcastle proceeded to tear the visitors to shreds with the sort of football that was a joy to behold. Beardsley in particular was on a different planet and the final 4-0 scoreline could have been doubled with ease.

One point was still needed from our last two matches to mathematically clinch promotion as Bank Holiday Monday's trip to Huddersfield Town came around. I was now back in Leeds and so only had to undertake a trip of some 20 miles to get to the Leeds Road ground. I'd picked up some kind of bug over the weekend which meant I was feeling sick, faint and, in a nutshell, pretty awful. There was no way in the world I was going to miss out on this though. Once I'd got into the ground I just stood at the back by myself away from all the heaving masses of supporters and, for the first time I could remember, didn't sing or shout but just stood quietly taking it all in. The quite amazing thing about this game was the fact that the Geordies occupied three sides of the ground; behind both goals (the only time I've ever seen this happen at any ground on an away trip) and part of the main stand to the left of where I was situated. It was such an amazing sight that if you hadn't actually witnessed it you would never have believed it – my conservative estimate of the number of supporters who made the trip down from Tyneside, by every means possible, would be 18-20,000, absolutely phenomenal.

Keegan had suffered a blow on the head 48 hours earlier against Derby so he was reluctantly forced to sit out his only game of the season. It didn't matter though as we earned a 2-2 draw and that was all that mattered. Very surprisingly, I don't think there were any cameras present to capture the game for posterity, as certainly I don't recall ever having seen any highlights. Apart from obviously being able to re-live the promotion celebrations, I would have loved to have seen Beardsley's goal again as all I can remember of it is seeing him smash a half volley into the net from 25 yards at the other end of the ground. This was just one of Beardsley's special goals that he scored during the season. I've already mentioned those that he delivered in stunning fashion against Carlisle and Derby, but the ones he got against Manchester City (home and away), Middlesbrough at home and especially at Fratton Park, Portsmouth, were as classy a couple of goals that you were likely to see in a lifetime of watching football. Beardsley must have the 'quickest' feet in the game and with a footballing brain to match he could outwit defences and goalkeepers at will, making them look so silly in the process.

I was back home on Tyneside for the final act which was also to be Keegan's farewell appearance in the Football League. Brighton were privileged to be the team sharing this joyous occasion, and once again the atmosphere within the ground had reached staggering proportions. BBC's *Match of the Day* had to be present and of course they were and it was nice to hear Jimmy Hill giving so much praise to Peter Beardsley who he has always had a tremendously high regard for.

Fate decreed that Keegan had to score and sure enough he did. It was fitting too that Waddle and Beardsley also got on the scoresheet (Beardsley's once again being a goal in a million which went on to make the BBC's 'The Greatest Goal in History' competition in May 1994) to crown a season in which the three of them had surpassed all expectations and given the club, and the whole of Tyneside, their pride back as well as countless fond memories to cherish for all time.

It wasn't quite the end though as the following midweek a special match against Liverpool was arranged to mark Keegan's farewell to football. I almost didn't make it as my car broke down just by Leeming Bar on the A1, but thanks to the A.A. I got going again and reached St. James' Park with only minutes to spare. It's funny, but on the countless occasions I've bombed up the A1 since, I always, without fail, think of this incident every time I pass Leeming. After a 2-2 draw, which was almost incidental, his departure from the pitch after the game by helicopter was superbly stage-managed. It was a fitting way to say good-bye to a man who single handedly did more for the club in two seasons than many could hope to achieve in a life time.

Tyne Tees Television did themselves proud at the end of the season by producing a special half hour programme called *Going Up*. It was a magical programme, recorded of course on video for posterity, which encapsulated all the highlights of the season and there had certainly been an abundance – Beardsley's brilliant goals, Waddle's precision passing and touch play and, of course, the inspiration of the one and only Kevin Keegan.

23/06/84 – FRANCE v PORTUGAL (3-2)

France were a brilliant football team. French football first came to my attention in 1976 when St Etienne reached the European Cup Final. Two years later they played in the World Cup Finals in Argentina and stood out as a team full of potential. Spain, and the 1982 Finals, was where the team really came to prominence. The incomparable Michel Platini obviously stood out but the likes of Marius Tresor, Jean Tigana and Alain Giresse were outstanding players in their own right.

The match against Portugal was in the semi-final of the 1984 European Championships which were played in France. I was devastated that neither the BBC or ITV were covering the tournament in any detail, indeed we only saw the briefest of highlights. Fortunately we received edited highlights of this match from Paris and we were treated to a classic. Portugal led 2-1 deep into the second period of extra time and, after France had conjured an equaliser out of nothing, it was left to Platini to put the seal on the evening. Tigana reached the bye-line after a mazy run, and when he pulled the ball back, Platini was waiting in the six yard box to first control the ball before lashing it joyously into the net. How he and his colleagues enjoyed it. The stadium erupted and the celebrations that followed were truly memorable. It's a shame that

Marseille have since gone on to sully the reputation of the game in France.

1983/84 – Season's Summary

League	P	W	D	L	F	A	Pts.	Pos.
	42	24	8	10	85	53	80	3rd

Top Scorers

Kevin Keegan	28
Peter Beardsley	20
Chris Waddle	18

1984/85 - COX OUT, CHARLTON IN

Despite Keegan having retired from the game, the future still looked rosy for Newcastle after the marvellous climax to the promotion campaign. I remember Keegan saying in an interview shortly afterwards that he thought, with two or three additions to the squad, the club could go on and achieve great things. But just when it appeared that the world was Newcastle United's oyster, the Board of Directors inexcusably decided that they didn't want to go along that particular road, preferring instead to choose a safe mediocre existence. It was criminal that they chose not to speculate and take the club to new heights, and it was all because the individuals in charge did not want to lose their control and power within the club.

The upshot of it all was that Cox resigned on a matter of principle having been offered only a two year contract instead of the four-year deal he wanted and indeed deserved. Jack Charlton, a Geordie lad himself, was appointed in his place and although he was a self-confessed supporter of the club and appeared a perfect choice for the job, his footballing principles and the subsequent style of play he adopted were foreign to us all.

25/08/84 - LEICESTER CITY v NEWCASTLE (2-3)

Not a bad fixture to start the season, one of those away trips you look forward to for a variety of reasons, and a game we were more than capable of winning.

The team that took the field at Filbert Street had seven North-Eastern born players in it and that certainly didn't do us any harm. David McCreery, one of the unsung heroes of the previous season (along with Glenn Roeder) popped up to score a rare goal, his only one of the season I might add, and together with strikes from Carney and Waddle we took all three points. It was a particularly warm day and I remember Jack sitting on the bench in a short sleeved shirt rising only to greet each goal and I'm sure inwardly feeling very happy with himself.

04/09/84 - ARSENAL v NEWCASTLE (2-0)

We arrived at Highbury on top of the league having also beaten Sheffield Wednesday and Aston Villa to claim a maximum nine points. It was a quite unbelievable situation.

This was a Tuesday night fixture and as fortune had it I had been working in London over the weekend and managed to extend my stay until the Tuesday. By chance Hally was also in town, and so the two of us met up at Kings Cross and travelled up to Highbury. I had my car and the first thing you found near the ground was that everyone just seemed to leave their cars anywhere, literally abandoned in the middle of streets. We had little choice but to follow suit and it was with some trepidation that we left the car in the middle of 'nowhere' before walking the short distance to the ground. After a recent diet of visiting small ramshackle grounds it was a pleasure to come to Highbury. It is an imposing stadium, well appointed and, above all, looked the part. The other interesting thing about visiting new grounds is that you get the opportunity to see all four sides of the ground. Watching on television you never see the stand where the camera position is located so apart from actually seeing the ground 'in the flesh' it's nice to get the full picture.

Although Highbury looked the part it was more than we did as Arsenal went on to play us off the park. We never got a sniff and got off lightly in the end by conceding only two goals.

The following weekend Manchester United put five past us without reply in front of 55,000 at Old Trafford and, suddenly, life in the First Division wasn't quite the bed of roses it had seemed. Mention of this fixture immediately brings to mind one player, Remi Moses, whom I didn't care much for – no particular reason other than I just did! There were many other players who over the years have come into this category, indeed a number of the present day Manchester United team would walk into such a team.

22/09/84 – QUEEN'S PARK RANGERS v NEWCASTLE (5-5)

Mention has to be made of this extraordinary encounter. I was actually back in Ponteland for the weekend and 'guesting' for Ponteland United (it was nice still to be wanted and I always kept my boots in the car anyway). It was the norm at half time during games, for the spectators who were watching to keep us fully in touch with how Newcastle were getting on, and when we found out that a Chris Waddle hat-trick had helped establish a 4-0 interval lead at Loftus Road it was quite unbelievable. The points were safe. As our second half progressed I became aware, during injury breaks or when taking a throw in, that Rangers were fighting back but surely not to an extent that we'd still not win. Come 4.40pm when our game finished I was astounded to hear that Rangers had pulled four goals back in the second half but Kenny Wharton had added a fifth for us and it seemed we were just going to hang on – I should have thought so too! Inevitably it wasn't to be as Rangers predictably knocked in an equaliser two minutes from time, to make the final scoreline 5-5, which I found out about when I came out of the showers. I'm sure only Newcastle United were capable of such play.

03/11/84 – LUTON TOWN v NEWCASTLE (2-2)

Not the most glamorous of places to visit but they were a first division club so going to Kenilworth Road was as much a part of the football season as going to Anfield or Old Trafford. The locals round and about Kenilworth Road don't care much for visiting supporters and we spotted several demented gangs roaming the streets around the ground before kick off.

It was a cold blustery day, our end afforded us no protection from the elements and so it quickly became a forgettable experience (playing in our dreary grey away shirts I'm sure didn't help either) bar two things of note. Firstly I thought Chris Waddle's display was shameful. As much as I admired his talent, his heart didn't seem to be in the game. Whether or not he'd had a bust up with Jack before the match I don't know, but he simply wasn't giving 100 per cent and that was criminal. Secondly, were the antics of several Luton supporters on a row of bench type seating on our left. When Luton went close to scoring, or even made a half decent foray into our half of the field, they would rise in unison off their seats and wave their hands in the air whilst making strange monkey like noises. No kidding. It was funny to watch them but only because you felt sorry for them! The 2-2 draw on the day seems hardly worth mentioning and it left us almost inevitably in our fated position of 11th in the table.

01/01/85 – NEWCASTLE v SUNDERLAND (3-1)

A magical game. Beating Sunderland in itself is normally good enough, but when you throw in a stupendous Beardsley hat-trick and the Mackems having two men sent off as well, then you can imagine how we felt. When I'm compiling my list of all-time memorable games, this one is right up there with the best of them.

Mingling around outside the ground before the game I remember seeing Chris Waddle in the car park, and when I overheard him talking to a couple of press representatives, and telling them he'd failed a late fitness test, my heart sank. Despite what I'd said about him after the Luton match we needed Waddle for this game as without him I wasn't as confident of the outcome as I might have been. We had slipped to 17th in the table, a position of some concern, and so the derby game took on a little extra significance.

There were loads of us from Ponteland in the Gallowgate End Corner and I remember Nick in particular going absolutely 'mental', I think a little worse for drink. In among us also was little Patty (Nigel Pattinson) who had recently begun following in the family tradition. He was perhaps the most boisterous and rebellious of all the brothers – remembering Andrew Pattinson's run across the pitch back in 1973 that was saying something. He would travel all round the country watching Newcastle and actually struck up quite a good affinity with John, who was now living in London, whenever Newcastle played in the south.

In the first half Beardsley rattled in his first with slide rule precision in front of the Mackems at the Leazes End but that was to prove only a taster for what was to be an explosive second 45 minutes. Beardsley, finding himself with a one on one situation with Chris Turner, comprehensively beat him with a shimmy and shuffle that Turner swallowed hook, line and sinker and followed that up with a penalty to complete his hat-trick. I suppose I've also got to mention the fact that Beardsley missed from the spot, but with the Mackems only claiming a single strike from Colin West our victory was never threatened.

Late in the game our jubilation reached levels never previously scaled as first Howard Gayle, and then Gary Bennett, both black players incidentally, received red cards. Sendings off are normally greeted with much pleasure, but that day they almost evoked as much joyous passion as the goals themselves. The floodlights beaming down on the turf added to the occasion, and I can still visualise it all as if it was yesterday, so clear is the memory.

We drew 0-0 at Roker Park later in the season and while we were effectively muddling around in the comparatively still waters of mid-table, Sunderland were desperate for points and the three

they failed to get against us contributed to their eventual relegation, yet again, at the end of the season. Happy Days!

27/04/85 – NEWCASTLE v SOUTHAMPTON (2-1)

A typical end of season encounter but one of special significance
for Chris Waddle. Jack Charlton's style of play had to an extent
alienated the likes of Waddle and Beardsley, and coupled with the
uneasy calm in the Boardroom and the club's apparent lack of
ambition and vision, Waddle in particular was fast becoming a
restless player. One incident in the closing minutes of this game
said it all. We were holding a 2-1 lead when the ball was played out
to Waddle on the wing. Beardsley quickly came to support him
and the two of them proceeded to engage in a delightfully skilful
passing game, messing about as if they were on the training pitch.
The crowd loved it and it turned out to be an excellent way of
keeping possession and thus playing out time. Charlton though
had different ideas. He was aghast at what he had seen, almost
apoplectic, and upon the final whistle strode angrily on to the
pitch to publicly admonish the two of them, Beardsley in particular. You can imagine, the relationship between the two players
and the manager was never quite the same again. I couldn't
fathom out Charlton's mood and if this was to be indicative of his
attitude towards skilful and entertaining players then we were
banging our heads against a brick wall if we ever wanted the game
in this country to progress beyond the big boot forward.

Two weeks later Waddle wore a black and white shirt for the last
time in a 0-0 draw at Carrow Road. During the summer he packed
his bags for London and a new career at Tottenham. Many fans,
myself included, mourned his departure and on the occasions he
has returned to St. James' Park in either a Tottenham or Sheffield
Wednesday shirt, I have never vilified him. Others though saw him
as a traitor for leaving and those people no doubt are the ones
who boo and chant 'Judas' at him. I'm not for one moment criticising them for doing so, but the true reason Waddle left has
never really been made clear. If it was a combination of Jack
Charlton and an unambitious board, then you could hardly blame
him, hard as it might have been to accept. As for his long term
future don't be surprised to see him end up in some capacity at
Roker Park. Despite his playing background at Newcastle he's
always been a Mackem at heart – witness his show of emotion on

Radio 5 when co-commentating on a Newcastle match when news of a Sunderland goal filtered through to him.

A final word on the 1984/85 season – The first appearance of Paul Gascoigne. I regret I wasn't there to see it but the penultimate match of the season against Tottenham Hotspur at St. James' Park saw the one and only occasion where the three Geordie magicians, Beardsley, Waddle and Gascoigne, played together for Newcastle United. No one knew of course what Gascoigne was going to achieve in the game, but the thought of their gracing St. James' Park for a decade or more would have been an idyllic scenario for every Geordie. Sadly it never happened and it makes you wonder just what we might have achieved in the game had the team been built around the three of them in the same way that Charlton, Law and Best lit up Manchester United in the late 1960s.

11/05/85 & 29/05/85 – BRADFORD AND HEYSEL

Two tragedies in the space of 18 days; one a result of fateful circumstances and the other mindless hooliganism, but both stomach churning occasions, which put football into perspective in terms of how much it really meant. I was only vaguely aware of the Ibrox disaster when it happened in 1971, which claimed 66 lives as a result of Colin Stein's last minute equalising goal for Rangers against Celtic. This caused hundreds of departing spectators on the steep exit stairway 13, to attempt to return to the terraces against the flow of other supporters moving in the opposite direction, only resulting in them being swept downwards in the chaos and thus causing the awful carnage.

Bradford and Heysel were two disasters I witnessed in their entirety as they had unfolded in front of my own eyes. First at Valley Parade, Bradford – I'd just returned home from playing football and switched on the television only to be confronted with horrendous pictures of fire sweeping through the main wooden stand, knowing full well that people were trapped inside the structure. The enormity of it all, 53 people losing their lives, was impossible to comprehend. And then Heysel, venue for the European Cup Final between Liverpool and Juventus. I was watching on television back home in Ponteland and as kick off approached it became clear that a tragedy was beginning to unfold right in front of us. The death toll of Juventus supporters who were crushed to death trying to escape rampaging Liverpool fans, would continue to rise throughout the evening and I'm certain the match would never have started had UEFA been fully aware of the numbers that had died, 39 in all, and all so needlessly.

1984/85 – Season's Summary

League	P	W	D	L	F	A	Pts.	Pos.
	42	13	13	16	55	70	52	14th

Top Scorers		
Peter Beardsley		17
Chris Waddle		16
Neil McDonald		8

1985/86 – BEARDSLEY FOR ENGLAND

Willie McFaul was installed as manager following Jack Charlton's surprising resignation a week before the season started. Charlton's departure had come after the friendly with Sheffield United at St. James' Park in which he had been verbally abused by supporters criticising his style of play. Who could blame them when he played the likes of Tony Cunningham and George Reilly up front as his main strike force which meant Beardsley having to stay out of the way on the wing – absolutely absurd. He didn't need that sort of thing so he simply walked out. I wasn't particularly sorry to see him go as I was one of those supporters who didn't care much for his managerial talent although his success with the Republic of Ireland, up until his resignation in December 1995, has been phenomenal – I do like him immensely though as a television pundit. Although we comfortably held our own in Division One, hovering around mid table for most of the year, it was a fairly mundane season. Early exits once again in both the Cup competitions were nothing new, and it was only the sparkling play of Beardsley and Gascoigne that kept us entertained.

24/08/85 – NEWCASTLE v LIVERPOOL (1-0)

I always seem to be on holiday in August, partly because it's the prelude to a new basketball season, so it's a good chance to watch a number of early season games and size up form and trophy winning potential (only joking, well I was in this particular era).

Against Luton Town the previous Wednesday night we'd had to come from 2-0 down to salvage a draw, late goals from Roeder and Beardsley doing the trick, and so a visit from Liverpool was bound to prove a good test. In the old days Liverpool arriving at St. James' Park would mean the 'house full' signs being put up, but a crowd of just under 30,000 said a tremendous amount about the apathy that had set in caused undoubtedly by a barren run of failure at the club, the 1983/84 promotion season notwithstanding.

One legacy that Charlton left us was a beanpole of a centre forward called George Reilly. He wasn't quite in the Shinton/ Rafferty class but I didn't think he was far behind. He did score the winning goal this afternoon though, heading home a right wing cross virtually under Bruce Grobbelaar's cross bar. McFaul did well to get rid of Reilly in November, but in replacing him with Billy Whitehurst he did himself no favours. Whitehurst arrived from Hull with something of a goalscoring reputation but proved only to be an overweight, over-zealous waste of money. Tony Cunningham was another poor quality player who led our attack during the season, and it made you wonder how people ever managed to rate these individuals to such an extent as to pay money for them and bring them to St. James' Park. It was incomprehensible and I can only think that if the Board had not been so parsimonious in its attitude, it might never have happened – surely the manager's judgement couldn't be that bad; or could it?

Talking of good and bad managers, down the road at Roker Park Sunderland had just appointed 'The Messiah', Lawrie McMenemy, as team manager. What an outstanding manager he proved to be! The Mackems promptly proceeded to lose their first five games of the season, and ultimately that contributed to a large extent to their eventual relegation at the end of the season. McMenemy was loved on Tyneside in the same way Terry Butcher would be in 1993!

26/12/85 – SHEFFIELD WEDNESDAY v NEWCASTLE (2-2)

For some reason, no doubt due to the insistence of the South Yorkshire police, this was a lunchtime kick off so it meant a particularly early start. Thank goodness it was only Sheffield for it has been known for the Football League fixture computer to have the occasional brainstorm. Take 1991/92 for example and what sane person would ratify Newcastle having to undertake a 650 mile round trip to Southend on New Year's Day and a noon start at that?

After my experience of Hillsborough two years earlier, I'd convinced the rest of the lads that the seats would be a prudent option. Although more expensive there was obviously no chance of another 'Cambridge' happening and we found ourselves with a perfect view high above pitch level. The good thing about these particular seats was the fact that they were wooden and hence could be banged up and down creating a lot of noise! The whole end was enclosed too, so it made for a pretty rarefied atmosphere, well, at our end of the ground at least – Sheffield Wednesday fans are notoriously quiet but not as bad as Ipswich!. The 2-2 draw that ensued maintained our position in the top half of the table, 10th to be exact, and made it a more than enjoyable day out. At least on the journey home we could listen to the rest of the day's action on the radio which made a pleasant change – we were even home for *Sports Report* on Radio 2, which is an institution for all football fans. Many a time after coming out of a ground you would dash back to the car to put the radio on before the clock ticked past 5.00pm. The title music is one of the most familiar introductory tunes on radio and following the afternoon's headlines the unmistakable voice of James Alexander-Gordon begins reading out the classified results. His tone and level of voice is so distinctive that even when he's half way through a particular score you know whether the away team has managed to earn a win or draw or has been defeated. There have been many presenters down the years, ranging from the inadequate Renton Laidlaw to the incomparable John Inverdale however the man who took over the microphone in 1994, Ian Payne, is proving an exceptional choice by the Radio 5 hierarchy.

01/01/86 – NEWCASTLE v EVERTON (2-2)

New Year's Day's matches are always special occasions and have that little hidden extra ingredient to whet the appetite. Usually they are fairly 'big' games and Everton, Football League Champions the previous season, certainly came into that category.

The first half was a fairly frenetic affair with Everton shading it but the second half that followed roused the Geordie passions to levels usually only associated with derby matches or big cup ties. Tackles began flying in, which is always a cue for getting the crowd worked up, and Billy Whitehurst in particular left a lasting impression on Paul Bracewell. Beardsley and Gascoigne scored two classic goals and it gave me extra pleasure to see Neville Southall left floundering. Although I rate him as an exceptional goalkeeper his time wasting tactics this afternoon had left me seething. A 2-2 draw was the final result, we stayed 11th, and Everton, I'm sure delighted, went back to Merseyside with a point.

I wrapped up the holiday period three days later with the FA Cup third round tie with Brighton at St. James' Park, and what a disaster this game proved. It was an icy pitch and totally unsuitable for football (undersoil heating at most of the major grounds these days makes such problems things of the past). Brighton scored in the first five minutes and after that we never looked like getting back in the game. They scored again in the second half and so for the second time in three seasons unfashionable Brighton had come to St. James' Park and dumped us ingloriously out of the most prestigious and glamorous cup competition in the world.

23/04/86 – ENGLAND v SCOTLAND (2-1)

Our hero Peter Beardsley was on the verge of gaining international recognition. He had made his full debut earlier in the year against Egypt in Cairo, and as there was a good possibility that he would get a game against Scotland, it became a match we couldn't miss.

The regular quartet, Hally, Goggs, Macas and myself met up again and, naturally sporting all our Newcastle United gear, set off down the M1.

One of the topics of conversation during the journey was the match Newcastle had played at West Ham 48 hours earlier. The result? 8-1 to the Cockneys and the heaviest defeat I have known in all my time of following Newcastle. There were mitigating circumstances though as during the course of the 90 minutes there were three different custodians of the number one shirt. Regular goalkeeper Martin Thomas had to leave the field with a shoulder injury early on and for the rest of the match Peter Beardsley, who had apparently always fancied himself as a bit of a Gordon Banks in training, and Chris Hedworth shared the duties in the green shirt. Perhaps we got off lightly on the night but even so, eight goals!

All was going well until we got about as far as Luton where we encountered a horrendous traffic jam. We contemplated shooting down the hard shoulder but I was driving I and considered the chance of losing my licence an unacceptable risk. We just had to sit it out and as kick off time drew closer so our frustration rose proportionally. When we did get off the motorway it took us only 15 minutes to get to Wembley and we arrived only five or ten minutes after kick off. Dumping the car without due care and attention we ran up Wembley Way and straight into the ground. It was only my third time inside the stadium and the feelings I had for the place remained intact, even though I wasn't able to savour the occasion as much this time.

We were all bitterly disappointed to find that Bobby Robson had left Peter on the bench but it didn't stop the four of us chanting his name non stop and making the Cockneys around us wonder who on earth these four nutters were! He didn't get a game, not even a few minutes, and although England beat Scotland 2-1 it was no consolation to us.

This was one of the last England versus Scotland matches to be played in the Home International Championship and the demise of the competition is rather sad. As a youngster I always looked forward to these games at the end of the season, with the England versus Scotland fixture, which alternated between Wembley and Hampden Park, always providing a fitting finale to the season. Two games in particular stick in my mind: the 5-1 thrashing we inflicted upon them in 1975 and the 2-1 win for the Scots at Wembley in 1977 which was followed by a pitch invasion by hundreds of drunken tartan clad hooligans who swung on the crossbars, eventually snapping them, and ended up taking half the Wembley turf back to Scotland with them. Aside from the hooligan problems influencing them, the decision of the English and Scottish FAs to draw a veil over the tournament, largely because matches against Wales and Northern Ireland were uneconomic, was very sad.

The lads fancied an Indian meal after the game, I didn't, but being in the minority I had to go along. Indian food makes me ill and so while the lads were tucking into some sort of Bombay curry I'd nipped next door to the chippie and brought a big plateful of traditional English fare back into the restaurant to sit down and enjoy with the rest of the lads. The owner didn't exactly approve but we told him where to go, politely of course!

03/05/86 – LEICESTER CITY v NEWCASTLE (2-0)

Mention has already been made of the infamous 'Macas' incident at the end of this match but I've got to mention the Beardsley factor too.

Bobby Robson had included our Geordie hero in his World Cup squad and with this fixture being the last of the season, he was determined to go out on a high note. Throughout the game the Geordies had been chanting 'Mexico', 'Beardsley for England' and other such Beardsley related World Cup ditties and Beardsley responded in the only way he knew how. He didn't manage a goal but his contribution to the game was phenomenal. One incident in particular stood out when he received a throw in at his feet, used the pace of the ball to flick it with the outside of his boot past the lumbering defender on his back before sharply turning around the other side of him to pick up the ball. Sheer class. Beardsley was lapping it up and it was a pleasure to witness. The match itself was lost 2-0, which didn't really matter, and we slipped one place in the table to a final end of season finishing position of, yes you've guessed it, 11th!

03/05/86 – ENGLAND v PARAGUAY (3-0)

The biggest thrill I got from the 1986 World Cup Finals was Peter Beardsley's goal against Paraguay in the second phase of the competition. Beardsley had cemented his place in the England team in Mexico providing an ideal foil for Gary Lineker. His creative performance against Poland, when England were in danger of elimination from the tournament, was outstanding and when we were eventually defeated by Argentina in the quarter finals it was a bitter pill to swallow especially as that footballing genius Diego Maradona was at his worst (his first goal against England) and brilliant best (his second in the same game).

The Brazilian full back Josimar was also a joy to watch, his stunning strike against Northern Ireland left Pat Jennings groping at thin air, as was Hugo Sanchez, the extrovert Mexican forward. The Final, between Argentina and West Germany was a game where I didn't particularly favour either side (unlike 1990 where I was firmly on the side of the Germans as opposed to the ultra negative South Americans) but when Burruchaga netted Argentina's winner I ended up on their side.

1985/86 – Season's Summary

League	P	W	D	L	F	A	Pts.	Pos.
	42	17	12	13	67	72	63	11th

Top Scorers		
Peter Beardsley	19
Paul Gascoigne	9
George Reilly	7

1986/87 – MACKEM RELEGATION

The dawn of a new season is always the most exciting part of the year and the 1986/87 season was no exception. On a personal front I'd just made a big investment in the shape of buying my own flat in Oakwood, Leeds (thanks by the way to John and Dave Ingham for their invaluable assistance with the removals). It wasn't really a gamble but it was a big step for me. However, I can assure you the thrill of having your own place, where you could come and go as you pleased and do whatever you wanted (not that I did anything out of the ordinary) was special. The location I had chosen was also ideal for the rock and pop concerts in Roundhay Park, a couple of hundred yards from my flat, and to see the likes of Genesis and Madonna live has been a real thrill. The fact that I was on the north side of Leeds and close to the A1 was useful too for obvious reasons.

My football programme collection, which took up a tremendous amount of cupboard space, unfortunately had to be sacrificed as I needed the capital for the essential expenditure I was about to incur. It was a sad day and, although it probably seemed to be the right thing to do at the time, it is a decision I regret very much today. Still, hindsight is a fine thing and we all make mistakes, so I've since adopted a philosophical and ambivalent attitude and that's got me through it!

I'd also managed to get my own footballing career back on the rails during the summer by joining Yorkshire Amateurs Football Club. The 'Ammers' are a club with a proud history and tradition and one of the best non-league clubs in Leeds. Although it would once more mean not being able to watch Newcastle as often as I would like, I was delighted to be back playing again – if you can play don't stop, nothing beats it. As it transpired it took a couple of seasons before I would manage to hold down a regular place in the side, partly due to work commitments, and so on the occasions I wasn't playing you can guess where I was.

The title to this section, 'Mackem Relegation', isn't of course anything to do with Newcastle United but the reason for the slight change in style is simply because there was nothing in the season at St. James' Park special enough to merit a headline. Thus the fate of our footballing foes from Wearside seemed a pretty apt substitution.

23/08/86 – NEWCASTLE v LIVERPOOL (0-2)

Liverpool did us again and the ease of their 2-0 victory was frightening. Ian Rush scored both goals, one in each half, and his was as impressive an all round display as you could wish to see. Liverpool were an exceptional side of course but if this was to be a sign of things to come then I feared for our fortunes in the months ahead. I wish I'd been wrong but when we went on to take only two points from the next five matches we unsurprisingly found ourselves once again rooted to the foot of the table. Mutterings of discontent were growing and it wasn't until Wimbledon came north to St. James' Park at the end of September that a Gascoigne goal registered our first win of the season and lifted us to the heady heights of 20th in the table – give me 11th place any day!

23/09/86 – BRADFORD CITY v NEWCASTLE (2-0)

It was handy having drawn Bradford City in the League Cup – for me anyway, as it's only 10 miles from Leeds. Bradford weren't back playing at Valley Parade yet and so we had the dubious pleasure of having to play at the Odsal Stadium, home of Bradford Northern Rugby League Club and a first for Newcastle. I'm nowhere near being a member of the '92' Club (I'm somewhere in the forties I think) but at least I was one up on many supporters who had never watched a match at this venue. The stadium is a huge exposed bowl but is ugly in character and the facilities were appalling. Leeds United had been the visitors a week or so earlier and typically caused havoc by setting fire to a mobile chip van. No such disturbances from the Geordies though, I'm pleased to say, other than on the pitch where Bradford beat us 2-0.

30/11/86 – NEWCASTLE v WEST HAM UNITED (4-0)

The era of live television coverage of Football League matches had recently begun and when the ITV executives selected this game for transmission at the start of the season it looked to be a good choice. Come November they were having second thoughts as they didn't want to broadcast two 'bad' teams playing out a relegation battle so early in the season. ITV were locked into the agreement though and weren't able to pull the plug. Thank goodness they didn't. It turned out to be a superb match (West Ham probably didn't think so) and I heard later those same ITV executives saying what fabulous entertainment the game had provided and what a good choice of match they had made!

All the pre-match build up had centred around the clash between Peter Beardsley and West Ham's Tony Cottee whom many people (those south of Watford probably) thought was a better player, an absurd suggestion.

In as charged an atmosphere as you could imagine, Newcastle laid siege to the West Ham goal and around the half hour mark scored twice in quick succession through Neil McDonald and Andy Thomas. Minutes later Paul Goddard went within inches of making it three, but second half goals from Darren Jackson and Thomas again gave us an emphatic 4-0 winning scoreline which moved us up a remarkable six places in the table from bottom to 16th place. Watching the match later on television it was nice to hear co-commentator Ron Atkinson say the passionate support of the Geordies was unrivalled anywhere else in the country – and of course he was absolutely right.

Like myself, Hally, Goggs and Macas had by now moved away from Tyneside, all because of work, and I'd linked up with a new generation of friends at the match. Nick was still going regularly and his younger brothers, Dave and Ritchie together with Simon McIntosh, had also become fanatics and the five of us are still going strong today. Doc (Mike), the second of the four brothers, was always interested but never had the same passion for the team as the rest of us and we always gave him a lot of good natured stick about his ambivalence. Like myself the Inghams were all keen golfers so it meant that we all got on very well throughout the year both in the football season and on the golf course during the summer. Dave, Ritchie and Sime are 'converted' Mags I suppose in that they didn't pick up the bug until their mid teens. I suspect this may have been due to their parents not taking them to games when they were young which is the way most football mad children first become involved. Nick was different only because I was his best mate at school and I quickly put him straight.

Two weeks later Nottingham Forest came to St. James' Park and were beaten by a supreme piece of finishing by, who else but, Peter Beardsley. He picked the ball up just inside the Forest half and sprinted clear before slipping his shot past Segers in typical fashion. It was around about this time that clubs had started to market video recordings of matches and it was perhaps inevitable that we all clubbed together to buy the Forest tape just so we could savour Beardsley's goal again. Things had begun to look much brighter all of a sudden, as 15th place in the table would testify, but it was to prove a false dawn as six consecutive defeats were on the horizon and with them the inevitable return to the bottom of the table.

01/01/87 – MANCHESTER UNITED v NEWCASTLE (4-1)

Old Trafford is certainly a very impressive stadium especially when viewed against the dilapidated St. James' Park although to be fair the new Milburn (West) Stand was in the process of being erected even though the Leazes and Gallowgate Ends remained a disgrace. Funnily enough I think the Milburn Stand, named after our legendary centre forward of the 1950s, looks better from the outside and I can only think this is because the roof jutting out on to the pitch looks a little out of place.

I was driving once again and this was undoubtedly due to the fact that I rarely, if ever, drink. This actually makes me a very rare breed – a football loving Geordie who doesn't drink. Apart from football, Geordies are synonymous with drink and indeed it is an integral part of the culture. Pre and after match drinking sessions are the norm for all Newcastle matches, home and away, but it's something that's never really bothered me. Some supporters I'm sure need a good drink to get them 'livened up' before games but, as all the lads will confirm, being completely sober on the terraces (but drunk with adrenalin) doesn't stop me from getting as carried away as anybody else. It's also ironic I suppose that I sing the 'Drink drink wherever you may be' song as heartily as anyone – all part of the fun really. At a conservative estimate I would say the average Geordie consumes at least five or six pints before a home game, and even more on away trips where double figures become the norm. At least with me driving the rest of the lads could drink without worrying about the consequences and sure enough upon arrival in Manchester we made a bee line to the nearest drinking establishment and set up camp. All the regulars had come down and, for the first time, Angus, who was one of those peculiar lads, a Manchester United supporter living in Newcastle. Angus is a really good mate but there must have been something seriously wrong in his upbringing for him to have his footballing allegiance at Old

Trafford. Of course there are thousands like him all around the country but you can never consider these people as 'true' football supporters. Another thing that really bugs me about Manchester United is that many football journalists, especially on television or radio, refer to them as 'United' even when they are playing another team with United in their name. What gives Manchester United a divine right to be known simply as 'United' is beyond me and the song 'Who the f*** are Man Utd' is always sung by me with particular relish. You may think we're jealous of Manchester United but any Tynesider will tell you they wouldn't swap their Geordie roots for anywhere in the world.

We were in the middle of our losing streak when we took the field and Manchester United were in no mood to do us any favours. The resulting 4-1 scoreline was as predictable as any in the division that afternoon, especially after Peter Jackson had scored in his own net. Mention of Jackson leads me to say that had he been blessed with pace he would have gone on to play for England. He took more pleasure from wearing the black and white shirt than almost any other player, was totally committed to the club, and it was a terrible shame that a player with his attitude and character didn't quite make it to the top of his profession.

It was the norm at the end of matches such as this for the away supporters to be kept locked inside the stadium at the end of the game for a period of anything between 10 and 20 minutes. It was a police measure designed to enable them to clear the streets of all the home fans, and of course much of the traffic, so as to give the likes of us as easy and trouble free an exit as possible. It didn't always work but even though it was annoying to be kept in (especially when you wanted to get back to the car to listen to the football results) I suppose there was a measure of sense in it.

21/02/87 – TOTTENHAM HOTSPUR v NEWCASTLE (1-0)

This was a fifth round FA Cup tie and we'd been fortunate to have drawn Northampton Town and Preston North End in the earlier rounds to give us a fairly easy ride to the last 16.

Virtually everyone on Tyneside (slight exaggeration) wanted to be at this game and the convoy of buses, cars, vans and the like that left Tyneside at dawn was a sight to behold. The official attendance for the game is recorded as 38,000 but to my mind there were thousands more in the ground. I think that the only reason that the true figure wasn't given was that the attendance had exceeded the official capacity of the ground and, had Tottenham admitted it, they may have been seriously admonished by the Football Association. Another thing of course is that they didn't have to declare the additional gate receipts – or am I being too cynical? In the light of what has recently come to light about Tottenham's alleged financial malpractice, which resulted in a six point deduction from their total in the Premiership for the 1994/95 season, coupled with a ban from that season's FA Cup competition, perhaps not. The fact that this ban was subsequently lifted doesn't alter these facts.

The reason for this overcrowding was that the Geordies took close on 14,000 supporters to White Hart Lane. Tottenham officials had naively anticipated less than half that number making the trip and so the away end got a little congested to say the least. It never got quite as bad as Hillsborough four years earlier but nevertheless being crushed against the railings wasn't exactly a bundle of fun. Macas and Lowsey were right next to me, literally, and we had to use all our combined strength to lift an elderly gentleman, who had all but passed out, over the railings to safety. As is the norm on such occasions the police and stewards just looked on oblivious to it all with our pleas for assistance falling on deaf ears. I remember, when I saw the highlights on television later on, thinking that I'd never seen an end so full of people before. Another unsavoury aspect of the afternoon was the tendency of a large proportion of Geordies to sing distasteful anti-Semitic songs aimed at the Jewish element of the Tottenham support.

Need I tell you who lost? Well we did, but only to a single Clive Allen penalty in the first half. Late in the game, at the far end of the ground, it looked on a couple of occasions that we were certain to score but failed to do so, television pictures only served to heighten the heartache when we saw them. With practically the last kick of the game Nico Claesen just missed making it two for Tottenham and this led to an ugly confrontation between Claeson and Kenny Wharton. I think Wharton attempted to head butt him, which of course is inexcusable in anyone's book, but Claesen was one of those players you didn't care much for and as we Geordies say, a 'worky ticket'. Claesen got what he deserved and Kenny became an instant hero. As for Wharton, he had learned his trade at Grainger Park Boys' Club in the Blakelaw district of Newcastle, and that told its own story. After the game, as the terraces slowly emptied, I found myself unable to move, I wasn't physically hurt or anything, just totally shattered by our defeat. This particular one hurt more than most.

21/03/87 – MANCHESTER CITY v NEWCASTLE (0-0)

Maine Road was a ground I was unfamiliar with. In fact, it was my first visit, which was quite surprising considering the number of times I'd been to Old Trafford and both Liverpool grounds. Anyway Macas was cajoled into taking his car, a clapped out Vauxhall if memory serves me correctly, and into it piled Ritchie, Dave, Sime and, of course, me. We had arranged to meet Hally somewhere in Manchester's Moss Side district (where Maine Road is situated) and having eventually done so, after driving round in circles after leaving the M63 at the wrong exit, we settled into the regular pre-match routine, partly to celebrate Ritchie's birthday. Macas had had rather too many so I was left with no choice but to assume the driving – I suppose I am always around as other people's insurance policy on trips such as this in case they decide to over indulge. Perhaps I should start charging them all a premium!

Parking the car somewhere near Maine Road was difficult as it appeared there was just one road leading down towards the ground. As this road was packed full of people walking to the match, we ended up just having to leave the car on this particular road and joining the procession. As for the match itself, which finished goal-less, the only abiding memory was the pleasure of seeing former Newcastle striker Imre Varadi miss a golden chance from only six yards out. City, as many of you will know, also have a supporter, a middle aged woman I think, who attends every game at Maine Road and rings an old school bell. I don't know why she does it but today, not surprisingly, was no exception.

08/04/87 – NEWCASTLE v NORWICH CITY (4-1)

Relegation was still a very distinct possibility. We were third from bottom but we'd just embarked on a little run that was gradually lifting us up the table. Gascoigne had been out of the side through injury since the beginning of November and it was his return to the team three games earlier against Tottenham that lifted the whole club. The other factor in our upturn in fortune was the goals of Paul Goddard who scored in seven consecutive games through March and April in which we were unbeaten, winning five of them.

The 4-1 win over Norwich gave me particular pleasure, not just as it moved us up to 18th in the table or because we scored three goals at the Gallowgate End in the second half, but because we put the ball past Bryan Gunn in the Norwich goal. Gunn antagonised me no end, certain players just have that effect on me, and I was delighted he and his team-mates deservedly left St. James' Park empty handed.

18/04/87 – NEWCASTLE v MANCHESTER UNITED (2-1)

This was to be Peter Beardsley's last match in a Newcastle shirt before departing in the close season for pastures new at Anfield. He cost the Merseysiders £1.9 million, which was almost three times as much as Tottenham had paid us for Waddle, but even at such a price Liverpool were getting a bargain.

As usual Manchester United were responsible for ensuring the gates were locked well before kick off and the atmosphere in the ground was boiling up nicely. Manchester had a certain Norman Whiteside in their team and he incurred the wrath of all those in the East Stand benches when he took Paul Stephenson out early in the game and went straight into the referee's notebook. Whiteside was undoubtedly a talented player but had a malicious mean streak in his make up and was prone to over physical and dangerous challenges. At least we were able to enjoy seeing Gascoigne take 'revenge', on behalf of the team, as he proceeded to give Whiteside a demonstration of football skill – we lost count of the number of times Whiteside was humiliated by Gascoigne's cheeky little nutmegs.

A lot of opposing players over the years have had to face venomous attacks from the benches (sometimes friendly in nature but more often than not aggressive) as they have been involved in incidents near the touchline. Standing as I did on the Gallowgate End you could see them all rising in unison with fingers pointing menacingly at the culprit, some even left their seats completely and ran down to the walkway at the front if they felt really irate! Linesmen weren't spared either and I'm sure some of the less firm officials have either raised or kept their flags down, as the case may

may be, in favour of Newcastle so as to avoid any aggravation from supporters behind them.

I suppose the converse may also have been true where you got a particularly obstinate or stroppy official who would take a perverse pleasure from upsetting the fans. On reflection though I'm sure that 99% of officials do the job to the best of their ability regardless of any outside influence or interference.

Dave and Sime went on to buy season tickets for the benches and I'm sure enjoyed the pleasure of abusing many a visiting player over the years. In all my years of supporting the club the benches are the only place in the whole ground (new and old) that I've never watched a game from and I include the Corporate Hospitality boxes and, believe it or not, the Directors' Box in that statement. Strangely enough it bugs me a bit but I would hope to remedy the situation at some point in the future.

As for the game itself I distinctly remember watching Beardsley stretch innocuously for a ball after only 20 minutes and quickly pulling up awkwardly. It was uncanny but I immediately thought to myself that he'd picked up a serious injury, would have to leave the field, and what's worse, be forced to miss the remainder of the season. Rumours had been spreading round Tyneside in recent weeks about the possibility of Beardsley leaving the club in the summer, Liverpool being the favourites to sign him. I was also more than concerned to think that it might even be his last appearance at St. James' Park – what a nightmare. He limped around for a few minutes and then the inevitable; my worst fears were realised and he left the field. I'm sure I wasn't the only person in the ground with the same feelings.

Beardsley's departure from the field was surely a mortal blow to our chances of winning the game but after Strachan and Roeder had scored a goal apiece in an even first half that man Goddard popped up inside the penalty area to rifle the winner under Gary Walsh in the Manchester goal. Pandemonium on the terraces and an anxious last few minutes before the final whistle blew. Not only had we put one over Manchester United but we'd virtually ensured our survival in Division One by moving up to 16th position and comparative safety.

Beardsley's injury was to his hamstring and although I suppose he could possibly have turned out in one of the final two games it wouldn't have been worth the risk. Most of us knew deep down that he wouldn't be playing on Tyneside next season although nothing was official, and it was terribly sad that he had to bow out of St. James' Park on such a low key note. When he did eventually sign for Liverpool later in the summer it was another kick in the teeth for the Geordie public. Waddle had already gone, the Keegan promotion bandwagon hadn't been capitalised on and here was another home-grown Geordie superstar being 'forced' out of the club primarily due to a Board of Directors, chaired by the miserly, but defiant, Gordon McKeag, who were a disgrace to the name of Newcastle United. It was rumoured, and probably not far from the truth, that the near £2 million received for Beardsley, went straight into the fund to pay for the new Milburn Stand.

09/05/87 – NOTTINGHAM FOREST v NEWCASTLE (2-1)

It's always particularly enjoyable to have a 'nice' away trip on the last day of the season. Nottingham Forest was certainly in that category and with Macas already in situ in Nottingham we thought it prudent to leave early in the morning to get down to Macas' place by mid morning.

Macas lived virtually next to the City Ground and as luck would have it pretty adjacent to the Trent Bridge Public House where we'd planned to spend a good few hours before the game – doing what I don't quite know! As it turned out though it was a wonderfully hot early summer's day and as we headed for the Trent Bridge at around 11.00am we noticed (well I did anyway) that at the other Trent Bridge (the Nottinghamshire County Cricket Ground) a zonal Benson and Hedges Cup match between Nottinghamshire and Derbyshire was just starting. Being something of a cricket nut I persuaded the rest of the lads that if we could wangle our way into the ground, they could still drink as much as they wanted in more relaxed convivial surroundings. It worked, I negotiated a 'special deal' with the turnstile operator who let us all in for £1 on the basis that we were Newcastle United football supporters, down in Nottingham for the day and would only be staying to watch the cricket for a couple of hours. As it was we ended up staying until 15 minutes before kick off time across the road at the City Ground and it was one of the best pre-match 'sessions' I'd ever had. I watched the cricket, lazing about on the grass by the boundary while the rest of the lads consumed numerous pints of Nottinghamshire ale in between snoozing in the sunshine. What a way to build up to a football match.

It was pretty inconsequential that we lost 2-1, which resulted in an end of season finishing position of 17th, but at least we had the pleasure of seeing Paul Gascoigne take Neil Webb to the cleaners. Gascoigne's influence on the team in the last month or so of the season, upon his return to the side from injury, cannot be over estimated. No less an authority on the game than the immortal Jackie Milburn had described Gascoigne as the best player in the world and, although he was going a little overboard in his assessment, he wasn't too far from the truth. Gascoigne had reassured Milburn that he wouldn't let his beloved Newcastle get relegated and he was true to his word.

17/05/87 – SUNDERLAND v GILLINGHAM (4-3)

A day that will go down in the annals of history as the day the Mackems achieved the stupendous feat of relegation to Division Three of the Football League for the first time in their history – it goes without saying that The Magpies have never stooped so low.

Sunderland had finished 20th in Division Two at the end of the season which meant they had to enter the Play Offs (more about them in 1989/90) to attempt to retain their place in Division Two at the expense of those clubs who had finished in positions three to five in Division Three. In the semi-final they were paired with Gillingham and in the away leg at the Priestfield Stadium they suffered a 3-2 defeat which clearly left them an uphill task in their return leg. There was a crowd of 25,000 at Roker Park and the visiting Gillingham supporters were joined by nearly 500 Geordies who were there with the express intention of cheering Sunderland into Division Three. It was an unbelievable situation and something the visitors found difficult to comprehend. After 90 minutes Sunderland led 3-2, which meant extra time, but when Tony Cascarino scored Gillingham's third it looked all over for Sunderland. They did manage a late goal to bring the aggregate scores level at 6-6 but it wasn't enough to prevent Gillingham winning on the away goals rule. When the final whistle sounded the expressions of despair on the faces of the vast majority of those in the ground was in stark contrast to the scenes of utter jubilation in the away supporters enclosure. It was amazing that the Geordies were more overjoyed and vociferous in their support of Gillingham's victory then their own fans! This one afternoon put into perspective everything that needed to be said about the relationship, or rather lack of it, between the Geordies and Mackems.

1986/87 – Season's Summary

League	P	W	D	L	F	A	Pts.	Pos.
	42	12	11	19	47	76	47	17th

Top Scorers		
Paul Goddard		13
Neil McDonald		7
Andy Thomas		7

1987/88 – BRAZILIAN MAGIC

Willie McFaul always did his best for the club and, although ultimately he was to fail, the 1987/88 season was to prove his most memorable and successful as team manager. Whether or not the signing of Mirandinha contributed to this is open to question, but there is no doubt that his signing was a bold move which took the whole of British football by surprise. Many clubs were sceptical about the potential success of the first Brazilian to play in the Football League; others were just plain envious. Sure a number of Argentinians, Ardiles and Villa at Tottenham and Tarantini at Birmingham being the most notable, had already played in the Football League, but the Brazilians had that extra little mystique about them and that's what made his signing such a mouth watering proposition for the Geordie fans.

15/08/87 – NEWCASTLE v ?

This was ridiculous. Here we were on the first day of a brand new season and we didn't have a fixture, talk about starting the season off on the wrong foot. The reason for this peculiar situation was that the Football League were in the process of reducing the number of clubs in Division One to 20 (from 22) and as it involved a two year process it meant that for this season only the number of clubs in the top division would be 21. Clearly not every team would be able to play on the same day and so on every weekend of the season one club wasn't allocated a fixture. Just our luck to be the odd one out on day one, one of the most exciting days in the whole of the football season. We couldn't even content ourselves with laughing at the Mackems, who were now gracing Division Three, as they sneaked a 1-0 win at Brentford. Still at least they had to look forward to glamorous home games against the likes of Walsall, Wigan and York later in the season. Now's probably as good a time as any to say it – the Mackems did, to their credit, manage to get out of Division Three at the first time of asking. If they hadn't I reckon they would have been stuck in the third or fourth division for ever. What a shame.

19/08/87 – TOTTENHAM HOTSPUR v NEWCASTLE (3-1)

Nick and I went to this game by ourselves and decided that going on the Supporters' Club coach was the most prudent choice of travel. Nick started his journey in Newcastle but as I was in Leeds I arranged for the bus to pick me up on the A1 outside the Alpine Inn in Wetherby. Long journeys on buses aren't exactly a bundle of fun unless you pay a little extra to travel on the video coach. Otherwise it's simply a case of sleeping (which is never easy), cards and other silly games or listening to your personal stereo. Recently I've started recording tapes of Newcastle matches from the radio, and having just acquired a radio with automatic recording facilities built in making life a great deal easier, the pleasure I get from reliving the magic moments in sound only is 'music' to my ears – you should try it.

The other good thing, or is it the only good thing, about coach travel to away games is the pleasure of being part of an enormous convoy of supporters travelling as one to follow your team. It's brilliant when you're in a car and you 'hit' the coaches and marvel at the huge numbers that are on the road. One match I'll never forget was at Hillsborough on one occasion when I was standing at the bottom of the dual carriageway near the ground and watched proudly, and in amazement, as bus after bus just kept on coming down the hill, each one packed full of Geordies. What a sight!

Coach travel is also a pretty reliable way of going to away games, although don't tell Nick that after his Wimbledon experience, which he was to suffer later in the year. It does take away your independence to a degree and, given the option, I would always choose to travel by car as you're in control of your own destiny throughout the day.

Some four hours later London eventually beckoned. Traffic levels in the capital are invariably worse than anywhere else in the country and so I was pretty relieved to see us work our way through North London to Tottenham with plenty of time to spare. Strangely, the coaches didn't drop us off anywhere near Tottenham High Road and we ended up down a back street a mile or so from White Hart Lane. Whether or not the driver got lost I don't know, but I suspect this wasn't quite what the plan was. Anyway we were left somewhat to our own devices to get to the ground and, with the street we were in being something of a dead-end, the way we headed was more or less predetermined for us. We wound our way through a small housing estate, mainly consisting of two or three storey dilapidated flats and it wasn't long before we cottoned on to the fact that we were actually walking through the notorious Broadwater Farm Estate, for the uninitiated the very place where only a week earlier there had been large scale violent riots which had even led to fatalities. Tensions were obviously still high in the area so the fact that several hundred Geordies were treading on their patch could have proved rather explosive. Thankfully it was only a few verbal exchanges that shook the night air and I for one was pretty relieved when we got back on the road and White Hart Lane appeared in the distance. The thought of an ambush by a load of north London nutters wielding knives and machetes had crossed my mind more than once; not something you would particularly care for.

For a Wednesday night in London the turn out of Geordies was magnificent and once again we put the Londoners to shame with our support for the team. Going 3-0 down by the interval wasn't quite what we'd hoped for but I'll never forget the chanting of 'Willie McFaul's Black and White Army' being sung non stop for at least 20 minutes. It was an incredible show of devotion, passion, call it what you will and honestly you had to be there in person to both appreciate its intensity and take it all in. Yet again the Geordies had shown themselves to be a race apart and the Tottenham supporters, standing up on the Shelf, could only stand and look on in appreciation. Similar scenes took place at Loftus Road in February 1995 when we were 3-0 down to Queen's Park Rangers in no time at all yet the support given to the team was phenomenal.

David McCreery, continuing his unusual habit of scoring his only goal of the season on the opening day (Newcastle's opening day anyway) of the season, pulled one back soon after half-time but that was to be the end of the scoring. After only one game we were already six points off the pace at the top of the table. The walk back to the coach thankfully passed off trouble free and we headed north dejected, but not too depressed.

22/08/87 – SHEFFIELD WEDNESDAY v NEWCASTLE (0-1)

I'd stayed on the coach coming back from Tottenham right through to Newcastle to spend a 'long weekend' at home before going to Sheffield with the lads on Saturday. Conveniently they would drop me off back in Leeds on the way home from Hillsborough.

As usual the Geordies descended upon Sheffield in huge numbers and we were sent into raptures by Darren Jackson's second half goal which gave us all three points. Towards the end a Wednesday equaliser looked inevitable as they were virtually camped in our penalty box. Hazel, a young black winger, was tearing us apart down the right flank and it seemed to me they missed an abundance of golden chances. Still, we rode our luck and my abiding memory of the afternoon was the deafening sound of the 'Blaydon Races' echoing out from our end of the pitch. Moments like this are what supporting the lads away from home are made of.

01/09/87 – NORWICH CITY v NEWCASTLE (1-1)

Mirandinha's (Francisco Emando Lima da Silva, to give him his proper title) debut and what an emotion charged night it was. Our Brazilian idol had first come to people's attention when England played Brazil at Wembley in May and after the game it was rumoured that several of their players were looking to get fixed up in Europe, not necessarily due to the quality of the football but because the money they could earn was much greater than in their homeland. Malcolm Macdonald was acting for some of the players and had tipped Newcastle off that Mirandinha would be available should they be interested. At first it was a little like the Keegan signing – unbelievable at first but, when it came close to fruition, a prospect of such gigantic and colossal proportions.

Mirandinha hadn't played in the first two games and indeed didn't actually arrive in England until the day before we were due at Norwich. As we set off for the long haul down to East Anglia we weren't even sure he would be playing due to his International Clearance not having arrived at FA Headquarters from his former club in Brazil, Palmeiras. Anticipating the fact that all the paperwork would be in place in time, we boarded the coach with the excitement level just that little bit higher. I joined the lads at Wetherby again and we even managed to pick up Macas (I'll be calling him 'Geordie' soon!) at Woodhall Services on the M1. It was amusing that Macas had to endure the indignity of having to join the Newcastle United Supporters' Club, in order to get a seat on the bus, which he had done only a week ago.

Even when we were getting towards 5.00pm, and well down the road to Norwich, no one could confirm whether or not Mirandinha had been cleared to play. The problem with Norwich is that it's so far off the beaten track. After you leave the motorway you've still got in excess of 60 miles to travel along single lane country roads and you're also liable to get held up behind lorries, tractors and the like. This is exactly what happened to us, and as kick-off approached it became frustratingly clear that we were going to be late. Carrow Road is on the 'other side' of the City, so to speak, which meant having to trail through the one way system when the match was kicking off. You cannot believe what this was doing to me; I was willing traffic lights to stay on green and hoping for the ground to come into sight. Eventually we rolled up outside Carrow Road only 10 minutes late and fortunately we were deposited right outside the away turnstiles. The first news of Mirandinha being in the team began to filter through and that made the rush to get into the ground even more desperate. It was every man for himself in the crush outside the turnstiles to get in as quickly as they could with scant regard for anybody else. Once in we hurtled up the steps and joined our fellow Geordies who were already in full cry. Even for Mirandinha's first game the Geordies had managed to get hold of Brazilian shirts and flags and one bloke even had a drum to beat out a distinctive South American rhythm – talk about jumping on the bandwagon, but really it was all about making our new hero as welcome as possible.

There he was, unmistakable with his dark skin and distinctive Latin features, every move he made was followed intently and every touch greeted with roars of approval. Believe it or not this was a night also that Macas and I led the singing, starting off new songs all the time until we'd exhausted our repertoire and found ourselves returning to certainly what is my favourite, 'The Blaydon Races'. When we start everyone else going with that famous first line 'We went to Blaydon Races, it was on the ninth of June', it's something else, it really is. It wasn't that we made a habit of this sort of thing, well we did occasionally, but it was just our night and that's sometimes how things happen.

Peter Jackson equalised Wayne Biggins's strike to give a 1-1 scoreline on the night which moved us up to 17th in the table, but no Geordie present at Carrow Road will forget the night Mirandinha made his debut in a black and white shirt. If there was one lingering memory it was the moment when we were awarded a free kick midway through the first half at least 40 yards from goal. Mirandinha took it upon himself to place the ball, clear everyone else out of the way (even Gascoigne) and attempt an audacious strike on goal. He never really stood a chance but the funny thing was we thought he could produce a miracle a la Eder or Branco, but he only flattered to deceive and that one moment probably summed up his whole career on Tyneside.

20/09/87 – NEWCASTLE v LIVERPOOL (1-4)

Defeat at Wimbledon followed Mirandinha's debut at Carrow Road but the following week the little Brazilian opened his account with two marvellous first half goals at Old Trafford to stun a Manchester United team who were riding high in second place in the League. St. James' Park apart, it was a fabulous arena to score your first goals in the Football League and the Newcastle fans present could hardly believe what they were seeing. Manchester United had also knocked in a couple of goals themselves in the first half and the interval score remained unchanged after 90 minutes. It was a well earned point and set up the visit of Liverpool, a match televised live by the BBC, perfectly.

The pre-match hype was tremendous but the bottom line on the day was that we simply didn't perform. It always seems more important to do well in front of the television audience – for a start the whole nation's attention is focussed on you and it's an ideal stage on which to perform. We were 3-0 down before Neil McDonald scored from the penalty spot, but Liverpool didn't let up and Steve Nicol found gaps as wide as the Tyne in the Newcastle back four to go on and complete his hat-trick. A resounding 4-1 win then (I wonder how Beardsley enjoyed his return to St. James' Park?) and yet another nation-wide humiliation from the Scousers – 3-0 in 1974, 4-0 in 1984 and now 4-1 – you could keep your live television!

23/09/87 – BLACKPOOL v NEWCASTLE (1-0)

I was pleased we had drawn Blackpool in the League Cup. Not only did it give us a good chance to progress into the next round but I'd be able to take the opportunity to visit relatives in Poulton-le-Fylde, five miles away from Blackpool. Mansel, my uncle, comes from Swansea, like the rest of my family, and had always taken a keen interest in football so he was only too happy to come along with me to Bloomfield Road. It was an awful night weather wise, wind and rain, and the open terrace reserved for the away fans afforded us no cover at all from the elements. While I was no stranger to such conditions Mansel didn't quite see it that way, but I told him the quality of our football would soon warm him up. And did it? Well Gascoigne did play one splendid through ball which led to the only goal of the game, the only trouble was he was facing the wrong goal at the time and Cunningham was only too eager to gobble up this gift wrapped opportunity to send the Blackpool fans wild with excitement. Make no mistake about it, beating Newcastle is still a big thing for the vast majority of Football League clubs and Blackpool couldn't be denied their hour of glory.

Two weeks later in the return leg I was flabbergasted when Blackpool scored in the first minute to open up a 2-0 aggregate lead but we hit back with four goals of our own to earn a third round tie at Wimbledon.

28/10/87 – WIMBLEDON v NEWCASTLE (2-1)

No one likes Wimbledon, not just because they're a Mickey Mouse club but because of their direct robust style and the fact that they kick everything that moves. A slight exaggeration perhaps but not too far off the mark. Their ground, Plough Lane, was the worst in the top two divisions by a street and, after combining all these factors, to have to go there for a midweek League Cup tie was a none too appealing prospect.

Nick and I had got into the routine of travelling together on the Supporters' Club coaches to long distance away matches but regretfully I had to leave him on his own tonight as I had to be in Leicester of all places for a meeting. Try as I did to get out of it I couldn't. You don't mind missing matches when you're actually playing yourself as it's your own decision; when the lads are playing and something else prevents you being there, it's soul destroying.

Nick first suspected it wouldn't be his day when the bus was held up on the M25 due to a combination of roadworks and very heavy traffic. If he knew then what was to be in store for the remainder of the evening he might have contemplated shooting himself there and then as the evening unfolded into a catalogue of disasters. Firstly the traffic delay never got any better, even after leaving the M25, and come kick off time they were nowhere near Plough Lane. Desperate attempts to phone the ground (by 'hijacking' a passing motorist's car phone) to get them to delay the kick off were never likely to succeed, so it became a case of following the match on poor quality transistor radios on the bus. As the match developed nothing much else did traffic wise and, come 9.30pm, with the scoreline tied at 1-1, the coach was still a painstaking ten miles from the ground so it was decided to take a quick leak (toilet stop), turn round and go home. You couldn't imagine things getting worse but they did, considerably.

Boarding the bus again news filtered through that Terry Gibson had snatched a ninetieth minute winner for Wimbledon. Sheer disbelief and total depression greeted this news and it was a very quiet bus that made its way back up the M1. The football highlights on the television would at least help pass the dreariness of a long journey home and, after enjoying the Liverpool-Everton highlights, the next match to be featured was to be from Wimbledon – at least they could watch the goals. That's where they were wrong though as just before Brian Moore started to introduce the teams the television set conked out and couldn't be repaired. If that didn't cap it all nothing could, and to round things off just nicely it took until 4.00am to get back to Newcastle – just an average day in the life of a football supporter.

As for me I didn't get away from Leicester until after 10.00pm and so decided against tuning into the late evening sports news to find out the score, choosing instead to shoot up the motorway as quickly as possible to watch the highlights on television and, in effect, watch the match 'live'. I did and when I saw Newcastle dominating the second half to such an extent that a winning goal looked inevitable at any moment, but in fact was never to come (how Beasant kept out one of Gascoigne's superb little flicks I'll never know), I got a terrible sickly feeling that Wimbledon were going to sneak a winner and that's exactly what happened. It's amazing how you just sense these things are going to happen and when they do it's just like waking up in hell.

28/12/87 – LIVERPOOL v NEWCASTLE (4-0)

Peter Beardsley had had a quiet game upon his return to St. James' Park back in September, which was perhaps to have been expected. Anyway for the thousands of Geordies who descended upon Anfield for this 'holiday' fixture the intention was to give Beardsley such a rousing reception that he'd be lost for words. We did, and when the Kop tried to respond, we simply raised the volume and drowned them out once again, which we were in the habit of doing, indeed it was quite simply the norm.

We went on to tear Liverpool apart on the pitch and put four goals past them – no sorry I was dreaming again, we lost 4-0 (predictable or what?) and headed home eating humble pie in a less than pleasurable 14th place in the table. I don't think adding up the aggregate scores from all our encounters with the Reds over the past 10 or 15 years would make particularly enjoyable reading – so I won't bother to get the calculator out.

At the end of the season the BBC put together a montage of all the best goals that Liverpool had scored throughout the year – it was effectively a Liverpool Goal of the Season competition, and to be fair it was justified because even I had to admit they had scored a number of absolutely stupendous goals. It helped that the *Match of the Day* cameras were always on hand to film them (Norwich City's fanzine is appropriately titled 'Liverpool are on the telly again') but I for one didn't mind watching them as they were playing magnificent football. One game in particular stood out when they destroyed Nottingham Forest 5-0 at Anfield and it could have been double figures. Barnes was at his peak and along with the likes of Houghton and Aldridge, not forgetting Beardsley of course, I am forced to admit they were positively brilliant.

01/01/88 – NOTTINGHAM FOREST v NEWCASTLE (0-2)

Another trip to the City Ground in Nottingham, but what a contrast in weather conditions to our trip only seven months earlier. Replace a lovely hot summer's day with a freezing cold damp day and you saw the two extremes of watching football in England. Having said that football is a 'winter' season sport and should always stay that way.

We were having an up and down season, winning one week then losing the next – in fact typical Newcastle United style inconsistency but better, I suppose, than being consistent losers. It wasn't too much to hope therefore that we could win at Forest and this is exactly what transpired. Gascoigne scored a well taken goal at the Trent End in the first half, and then as the minutes ticked by towards the end of the match Mirandinha sealed the points for us and celebrated in typically wild South American style by running round the corner flag – shades of West Ham's Frank

Lampard in the 1980 FA Cup semi-final replay at Elland Road.

I don't think our two goal scorers this afternoon were ever destined to quite hit it off together. Mirandinha fell into Gascoigne's 'company' in his early days at the club, and the standing joke was that Gazza was teaching Mirandinha to speak Geordie. The two of them would sit together on the back of the team bus with Gazza's non stop clowning and childish pranks possibly not being the best thing for Mirandinha to be a part of in his formative days in English football. The only thing about them was that they were both headstrong characters and very much individuals on the field of play. I think it got to a stage when it didn't do us any good to have them both on the same pitch together as it seemed at times they 'fell out' and just went off and did their own thing to the detriment of their team-mates. Paul Goddard in particular must have suffered more than most at the hands of Mirandinha, and all credit to him for maintaining his dignity throughout his time with the club. Many a time Goddard would be ideally placed in the penalty area to receive a pass from Mirandinha, but instead the Brazilian would shoot from an impossible angle or try to dribble past three or four defenders before invariably losing the ball – poor Goddard was left only to despair and wonder what might have been.

Nevertheless, and having said all this about Mirandinha, his influence on the club did far more good than harm and I wouldn't have missed the 'Mira' era for anything.

A quick word about the journey home. I was driving Dad's Ford Sierra (christened 'HMS Slop' by Lowsey and used so all the lads could squeeze in) and in trying to find a short cut through the congestion on the roads outside the ground came within inches of knocking a police motorcyclist off his bike – thankfully he was too busy doing other things to pursue us! Even to this day the lads never stop reminding me about it, but my excuse was that rain and the dark conditions made for poor visibility.

20/02/88 – NEWCASTLE v WIMBLEDON (1-3)

The FA Cup fifth round and Cup fever on Tyneside had reached unparalleled levels, this year our name was on the Cup. We had put together a nice little run since the Liverpool defeat at Christmas and were in confident mood as the match approached. There had been one hiccup though which occurred only the previous week when Norwich had come to St. James' Park and beaten us easily 3-1. Perhaps the players had had their minds on the Cup game or they simply played poorly, whatever, we saw it as being a fairly insignificant result and thought that it would be 'all right on the night' come Wimbledon.

Our progress to the fifth round had been pretty spectacular. In round three Paul Gascoigne scored the only goal of the game, a spectacular 30 yarder against Crystal Palace at St. James' Park. Where was I? Well I was attending the wedding of a work colleague in Leeds. Round four brought Swindon Town to Tyneside and they were despatched back to Wiltshire with the memory of a 5-0 thrashing still fresh in their minds. We were outstanding, Gascoigne in particular, and I think it was this game that really made us think it was going to be our year.

Wimbledon's style and rough house tactics have already been commented on and, as often happens in football, when you draw a team in a cup competition you invariably find yourself playing against them in a league match also either the week before or week after – an uncanny situation.

The League match at Plough Lane had been played two weeks earlier. It finished goal-less but will always be remembered for the infamous incident when Wimbledon's self appointed 'hard man', Vinnie Jones, who had been assigned the job of marking Gascoigne during the match, went beyond the bounds of acceptable conduct by grabbing Gascoigne's private parts during a particularly close marking encounter. The photograph from the incident became the most frequently used shot that season and even today still pops up every now and again. Jones had a dog-like growling expression on his face while a still young fresh faced Gascoigne looked, as you can imagine, as anyone would in his situation.

Strangely enough the two of them had a degree of respect for each other despite their talents and skills being at opposite ends of the footballing ability spectrum and in the months to come they were to strike up a good friendship off the field. Two oddball characters, so I suppose it wasn't that difficult to believe they would find things in common. Without overly criticising Gascoigne, because his playing ability still leaves me drooling, his questionable mentality and foolish antics can only be harmful to his career. The knee injury he sustained during the 1991 FA Cup Final (and the night-club incident which exacerbated the injury that followed) bear testament to this and having sustained a broken leg in 1994 it makes you wonder whether he will ever be back to his impudent best – sadly I doubt it. Jones on the other hand demonstrated his total imbecility when producing his video which focussed on dirty and foul tactics in football. He was rightly pilloried by his fellow professionals in the game for such a crass venture. Still on the Jones front how on earth did Mike Smith see fit to call him up into the Welsh squad for the game against Bulgaria in December 1994. Earlier in his career he had tried to claim Irish ancestry in order to attempt to get a game for Big Jack's boys but the bottom line is that if Jones is an International player then I'm a Mackem.

The atmosphere in the pub (we used the Whistle Stop in the Haymarket this season) before the game was marvellous. All the lads were together again, including the exiles, and the level of anticipation and uncontrollable excitement was bubbling up nicely. Into the ground shortly after 2.30pm and time to really get started. Such games generate unique feelings so I took it upon myself to climb on the barrier, not for the first time I should add, and generate an even greater frenzy in the Gallowgate Corner. What an occasion, electrifying, intoxicating and the most animated crowd on fifth round day anywhere in the country was getting ready to savour our relentless march towards Wembley. When Mum read this she wondered what sort of son she had! – a real Jekyll and Hyde character – perfectly normal and respectable at home but transformed into a 'football animal' on match day.

Why, oh why, do Newcastle United take you to such heights only to let you hurtle to the depths of despair? We didn't play, we didn't compete and we crashed out of the Cup, Wimbledon running out 3-1 winners. Lots of matches are capable of raising the spirits but ultimately providing false dawns, but there was something different about this occasion that made defeat more unpalatable than most.

Wimbledon went on to win the FA Cup at Wembley in May against Liverpool. Could it have been us instead? You bet it could have been!

A final word on Wimbledon and their Cup triumph. Why is it that, with all due respect, second rate 'Mickey Mouse' clubs (in comparison to ourselves) can reach Wembley and win major cup competitions? Coventry had done it the year before and with teams like Oxford, Norwich and Luton having done likewise in the League Cup, it was something that, to put it mildly, left me fuming.

24/04/88 – NEWCASTLE v LUTON TOWN (4-0)

The season was effectively over now, it had been since the Wimbledon defeat, so the visit from the Hatters promised little else than typical end-of-season fare. How wrong could you be, over 20,000 were inside St. James' Park and for those who weren't they missed a game never to be forgotten – primarily due to Kenny Wharton and Paul Gascoigne.

It had all begun in November when we had been well beaten, 4-0, on Kenilworth Road's plastic pitch and, at the same time, Luton had given us a lesson in playing football and hadn't been shy to let us know. Revenge could never have tasted sweeter. It wasn't just the fact that we reversed the 4-0 scoreline, young Irishman Michael O'Neill scoring a hat-trick, but the way Wharton and Gascoigne humiliated their opponents with Les Sealey and Steve Foster being the two particularly targeted.

After knocking in the fourth goal, with about 15 minutes left in the game, Kenny Wharton picked up the ball just outside his own penalty area, at the Gallowgate End, dribbled into the box and, finding no Luton players near him, proceeded to sit on the ball. It was hilarious and Wharton had a grin on his face as wide as the Tyne. It was also an insult to your fellow professionals and Wharton's behaviour could, and indeed was, viewed in this manner by Luton Town. They were incensed, maybe rightly so, but we were loving every moment of it. Some five minutes later the inimitable Gascoigne could not resist rubbing their noses in it even further. Finding himself roughly in the same position as Wharton, and again unmarked, he began a solo game of 'keepy-uppy', flicking the ball up as if he had it on a piece of string. It was an outrageous display of arrogance and it brought the house down. Needless to say few handshakes were exchanged between the players at the end of the match, but I absolutely loved it.

07/05/88 – NEWCASTLE v WEST HAM UNITED (2-1)

Why is it that at the end of many a season I finish up reporting on the departure of yet another quality player from St. James' Park? Of course we didn't know for sure at the time but there was still an air of inevitability about the fact that Gascoigne might be on his bike in the summer. In the 1980s the one thing the club were more famous for than anything else was the sale of all three of its home produced Geordie superstars. The bottom line was that they wanted success, who could blame them, and at the time each departed there certainly wasn't much hope of it on Tyneside. Do I blame them for going? Well yes, to a degree, because Newcastle United should have been the only club in the world they should have wanted to play for, and no because their ambition led them to want to perform on a bigger stage. Sadly in the 1980s that stage could never have been St. James' Park.

Gascoigne scored the winner in the 2-1 defeat of the Hammers and we earned a respectable finishing position of eighth. He left leaving a thousand treasured memories – impudent skill, breathtaking goals and above all else that extra buzz of excitement special players give you when they are on the ball. 'Wor Jackie' wasn't too far off the mark with his assessment of Gazza – a truly unique footballing talent the like of which I may never see again in my lifetime.

1987/88 – Season's Summary

League	P	W	D	L	F	A	Pts.	Pos.
	40	14	14	12	55	53	56	8th

Top Scorers		
Michael O'Neill	13
Mirandinha	12
Paul Gascoigne	11

1988/89 – THIRTY FOUR SECONDS

Thirty four seconds perhaps sums up the season perfectly. From the time it took Tony Cottee to score on the season's opening day at Goodison Park, our season, which was to dismally end in relegation, was set to go from bad to worse and plummet to new depths of despair previously unexplored (I can cite Millwall and Wimbledon away in the League and Sheffield United at Bramall Lane in the League Cup to name but three) with only fleeting moments of glory thrown in (Liverpool away and the first half against Tottenham at St. James' Park).

Pre-season optimism, despite the sale of Gascoigne, was high (some things never change) primarily because the Board had at last, reluctantly I'm sure, given Willie McFaul money to spend on the team. In came Dave Beasant and Andy Thorn from Cup winners Wimbledon, along with the two Johns, Hendrie from Bradford and Robertson from Heart of Midlothian. On paper they all looked exceptionally good investments, especially as we still had the likes of Mirandinha at the club along with exciting young talent in the shape of Darren Jackson and Michael O'Neill. The hype being generated at the club was exceptional and the excitement as the opening day fixture at Everton approached was incredibly high – but not unexpected for it just needs the slightest hint of success to set the passions of a Geordie racing. On the down side the hopes and dreams of the Geordies have been raised on so many occasions that you hoped that this would not be another case of a false dawn. At least we could enjoy it whilst it lasted and that we certainly did.

One more item of interest concerned the summer wrangling between the Football League and the television companies in respect of the 'deal' that was to be struck for the 1988/89 season. It got to a stage where it looked almost certain that there would be a split in the Football League, instigated by the 'big five' (Liverpool, Everton, Manchester United, Arsenal and Tottenham), and supported to an extent by the 'second five' (Newcastle, Aston Villa, Sheffield Wednesday, Nottingham Forest and West Ham). I remember Nick being particularly indignant about the whole affair, he vehemently believed that football belonged to the ordinary person in the street and not the 'money men'. I was surprised at how strongly he felt, but fortunately in the end all parties eventually saw sense and the matter was resolved without any rift taking place.

27/08/88 – EVERTON v NEWCASTLE (4-0)

Trips to Merseyside are always enjoyable occasions and whether it be to Anfield or Goodison the 'crack' is always good. Ten thousand Geordies helped swell the attendance to nigh on 42,000 and the pre-match atmosphere was something else. Dave Beasant, who was making his debut, was warming up in the goalmouth in front of us and you could see he simply couldn't believe the level of noise we were generating. It was a whole new world for him and he was loving every moment of it – if only he knew what the fates had in store for him.

Everton had also splashed out in the transfer market in the summer, paying West Ham £2 million for Tony Cottee and it was he that set the ball rolling at 3.00pm on a fine late summer's afternoon. I remember we were half way through a deafening rendition of the 'Blaydon Races' when straight from the kick off the ball was played around by Everton, pumped forward, missed by John Anderson, and following a shot by Graeme Sharp which Beasant did well to parry, Cottee gobbled up the game's opening goal. Thirty four seconds into a brand new season and a goal down. It was a sensational start for Cottee but for Newcastle absolutely unbelievable. We never recovered from that mortal blow and when Mirandinha limped off soon afterwards you could only shake your head in disbelief. Everton rattled in another three goals, including two more for Cottee giving him a dream debut hat-trick, and the 4-0 opening day reverse was as decisive a result as you could have got. Poor Willie McFaul must have felt suicidal and you genuinely felt for him.

I travelled back to Leeds with Hally while the rest of the lads headed back to Newcastle. We hardly spoke – I think we were still numb with shock. Football more often than not gives you the opportunity to put things right and at least we could look forward to the following weekend when Tottenham, with Waddle and Gascoigne within their ranks, were due on Tyneside.

03/09/88 – NEWCASTLE v TOTTENHAM HOTSPUR (2-2)

Matches at St. James' Park always mean a little more when the visiting team contains a player who used to perform for Newcastle United. When that player is a former Magpie hero, and in Tottenham's case they had two of them, it's even better. Local confectionery stores had done a roaring trade in Mars Bars for the obvious reason that they were intended for throwing at Gascoigne (for the uninitiated Gascoigne had a penchant for eating them in abundance during his time on Tyneside). Some supporters stupidly froze them in advance, thus making them into dangerous projectiles, before taking them into the ground and clearly this was taking the 'fun' element of the Mars Bar theme to absurd malevolent levels.

Of course there was a full house and when Jackson and Thorn opened up a two goal lead early in the game all thoughts of the previous week had been totally forgotten. St. James' Park was awash with emotion and perhaps after all we were about to come good. Straight from the kick off though at the start of the second half Waddle cut through our defence like a knife through butter to pull one back, and when Terry Fenwick (unfortunately a Mackem) headed in from a Gascoigne left wing corner Tottenham were back on equal terms. For visiting players, taking corners at the Gallowgate End is not a pleasant experience. Many get pelted with coins and it is an action you cannot condone. Worse still is the treatment dished out to anyone unfortunate enough to get injured in that corner of the ground, and it was shameful to witness Charlton's Colin Walsh being subjected to such treatment after he'd broken his leg and was clearly lying in agony on the turf.

Briefly back to the Paul Gascoigne theme and to a player called Ian Bogie who was playing for us today. Bogie had played with Gazza in the FA Youth Cup winning team of 1985 and although always appearing to be in Gazza's shadow this was seen as being a great opportunity for him to 'come of age' with Gazza having left the club. Unfortunately he never managed to do so, perhaps the weight of expectation was too great for him to cope with but nevertheless it's always a shame to see young talented players built up by the media as potential superstars only for them to fail to make a real impact in the game and drift sadly into obscurity.

Tottenham had got out of jail and it was a bitter disappointment. The next three fixtures only brought one point and after only six games we were back in the by now familiar position of propping up the rest of the division – at least we could claim to be the strongest team in the League! The media were postulating that Willie McFaul's position was becoming untenable and after defeat at Sheffield United in the League Cup speculation was rife that if we were to lose at Liverpool on Saturday McFaul would be out. I'd gone to Sheffield with Kevin Stephenson and, after the kick-off had been delayed for 15 minutes, to give all the supporters outside the ground time to get in (a rare occurrence at the time but far more common practice in the 1990s), we witnessed a performance which had to go down as one of the most spineless I can recall. I rarely, if ever, vent my displeasure at the players, preferring vocal encouragement to detrimental abuse, but on this occasion my anger got the better of me and I joined in with the rest of them. Changing the subject slightly, the away end at Bramall Lane isn't the best for watching your football as there are a number of high concrete supports which block your view of the action wherever you choose to stand. I guess the answer must be to get one of the seats above next time.

01/10/88 – LIVERPOOL v NEWCASTLE (1-2)

If there was one game during the season I would have loved to have been at it would have been this one. I was back playing again and missed an unforgettable occasion. It was a result completely out of the blue. John Hendrie had cancelled out Gary Gillespie's opener for Liverpool and it was left to none other than Mirandinha, scoring a penalty in front of the Kop 10 minutes before time, to send the Geordie hordes at the Anfield Road End delirious. At least I could imagine what the scenes were like that afternoon – I only wish I had been part of them.

Willie McFaul had been spared and could this be the turning point in the season? Coventry arrived at St. James' Park the following week, scored three in the first half, and condemned Newcastle to a defeat which would effectively signal the end of McFaul's reign at the club – he was sacked 24 hours later. How could the same group of players turn it on at Liverpool only seven days earlier and then proceed to produce a performance so lacking in aptitude? It was unfathomable and in the end the buck had to stop somewhere and that ultimately meant the manager.

JACKIE MILBURN

Jackie Milburn died on 9th October 1988 at the age of 64. There were lot of heroes down the years at St. James' Park but 'Wor Jackie', because of his Geordie roots, was probably the greatest of them all. In 397 appearances for the club (excluding war time games) between 1943-1957 he scored 200 goals and forged a unique relationship with everyone on Tyneside and I include the housewives in that statement such was the popularity of the man. It was appropriate that his funeral procession went down Barrack Road, past St. James' Park, and the numbers that lined the streets were a testimony to his greatness. A magnificent stone statue of Milburn stands proudly in Newcastle City centre and that, perhaps more than anything else, will ensure that our memories of the man will live for ever. I never even saw him play but such was my upbringing in the game he was still a very special person in my estimation.

10/12/88 – NEWCASTLE v WIMBLEDON (2-1)

The Bald Eagle, Jim Smith, had been installed as team manager at St. James' Park on 4th December, after quitting his post at Queen's Park Rangers, and to all intents and purposes his was a reasonable appointment in most people's eyes. Not in mine though – he was an experienced professional but had never really done it at the top level, and I thought he was never going to be more than a second class citizen in the managerial ratings. It actually took eight weeks for the club to install a new manager to replace McFaul and that was a ridiculous amount of time in anybody's book. The reason for the delay was that the Directors couldn't get the man they wanted for the job as first Arthur Cox ruled out a return to Tyneside and then Athletic Bilbao's Howard Kendall also decided to stay put, rather than take on the daunting task that Tyneside had to offer. Why did they turn down the chance to manage such a great club? Fear can be the only answer. It wasn't that it would have been too big a job for them but the political situation at the club would almost certainly have prevented them from achieving everything they would have wished. Jim Smith was therefore third, or even fourth choice, but it didn't seem to bother him as he strode confidently into the St. James' Park hot seat – and there weren't any hotter seats in the whole country.

We all knew of his reputation for losing his temper when conducting team talks, cups of tea having been known to have been seen flying through the air in the changing rooms, but perhaps more revealing was the destroying of the myth that he liked to play good football. Perhaps he did at times but I'll never forget watching a documentary on the club at the end of the season when the cameras closed in on the dug out during the home game with Luton Town. All he was shouting and encouraging the players to do was to 'hoof the ball forward' – that tells its own story and needs no further comment. Watching football regularly played like this must be soul destroying and how supporters of 'long ball' teams put up with it I just don't know. In my view that's why Graham Taylor was unsuccessful as England team manager as success at international level requires a more skilful and sophisticated approach, one that Terry Venables brought to the job, and hopefully, a philosophy that Glenn Hoddle will continue to develop.

Prior to the visit of Wimbledon we had failed to score in six consecutive matches and our position was desperate to say the least. At least the Dons allowed us the luxury of breaking that unenviable record and with John Hendrie scoring twice, the 2-1 win was hugely welcomed. A point against Southampton the following week moved us up to a pleasant 18th!

26/12/88 – SHEFFIELD WEDNESDAY v NEWCASTLE (1-2)

We were on something of a mini revival, if you can call three draws and a win a revival, and Jim Smith at least appeared to be injecting some life into the club. The Boss liked a bit of experience around him and so the purchases of Kenny Sansom and Ray Ranson were predictable. Both played at Hillsborough and made vital contributions to our 2-1 victory. The first goal was scored by centre forward Rob McDonald, a player who unbelievably managed 20 first team appearances for Newcastle. He was brought from the Dutch League and my feelings about these type of players are that they only go abroad because they're not good enough to make it in the Football League. If you haven't got the message yet he was absolutely useless. Later in the season, at home to Queen's Park Rangers, he missed the biggest open goal you could possibly wish to see – literally three yards out and he put it over the bar. With that, he virtually sealed his fate at St. James' Park.

Irish youngster Michael O'Neill scored the second, although I don't think he knew too much about it as it appeared that an attempted clearance ricocheted off his shin before trickling into the corner of the net.

At a number of away matches I'd been taking a fog horn into

the ground to blast out as much noise as possible in order to get the crowd going – you may be aware that the sport of basketball uses such devices for timing purposes and so it was fortunate that I could easily get my hands on them at work. Their use wasn't only limited to the terraces as Macas will testify. Driving down the motorway on one occasion, with Macas at the wheel and me in the back with the rest of the lads, we wound the window down and started pumping out the volume as we raced along past our fellow supporters on the road. Perhaps not the sort of responsible or mature behaviour you might expect from me, but really it was only a bit of harmless fun.

This was also the era when the dreaded ID card proposals were being pushed through government by Prime Minister Margaret Thatcher and Sports Minister Colin Moynihan. Quite frankly neither knew the first thing about football and it was the most ill-conceived piece of legislation imaginable. For a short while I was very concerned that it might cause havoc in the game, killing off the floating supporter for one thing, and when it eventually fell through it was greeted with huge relief by everyone involved in the game – that is with the exception of Luton Town Chairman, Conservative MP David Evans, who had already introduced a much detested membership scheme at Kenilworth Road.

16/01/89 – NEWCASTLE v WATFORD (0-0)

This was the third game of the four it took to separate the sides in the FA Cup round three. It was played on a Monday night, an unusual day for football in the pre-Sky Television days, and inevitably another draw resulted, even after extra time, which meant a third replay would need to be staged at Vicarage Road 48 hours later.

Replaying FA Cup ties until they finally produced a winner was one of the factors that made the competition the greatest in the world. Letting the drama of each game unfold, the tension of extra time and the absorbing fascination of following a tie to its natural conclusion were elements inherent to the FA Cup. When the ever-growing influence of the police 'forced' the Football Association to bring in penalties to decide a tie after the first replay because they insisted three to four days wasn't enough time to organise the policing of a replay, it was a sad day for football. Sure the police should have a voice in the game, but not to an extent where they can dictate policy, and I really believe the Football Association should demonstrate its authority and revert to the old system which, after all, has served us perfectly for well over a century! Incidentally, why were Oldham and Manchester United able to play their 1994 FA Cup semi-final replay at Maine Road only three days after they had fought out a 1-1 draw at Wembley? You might think I dislike penalty shoot outs. Well I don't, I absolutely love them but not in the FA Cup. Clearly in competitions where time is a factor, World Cup semi-finals for example, a penalty shoot out is a true test of skill and nerve and seems an appropriate way of settling a game. They're not luck, in my opinion, as many commentators would have you believe, but they do have one negative point. If a team knows that there are going to be penalties at the end of extra time they can play defensively, boring and tedious in other words, as they believe their best chance of winning is to do so through scoring their penalties. Red Star Belgrade, in winning the 1991 European Cup Final, and Argentina in the 1990 World Cup Finals against Yugoslavia and Italy, were two classic examples of this and on all three occasions it was regrettable that the 'negative' team triumphed each time.

Now we're apparently stuck with penalties in the FA Cup, although as I've said I really hope it won't be for long, you often end up listening to matches on the radio or watching them on television hoping that as extra time draws to a close neither team will score the winner so you can enjoy the excitement of penalties – well I do anyway. Commentators on the other hand always prefer one or other of the teams to score – but I'm sure most of them quite enjoy the penalties too! Don't get me wrong, I really enjoy the incomparable drama of penalties but not in the FA Cup, and I would gladly sacrifice this pleasure, which you get at least three or four times in each season's competition, for a return to the good old days of classic replay football – Arsenal versus Liverpool in the 1980 FA Cup semi-final immediately comes to mind, and just remembering such encounters simply re-emphasises the absurdity of the whole penalty scenario.

Perhaps it would have been better to have taken Watford on at penalties (only joking) as we fell victim to a cruelly deflected goal, eventually debited as an own goal against Glenn Roeder, during extra time at Vicarage Road in the fourth game. Of course it was disappointing and, as is always the case after a replay, it was made worse because you knew you had a plum home tie to look forward to in the next round if you could have won the replay – that's football for you though!

04/02/89 – NEWCASTLE v LIVERPOOL (2-2)

After the FA Cup dreams had been washed away it was back to the grind of the League and trying to cobble together enough points to avoid the dreaded drop once again. Liverpool at St. James' Park could never be considered a grind, the only problem was having to watch the match in cold soaking wet conditions.

There wasn't really much to report on this day. Frank Pingel, our bungling Danish import, not quite in the Laudrup class, managed a goal that he didn't really know much about and Mirandinha scored the other in a 2-2 draw which left us in 19th position and clearly still in a lot of trouble. There was also a shot from Mirandinha from all of 35 yards that Bruce Grobbelaar in the Liverpool goal could only watch fly past him before smacking into the right hand upright. It would have been the goal of any season and left us all gasping for breath afterwards so stunning a strike was it.

Grobbelaar had earlier treated us to a fine display of his extra-ordinary talents and displayed his exuberant personality to the full. He is one of the game's true characters (witness the extra-ordinary bribery allegations that were made against him) and his relationship with away supporters, Newcastle 's being no exception, was superb. We would chant 'Brucie give us a wave' and of course he obliged, followed by 'Brucie give us a handstand' and would he let us down – of course not. During all the matches at this time one lad up in the East Stand, Gallowgate Corner, would come out with an amazing and very distinctive Indian like (Wild West as opposed to Asian!) battle cry which of course Brucie responded to and milked the occasion to the full.

It's said Liverpool's Kop always appreciates and applauds visiting goalkeepers and I like to think we do the same at St. James' Park, although to be fair it's tailed off a bit since the 1970s and now we resort to chants of 'dodgy keeper' which in it's own way I suppose is far more entertaining – just ask Chris Woods! Peter Shilton, on his visits to Newcastle, has always been greeted especially well as have other such greats over the years such as Pat Jennings, but strangely I can never re-call Ray Clemence being accorded as good a reception as the others.

27/03/89 – NEWCASTLE v SHEFFIELD WEDNESDAY (1-3)

The return game with Sheffield Wednesday on Easter Monday and once again, as had been the case on Boxing Day, we were just beginning a little revival that we all prayed would take us clear of the relegation zone. We'd drawn at Forest, beaten Everton at St. James' Park, where I remember a snow storm accompanied Liam O'Brien's goal in the second half, and two days earlier on Easter Saturday had surprised everyone by winning 2-0 at Norwich with two excellently taken goals from Mirandinha and O'Brien again. Things really were looking up, confidence was high and this was reflected by the 31,000 that turned up at St. James' Park. Need I go on, I think you can guess the rest as we proceeded to crash to a 3-1 defeat. Wednesday were wearing horrible green and black hooped shirts (where do the manufacturers get these designs from?) and looked a total mess. Still, not looking the part and not being able to play football unfortunately aren't always linked and we hardly got a look in. Were we that bad, did we freeze on the big occasion or were Wednesday just too good for us on the day? Two players stood out for the visitors on the day: David Hirst for looking an exceptional talent – he scored a brilliant goal today and it's a shame his career has been blighted by injury since, and Carlton Palmer who had just broken into the team and even then looked like the most ungainly footballer you could wish to see. Okay so he could run and chase but could be play? Could he heck, and how he managed to get a game for England I'll never know – only a certain Graham Taylor would know that – certainly his £2.6 million transfer to Leeds prior to the 1994/95 season was a mystery to all the Leeds supporters I know.

Football supporters are eternal optimists and even after this catastrophic defeat, and the miserable drive home with the lads, each as disgruntled as me and each offering their own opinion as to where we had gone wrong, I still felt that if we could win next Saturday at Southampton we would still be in with a fighting chance of saving ourselves. I was working across in Manchester on the evening of the game and so had to leave home at 4.30pm in order to arrive in time. I'd been tuned into *Sport on 2* throughout the afternoon and as I embarked on the journey the match was still scoreless. As I reached the M62 heading out of Leeds some 10 minutes later it appeared we were going to have to settle for a draw. Suddenly, the radio commentary game, I think it was

Liverpool and Norwich, was interrupted from the studio with the words 'And we're just quickly going off to the Dell where I understand we've news of a goal'. My heart skipped a beat and for a second or two the tension was unbearable as I waited for BBC Southampton's John Hughes to say something like 'And Newcastle have snatched a vital victory in the last minute through a superb John Hendrie goal'. He didn't. I can still to this day recall his exact words, 'It's a penalty for Southampton, Ruddock against Kelly' and, after a momentary pause, 'Ruddock scores'. I was devastated, so much so that I found myself screaming out loud in the car – any passing motorists overtaking me must have thought I was mad had they seen me. Later in the evening I watched the goal on television and when I saw how reckless, foolhardy and needless Gary Kelly's challenge on Wallace had been, it made me feel even worse and, considering how I felt at the time, that must have been pretty bad!

15/04/89 – HILLSBOROUGH

Arsenal versus Newcastle United at Highbury was a totally insignificant sideshow in the light of the horrific and appalling events that were unfolding simultaneously at Hillsborough on the occasion of the FA Cup semi-final between Liverpool and Nottingham Forest.

They say you can remember exactly where you were when first news of a real tragedy breaks and this was certainly true for me. I wasn't playing or watching but was in the Press Lounge at the National Exhibition Centre, Birmingham for our National Championship Basketball Finals.

Shortly after 3.00pm *Grandstand* interrupted its coverage of all other sport to go live to Hillsborough to report on what was beginning to unfold and, as is the case on such dreadful occasions, the full extent of what is happening can never be conveyed to the onlooker simply because those bringing you the story are themselves ignorant of the full facts – I'm not for one moment blaming them for that. When the reports of 25 deaths rose to 50 and then higher still, I felt numb and I realise I'll never be able to understand or appreciate how those either directly, or indirectly, affected felt.

Liverpool and Forest had met at the same venue 12 months earlier at the same stage of the competition, and even then I can remember thinking the Leppings Lane End looked dangerously full as indeed it did when Leeds United's supporters filled it for the 1987 FA Cup semi-final. I've already detailed our visit there in October 1983 and it really does start you thinking.

The Hillsborough tragedy can't be blamed on one single factor, but the fact that fences prevented people escaping onto the pitch was inexcusable. Photographs printed in the newspapers the next day of people pressed up against the fences were sickening images, and their dismantling came not a day too soon. You can never say anything good came out of the tragedy, but at least Lord Justice Taylor's report has led to long-overdue ground improvements up and down the country which has resulted in many stadiums being unrecognisable in the 1990s from what I knew them as in the 1970s.

A word too for the late Peter Jones. He was present at Hillsborough on 15th April and his radio reporting on the day was as good as you could hear – sensitivity coupled with a deep understanding of the enormity of the occasion. The final death toll of 96, like the two disasters in 1985, put the meaning of football into true perspective – who cares if we get relegated when things like this could happen to you. As for the FA Cup Final itself, and whether or not it should have been played, I think the Football Association got it right when they continued with the competition. No doubt they consulted with Liverpool Football club prior to announcing their decision but I'm sure the people of Liverpool would have wanted the game to have gone ahead in memory of all those who lost their lives. As it turned out the final, an all Merseyside affair, proved to be a fitting tribute to Hillsborough.

29/04/89 – WIMBLEDON v NEWCASTLE (4-0)

Relegation was a virtual certainty when we travelled to Plough Lane to face Wimbledon with only four games left to play in the season. Even so the manner of our demise on the day, 4-0, was as gutless and humiliating a defeat imaginable (visions of Exeter in 1981?) and Jim Smith rightly accused his players of lacking character and pride. No-one came out of the game with any credit and the manager was under no illusions that if he wanted to get us straight back into Division One at the first attempt then quite a lot of transfer business would need to be done in the summer.

Looking back on the last few weeks of the season after the win at Norwich on 25th March the final nine games of the season were to bring only two points, a pathetic return. Thirty five players had pulled on the black and white shirt during the season and, as in seasons past, that is a tell tale sign of a club enduring a season of struggle. It was amazing that a season that had started off with so much to look forward to at 3.00pm on the 27th August at Goodison Park, would turn into a total nightmare. Of Willie McFaul's four major summer signings two, Beasant and Robertson, lasted barely half a season (strangely I had, and still have, a soft spot for Robertson even though he failed to hit the back of the net for us during his time on Tyneside) while Hendrie was sold to Leeds in the close season and Thorn lasted only 10 matches into the 1989/90 season before being off-loaded by Smith. He also got rid of Mirandinha in the summer and clearly their personalities didn't exactly go together particularly well. The little Brazilian's last appearance in a black and white shirt was against Luton Town at St. James' Park on 22nd April, and I think maybe 90% of the Geordies were a little sad to see him go even though they realised that he was never quite going to integrate fully into English football and we'd be better off with someone else. I still to this day wear my bright yellow Mirandinha T-shirt with the words 'Now he's one of the Lads' emblazoned on the front together with a caricature figure of a 'Brazilian' Geordie – absolutely brilliant. I would certainly miss Mira but not the likes of John Cornwell or Archie Gourlay, who also made first team appearances during the season. I've nothing personal against these players, it's just that they weren't good enough to play for the club and that has to be the bottom line.

It was around this time that supporters' action groups, namely the 'Magpie Group' and 'Supporters for Change' – both incidentally backed by the Newcastle *Evening Chronicle* – took off as discontentment reached unparalleled heights. Nick joined the latter as his frustration was reaching boiling point whereas I took a more stand-offish view, but that's not to say I wasn't concerned. I was, deeply, but felt powerless and inadequate as my football club was being slowly strangled and destroyed. The Board members became figures of derision and, as we have seen in recent seasons at clubs such as Everton, Southampton, and in particular Manchester City, feelings of hatred against them took on whole new proportions. Although the Maine Road fans' actions against Peter Swales have been well chronicled, I cannot imagine the campaign to 'Sack the Board' being as concerted, intense or vitriolic as it was on Tyneside throughout the late 1980s and early 1990s.

1988/89 – Season's Summary

League	P	W	D	L	F	A	Pts.	Pos.
	38	7	10	21	32	63	31	20th

Top Scorers		
Mirandinha		11
John Hendrie		5
Liam O'Brien		4

1989/90 – PLAY OFF MISERY

T he season immediately following relegation is always a difficult one – for the club, the players and the supporters. The club are naturally going to be worse off financially, the players have got to adapt to a different level of football, and people like me have got to watch lower quality fare. There's only one place to be and that's in the top division – anything else is both inferior and inconsequential which was perfectly and humorously illustrated in *Fantasy Football's* take off of Saint and Greavsie being 'forced' to cover the Endsleigh League.

It was also pleasing to report that the Newcastle strip once again had the famous and distinctive club crest on the breast as we kicked off the new season. It's amazing how often badge designs, let alone strips, change and the previous design of the letters NUFC in a circular style was a poor and cheap imitation of our true heritage.

19/08/89 – NEWCASTLE v LEEDS UNITED (5-2)

Leeds United were about to begin their eighth successive season of second division football and for a club their size it was disgraceful. The great days of the Don Revie era had long gone and a succession of managers, Bremner, Clarke and Gray, all of whom had played under Revie, had all failed to take the club back to its former glory. It was the best possible game for us to kick off the new season, but I could never have dreamed quite how it would turn out.

Jim Smith had had a busy summer. He was determined to turn the club round and among his signings were a couple of new strikers, Mick Quinn from Portsmouth, who came to St. James' Park with a reputation of being a prolific scorer in the lower divisions, and Mark McGhee from Celtic, who was returning to Tyneside for a second stint at the club following his unsuccessful spell over a decade earlier. As is the norm in these cases new signings always tell the media that they're joining a club with unlimited potential, with promotion being their sole aim for the season. The potential has never been in doubt, what has been is the dedication and ability of the players and they, and indeed the whole squad, had a lot to live up to in the forthcoming nine months with the massive expectations of the supporters being heaped upon them from day one.

Before we start I have to report the embarrassment, in my opinion anyway, of having to wear 'Greenalls' on the front of our shirts. We had lost the Scottish and Newcastle Breweries deal shortly after the 1984/85 season when relationships between the club and the brewers regretfully took an adverse turn and the sponsorship was severed. Scottish and Newcastle (now Newcastle Breweries) are synonymous with Newcastle United, it was a perfect match (as Arsenal and JVC would say) and someone somewhere had to be held accountable. Anyway to have to wear the name Greenalls, a 'Mickey Mouse' brewer in comparison from the North West of England, was something that really bugged me.

As is often the case, the opening day of the season brought with it a lovely warm summer's day, well it was mid-August after all, and consequently a perfect day for playing football. Incidentally I'm not one of those people who advocate the football season being moved to the summer. Firstly because it would intrude into traditional summer sports such as cricket, golf and tennis (all of which I enjoy immensely), secondly because pitches would become too hard and bumpy, thirdly it would do away with floodlit football which would be awful, and, finally, because I'm a traditionalist!

When the match got under way the first thing I remember was Leeds' David Batty kicking everything in sight. I must confess, as a result of this, I immediately took a dislike to him however have more recently given him the benefit of the doubt – he can play a bit. When Blackburn visited St. James' Park in November 1995, he again infuriated the home supporters by blatantly elbowing David Ginola in the face. It will be interesting to see how he settles into the squad now that he's one of our own. Back to the visit of Leeds, and at least Batty's destructive play got the crowd worked up. It's amazing how a bit of kicking can raise the passions so quickly, and they were really screaming when Jim Beglin brought down John Gallacher in the box. Penalty. Quinn, who else, grabbed the ball and planted it wide of Mervyn Day in the Leeds goal. The fact that Leeds replied with two goals of their own shortly before half time put a damper on things, but the second half was to prove a nightmare for the Yorkshiremen. Four goals were smashed past a bemused Day, three for Quinn and one for Gallacher, and Leeds had been well and truly dismantled. Four goals for Quinn on his debut was sensational and his fourth in particular stood out. Kevin Dillon, a Mackem who never quite won over the fans at St. James'

Park – he never managed a single goal either – put Quinn clear on the half way line and the predatory striker homed in on the Leeds goal before striking a superbly placed shot wide of Day. It was as lethal a piece of finishing as you could wish to see. Quinn became an instant hero (relatively speaking) and we all believed a great season was set to follow.

16/09/89 – NEWCASTLE v PORTSMOUTH (1-0)

None of us were at St. James' Park today and that was because we were all across at Rowlands Gill for Michael Lowes' wedding; congratulations to him and Paula by the way. We arrived for the reception at the Holiday Inn at Seaton Burn just before half time and were disappointed to find out the scoreline was still blank. After the usual pleasantries the meal began but was interrupted just before 4.30pm with news that Andy Thorn had scored to secure a 1-0 win and sixth spot in the table. Lowesy had certainly scored today and this was obviously good reason for a double celebration. One of Lowesy's workmates was a Mackem, a real one, and he was sitting with the rest of the lads on our table and did he get some abuse! Nick was Best Man and while his speech contained some definitely libellous remarks against me, it was all good fun and a great night was had by all.

02/12/89 – LEEDS UNITED v NEWCASTLE (1-0)

Leeds, Sheffield United and ourselves were well clear at the top of the division and it was apparent, even at this early stage of the season, that the two automatic promotion spots would fall to two of these three teams.

David Holding, a blast from the past, had been working in America for the past five years and had only just returned to England and to his parents, who had relocated to Leeds. When he called me the week before the game it was totally out of the blue but the chance to renew our 'partnership' was irresistible. We went to Elland Road ticketless and as Newcastle had only been allocated something in the region of 1,200 tickets, a scandalously low amount, getting hold of a ticket was going to be difficult. Hanging about outside the ground looking rather conspicuous wasn't much fun and if the police weren't moving you on, threatening taunts from the home supporters weren't exactly appreciated either. These sort of occasions always bring the scum of football, namely the ticket tout, out of the woodwork and we had no choice but to eventually resort to buying two hideously over priced tickets from one of these loathsome individuals. I know we wouldn't have got into the ground without him but they still make your blood boil. On occasions in 1993 touts have been left with their fingers 'burnt' as they have been unable to shift their merchandise and when that happens you can't help but gloat. Back to Leeds and the tickets we got put us in with the Leeds supporters, unfortunately in the Lowfields Road Stand. The worst thing about this was that we couldn't reveal our support for Newcastle otherwise we would have been 'kicked in' not to put too fine a point on it, as there were many 'asylum' type characters lurking around near us.

In the first half Mervyn Day pulled off an unbelievable save from Mark McGhee and that was to be our only real chance of the game. After the break Mel Sterland galloped down the right hand touchline and, to give him credit, put over a superb cross for Ian Baird to power the ball past John Burridge. The Elland Road crowd rose as one whereas my heart just sank. The Kop sang the only song Leeds have got, 'Marching on together', which is my most hated football song – it really makes me cringe, not just because it's Leeds United but because I simply hate its tune, lyrics and everything about it; abysmal is too good to describe it. We saw out most of the remainder of the match, hating every moment, before quietly sloping out of the ground with a minute or so left on the clock. Some of the Leeds lunatics had cottoned on to us and chased us down the steps. Turning to fight would have left us in hospital so we sensibly took the cowardly option and ran as fast as we could and, I'm pleased to report, escaped unharmed. Stories of similar violence would regretfully surface once again when we next travelled to Leeds in April 1994.

01/01/90 – NEWCASTLE v WOLVERHAMPTON WANDERERS (1-4)

December was a disastrous month for us – four league games had resulted in three defeats and one draw and we were to pay the ultimate price for this poor run later in the season. Apart from the defeat at Elland Road on the first Saturday of the month, Oxford, fast becoming our bogey team, beat us as did Stoke on Boxing Day. Swindon on the last Saturday of the year almost brought three points but a last minute goal was to cruelly deny us. I'd been working in London during the day and journeyed back to Newcastle on the train arriving back at the Central Station just after 6.00pm. The frustration of not knowing the score on the train was immense and as soon as I dived off the train I made straight for the Newspaper Stand to get the Pink. Seeing the number '90' next to the Swindon scorer was such a bitter disappointment it's really difficult to put into words. There are numerous ways and means of hearing disappointing results – this was a new one but as shattering as any of the others.

Wolverhampton were no great shakes and arrived at St. James' Park occupying only a mid-table position and with only one string to their bow in the shape of prolific striker Steve Bull. No goals at half time didn't afford any clues as to what was about to unfold. Bull rattled in four goals past a mesmerised and static defence and although Brock pulled one back the crowd were almost too stunned to think about getting on the backs of the players. Visions of the 1979/80 season, when we'd led the table at Christmas only to sink into oblivion in the New Year, came flooding back. I know we were only seventh but the feeling was there nevertheless. Jim Smith had to do something and this he did by bringing the former Celtic and Scotland captain, Roy Aitken, to St. James' Park. On the face of it, Aitken was a good buy. Here was a vastly-experienced player capable of leading the team out of its slump in form and back onto the tails of Leeds and Sheffield United. I took to Aitken pretty well at first but became slowly more disenchanted with him as the season reached its conclusion. It wasn't that he didn't perform well on the majority of occasions, it just seemed to me there was something missing from his make-up but, what that was I couldn't tell you. Aitken couldn't have picked a better game for his league debut, a 5-4 win at St. James' Park against Leicester in mid January – a match in which we'd had to come from 4-2 down to win with Aitken's big mate Mark McGhee scoring the winner in the last minute. McGhee was becoming good at late winners, but even this effort couldn't match the amazing winner he'd got against Bradford City back in October when, after dribbling past four or five defenders, he shot past Tomlinson with virtually the last kick of the game.

04/02/90 – NEWCASTLE v SUNDERLAND (1-1)

This match was almost called off shortly before kick off due to high winds which were threatening to cause structural damage to St. James' Park. There was also a potential risk to the safety of the spectators but in the event the match proceeded. I wish it hadn't. It was a farce, caused entirely by the wind which meant playing any sort of football was impossible – Sunderland probably didn't mind the levelling out of conditions though as they were a much inferior footballing side.

It was another of those ridiculous Sunday lunchtime starts which again was entirely down to the influence of the police. Why were derby matches in Liverpool and Manchester able to be played at 3.00pm on a Saturday afternoon with no apparent problems when we had to suffer a move to Sunday afternoon? For one thing the atmosphere isn't quite the same and surely the respective police forces cannot be so far apart in terms of their philosophy and competence over such matters. At least as we're not likely to be playing Sunderland for some time, it may not even be until the next century, it gives the authorities ample opportunity to sort themselves out and get their house in order.

Marco Gabbiadini scored for the Mackems with McGhee equalising shortly after, but it was a dreadfully poor match and regrettably one of the most forgettable derby matches I'd ever seen. The whole day proved to be a complete anti-climax.

18/02/90 – NEWCASTLE v MANCHESTER UNITED (2-3)

Although this was a fifth round FA Cup tie and the BBC *Match of the Day* cameras were present, there was something a little unusual about the day and I've never really been able to put my finger on it. We lost the game 3-2 and only came that close because the referee allowed a blatant foul by Mick Quinn on Jim Leighton to go unpunished as we scored our second goal to draw level early in the second half. I've still got the game on tape at home but can't recall ever having the inclination to watch it again which more or less sums up the whole occasion.

24/02/90 – SHEFFIELD UNITED v NEWCASTLE (1-1)

Much to my chagrin and annoyance, Sheffield United, a team of such limited ability and stereotyped quite rightly as long ball cloggers, were above us in the table when we went to Bramall Lane for a game we couldn't afford to lose. If nothing else Bramall Lane is pretty good for close side street parking and we found a place only a hundred yards or so from the ground. Macas came up from Nottingham and we met him outside the ground with a couple of Sheffield United friends of his he'd brought with him. Quite what we were doing fraternising with the opposition before the game I don't know, but you kind of had to go along with it.

Quite frankly we bossed the game and were cruising at half time even though we'd only scored once through Kevin Brock (later to be debited as a Mark Morris own goal). The second half continued in much the same vein but no further goals followed. No further goals for us that is, but with only two minutes left Sheffield United fluked (there were a lot of deflections in the penalty box) an equaliser through Brian Deane (later to become one of the costliest big money flops at Elland Road) which must go down in history as one of the most undeserved goals ever. We were distraught. I recall that Sheffield had, over the past few weeks, made a habit of scoring last minute goals to either draw or win games, and the fact that they'd done it again today was too much to take.

The great boardroom battle was still raging as we entered a new decade with the 'United Supporters for Change' group particularly prominent. Sir John Hall had eventually been given a seat on the board after spending an inordinate amount of money acquiring shares at hugely inflated prices. Back in October 1988 he raised his offer for shares from £500 to £1000 which was an incredible show of commitment to the cause. It was a necessary course of action to have pursued, but in reality so wasteful when you stand back and look at the overall big picture of the ultimate health, viability, status and success of the club. A failed share issue at the beginning of the 1990/91 season, under the Chairmanship of George Forbes (a dedicated supporter of the club but with no real financial clout) did the club no good at all, and it wasn't until October 1991 that Sir John stepped in as Chairman with Gordon McKeag and Stan Seymour moving in the opposite direction.

05/05/90 – MIDDLESBROUGH v NEWCASTLE (4-1)

The last game of the season, hopefully, and the automatic promotion places were still not settled. It was an absolutely intriguing situation and one which was set to test the nerves to the limit.

After the Sheffield United game we embarked on a very useful run, interrupted by consecutive defeats at Bradford and Blackburn at the end of March, but then hit back with a vengeance with an amazing six-game winning streak. The last of those games, against Stoke City at St. James' Park on Easter Monday, (historically a pretty good day for Newcastle winning important matches) even took us up into second place, below Leeds but above Sheffield United. Four matches to play and our destiny was in our own hands. Although we beat West Ham, draws against Swindon and Plymouth let Sheffield sneak back above us in to second place before the visit to Teesside.

The scenario on 5th May before kick off saw Leeds top with 82 points and away to Bournemouth, Sheffield second, also with 82 points and away to Leicester; and us in third, two points behind with the derby at Ayresome Park to come. A win for us, coupled with either of the other two failing to win, would almost certainly have brought promotion. Incredibly relegation issues were also at stake in the equation as Middlesbrough needed to win to ensure their place in Division Two remained intact. What an amazing situation it was. I really thought that we'd win, Leeds would win too, but Leicester would do the business for us and so we'd finish second. I have never won anything on the pools, not surprising really, as the day turned out to be an unmitigated disaster. Leeds and Sheffield both won which meant our result was irrelevant (of course the players didn't know that at the time) but the 4 -1 defeat we suffered, which kept Middlesbough up, was as bad a performance as we had put in all season – maybe Wolverhampton's win at St. James' Park was as bad, scoreline wise, but in terms of the importance of the occasion nothing like as serious, I think we just bottled it. I couldn't even blame players such as the woefully ineffective Wayne Fereday and wholly inadequate Billy Askew who had played during the season but not today. I'm sure they were both smashing lads but they certainly weren't good enough to play for Newcastle United.

I was ticketless for the big game at Ayresome Park and as so many other Geordies were in the same predicament the club at least had the foresight to install a giant screen at St. James' Park so people could buy tickets to go into the ground and watch the game live. I went along (so did 17,000 others, many with their giant Newcastle Brown Ale inflatables which were popular at the time) but it was something of an unreal atmosphere and as the picture quality left a lot to be desired it ended up being a totally unrewarding and fruitless afternoon. We were so near and yet so far and having finished six points clear of the three clubs placed fourth to sixth we had to join them in the Play Offs to determine the third club to be awarded promotion to the promised land. Swindon and Blackburn were fourth and fifth respectively and by a quirk of fate Sunderland were sixth, which meant the two of us meeting in the semi-finals of the Play Offs.

13/05/90 – SUNDERLAND v NEWCASTLE (0-0)

Firstly a little word on the Play Offs. Although we finished well clear in third place yet failed to win automatic promotion, I am still very much in favour of their concept. There are a number of reasons – all the teams know the rules of the competition at the start of the campaign, they generate tremendous extra interest and excitement at the end of the season coupled with the thrill of a Wembley Final and, more than anything else, they keep the regular season alive for all the teams in the top half of the table as they strive to reach a top six finishing position and that's a tremendous incentive for any team. Okay, so the sixth placed team can knock out the third placed team – tough! That's football and, as they say, it's all part and parcel of the game.

The Play Offs pitted third versus sixth and fourth versus fifth in the semi-finals over two legs with the highest placed team having home advantage in the crucial second leg. The two winners would meet in a showpiece Wembley occasion and, unlike the FA Cup Final, it would be a day for the fans with each club receiving 40,000 tickets each – I couldn't wait.

I was home for the weekend, ticketless for Roker but safe in the knowledge that I'd be at St. James' Park three days later. I think it's fair to say we set our stall out for a draw at Roker Park. Jim Smith had decided to play defensive rather than attacking midfielders, and it meant Quinn and McGhee hardly got a look in all afternoon. I suppose it was a tactically acceptable approach – however it still goes against the grain for me. Teams who adapt their formations to stifle their opponents or play three centre halves with a single striker up front really annoy me, and how supporters of teams like (Boring) Arsenal must suffer. I almost feel sorry for them but, unfortunately, can't quite bring myself to do so.

We got the draw we came for, 0-0 as it happened, but if it hadn't been for John Burridge we would have been on the wrong end of a 1-0 defeat. Picture the scenario. Time had virtually expired when Gabbiadini broke clear on the left, across came Stimson and as Gabbiadini raced into the penalty box Stimson challenged him knocking the ball out for a corner. Meanwhile our pleasant, fair playing, mild mannered Mackem had thrown himself to the ground desperately claiming a foul. No chance, but with referee Vic Callow well adrift of the action it was left to the linesman to put his flag across his chest which meant a penalty. It was an incredible decision. Gabbiadini had a little chuckle to himself, the Fulwell Enders went crazy whilst Aitken and Stimson led a furious assault on Callow. In all my years of watching football I've never seen a referee change his mind and so arguing, although understandable, was futile and would only result in a yellow card. I digress slightly here just to report the fact that throughout my whole playing career, spanning nigh on 20 years of competitive football, I am very proud to say that I have never been cautioned by a referee (nor sent off I hasten to add) and I suppose you could call me the Gary Lineker of non-league football. Indeed I've only ever been spoken to once and that was for a mild piece of time wasting back in my early days at Ponteland United.

The whole affray took several minutes to settle down before Paul Hardyman was able to place the ball on the spot. Meanwhile back in Ponteland I was lying on my bed listening to the radio, heart pounding rapidly, fist banging on the pillow in disbelief, and praying that he would miss. Hardyman obliged – it must have been the worst day of his career (he was also dropped for the 1992 Cup Final!) as he saw Burridge dive to his right to save his shot and, when he followed up, kicked at the ball as Burridge laid on top of it. It was probably out of sheer frustration, to give him the benefit of the doubt, but he promptly received the red card from Callow. How fortunes could change. Thirty seconds ago the Mackems were in full cry but now they were stunned into silence whilst the Geordies occupying the Roker End lost all self control and celebrated like never before. Moments like this sum up every emotion football can provide, good and bad, and that's the beauty of the game. The floorboards in my bedroom had by now taken a hammering as I was jumping up and down with joy. We'd got the draw we wanted and everything was perfectly set up for a night to savour at St. James' Park.

16/05/90 – NEWCASTLE v SUNDERLAND (0-2)

I'd taken the first part of the week off and really just lazed around the house – Wednesday simply couldn't come quickly enough. There was constant newspaper and radio speculation and it was almost like the build up to an FA Cup Final in respect of the coverage the game was attracting. On Wednesday morning I went for a run out into the countryside (through Primrose Wood, a favourite childhood haunt) and even now I can remember where I went and exactly what I was thinking. My mind was so active with nothing else but the game in my thoughts – Would we win? Would Quinny score? How would Burridge play? I could have just run and run – such was the distraction from the match that any fatigue in my limbs was totally unnoticeable.

We all had tickets for different parts of the ground and I ended up with Lowesy in the Gallowgate Centre Section. Feelings were so intense all round St. James' Park and I would have loved to have been a fly on the wall inside the dressing rooms to have seen what the mood of the players was like. Everything was in our favour; home advantage, the knowledge of having gained the upper hand at Roker Park, and current form. In the final analysis it didn't mean a thing. Had we peaked two or three weeks ago and gone into an irreversible decline? Whatever the reason you have to say Sunderland deserved their victory. Eric Gates put the Mackems ahead early on before Gabbiadini scored the second in the final minutes. The second 'killer' goal was the signal for the lunatic fringe in the Gallowgate End to invade the pitch (no fences now of course) and as many as 500 got on to the playing surface. What was the motive, an abandonment, or was it just plain stupidity and senselessness? Whatever it was the outcome was that the match was halted for no more than 10 minutes while police horses ushered all the moronic youngsters (they were mainly teenagers) back on to the terraces. The Mackems to their credit stayed put in the Leazes End, content I'm sure to celebrate their imminent and momentous victory. They'd won 9-1 at St. James' Park back in 1908 but in terms of history making, important and significant victories, this one would surely top the lot.

After referee George Courtney brought the players back on to the pitch the final moments were played out in an eerie atmosphere, and as soon as the final whistle sounded Lowsey and I just left the ground in silence. It was almost unreal and I for one found it difficult to come to terms with.

I suppose it wasn't until the following morning that the realisation of the events at St. James' Park the night before really hit home. The bottom line was that we had blown the chance of promotion, would be missing out on a dream trip to Wembley, would have to endure another season (at least) of second division football, and perhaps worse than any of these was the small matter of Mackems taking all of these things from us. We were inconsolable for days on end but when the Mackems went on to lose to Swindon at Wembley in the Play Off Final, at least we knew they wouldn't be promoted after all. A final word on Wembley and it goes without saying that Macas was there and for the second time he had seen Sunderland lose to an own goal! Gordon Chisholm did the trick in the 1985 League Cup Final against Norwich and against Swindon it was a bit like snooker – in off the black as the joke went – a Gary Bennett own goal.

A week or so later rumours began circulating that Swindon were likely to be punished by the Football League for serious financial irregularities, and stories even went as far as to suggest that they would be demoted. When this became a reality the question on everybody's lips was who would replace them in Division One? Newcastle as the third placed club in the regular league season, Sunderland as Play Off Finalists or Sheffield Wednesday who were the 'highest placed' club to be relegated from Division One. The final option was quickly discounted by all of those 'in the know' and speculation was rife on both Tyneside and Wearside as to which way the Football League would fall. Each thought they had a good case but the consensus of opinion emanating from within the corridors of power at Lytham St. Annes seemed to be favouring the Roker cause. When the decision was finally confirmed, I remember it being officially announced by Des Lynam on *World Cup Grandstand*, it didn't really come as a great surprise as I had braced myself accordingly. And so that was it, the Mackems went into Division One through the backdoor and we were going nowhere.

At the time it was a devastating blow to all connected with Newcastle United, but looking back it turned out to be one of the best things that happened to the club. A strange thing to say you might think but this is why. If we had gone up, Jim Smith and his ageing squad would have drifted along aimlessly in the bottom half of the league, the Board of Directors would have remained unchallenged and even worse unambitious; it might never have given Sir John Hall an opportunity to take control of the club and there would have been no return for Kevin Keegan. Looking at where we are today it's frightening to think what might have been if the fates had taken a different turn – in fact it's barely worth even contemplating, so ruinous and hideous would have been the consequences. So, thank you Sunderland, and no you are not hearing things, I really mean it.

04/07/90 – ENGLAND v WEST GERMANY (1-1)

Regardless of whom England are playing the result that matters, more than any other, is that of Newcastle United. Tonight England were playing in the World Cup semi-final, the biggest game in England's history since 1966, and I was glued to the television set along with 25 million others. What made the occasion even more splendid was the fact that our three Geordie heroes, Waddle, Beardsley and Gascoigne, were all on the field in Turin, and it was as strong an England team as you could imagine – certainly no quibbling over players who may not have been selected. The Germans as expected were as tough as nails though, and come the end of 120 minutes the score was tied at 1-1. Gazza was already in tears, having been booked in the first period of extra time, his second of the tournament, which would mean him missing the final had we won the game. The emotion and tears he produced were some of the most genuinely touching moments I have ever seen – can you imagine having to miss out on the biggest game of your whole career because a German had conned the referee into issuing a yellow card? It was tragic, galling and heartbreaking for the lad and I even thought I wouldn't mind if we lost the game so Gazza wouldn't have to endure the pain of missing the final. It's history now that Pearce and Waddle missed their penalties, thus granting the Germans a passage into the final, but what a sad night it turned out to be.

1989/90 – Season's Summary

League	P	W	D	L	F	A	Pts.	Pos.
	46	22	14	10	80	55	80	3rd

Top Scorers		
Mick Quinn		34
Mark McGhee		25
John Gallacher		7

1990/91 – ARGENTINIAN DELIGHT

This season was one of the biggest non-events in the club's history. From day one where it all started with a mundane opening day fixture against Plymouth Argyle, all the way through to the final fixture against Hull City. There was virtually no excitement and nothing out of the ordinary bar the home FA Cup tie with Nottingham Forest. We flirted briefly with the bottom of the table in November, but were never really likely to get embroiled in a relegation battle, had no glamorous fixtures, got knocked out in the early stages of both cup competitions, never got higher than 11th in the table after Christmas, and only the resignation of Jim Smith followed by the appointment of Osvaldo Ardiles in late March, saved the season from being a total write off. After coming so close to promotion in the 1989/90 season we deserved far more than we got out of this season.

25/08/90 – NEWCASTLE v PLYMOUTH ARGYLE (2-0)

The first time we had all been back at St. James' Park since the Sunderland debacle in May. The attendance of 24,000 was reasonable considering that the bitter anti climax of play off failure was still fresh in everyone's minds.

I'd chosen to go in the Leazes End, just for a change, perhaps it was because I couldn't drag myself back in the Gallowgate just yet – bad memories and all that, and I stood immediately behind the goal. It had been a long time since I'd stood so close to the goal and looking through the net to the other side of the ground brought back many memories of years gone by. The pitch, as you would expect on the opening day of the season, looked in immaculate condition, really lush grass and ideal for playing bowls on let alone football.

We got off to the best possible start. After only a couple of minutes Benny Kristensen strode forward and, from 25 yards, directed a perfect right-foot shot into the corner of the net. I had a superb view of the goal and remember thinking just before he scored that it was all opening up for him and a shot was on. It was a goal from the moment it left his foot and I followed it all the way into the back of the net. It was almost as if I was watching one of those ball tracking devices that television were so keen on in the 1970s, to follow the path of a ball on its way into goal.

Steve Howey, a young lad of only 19 who is now established in the team and fully deserving of his England debut in 1994, was playing alongside Mick Quinn in the front line. I can vividly remember him missing a good opportunity to put us two up and I watched Quinn becoming exasperated with young Howey almost to the extent of 'black balling' him. It was a disgraceful way for a senior professional to act towards a young player trying to make his way in the game. It could have destroyed Howey there and then, but thankfully he's had the strength of character to come through in the game and emerge, in a new position, as one of the country's outstanding central defenders.

Quinn didn't endear himself to me either in the League Cup tie against Middlesbrough at St. James' Park. It was a second leg match and having lost the first leg 2-0 we needed a concerted effort from all 11 players if we were to get anything from the game, but Quinn regretfully let everyone down, himself particularly, by getting sent off. Stephen Pears, the Middlesbrough goalkeeper, wasn't totally blameless but when the two of them clashed early in the game the pettiness in Quinn's character led him to take the law into his own hands and a red card was inevitable. With only 10 men and our main goalscorer in the bath, we faced an awesome task. Not surprisingly it proved too great an obstacle to overcome, and although 1-0 winners on the night we were 2-1 losers on aggregate and that's what mattered.

Quinn, in all his time at the club, never managed a goal against either Sunderland or Middlesbrough and this really annoyed him. Overall I suppose he did a good job for the club but his mean streak, not to mention his weight problem, probably held him back from achieving greater things in the game. He has since earned the nickname 'Sumo' and at least receives a warm reception from the fans whenever he comes back to St. James' Park.

The Mackems, making their first appearance back in Division One at Norwich, lost 3-2 and set the tone for another season of failure which was set to climax in glorious ignominy at Maine Road nine months later.

01/01/91 – OLDHAM ATHLETIC v NEWCASTLE (1-1)

If you looked at the list of players who were to represent us throughout the season it didn't exactly fill you with much enthusiasm. Quite honestly from all 36 of them there wasn't a single one who was either very good or exciting. There were the reasonable ones – such as Scott, Anderson and Peacock, the ones who could maybe play well one week but not the next – O'Brien and Stimson come to mind – and of course there were the total no-hopers like Sweeney, Fereday and Robinson. We also took a number of players on loan, always something of a strange arrangement and you have to be eternally thankful that we didn't agree transfer fees for Paul Moran, Tommy Gaynor and Dave Mitchell because all three of them would have walked into an all-time Newcastle United worst players team – yes they were that bad and summed up jim Smith's assessment of a player down to a tee.

Our visit to Oldham on New Year's Day, we were 15th in the table at the time, was a relatively nice change of scenery for a Christmas holiday trip. Boundary Park must be one of the easiest grounds in the Football League to find as you simply leave the motorway, drive along a short bit of dual carriageway, turn off left for Oldham and you see the ground immediately on your left. Oldham is one of your typical Lancastrian 'Industrial Revolution' type towns with old cotton mills and the like clearly in evidence. It also suffers terribly from being in the shadow of Manchester, so all credit to their small band of supporters for remaining loyal to the club rather than deserting to one or other of the 'big two' down the road.

The match itself was a tough proposition as well. The Latics were riding high in the table and would ultimately go on and win the League. The year before they had done marvellously well to reach the League Cup Final and the semi-finals of the FA Cup, and it was surely only the distraction of the Cup success that cost them promotion.

I had missed a few matches before Christmas but the lads told me I hadn't missed anything. If the form I saw them in three days earlier against Notts County at St. James' Park was anything to go by, we would be lucky to get off with a three or four goal roasting. As it was Quinn opened the scoring after a goalless first half and our celebrations, even though there was nothing really to cheer about when you looked at the season as a whole, were in full swing as 90 minutes expired on the clock. The three points were to be ours after a battling yet composed performance, but we'd reckoned without the intervention of Mark Stimson. The moment that followed had shades of Willie Donachie written all over it as we proceeded to concede the most bizarre own goal of the season to gift Oldham their equaliser. I can't imagine what John Burridge said to Stimson in the privacy of the changing room but you can be sure some rather choice expressions were passed his way. Budgie wasn't afraid to give people a piece of his mind and, for someone who always took so much pride in his performance (when he first signed for us he famously stood on the terraces behind the goal Newcastle were defending so he could see at first hand how the back four played), it must have been a bitter pill to swallow.

13/02/91 – NEWCASTLE v NOTTINGHAM FOREST (2-2)

It was FA Cup time again and even though we were a second division side we certainly didn't have an inferiority complex. Any home draw is welcome and regardless of who they are, be it Lincoln or Liverpool, Mansfield or Manchester United, we fancy our chances of turning them over at St. James' Park. In round three, Derby, a first division side, albeit a struggling one, were well beaten and we were now lined up against their East Midland rivals Nottingham Forest. This was the third time in 17 years Forest and ourselves had been drawn out of the hat together, a coincidence obviously, but it's strange how we've never met in recent years the likes of major clubs such as Arsenal, Leeds or Everton in the competition – it could be something to do with the fact that getting knocked out in the early rounds lessens your chances of meeting the better clubs!

The match had been postponed from the originally scheduled date in January due to bad weather but a midweek fixture suited me as it would guarantee my attendance and we all enjoyed the night match atmosphere much better. What a dream start we got. Quinn and McGhee quickly put us two up and although Pearce pulled one back early in the second half we were still coasting and looking forward to a visit to Southampton in the next round. Youngster Steve Watson, he of the famous back-flip throw in, went so close to adding the decisive third goal but then two minutes from full time Nigel Clough strode unchallenged through the heart of Newcastle's midfield to strike a superb shot past Burridge. The goal had class written all over it and Forest, so relieved to 'get out of jail', beat us 3-0 in the replay at the City Ground. Remarkably, for the third time in four seasons the club who had knocked us out in either the fourth or fifth round went on to reach Wembley – sooner or later it would be our turn.

This was effectively Jim Smith's swan song. He could possibly have survived had we reached at least the semi-finals but as our league position was poor, in fact it was downright appalling, his reign at the club, just over three years, was shortly to be terminated and I for one wasn't sorry to see him go.

01/04/91 – NEWCASTLE v BRISTOL ROVERS (0-2)

As the season was going nowhere, that is we weren't anywhere near relegation and the promotion play offs were a wild fantasy, it was important to get a new manager installed as quickly as possible, effectively to give him a chance to look at the players over a period of 10 games or so in order to assess what he would need to do to build a promotion-winning squad for the following season.

Osvaldo Ardiles, World Cup winner with Argentina in 1978, FA Cup winner with Tottenham in 1981 and a figure hugely respected in the game, was a popular choice to lead the club back to the top. Ardiles had been manager of Swindon, and ironically was still at the County Ground as Swindon's manager for the game there the previous weekend when we'd lost 3-2 and stayed anonymously in 14th place in the table. A nice way for Ossie to say farewell to Wiltshire but not the best thing to do to a club you knew you would be joining within 24 hours. It was no secret that he had been 'tapped up' by Newcastle and understandably the Swindon public were not best pleased. Ossie brought his right hand man from Swindon, Tony Galvin, to St. James' Park with him. He was another former Tottenham player and although I always thought of him as a reasonable player he didn't strike me as being managerial material – a little too dour for my liking.

Before the Rovers game Ardiles was given a rousing reception when he stepped out onto the turf at 10 minutes to three. He was a small, proud man with fine footballing principles and he couldn't have wished for a better stage on which to realise his ambitions in the game. Usually when a new manager takes over at a club all the players try extra hard to impress, especially in his first game, but although this may have been the case Bristol Rovers didn't give Ossie a dream managerial start and deservedly won 2-0. A setback, that's all, and not too disappointing but when the remaining matches only brought two wins, surprisingly against two of the three promoted clubs, Oldham and Sheffield Wednesday –

the latter being particularly sweet as it would have been nice to have denied the Owls promotion – the confidence we all had in Ardiles when he first came to the club wasn't as high as we would have liked. It was perhaps an ominous sign of things ahead.

11/05/91 – NEWCASTLE v HULL CITY (1-2)

Nothing really to report here, a drab dreary way to finish the season, except that it was nice to see Ossie showing faith in the outstanding young talent at the club. Lads such as Lee Clark and Steve Watson were in the side on merit and believe me there was nothing better then seeing dedicated born and bred Geordie lads wanting only to play for Newcastle United.

We were 11th once again and, as it happened, the 2-1 defeat didn't matter too much since most of the attention was focussed on Manchester where once again, it's amazing how often it happens, Sunderland went into their last fixture needing a win to stand any chance of avoiding relegation. Credit to the Mackems, they took over Maine Road, but alas lost 3-2 and nose dived straight back into the second division – just desserts really for their ludicrously fortunate promotion a year ago.

1990/91 – Season's Summary

League	P	W	D	L	F	A	Pts.	Pos.
	46	14	17	15	49	56	59	11th

Top Scorers		
Mick Quinn		20
Gavin Peacock		7
Mark McGhee		6

1991/92 – THE PRODIGAL RETURNS

Need I even say it, Ossie was going to take us storming back into Division One and under his guidance we would re-establish ourselves in the British game while at the same time playing stylish and entertaining football. We all thought it could happen and I'm sure Ossie believed it would too – the fact that it didn't not only led to his departure from the club in February but threatened the near extinction of the club, and that's no exaggeration, as Division Three loomed large.

24/09/91 – CREWE ALEXANDRA v NEWCASTLE (3-4)

This was another first for me, a visit to Gresty Road and a sighting of the famous railway lines, junctions, and what seemed like hundreds of signal boxes in close proximity to the ground. None of the usual crew could make it so I took a couple of lads from Leeds to treat them to an away day with Newcastle – better than anything they could experience with Leeds! We were a shambles in the first half hour, 3-0 down and seemingly out of the competition at the first hurdle once again. Newcastle never cease to surprise you though and thanks to a Peacock hat-trick and one from Andy Hunt, we fought back magnificently to win 4-3. At least pride had been restored for the 1,000 or so fans who had made the journey from the North East. It was a match they'll never forget, not a classic of course, just one of those games that will stick in the mind. As for my two mates, they witnessed the anger of the fans during the first part of the game, followed by such overwhelming scenes of excitement and jubilation that even they found hard to comprehend – and this was only for Crewe Alexandra on a bleak autumn night in Cheshire.

05/10/91 – PORTSMOUTH v NEWCASTLE (3-1)

We'd never been 24th in a division before (Division One had only ever had 22 teams on the occasions when we were rock bottom) but after this match we were. The expanded second division meant a 46 game league programme and it was hard to believe that of all the unbelievably poor sides in the division, Port Vale, Barnsley, Bristol Rovers to name but three, we were worse than any of them! Incredible but true – league tables never lie.

This was our 11th match of the season and we had only managed a solitary win. It was classic relegation form and although we were to win our next two matches the revival wasn't set to last as another run of only two victories in 12 games was on the horizon. It wasn't that we didn't have any decent players. Gavin Peacock was a class act, Tommy Wright and Pavel Srnicek were both good keepers and David Kelly, whom Ossie brought to the club a month or so before Christmas, was a player I'd always admired in the past. Could it be that Ossie was losing control – certainly he must have been beginning to feel the pressure although, to be fair, the crowd never once got on his back.

26/12/91 – NEWCASTLE v MIDDLESBROUGH (0-1)

Middlesbrough will never be as big a game for the Geordies as Sunderland but nevertheless it's always more than just a run of the mill fixture. Everyone on Tyneside also built up this match as the most important of the season so far, purely because of our precarious league position. Three points were an absolute must – I know that's a cliché, and it's often an over used expression, but on this occasion it really was a 'big' game.

It didn't help our cause that Middlesbrough were having a good run, third in the league (they would end up getting promoted at the end of the season) and full of confidence. We played reasonably well but naively and that couldn't have been better illustrated than when Middlesbrough scored the only goal of the game minutes after half-time. We had thrown virtually everybody forward and when the attack broke down the ball was played up to Paul Wilkinson standing in the centre circle. I couldn't believe it, there was absolutely no one near him, the defence was absent without leave and Wilkinson simply had to turn, advance towards goal (even he cannot have dreamed how much space he was in) and knock the ball past a bemused Tommy Wright. Given the amount of time he had Wilkinson took the goal well, which you might think is a strange thing to say but you often find strikers are better at tucking away sharp chances instinctively rather than having too much time to dwell on the ball and, as a result, making a mess of the opportunity – witness Geoff Thomas's appalling miss against France at Wembley in 1992.

The following weekend Richie, Angus and myself went off for a week's skiing in Livigno, Italy. It did mean missing two games though so our first priority on New Year's Day afternoon was to phone home and find out the score of the match at Southend. Ritchie made the call, hoping to speak to one of his brothers, but finding none were at home ended up speaking to his Dad. Mr. Ingham could never be described as a football fan but has always had a sharp sense of humour, particularly as far as I have always been concerned, so when Ritchie conveyed the news to us that we had suffered a 4-0 defeat I thought it was a wind up and simply refused to believe that Southend, a club of such minnowesque standing in football, had humiliated us so badly. It wasn't until we got the English newspapers two days later that the result was confirmed, as was our perilous position of 20th, and only then did it really sink home. At least I had the pleasure of being able to tell Angus that Manchester United had also been thumped, 4-1, at home to Queen's Park Rangers. On the subject of newspapers the Italian media is absolutely football crazy and, had I been able to read Italian, there were numerous football newspapers I could have bought – not a bad place to live if you're a football nut.

We flew back from Bergamo to Gatwick (quite why we were flying from Gatwick I'll never know, I blamed Ritchie for making the bookings) on the first Saturday of the New Year which, of course, was FA Cup Third Round day. The draw had pitted us against Bournemouth at Dean Court and as we touched down it was about 5.30pm and I couldn't stop wondering if we were still in the Cup. We managed to catch a courtesy bus from the airport to the place our car had been parked, but unfortunately the only score the driver was able to tell us was that Wrexham had knocked out Arsenal. That was no good to us and we had to wait for the second reading of the classified results on Sports Report to learn of our fate. The 0-0 scoreline was greeted with huge sighs of relief and I for one was overjoyed to still be in the Cup – it certainly made the long drive home a great deal more bearable.

22/01/92 – NEWCASTLE v BOURNEMOUTH (2-2)

The weekend before this third round replay we had virtually committed footballing suicide by managing to lose 4-3 to Charlton Athletic at St. James' Park after leading 3-0 midway through the first half. The fact that Liam O'Brien scored an own goal to give the Valiants their winner made it even more galling and it also meant we were only one place off the bottom of the table. Even though our position was absolutely desperate I never once thought that we would end up getting relegated. I don't know why this was, perhaps I simply refused to believe it was possible or was too fearful to even contemplate such a fate.

This match was the second attempt at playing the game as the first had had to be abandoned a week earlier after only 17 minutes, due to fog. If we weren't capable of beating a mid-table third division side at St. James' Park then we really were in trouble. As things turned out we played okay without ever looking like getting out of third gear, but could only end up sharing a goal apiece after 90 minutes. Almost immediately extra time began Andy Hunt scored his second of the game to seemingly put us into the next round, but Kevin Bond popped up near the end with an equaliser. No second replay to come, just penalties, and so we braced ourselves for the drama about to unfold before us. Was it an omen that the Gallowgate End was once again selected as the end of the ground where the penalties would be taken? Remembering Jim Pearson's infamous miss, I didn't much care for that particular train of thought.

Earlier in the competition both Rotherham and Exeter had progressed by virtue of winning penalty shoot-outs against Scunthorpe and Colchester respectively; we at St. James' Park were about to witness the third penalty occasion in the competition, but the first in the third round. It started well enough but then, almost as if time stood still, Kevin Brock and Liam O'Brien both missed their kicks and before we knew it Bournemouth were through and our cup dreams were once again left in tatters. Exasperation, raging fury and emptiness were but three of the emotions driving me towards unparalleled depths of despair. I drove back to Leeds straight after the game and what a miserable journey it was.

01/02/92 – OXFORD UNITED v NEWCASTLE (5-2)

If Custer could have a last stand then so could Ossie, and to all intents and purposes this was his. Apart from the fact that the club were £6 million in debt, our position in the League was dire, second from bottom, and the downward spiral we were on was threatening to become irreversible. Sir John Hall had publicly backed Ossie in the week leading up to the game and ironically, in many people's eyes, that meant the sack was imminent.

The Manor Ground was fog bound and I suppose you could say

we lost our way. If that's an explanation for losing 5-2 then it's a pretty inadequate one. What was it about Oxford that saw us continually turn in woefully pitiful performances? Ossie was at a loss but John Hall, in typically decisive style, wasn't. He decided that unless he acted immediately the rescue package he had put together would fail because the only place the club was heading was into division three. He sacked the little Argentinian and later admitted it was one of the hardest decisions he had ever had to make. Ossie may even have been relieved to have been put out of his misery, but I'm sure while understanding why it had to be done, his professional pride had been severely dented. Ardiles left the club with dignity and both he and the supporters still today retain a genuine affinity for one another. In other circumstances Ossie's appointment may have been the ideal one for the club, on this particular occasion fate decreed that it simply wouldn't work out.

A final word on Ossie, with him being dismissed by Tottenham after failing to make an impact at White Hart Lane, perhaps all the hype about him being a top class manager doesn't quite ring as true as many people, including myself, once thought.

08/02/92 – NEWCASTLE v BRISTOL CITY (3-0)

The Messiah, the King, the Saviour, call him what you will, had returned to his spiritual home – Tyneside. As they say it was a marriage made in heaven and we knew he would save us. Some individuals have such an awe inspiring inspirational effect on you, and in this context Kevin Keegan was unique.

The deal that brought Keegan back to St. James' Park was clearly the brainchild of Sir John Hall but was heavily backed by Newcastle Breweries. It was fantastic that everyone was pulling as one for the first time in many a year, and there was genuine optimism and expectation emanating from the whole of Tyneside.

Keegan appointed another Newcastle favourite, Terry McDermott, as his 'buffer' and it was no surprise that 30,000 turned up at St. James' Park for the visit of Bristol City, Keegan's first match as manager. Looking back only 12 months ago the other Bristol side, Rovers, were the visitors for Ardiles's first match in charge – how different the two days turned out to be. No score at half time but the atmosphere in the ground was so changed from anything that had gone before. I've said it already but it's worth repeating that only Keegan could have brought about this transformation in fortunes, and when the deadlock was broken by David Kelly the roar that went up from St. James' Park was immense. Two further goals followed and the resulting 3-0 victory was, not surprisingly, our most conclusive of the season. The win only moved us up one place, to 22nd, but you had that special inner feeling that this was to be the start of our ascent.

A week later at Blackburn, in the media-titled 'Keegan versus Dalglish' encounter, Kelly was on the mark again to put us ahead, but a David Speedie hat-trick, the first of which followed a blatant foul on Tommy Wright, sent us all back to reality after a week of living in dreamland. Talking of David Speedie, I can't think of another player who has been subjected to as much abuse by the Newcastle supporters. Much of it was good natured taunting but it did go a little over the top, certainly as far as Speedie was concerned, when insinuations about his wife were made. It's fair to say Speedie brings much of this on himself due entirely to the sort of character he is: volatile, fiery, impetuous and easily provoked. Sunderland's Gary Bennett, famous for being sent off at St. James' Park in 1985 and for scoring the own goal at Wembley in the Play Off Final in 1990, did everyone a favour when he clashed with Speedie during a fixture at Roker Park and near enough ended up throttling him – very amusing. From my point of view, and indeed on behalf of all Geordies, we relish such confrontations.

14/03/92 – NEWCASTLE v SWINDON TOWN (3-1)

I wasn't at this game but having got home after my own match, knowing that we had secured an important 3-1 win, I put Ceefax on for the match report and saw the most incredible headline you could ever wish to see, 'Keegan walks out on Newcastle' it said and with Radio 5's *6.06* programme confirming the story I was astounded, horrified – you name it, I was it. What a bolt from the blue it was. Apparently Sir John Hall had reneged on a promise made to Keegan when he was appointed and Keegan, being a man of fine principles, had walked out. It was all done in the heat of the moment though and we all have to be extremely thankful to Terry McDermott, who managed to calm Keegan down, made him reconsider his rash decision, and coaxed him back to St. James' Park. Hall and Keegan quickly made up, and on reflection it may have done both men, and ultimately the club, a great deal of good. It showed that the bottom line was that no one individual was bigger than the club.

29/03/92 – NEWCASTLE v SUNDERLAND (1-0)

The Mackems were also struggling at the foot of the table but they at least had an FA Cup semi-final against Norwich at Hillsborough the following weekend to look forward to. Sunderland's Cup success had adversely affected their league form and they were in danger of winning the FA Cup and being relegated in the same season. Some double that would have been although in the end they achieved neither. We were worse off because we had played two or three more games than most of the other teams involved in the relegation dog fight so, when Kelly's header from Sheedy's left wing cross hit the net, scored incidentally in front of the Mackems at the Leazes End, it was to prove enough to win the game and move us three places clear of the relegation zone into 18th place. Relative safety it seemed but when we proceeded to lose the next five games on the bounce, including a 6-2 hammering at Molineux, we were back down into the bottom three, in a relegation position and with only two games left to save ourselves from a fate worse then death – and it would have been as bad as that!

20/04/92 – DERBY COUNTY v NEWCASTLE (4-1)

My first visit to the Baseball Ground was the fifth of those defeats I've just mentioned. Derby were on the verge of automatic promotion and there was added interest in the game with the meeting of Arthur Cox and Kevin Keegan, since it was Cox who had first brought Keegan to Tyneside back in 1982. Sime took his car today and with Dave, Ritchie and myself on board we arrived in town at 11.00am leaving plenty of time to locate a suitable hostelry. The Baseball Ground is virtually in the middle of nowhere. There's a railway line on one side which restricts access and, after walking for what seemed at least a mile round run down old factory buildings, we found a good chip shop, stuffed down a few chunky meat pies, and headed straight for a pub we'd spotted about four hundred yards behind the away supporters end. As usual it was heaving with Geordies, a fact that I always find amazing. The Geordies 'take over' numerous pubs on every away excursion but never has this happened when anyone comes to play in Newcastle. The locals must be thrilled at the business they can do. I'm sure it's even more profitable than they would do on New Years Eve, but it's a shame that sometimes some of us can't behave ourselves and the vandalising of fruit machines or even just tables and chairs by a very small minority is scandalous and inexcusable.

The match itself was one of the most 'memorable' I have ever seen for a number of reasons. The 4-1 scoreline in Derby's favour doesn't even begin to tell the full story, as I witnessed the most crass refereeing performance I had ever seen, but at the same time felt so proud to watch the performance put in by the players, notably David Kelly.

First of all Kevin Brock was sent off for a dubious handball which at worst was accidental, Derby scored from the resulting penalty. Next, Kevin Scott was shown the red card after Marco Gabbiadini had thrown himself to the ground as if he had been knocked down by a bus – shades of Roker Park in the Play Off semi-final in 1990. Steve Watson then made a horrendous error and so at half time we were 2-0 down facing a further 45 minutes with only nine men – not good. Incredibly Peacock pulled one back immediately after half-time to send us delirious. Could we pull off the impossible? For 10 minutes the nine men played above themselves and made Derby look foolish, but on the hour, when Liam O'Brien became the third Newcastle player to be dismissed, quickly followed by Terry McDermott being removed from the dug-out area, the task became an impossible one and Derby inevitably found enough space to add two further goals. Peacock and Kelly had run themselves into the ground, with the latter's display being the most committed and gutsy performance I have ever seen from anyone in a black and white shirt. At the end of the game he threw his shirt to the fans – a gesture that will never be forgotten, and one that endeared him to every Geordie heart that afternoon.

So who was the guilty man? His name was Brian Coddington and he simply couldn't relate to the game. He had absolutely no empathy with the players, was far too officious and used his position of authority to denigrate the good name of football. His name did crop up again in the news towards the end of 1993 when he was involved in an incident with 'Mr Blobby' who was alleged to have tripped him up and caused him a great deal of personal embarrassment. His 'retirement' from the Football League list at the end of the 1993/94 season said it all.

A final footnote on the game goes to the Derby supporter who was sitting in the stand not far from where we were. All through the game he was inciting us, actually all credit to him, and we got round to calling him a 'fat git' as he would rise from his seat, pot belly hanging out, in his yukky yellow, red and blue Derby away shirt to taunt us with jibes of relegation. He was loving it (having the Geordies in town always gives the home fans a chance to express themselves and don't they love it) and it was so nice that he (and Marco Gabbiadini) had to suffer second rate Endsleigh League football at the Baseball Ground for a further four seasons, until their eventual promotion in May 1996, while we basked in the glory of the Premier League – it just emphasises that foot-balling fortunes can turn right round at the drop of a hat.

25/04/92 – NEWCASTLE v PORTSMOUTH (1-0)

The worst thing about going into this game was that our fate wasn't entirely in our own hands. There were numerous permu-tations and if you studied the league table in detail you would drive yourself scatty by trying to work out what might happen: if Oxford win but lose their next game, if Plymouth only draw or if Brighton do this or that. 'If' was the key word and there were far too many of them for comfort.

If David Kelly hadn't already done enough to endear himself to all of Tyneside by virtue of his performance at Derby, his goal today, of such monumental and far reaching proportions, sealed a life-long affinity with Geordies all round the world. Yes it was that important and with it coming so late in the game the relief it brought was quite simply immeasurable.

02/05/92 – LEICESTER CITY v NEWCASTLE (1-2)

The day of destiny had arrived. Only 1,800 Geordies would be able to obtain tickets. As for me, I was lying on my bed at the Wembley International Hotel waiting for the evening's basketball finals to begin!

Leicester needed three points to stand any chance of automatic promotion and with our need for points self evident the tension must have been unbearable. Had I been up in Newcastle I don't think I could have stood listening to the radio commentary. Ritchie was the same, he couldn't get a ticket and ended up mowing the lawn halfway through the second half just to get away from it all. It was entirely understandable and with me being stuck in London I had no choice but to stick with the intermittent reports from *Sport on 5*. I suppose I could have opened a permanent telephone line through to Newcastle but that was an idea that never really appealed!

When Peacock opened the scoring in the first half I almost hit the roof and gave the bed springs such a hammering I wouldn't have been surprised if they have had to replace them. Come 4.40pm and there still had been no update so it had to mean it was still 1-0 and with the other results looking good, especially Plymouth's demise against Blackburn, we were safe if nothing changed. Suddenly the ecstasy turned to agony as news of a last minute equaliser for Leicester came through but almost immediately it was updated with another score flash, this time a winning goal, albeit an own goal, for Newcastle. I've never suffered like it before and would never want to go through the same ordeal again. To experience such totally contrasting feelings in such a short space of time was enough to drive you insane. Once the dust had settled it transpired that even if we hadn't scored the second goal in injury time we still would have stayed up. The players and supporters at Filbert Street didn't know that of course, and if I thought I was having a rough time then it must have been far worse for them.

The Leicester supporters couldn't stomach defeat, even if they had won Middlesbrough would have pipped them for second place, but that didn't stop them from rioting after the final whistle, which from all accounts was a very frightening and unpleasant experience. Looking back at the season we had just endured it makes you wonder whether pressure on players and supporters is worse when you're at the top of a division challenging for promotion, or at the bottom when you need points to avoid relegation. Having experienced both at close quarters I find it extremely hard to split the two, but if forced to I would have to conclude it's worse down at the bottom end.

I know it's easy to say now, but over the last few weeks of the season, when things looked really bleak, I never seriously thought about the possibility of relegation, indeed it rarely crossed my mind. It was almost as if I had subconsciously blocked it out of my mind, or perhaps it was just too scary a thought to contemplate. Strangely enough, I had the same feelings at the end of the 1995/96 season as we were faltering in our challenge for the Premiership title, only this time it was a case of never stopping believing that, come the end of the season, we would be Champions – and that was despite the defeats at Liverpool and Blackburn which led many Geordies to believe our dream was over. Sadly, on this occasion, it was not to be.

At least we could relax a week later and sit back and watch the inevitable demise of the Mackems at Wembley in the Cup Final. Can you imagine what it would have been like had they won and qualified for the European Cup Winners Cup? – it doesn't even bear thinking about.

I round off the season with the thought that Keegan had done what Sir John Hall had brought him to the club to achieve. It had been a tough yet rewarding last three months (probably the understatement of the year) and we were now well and truly set to lift off.

1991/92 – Season's Summary

League	P	W	D	L	F	A	Pts.	Pos.
	46	13	13	20	66	84	52	20th

Top Scorers		
Gavin Peacock	19
Andy Hunt	12
David Kelly	11

1992/93 – ELEVEN ON THE TROT

Y ou couldn't help but feel excited come 15th August. Keegan had brought such a transformation to the club that any lingering memories of the traumas of the 1991/92 season had long been washed away. We had invested wisely in three major summer signings, not necessarily big money buys but players who had both class and character. First there was the quintessential Barry Venison, a former Sunderland captain but more recently Liverpool reserves, then Paul Bracewell, League Championship winner with Everton in the 1980s and stolen from Sunderland during the summer because Bob Murray was too miserly to offer him a decent contract, and finally John Beresford, who ended up at St. James' Park after turning down Sheffield Wednesday and failing a medical when Liverpool were on the verge of signing him. You might have thought the signing of two former Roker heroes would not have gone down well with the Geordies but, maybe a little surprisingly, they were both welcomed with open arms and accorded a rousing Geordie reception.

This was to be the first season of the FA Premier League and being on the outside looking in was a very unenviable position. For a start at least 90% of the nation's media attention focussed on the Premier League, to the exclusion of virtually all other football, and the financial returns from being a member of this elite club were massive in comparison to the shallow waters of the Football League. Even worse was the fact that the Yorkshire media (television, radio and newspapers) afforded practically zero coverage of Newcastle. Promotion had to be a priority and the season ahead took on gigantic proportions, almost to the extent of being seen as win or bust.

It was also to be the season when the 'Toon Army' came to prominence on a nation-wide basis. The origin of the word 'Toon' comes from the Geordie expression of 'going into town', i.e. Newcastle, and the local dialect which pronounces the word town as 'Toon'. All Geordies view Newcastle simply as the 'Toon' and so it was therefore a natural progression to become the 'Toon Army' and the most famous group of travelling supporters in the land.

The 1992/93 season proved to be packed full of so many highlights that I could virtually write a chapter about every single game we played. So, at the risk of missing out the odd little incident, here is an attempt to pick out the salient features of a season which was just one big roller coaster ride – exhilarating from start to finish.

22/08/92 – DERBY COUNTY v NEWCASTLE (1-2)

A somewhat scrappy 3-2 home win over Southend had heralded the start of the new season in front of a good crowd of 28,000. A visit to Derby County's Baseball Ground would prove a sterner test especially with the Rams having been installed as the pre season promotion favourites by the bookies. When we arrived at the ground it was impossible not to cast your mind back only four months to that fateful April day when it looked for all the world that relegation was the only 'prize' awaiting us. On that occasion at least we had had the backing of 5,000 plus supporters but today, Derby, in their wisdom, had cut our allocation to under 3,000 and worse still moved us from behind the goal to a horrible trench like area on the side of the pitch. Not to be outdone though, the backing the team received was once again second to none and when the lads left the field with a 2-1 victory under their belts, apart from feeling immensely satisfied, I knew that we were really going places this season.

Three weeks later, in front of a vibrant crowd at St. James' Park, a 3-1 defeat of Portsmouth took us to the summit, six wins from six and a maximum 18 points in the bag. You might think it strange to find it took six matches to reach the top of the table but it was only due to other teams in the division having played more games than us. We had missed out on two fixtures by virtue of having to play in the first round of the League Cup – punishment for our lowly finishing position in the league the previous season.

26/09/92 – PETERBOROUGH UNITED v NEWCASTLE (0-1)

I'd gone to Peterborough back in October 1991 to see our demise in the League Cup competition, Justin Fashanu and all, but this was something else. Conveniently Angus was working in Peterborough and so we all descended on him on the Friday evening. Driving down the A1 with Ritchie and Jim we came across the team bus and were delighted to get a wave from Terry McDermott when we deliberately drove in front of the bus and made our presence known – it's little things like this that make the world go round!

The Toon Army were out in force and as it wasn't designated as an all ticket game, Peterborough obviously thinking they would be 'quids in', no less than 8,000 Geordies descended upon London Road. As we were early we found a nice pub on the main road right at the top of the ground – an ideal location and soon to be filled to overflowing. Harry Palmer, a Tyneside guitar playing lyricist (club entertainer) was just coming to prominence for following the Toon Army around and entertaining the fans with little ditties mainly relating to old football songs. Such classics as 'Terry Hibbitt on the wing' were plucked out of the archives and he became so popular that a compilation tape was regularly played on match days at St. James' Park. He even graduated to a national audience when Radio 5 did a special feature on him and, although he could never be described as exceptionally talented, he became a cult figure and will rightly take his place in Geordie folklore history when the 1992/93 season is looked back on in the future.

The level of noise generated by the Geordies at away games is often greater than at St. James' Park, (except on special occasions when the whole ground, and I mean every single supporter, is up on his or her feet making enough noise to shatter all previously recorded decibel levels). Away trips though, for a variety of reasons, generally make you sing louder and longer and anyone who hasn't enjoyed the unique pleasure of travelling away with the Toon Army simply hasn't lived. Speaking of away trips, those Geordies who travelled to Italy to watch the lads play in the 'meaningless' Anglo Italian Cup ties can only be described as a rare breed and I for one take my hat off to every single one of them.

Kevin Sheedy scored the only goal of the game to make it eight straight wins, but my abiding memory of the game was walking away from the ground after the match and seeing thousands of black and white clad supporters streaming over the bridge outside the ground. It was an incredible sight and the good folk of Peterborough were simply unable to comprehend what was going on around them.

07/10/92 – MIDDLESBROUGH v NEWCASTLE (1-3)

The first of two derby matches within the space of 11 days. The Middlesbrough game was a second leg tie in the League Cup and, with the first leg at St. James' Park having finished goalless,

Premier Division Boro' were supposedly the favourites to progress in the competition. Ayresome Park had not been a happy hunting ground for us in recent seasons but that didn't stop the Geordies turning out in force. After David Kelly opened the scoring towards the end of the first half I'll never forget the enthusiasm with which the 'Blaydon Races' was sung – as loud as I can ever recall. It was magic and although Boro' equalised in the second half two further goals, from O'Brien and Kelly again, sealed an impressive 3-1 victory. In the next round at Chelsea I don't think the Londoners could believe it when they saw the huge number of Geordies piling off the buses outside Stamford Bridge for a Wednesday night fixture and it was a bitter disappointment to go on to lose the game 2-1.

Fanzines were now well established in the football world and Newcastle supporters are especially fortunate to have a good number of high quality publications in circulation, certainly they do a tremendous service to the game. As well as being terrifically witty and irreverent they deal with the real issues of the game and appeal to the 'real' supporters. The Newcastle fanzines are for ever taking the mickey out of both Middlesbrough and Sunderland and the issues covering these two games were full of such material. All credit to the editorial teams of the various publications for providing an invaluable service to the likes of people like me.

18/10/92 – SUNDERLAND v NEWCASTLE (1-2)

The Mackems were desperate to put an end to our winning run, but Willy Wonka (Malcolm Crosby), who was Chairman Bob Murray's puppet, and his team of 'has beens' and 'never will be's' never stood a chance. All that needs to be said is: 'free kick, O'Brien over the ball, O'Brien strikes it, Carter, flatfooted and floundering, ball hits the back of net, equals eruption in Roker End and 11 out of 11'.

Grimsby Town put an end to dreams of re-writing every record in the book by winning at St. James' Park the following week. Our brilliant start, 11 straight wins, had to give some time and no one really begrudged Grimsby their victory even though it took a last minute goal to win the game. This was the first home game which had been designated all ticket – inevitable really since at the last home match with Tranmere the gates had had to be locked more than half an hour before kick off with in excess of 7,000 locked out. Quite simply, the ground wasn't big enough to hold every-body who wanted to see the Toon play.

Talking of new stadiums the plans to rebuild the Leazes End at the end of the season were exciting. Certainly the artist's sketches had looked pretty impressive, and with the Gallowgate End following suit in 1994, we were going to have a stadium to match the very best in Britain – a mini Maracana in my opinion with its cantilever stands fully enclosing the whole ground. When the European Championships were played in the summer of 1996 I'm sure the Bulgarians, French and Romanians were thrilled at being drawn in the North East group and really savoured the pleasure of playing at St. James' Park.

Before its final re-development, St. James' Park could have become a thing of the past as Sir John Hall had floated the idea of building a brand new stadium near the Metro Centre in Gateshead, but this was a vision not shared by any of the support-ers who wouldn't watch Newcastle United play anywhere but St. James' Park. There were also grandiose schemes going as far back as the 1960s to re-develop St. James' Park into a super stadium, but although we've had to wait a long time for it, the new St. James' Park is a magnificent monument for every Geordie to be proud of and make pilgrimage to. I realise I'm probably getting a bit carried away here but I'm devoted enough to even think of it as the mecca of world football, and that just about sums up what the club means to me.

On the other side of the fence of course is Roker Park which is as run down now as St. James' Park was in the early 1980s. The Mackems had visions of a super stadium in Washington but failed to obtain the permission of Japanese car giants Nissan to build on land adjacent to their plant. That permission was about as likely to be granted as a statue of Bobby Shinton or Rob McDonald being erected in Newcastle City Centre. The whole exercise was a public relations disaster but now that they are committed to a new site at Monkwearmouth, the Mackems may at last have something to look forward to – someone should tell them that they will need a few decent players on the park unless they will remain living in fantasy land for eternity.

20/12/92 – NEWCASTLE v MILLWALL (1-1)

I was home once again for Christmas and after a morning in church, listening intently to one of Dad's sermons and, at the same time, praying for a good result later in the afternoon, I got dressed for the match. For the first time ever I put on a shirt and tie to go to the match. Why? Well I was to be the guest of one of our church members, Alan Ross, who also happened to be the sponsorship manager for Newcastle Breweries and replica shirts were not permitted in the Executive Box areas. Dad had been with him earlier in the season, to the scoreless Middlesbrough game in the League Cup, had thoroughly enjoyed himself and fixed this special treat for me. Everything was different, I drove the two of us in and parked my car in the confines of the ground in a reserved parking spot and it was almost as if I was one of the players arriving for the game. I was ushered into the ground through the main entrance, again a first, and up into the hospitality boxes at the top of the Milburn Stand. Naturally we headed for Newcastle Breweries own private box, passing Sir John Hall's luxurious box on the way, and proceeded to have a good meal in more than comfortable surroundings. The view was terrific and looking down at the rest of the ground just before kick off I could even spot the lads on the terraces below. It was the sort of experience I'd never had before, and when Sir John Hall, along with club Chief Executive Freddie Fletcher came into the box to say a few words, I found myself in exalted company. Alan actually had two seats in the Directors' Box itself, so rather than watch the game from behind the glass windows it was a much better option to move out into the Directors' Box. This was totally beyond my wildest dreams and who should be sitting just in front of me – none other than Gordon McKeag. The game itself was no great shakes and ended in a disappointing 1-1 draw thanks to a second half equaliser from a David Kelly penalty.

And that was it really, a whole new ball game as far as I was concerned. Enjoyable? Yes very much so – but just as a one off. Strange as it may seem I wouldn't want to be afforded V.I.P. treatment every week – give me a spot on the terraces with the lads any time.

Later in the season Newcastle earned a marvellous 2-1 victory at Millwall's Den which, perhaps more than any other result, confirmed our right to the Championship. After that match a number of Geordies were subjected to despicable and terrifying physical abuse by the hardcore of the Millwall hooligan element and when I heard of the trouble that had occurred after Millwall's play off fixture with Derby County in May 1994, I really felt for the genuine Derby supporters as they left the ground (The New Den, as opposed to the old ground) after the match. A final word on Millwall concerns the time back in 1978 when John went to see Newcastle play at The Den. It was the opening fixture of our first season in Division Two after relegation and our first visit to Millwall for a number of years. Not many away supporters went to The Den in those days, for fear of violence, and come 15 minutes before the start there was only a sprinkling of Geordies in the ground which of course didn't look very good. However, when thousands of Geordies poured into the ground virtually at kick off time, no doubt from the local hostelries, the Millwall supporters applauded the Geordies for such a good turn out – I'm sure that's where the good feeling stopped though!

02/01/93 – NEWCASTLE v PORT VALE (4-0)

An emphatic 4-0 FA Cup victory and a match that I should have been at but, due to circumstances beyond my control, wasn't. An explanation is due and it all revolved around another skiing holiday. We'd all gone off to Val Thorens in France the previous Saturday, safe in the knowledge that the return flight was due to touch down in Newcastle at 10.45 on the morning of the Port Vale game. As we only lived a couple of miles from the Airport there would obviously be time to nip home, say hello to Mum and Dad, before shooting off to the match – well you had to get your priorities the right way round.

We were flying from Geneva and arrived there in plenty of time for the early morning flight having left the resort at three in the morning. That's when things started to go wrong. The travel company 'rep' did a runner and it was soon clear why. We found out to our horror that the flight arrangements had been well and truly cocked up and we weren't due to fly for another six hours! We worked out that we would still arrive home at 3.45pm so we could still race into town for the second half, but as time passed even that possibility evaporated as delay after delay was announced and it wasn't until 5.30pm that we finally touched down on Tyneside. Even that was a little dodgy as the pilot had apparently handed over the controls to the co-pilot who almost put down on the grass verge rather than the runway! I should know as I was looking out of the windows wondering exactly what was going on. I rushed through to the baggage reclaim area, found a pay phone and let out a mighty roar when Mum told me the score. At least the day had ended on a high note, certainly hanging around Geneva Airport knowing the Toon were about to step out at St. James' Park was a none too enjoyable experience.

A quick word on the actual skiing, we'd all brought over our new 'Toon Army' hats and wore them proudly on the slopes of Val Thorens and of course the black and white shirts were given a good airing in the evening. Strangely enough we didn't see any other football clothing being displayed by any other skiers during the week – perhaps it was only the Toon Army who were daft enough to do so. On the other hand summer holidays abroad always bring the football shirt to prominence, and from what I've heard the black and white stripes are more visible than any other, and there are no prizes for guessing why either.

23/01/93 – ROTHERHAM UNITED v NEWCASTLE (1-1)

An FA Cup fourth round tie at Millmoor wasn't a bad draw. What was unacceptable was the way Rotherham, and in particular their secretary, a Mr. Darnill, treated us. Knowing that thousands of Geordies would travel to South Yorkshire they raised the price of terrace tickets for us only, while keeping the price down for their own supporters. It was sheer exploitation and the popular chant from the Geordies all throughout the game was 'You greedy Yorkshire B*******', which of course they were. Mr. Darnill further infuriated the Tyneside public by the comments he made in trying to justify his action – as he couldn't possibly do so, he ended up just digging himself further into the mire.

Dave, Sime and Ritchie came down from Newcastle and picked me up in Leeds before continuing the journey to Rotherham. They all had tickets, I didn't, but was confident I'd be able to pick one up outside the ground at a reasonable price. It was easier said than done and eventually I had to resort to paying £15 for a place in the Rotherham End. There must have been nigh on 50 of us in there and the police put us all in one corner of the terrace, separated from the home fans only by a piece of plastic tape. Needless to say about 15 minutes before kick off feelings got a ittle out of hand, both sides to blame I suppose, and the only course of action was to vacate the terrace and walk down the side of the pitch to the Newcastle end. I'm sure you would have done the same if you had been faced with a load of demented Rotherham miners charging at you with only one thing on their minds. Still it was all a bit of fun. I was then fortunate to spot the rest of the lads at the back of the terrace and so happily joined up with them again. After the game, a 1-1 draw, we were walking back to the car when one of those little 'hopper' buses went past with Rotherham supporters in the back seat making rather rude gestures towards us. Unhappily for them traffic congestion caused the bus to slow which immediately prompted a couple of Newcastle loonies to pull open the emergency door on the bus, pile in, and start wading into the Rotherham supporters. Violence of this type can never be condoned, but the way it happened was rather amusing at the time.

We polished off Rotherham 2-0 in the replay at St. James' Park 10 days later which left us with the unenviable task of having to go to high flying Blackburn Rovers in round five. Ritchie had gone to St. James' Park shortly after 6.00 in the morning to get our tickets but with the ticket office not due to open for another four hours he couldn't believe it when he saw 'Sold Out' signs at the main gates. Surely there was a mistake but no, it transpired that supporters, once again gripped by Cup fever, had begun queuing the previous night and when police reported that the queues had reached gigantic proportions by as early as three in the morning, they advised the club officials that it would be a prudent move to open the ticket office there and then. This they did and all the tickets were snapped up before 5.00am. No surprise really. I should have talked Ritchie into going in the night before to start queuing. As it happened Blackburn beat us 1-0 with the goal which broke every Geordie's heart coming, agonisingly, in the last minute. Well, at least we could now trot out the familiar excuse of saying we could now concentrate all our efforts on the league.

A word on Blackburn Rovers who have risen to prominence in the past few seasons, culminating in winning the Premiership title in May 1995, largely through the millions of pounds put into the club by Jack Walker and also of course the management skills of Kenny Dalglish. Whilst they may be a top level club by virtue of their position in the league, I cannot include them in the big club category, despite their long history, purely because they don't have the support (in numbers or fanaticism) – an essential element in this respect. Even the Mackems are a bigger club than Blackburn!

13/03/93 – SWINDON TOWN v NEWCASTLE (2-1)

The fact that we lost this match was pretty insignificant because it marked the first appearance in a black and white shirt of Andy Cole.

During the week Dave had phoned me at the office to tell me we had just paid £1.75 million for a player from Bristol City. I knew a bit about him but must confess that at the time I was a little sceptical and thought it was an awful lot of money to spend on a relatively unknown and unproven talent. How wrong I was. Cole knocked in 12 goals in the run in, virtually clinched our promotion single handed (on reflection that's not a fair comment because all the team played their part) and endeared himself to every Geordie in a manner no one had done since Keegan himself was a player at the club. The adulation he would go on to receive would be phenomenal and once again Keegan had come up trumps in the transfer market. It was a dream move for the player, the club and the supporters.

Back to matters on the pitch and our form since Christmas had been a little patchy and the massive 15 point lead we had established had been eaten into by Portsmouth and West Ham. There had been some more marvellous moments though: a superb 3-0 win at Tranmere in front of a live ITV television audience and a wonder goal by Robert Lee against Brentford, scored from inside his own half, which was disallowed by the referee as he brought play back in order to give a free kick to Newcastle!

In the weeks to come Barnsley would be dismantled 6-0 at St. James' Park (three more goals for Cole) and Cambridge United torn apart 3-0 at the Abbey Stadium. Around about this time I would have privately settled for promotion alone, that is a finishing position of either first or second such was the desire to get into the Premier League, however as the season's end drew nearer I realised how much it would mean to actually round the season off in style by taking what our efforts throughout the season had merited – the First Division Championship Trophy.

25/04/93 – NEWCASTLE v SUNDERLAND (1-0)

The Toon flying high, the Mackems staring relegation in the face – what a perfect time to play a derby match. Well almost perfect, if it hadn't been for the monsoon conditions which left ridiculous amounts of surface water on the pitch. Of course it affected the flow of the game but thankfully it never reached a farcical stage. There was only ever one side going to win and it was surprising it was only by a one goal margin. Having won at Roker Park back in October with a stupendous Liam O'Brien free kick it was another such effort, this time from the silky left foot of Scott Sellars, that condemned the Mackems to defeat. I don't know what gave me more pleasure, the ground reverberating to 'Championi' (Italian lingo for Champions!) or 'Terry Butcher on the dole'. Butcher was Sunderland's beleagured manager and the cry was in anticipation of his imminent, or so we hoped, sacking. It was such a tremendous occasion and must go down in the annals of Mackem taunting history.

This fixture was also one of the first where our giant flag appeared in the East Stand. It was a magnificent creation, with the words 'Toon Army' and 'Champions 1992/93' emblazoned on it, it was a dazzling and spectacular sight. The flag would be passed overhead along the whole length of the stand and looking at it from a distance it made you swell with Geordie pride. If we thought this flag was something special, the new enlarged version that would herald the start of the 1993/94 season would take our breath away, such was its sheer splendour.

04/05/93 – GRIMSBY TOWN v NEWCASTLE (0-2)

Promotion could have been clinched the previous weekend, without us even playing. If West Ham had failed to win at Swindon it would have been enough, but the Hammers did win and in a way I think we were all pretty pleased as it would make Tuesday's trip to Grimsby more worthwhile.

On the Saturday of the aforementioned Swindon fixture my work had actually taken me to Wembley Arena for the end-of-season basketball finals. I'd arrived on the Friday afternoon and after checking into the Wembley International Hotel, adjacent to the stadium, I decided to go for a training run around the Wembley complex as it was a pleasantly warm May afternoon. Had someone told me what was to be in store for me I would have never have believed them! You know my feelings about Wembley so obviously I headed straight for the stadium, just to enjoy the pleasure of running around its outer confines. The Rugby League Cup Final was due to be played the next day and as I reached the tunnel end I noticed that the large fortress like doors were open, for the benefit of the various contractors who were putting up advertising signs and the like, and I could see right up the tunnel and into the stadium. That was a sight in itself but I then hit upon the idea of asking the security guard at the entrance if I could walk up the tunnel to take a little peek inside. I was only wearing a T-shirt and shorts so without looking entirely respectable I could never be thought of as a potential security risk. My heart missed a beat when he agreed to my request and I began the walk up the tunnel almost overcome with emotion, incredible really, and almost not believing this was actually happening to me. I walked past the dressing rooms, one on either side, and pretending I was about to walk out on to the pitch for the FA Cup Final, slowly made my way up the tunnel. Suddenly the sunshine hit me and I walked spellbound into the stadium itself, across the sand track until I reached pitchside. That was as far as I could go as, with people working all around me, I could hardly continue walking onto the pitch. Thankfully no one asked any questions and so I took the opportunity to walk around the whole pitch just looking up at the stands. As I did, I was in virtual dreamland and was to savour the moment like none before. I actually stayed in the stadium for at least an hour, just standing and staring around the place. It was a day I'll remember for the rest of my life and how I managed to drag myself back to the hotel I'll never know.

On a previous visit to Wembley for basketball back in 1985, a few of us had gone to watch the greyhound racing the night before our games took place. We dined in the main restaurant overlooking the track whilst placing our bets, what style, and although I didn't have any winners it was still a very gratifying evening. Things were rounded off perfectly when I found I was able to take the opportunity of stepping out of the restaurant into the Royal Box and seeing exactly where the Queen sat on Cup Final day – there is no doubt she has the best seat in the house!

During the basketball matches on Sunday afternoon, the only thing I wanted to know was the score from the County Ground. I managed to get a half-time update from one of my press friends (thanks to Nic Harling of *The Times*) but then, much to my consternation, couldn't find anyone to give me a final score at the end of the game. Imagine my frustration at wandering around Wembley Arena, desperately trying to find out whether our season's dream had been achieved. Then, right out of the blue, I spotted two lads walking around the concourse wearing black and white striped shirts! It's said Newcastle supporters can be found in all corners of the world but to find a couple of lads in these circumstances made me feel as if some sort of magical force had brought them especially to Wembley to see me! Anyway I made a beeline for them and immediately asked them the vital question; no need for any polite introductions. As I've said, finding out the answer was initially disappointing but what a week was now in store.

Grimsby's Blundell Park, as you probably know, is actually in Cleethorpes and my previous visits to this ground, usually on Boxing Day or New Year's Day during the dark days of Division Two back in the late 1970s and early 1980s, were not exactly filled with many good memories.

The game had been switched from the Bank Holiday weekend to the Tuesday night as the home club were concerned about the number of Geordies likely to descend on their patch. They certainly had cause for concern but there was never going to be any trouble on this occasion. The official ticket allocation was 3,000 for a ground capacity of 12,000, however that didn't stop 8,000 plus Geordies hitting the road. I'd made plans to meet Richie at Ferrybridge Services, having got our two tickets only the previous day from a friend of the family, Les Donald. Naturally we would have gone ticketless, as indeed many did. We didn't arrive at the ground until about an hour before the start but by then it was clear that many of our fellow supporters had been in Cleethorpes since early morning making a day of it. The whole area was a seething mass of black and white and many fans were also sporting the natty new blue Asics away strip.

Chippies were overflowing and, needless to say, the local pubs and clubs had their best day's business for a long time, if not ever. If there were any home supporters around we didn't see them, which isn't untypical when the Geordies play away at relatively small clubs (i.e. the majority of English League clubs). Our seats were in the quaintly named Findus Family Stand, normally filled by home supporters, but tonight contained an amazingly high proportion of Geordies. The Grimsby supporters we were sitting next to welcomed us with open arms, except for one rather mean looking individual who was rather irritated by our presence. They were pleased to be involved in such a big match and were totally in awe of both the numbers and noise of the Geordies in the ground. Our seats afforded us a view to a number of trawlers at work out in the North Sea and I remember thinking, rather oddly, of that famous Geordie folksong 'When the boat comes in' and trying to make it become some sort of omen for the match ahead.

Three points would give us the Championship but by half-time a blank scoresheet was all that had transpired. Straight after the resumption came our salvation. Robert Lee went on a mazy dribble and released Andy Cole, still something of an unknown quantity at this time, to slot the ball past Rhys Wilmot. Pandemonium ensued and it's hard to recall as joyous a celebration. I've always thought I was so lucky to be born a Geordie and this was one of those occasions I'll never forget. Supporters of other teams simply can't generate the same sort of passion and feeling for their team, and when David Kelly clinched our 2-0 victory in the dying minutes, our day was complete. Needless to say the ritual lap of honour followed and it was a good 45 minutes after the final whistle had blown that we eventually left the ground in a state of delirious and unbounded happiness.

The journey home, amid a mass of trailing scarves, tooting horns and joyous faces, went a long way to leaving behind those distant memories of driving grimly home from Grimsby on a cold winter evening after yet another away defeat. Some Geordies even stayed the night in Cleethorpes and revisited the scene of our triumph again in the morning before making their way back to the North East. We stopped at Ferrybridge and made straight for a pay phone to give Dave a ring. We knew he was going to watch the highlights on television later in the evening and didn't want to know the score in advance but we just couldn't resist calling him as we were in a totally euphoric mood. He wasn't best pleased, but I'm sure fully understood!

09/05/93 – NEWCASTLE v LEICESTER CITY (7-1)

Three days previously Oxford United had been despatched 2-1 at St. James' Park in a match that had turned into a total anti-climax, but this day would surely be different. Myself and 30,000 Geordies weren't to be disappointed.

The first problem to be solved was obtaining a ticket. In the days leading up to the match all attempts had brought no joy, however, I left home for the match as usual with the lads determined that I'd get into the ground by whatever means and whatever cost. Two hours before the kick off the lads went off for the habitual pre-match drinking session at the North Terrace while I headed straight to the ground to find a way of getting in. This match was more than just your typical end-of-season fixture; a carnival atmosphere was promised, the Geordie folk group Lindisfarne were playing live and the Championship Trophy was to be presented just before kick off – the football would just be incidental – or would it?

Come 1.30pm I was still frustratingly outside the ground as at least 10 attempts to slip a turnstile operator a large sum of money (instead of the required ticket) had failed miserably. All credit to the operators for refusing my offer, which I know would have only ended up in their pockets. Security at the ground was such that any unauthorised entry was out of the question, which reminded me of those occasions in the early 1970s when I regularly watched people scaling the walls at the Gallowgate End to attempt to slip unnoticed into the ground. Not all of them were successful of course and the unlucky ones were quickly frog-marched to the police detention cells in the south east corner of the ground. I often wondered what the conditions were like inside, but fortunately never got the chance to find out. At the beginning of 1996, in time for the European Championship matches being played at St. James' Park, a new 'mini' Police Station was opened at the ground which housed a computerised custody suite, apparently one of the most modern in the whole of Europe. Let's hope it doesn't get used much, if at all, on match days at St. James' Park.

As 2.00pm approached it was clear a new strategy was required. Could I find a ticket tout somewhere? A quick visit to a handful of local public houses proved fruitless before I hit the jackpot when I found a Newcastle supporter outside the Leicester end of the ground with two tickets for sale for the Leicester section. Not ideal, but I snapped one of them up instantly at the remarkably cheap price of £10 (face value £7.50) as it would at least give me access to the ground. Not unnaturally I wasn't the only home supporter in this section of the ground but there was never going to be any sort of aggro inside (despite some recent cases of trouble between the two sets of supporters) due to the nature of the occasion. Leicester's supporters had already seen their side clinch a Play-Off place and had come to Tyneside more for an enjoyable day out rather than the essential nature of seeing their team win. As often happens on these occasions the home fans were moved to the adjoining section which caused it to be somewhat overfull, but not dangerously so, and everyone seemed happy enough about it.

And so to the afternoon's entertainment. Lindisfarne trotted out their classic oldies such as 'Fog on the Tyne' which acted as a prelude to the team being presented with the Championship Trophy 15 minutes before the start of the game. This was the culmination of a magnificent season and the whole stadium (including the Leicester contingent) roared their appreciation to such an extent that every hair on your body stood up. I'd seen television pictures of Manchester United receiving the Premiership Trophy earlier in the week and the ensuing celebrations, but they were nothing compared to what I was witnessing now. The Reds had of course won a higher level competition than us so to be fair theirs was a greater achievement in comparison.

The game itself was almost incidental as it kicked off with no one really sure what to expect. Keegan had promised a great send off for the fans but even he couldn't have imagined what was to follow. Six magnificent first half goals, all for Newcastle, sent the fans delirious and the atmosphere in the ground was possibly the best I can remember. Literally everyone, including those in seats, was standing and singing at the top of their voices and it was a truly remarkable sight. Perhaps the most memorable moment was the ovation and adulation accorded to Andy Cole with the 'Andy Cole Scores a Goal' song being launched at St. James' Park. You had to be there to see it and savour it and, despite only two more goals being added in the second half, one for each team, the season finished on an unbelievably high note.

The match also marked the first viewing of our new Asics strip. Our success had prompted the Japanese clothing manufacturers to take us on board as one of their teams and it proved also to be a very good deal financially for the club. While this fact wasn't necessarily uppermost in the eyes of the supporters, the new strip most certainly was. The traditional home shirt had reverted to equal size black and white stripes (as opposed to wide and narrow ones which I never liked) and with the blue star of Newcastle Breweries adorning the front it looked superb. I would say that at least nine out of every ten Geordies invested in the shirt which, as well as being a means of identification, was also a leisure shirt such was its design. The shops on Tyneside couldn't sell enough and over the summer it outsold every other strip in the country, providing massive profits for both Asics and the club. Later, in the 1993/94 season, the shirt was voted as the most fashion conscious in football by an independent panel and that was praise indeed. The away shirt was all blue with just a tinge of white and while not being quite as popular as the home shirt it was always very evident wherever the lads played. For the 1994/95 season the club market-ed a third strip, primarily green in colour, which was used on one occasion during the 1993/94 season (at Sheffield Wednesday) before being auctioned off apparently not to be seen of again! Of course it's going to help swell the coffers but really I cannot see the need for it and don't think it will prove to be too successful.

The following evening, the team, as is the norm on such occasions, drove through the city in an open top double decker bus to a special reception at the Civic Centre. Thousands lined the route and the bus was forced to move at a snail's pace, inevitably making the team late for the reception. Who cared? It was another marvellous night for the club, the city and, above all, the Geordie supporters who had waited so long for any sort of success. My generation in particular has been shabbily treated in respect of success – too young for the Fairs Cup triumph, lifted briefly by the Supermac and Keegan eras, but, with everything else in between being second rate.

1992/93 – Season's Summary

League	P	W	D	L	F	A	Pts.	Pos.
	46	29	9	8	92	38	96	1st

Top Scorers		
David Kelly	27
Gavin Peacock	16
Robert Lee	13

1993/94 – THE ENTERTAINERS

Having waited so long for a sniff of success, here we were ready to launch an assault on the Premier League with a first class team in a first class stadium to match (come 12 months' time and the completion of the Gallowgate stand, bar the two corner sections, and I'll be totally lost for words). I've said it before, but if anyone deserved success, and tangible at that, it was the Geordie public and the unparalleled enjoyment the season would bring would warm the cockles of your heart so that they burned inside you.

Being an exiled Geordie isn't exactly a bundle of fun. There are countless things you miss and without naming them all, the worst might just be living so far from St. James' Park. Like the previous season virtually every game would prove to be 'special', and one of the best things was actually knowing that when you went to a match you were guaranteed entertaining and exciting football. Even better you knew, as opposed to being hopeful, that we were strong favourites to win the game, and that's not something Newcastle supporters have been able to say for a long long time.

25/08/93 – NEWCASTLE v EVERTON (1-0)

Our fourth game of the season, but my first. Not an ideal situation of course, but brother John didn't mind as he travelled up from London on the first day of the season to use my season ticket for the opening fixture against Tottenham. Season tickets were like gold dust (I remember them being like that in the early 1970s for the old West Stand where the only way you could get one was either by having it passed down through the family or when someone died!) and with 30,000 being sold in the close season it also meant a tremendous amount of revenue for the club. In addition the 'Platinum Club' had been formed by Sir John Hall which, to tell you the truth, I would have thought very strongly about joining had I been resident on Tyneside. I would have had to find an initial outlay of £3,000 to have done so though, so perhaps that idea was just a pipe dream. The benefits of membership were very rewarding though, and as long as the average fan wasn't going to be priced out of attending matches then I see no reason for not having a thriving Platinum Club at St. James' Park. Incidentally, the stories that surfaced in 1995 and 1996, that some

Platinum Club members were selling their tickets for £6,000, were a disgrace, and a kick in the teeth for the real fans. At the end of the 1993/94 season plans were also announced for the formation of a bond scheme whereby supporters were invited to put forward £500 to give them a guaranteed right to buy a season ticket for the next 10 years, free home cup-tie tickets for the first three years and a further option to tickets for the remaining seven years. The club apparently hope to sell 10,000 bonds however I am not convinced it is the right thing for the club as the primary concern of many supporters is that it threatens to price out the ordinary fan, as well as children, who have always been the lifeblood of the club (especially in the dark days of Division Two). This is a really major worry, how would I have ever have begun my attachment to the club had this situation existed in 1969? I feel for the likes of the Watson children from our church in Ponteland who are just at the age I was when I started going regularly and appear to be as interested and devoted as I was all those years ago. It also means that some long term season ticket holders may not be guaranteed their ticket in years to come which again cannot be right – as for me, I've managed to re-locate to a seat in the new Gallowgate End stand with the rest of the lads so I can't really complain.

On the subject of season tickets, there was an amazing story, true and very amusing, that came to light as the season unfolded. Early in the season a supporter in the Leazes End found it very unusual that the seat next to him was never occupied. He enquired at the Ticket Office and they confirmed that the seat had been sold so there was no logical reason for it always being unoccupied. This situation continued up until Christmas and then suddenly, right out of the blue, a chap appeared in this mystery seat for the first game after Christmas. It transpired that the new-comer had been given the season ticket by his wife as a Christmas present, having bought it earlier in the year. And they say that women don't know anything about football!

Extra revenue for the club was also provided through the 'Club-Call' line which was so successful that Newcastle United were the first club in the country to top the £1 million mark in income generated through the supporters telephoning the club for news updates. On a Radio 5 football discussion programme the inimitable Alan Green jokingly said the Newcastle public must have been 'daft' to have kept calling in at 48p per minute, he didn't mean it as it sounds, but the remark does have an element of truth in it!

John was pretty unfortunate at first as in the first four matches he came up for, the Toon hadn't turned in a winning performance for him. Apart from Tottenham spoiling the party, Queen's Park Rangers, Manchester United and Southampton have all given him a frustrating time at St. James' Park. He broke his duck in grand style when Swindon came north and were sent packing on the wrong end of a 7-1 hammering. At least he's managed to celebrate our London victories in style.

Taking only one point from the first nine was something of a shaker, but it could all be explained away. The opening defeat against Tottenham proved too big an occasion for the players, even though we could have sneaked an equaliser right at the death, but losing to Coventry the following Wednesday was bitterly disappointing. We played well, lost goalkeeper Pavel Srnicek (for a professional foul), and one of our former strikers, Mick Harford, came back to haunt us with a late winner. Game three was at Old Trafford, home of the first FA Premier League Champions, and we gained a magnificent point which was to prove the real launching pad for the season. The team, and the Toon Army, silenced Old Trafford with outstanding levels of skill and passion, and that man Andy Cole opened his account for the season – what was to follow for Cole in the months ahead would be far beyond his wildest dreams.

Throughout the summer months I had seen the new Leazes End Stand take shape as it grew into the Newcastle sky line. Note I refer to it as the Leazes End, rather than the North (Sir John Hall) Stand, as indeed the Gallowgate End will always be the Gallowgate End rather than the South (Exhibition) Stand, it simply can't be called anything else. It looked imposing when it was still a shell but when the roof went on and it joined up with the Milburn and East Stands it looked absolutely awe inspiring. Magnificent doesn't do it justice, and with 11,000 Geordie season ticket holders packing it to the rafters every game, St. James' Park established itself as *the* ground to watch your football in this season.

It was nice also to be able to walk into St. James' Park through the main gates at the Leazes End of the ground and admire the large Newcastle United crest that was on the gate – just a small thing but it added to the atmosphere of the place. Later in the season the crest would also appear on the East Stand roof which again was a nice touch.

A new flag, at least three or four times as large as the old one, well last season's one, was unveiled before the game. Decorated with Magpie motifs and looking marvellously resplendent, it could now be passed round from the East Stand into the Leazes End where it could be seen in its full glory. Later in the season against Liverpool it even made its way round the Milburn Stand and into the Gallowgate End. It travels round the country as well, provided the home club has no objections, and with plans to produce an even larger one in the near future (goodness knows what size that will be) it's another example of how the Geordies never cease to amaze you, surpassing themselves with their devotion to the club. Let's just hope that the powers that be relax the 'flag ban' that they have introduced at the ground, as the sight of the flag in its full glory quite simply helps make St. James' Park the place it is – the best football arena in the country.

Everton came to Tyneside with a 100 per cent record from their opening three games and, in my eyes, have always been a decent footballing side. This was clearly an opinion I would need to revise after their next visit to Tyneside in February 1995. The pitch was in pristine condition and the best I had ever seen it. I play on pretty good pitches myself, but when I took a really close look at the surface it was immaculate although it was to deteriorate markedly as the season progressed. An hour or so before the game I was outside the Trent House at the back of the East Stand when the Everton supporters were being escorted by the police to the ground. The only thing they were chanting was 'Ever-ton, Ever-ton' which struck me as being as boring a chant imaginable – it transpired that during the game they couldn't come up with anything else either. No imagination these blue Scousers. As you would expect a good free flowing game ensued and, thanks to Tony Cottee hitting the Leazes End bar from inside the six yard box (I'll never believe how he missed), it was left to Malcolm Allen to shoot past Neville Southall for the decisive winning goal. We were on our way, and I for one was mighty relieved.

13/09/93 – NEWCASTLE v SHEFFIELD WEDNESDAY (4-2)

Monday Night Football, as the Sky Television executives billed it, even if the match was being played on a Tuesday or Wednesday night, was here to stay. With the satellite television company having bought the rights to the FA Premier League at the beginning of the 1992/93 season, it meant a live game virtually every

Sunday and Monday of the league season. Being a football nut I'd invested in my Sky dish earlier in the year and for those people who complain that football is being taken away from those with access only to the terrestrial channels, I've no sympathy. Life is full of choices, and I've chosen Sky as one of my companions.

Sky TV games are perfect for me as it means being able to play on the Saturday and watch the Toon all in the same weekend – a dream combination. It also means a chance to pop home as well to raid the larder! I was back in Newcastle shortly after 6.00pm and met the rest of the lads in the North Terrace, which has been our regular pre-match meeting point for a couple of years now. Before that it used to be the Whistle Stop in the Haymarket and then The George in the Bigg Market. We also occasionally frequent Inventions in the Haymarket, a pub famous for its caricatures of Beardsley, Clark and Cole on a Newcastle United chalk board.

This wasn't our first appearance on Sky, as we had been featured against Blackburn Rovers at St. James' Park two weeks earlier. That game though proved to be something of a damp squib, memorable only for the return from injury of Alan Shearer who scored the equalising goal minutes after appearing as a second half substitute. Sky Television do things in style. Their studio presentation is first class with the highly professional, smartly attired, Coventry City supporting front man Richard Keys being the ideal man for the job. First rate commentators, including Martin Tyler, bring a refined quality behind the micro-phone, summariser Andy Gray brings such an enthusiastic approach to the job that he is unrivalled in his role and really the only 'downer' about the presentation is reporter Nick Collins whose style I don't really care for. Sky's coverage of football also begins an hour before the game and this gives plenty of time for a full preview and an in-depth analysis of the game. I also particularly enjoy the last hour of the Sunday afternoon programme when Andy Gray and the studio guests analyse all the games and goals from the matches played the previous afternoon.

Another plus that Sky's coverage of football has brought is all the additional programmes during the week. *The Footballers Football Show* is a superb talk show, Andy Gray's *Bootroom* is a tactical fasci-nation, while the *Sky Soccer Weekend* and *Goals on Sunday* shows, hosted by the excellent Paul Dempsey and Anna Walker, are equivalent to BBC's *Football Focus* and *Match of the Day*. Me, I can't get enough of it. Throw in the top quality cricket, golf, basketball and tennis as well, and you can see why Sky Sports has just that little bit of appeal to me!

I couldn't believe it when the lads ran out onto the pitch in blue shirts, our change strip. Apparently Sheffield Wednesday couldn't provide a suitable strip (even though they had three to choose from) that wouldn't clash with our black and white stripes – at least according to referee Roger Dilkes anyway. It was scandalous that we were prevented from playing at St. James' Park in our traditional home colours, but as it turned out it didn't matter come the end of the evening. We were 2-1 down with only 14 minutes remaining, but after Andy Cole had equalised, reserve Scottish striker Alex Mathie, a second half substitute, scored a 'wonder goal' to give us the lead, and with Malcolm Allen wrapping things up in the final minutes it finished off a stirring comeback which set St. James' Park alight. Mathie's goal for some reason didn't even make those featured on the September Goal of the Month Competition which amazed me. Still it had been a fantastic night and I even managed a little cameo role in front of the roving Sky cameras at the end of the game as they focussed on the joyous fans. After quickly popping home I drove back to Leeds with a cassette tape of the game to listen to (Mum had kindly recorded it for me), and wasn't it just great to listen to the commentary knowing exactly when we were going to score and reliving every kick of the game. Back to my flat at about half an hour past midnight and I had no choice but to rewind the video and spend the next 90 minutes watching it all over again. What a game, what a day, what a life.

24/10/93 – SOUTHAMPTON v NEWCASTLE (2-1)

Newcastle United were setting the Premier League alight. The whole country had cottoned on to the fact that we were a top quality side and the season was fast becoming the most enjoyable I could remember as we went from strength to strength. Sky Television had taken a special liking to us and dubbed the team 'The Entertainers'. The Toon Army were becoming part of England's footballing culture, and Beardsley and Cole in particular were England's hottest striking partnership. Even training sessions at our Durham headquarters were watched by upwards of 3,000 supporters, such was the interest in the team and the desire of the Geordies to see their heroes in the flesh.

Attendances at the reserve team fixtures in the Pontins League also soared with the game against Sunderland almost reaching 10,000 – remarkable you might think but not unexpected, just proof if it was needed of how much the Geordies love their football.

Earlier in the month I was privileged to be at both Villa Park and Meadow Lane to see two away victories, both memorable in their own way, with the latter producing a sensational seven-goal haul for the Toon. For the game against Southampton the lads weren't able to get enough tickets so the crew, Nick, Ritchie, Dave and Sime, all descended upon my Leeds flat to watch the game. I can't imagine what my neighbours thought when their car screeched into the car park and four 'drunken' Geordie yobs (sorry lads!) piled out in their black and white shirts, arms full of cans of Newcastle Exhibition. I quickly ushered them inside without my reputation (a quiet unassuming lad!) being torn to shreds and we took our places in front of the television, all set for a football feast. As it turned out Southampton's Matthew Le Tissier scored two goals, the like of which he was well capable of, but likely to score maybe only once every two or three seasons (on reflection this statement has a hollow ring to it as he continued to score spectacular goals throughout the 1993/94 and 1994/95 seasons), and we ended up shell-shocked 2-1 losers. The lads left quietly and I was left to tidy up the 24 empty cans (yes, 24) which between three of them (Nick was driving) was some going, and that's not counting what they had had on the way down, or would be having on the way back. Personally, it's beyond me how people can consume so much alcohol.

In the build up to the match one of the guests in the Sky studio was the impressionist Mike Osman. If you haven't seen him I would thoroughly recommend him – his impersonations of Lawrie McMenemy and Peter Beardsley are absolutely brilliant. I was fortunate to see him 'live' at the Café Royal in London during a basketball function in 1991 and have held him in high regard ever since.

During the game at the Dell, Keegan had brought off young Lee Clark, a genuine potential Geordie superstar, as things had not been going too well on the field and it was felt a change was needed. Unfortunately Clark reacted petulantly, but after a public rollicking from Keegan and a few days of brooding he was welcomed back into the fold. Clark very much regretted his actions and offered profuse apologies to all concerned. After all, all he ever wanted to do was play his heart out for the Toon.

More internal turmoil hit the club full in the face the following Wednesday when Keegan dramatically left Cole out of the team for the League Cup tie at Wimbledon. It transpired that Cole had complained of feeling homesick prior to the game (a portent of things to come?) and Keegan, believing him to be in the wrong frame of mind, decided not to play him. The papers had a field day and, to my mind, overreacted and tried to sensationalise the dispute. With the Clark incident still bubbling it was a testing managerial situation for Keegan to deal with, and he could have done without the rash and idiotic speculation that both players might be leaving the club. I was sure that it was all a storm in a tea cup, and that Keegan would soon bring harmony back to the club, and I was delighted that this proved to be the case. Against Wimbledon in the League the following weekend Cole and Clark were loudly cheered when they took the field – you wouldn't really have expected anything else would you – and between them they helped demolish the Dons 4-0, albeit with just a little help from Peter Beardsley who notched a magnificent hat-trick.

Back to the League Cup tie and this was one of the rare occasions that I've 'watched' the game on Ceefax as I was unable to get the afternoon off work in order to travel down to London. If for whatever reason you're not able to get to a game, and radio commentary is unavailable, then Ceefax provides an interesting alternative. It's as up to date a service as you can get, and keeping your eyes glued to the screen is a very tense affair as you wait for score changes to suddenly appear on the screen. On this occasion the failure to get an equaliser as the second half minutes ticked by was infuriating.

08/11/93 – OLDHAM ATHLETIC v NEWCASTLE (1-3)

This was the first of two consecutive appearances on Sky with Liverpool's visit to St. James' Park coming up in two weeks' time. Boundary Park is only a 45 minute drive for me, which is ideal and, unusually, I ended up going by myself. The Blobbys were out in force together with the painted faces and black and white wig brigade. It was a real carnival atmosphere and a privilege to have been there. The performance the lads produced was sensational – 19 shots on goal (according to the Sky statistics I saw later in the evening) and the 3-1 victory was as comprehensive as you could wish to see – absolutely brilliant.

Some flurries of snow greeted Liverpool's arrival at St. James' Park. It was a cold winter's day and the Reds would end up wishing they had never left home. An Andy Cole hat-trick inside the first 30 minutes sent the Geordies into total ecstasy – at long last the ghost of Anfield had been exorcised. I know Liverpool aren't quite the force they were throughout the 1970s and 1980s, but they are still the bench mark against which to measure your progress and that's what made the victory, or should I call it annihilation, so sweet. Peter Beardsley's influence on the game was also highly instrumental, and the way he mesmerised Liverpool's Neil Ruddock for the whole 90 minutes was particularly poignant as it was Ruddock who had been involved in the incident that had shattered Beardsley's cheek bone in a pre-season friendly at Anfield which resulted in him missing the first seven league fixtures of the campaign. Needless to say Ruddock also suffered mercilessly, and deservedly so, at the hands of the St. James' Park crowd. It goes without saying that I was truly elated on the day Beardsley re-joined Newcastle from Everton in the summer, my admiration for his talent is second to none and I've even got a Peter Beardsley calendar hanging in my office at work!

It was only a shame that we didn't add to our tally in the second half. Certainly the performance merited it, but it didn't stop Andy Gray from eulogising over the Newcastle display during the game and later in the week in his *Bootroom* programme.

22/12/93 – NEWCASTLE v LEEDS UNITED (1-1)

The big games just kept on coming at St. James' Park. Manchester United had already been earlier in the month, a match that none of the lads had seen as they had all been at Angus's wedding. Fancy getting married in the middle of the football season, I mean how inconsiderate! (only joking Angus, but at least choose a day when the Toon aren't playing. Hally, for example, got married on a Friday in Northallerton which showed great foresight!). As for me I had a different sort of predicament: to go to the wedding or play for Yorkshire Amateurs in a crucial FA Vase game. I chose the latter purely because it was such a big game; obviously it wouldn't have mattered missing a normal league game and I must thank Angus as well for being so understanding of my decision to miss his big day.

The Leeds fixture had been brought forward from Boxing Day, which made sense as it would help to ease the fixture congestion over the holiday period. Quite frankly Leeds were boring and dirty. Only McAllister stood out, and all I can say is thank goodness Andy Cole managed a late equaliser to prevent Leeds stealing the points. I was pleased Howard Wilkinson wasn't going to get the England job, long ball men never change their spots and it would have been a backward step for the FA to have appointed another Graham Taylor clone. Speaking of the England job, Kevin Keegan was many people's favourite to be given the huge responsibility of managing the national team. Yes he would have been a good appointment, but with every Geordie urging him to remain on Tyneside, Keegan gladly committed his immediate future to Newcastle United. There's no doubt though that his time will come, but only if he wants it. In the meantime, Terry Venables, the popular choice for the vast majority of English football fans despite the fact that, like his predecessors, was never absolutely sure what his best eleven was, did a splendid job even though he felt it necessary to resign at the end of the 1996 European Championships.

09/02/94 – LUTON TOWN v NEWCASTLE (2-0)

Our third meeting with the Hatters in the FA Cup and coincidentally all had been at the fourth round stage. After a 1-1 draw at St. James' Park, on a rapidly deteriorating pitch (it was relaid before the start of the 1994/95 season) which doesn't do anything to assist our free flowing passing game style, I went down to Luton as confident as ever. As is the case these days when you return to a ground you haven't been to for a while you find it's all change, with new stands shooting up everywhere. Kenilworth Road was no different and we found ourselves seated in a nice little stand behind the goal. It was a bit too small to fully unfurl the flag but nevertheless afforded us a good view, even though the seats themselves were a little on the small size – a classic case of a club implementing the Taylor Report 'on the cheap'.

It was one of those games where after only 10 or 15 minutes I got the horrible feeling that we weren't going to score. It's difficult to explain but it's just one of those gut feelings that I'm sure all football fans experience at one time or another. Despite the constant chanting of 'Toon Toon, Black and White Army', the latest 'in' song, my worst fears materialised and we crashed out of the Cup, eventually losing 2-0. It was incredible that we were actually installed as second favourites for the competition as early as the third round, and I bet none of you can remember when that last happened, if indeed it ever has.

This defeat was a disaster (relatively speaking of course), nothing more – nothing less. Coupled with the league defeats last time out against Southampton, and the following weekend at Wimbledon, we were in something of a mini crisis, especially as Keegan had had to discipline club captain Barry Venison, Steve Howey and Alex Mathie for a spot of unauthorised drinking in a Bournemouth wine bar before the Wimbledon game. Mention of the game at Selhurst Park leads me to mention Justin Fashanu who had recently been sacked by Hearts, possibly for alleged mis- demeanours with a Conservative M.P. As his brother John played for Wimbledon he was subjected to taunts of 'You'll only score with your brother' which, although a little cruel, were largely good humoured.

This was the time to stand up and be counted and that applied in particular to the supporters. It was sad, and distressing, to hear a very small minority abusing the team and booing. Short mem- ories they have. It appears they don't seem to appreciate what gigantic steps the club has taken since division three was staring us in the face only two years earlier, and the message has got to be to get behind the team at all times. I am as genuinely disappointed as anyone when we don't perform, but I'm not foolish enough to unjustly criticise the team. Occupying fourth place in the Premiership, as we did today, is an unbelievable achievement considering where we've been for the past five years. I know we all desperately want to reach the top, and we will, but it's not going to be achieved overnight.

12/03/94 – NEWCASTLE v SWINDON TOWN (7-1)

A superb 7-1 win was the only bright spot of a thoroughly de- pressing day, in fact, had we not won so emphatically, I would have been in an even worse state, read on.

I was playing once again (I even gave Doc's stag night a miss) so John came up from London to see the game and I was really pleased that the lads turned on a show for him so he could savour his first home victory of the season. It was the Toon's third 7-1 victory inside the last 12 months which was an incredible feat in today's football where teams are generally more organised defensively than say in the 1960s – certainly such performances reflected the attacking flair and strike power of the team. Amazingly, goal king Cole didn't get on the scoresheet, but it was nice to see Steve Watson and Robert Lee both score two each and also Ruel Fox, our new £2 million acquisition from Norwich, open his account. Later that weekend, the Arsenal manager, George Graham, even went as far as to pay us a rare compliment when he described their European Cup Winners Cup semi-final opponents, Paris St. Germain, as 'being like Newcastle United', i.e. a good attacking team.

Back to my own game, and after only a couple of minutes I was involved in a collision, completely accidental I should add, which left me with what felt like a broken finger. Although incredibly painful I wasn't really sure of the extent of the injury and so played out the remaining 88 minutes – after all I could hardly tell the manager I wanted to come off because I had a sore hand! I tried to keep clear of any other physical challenges but it was inevitable that sooner or later I would need to 'get stuck in' again, and sure enough on one occasion in the second half when a sliding tackle was called for, the pain I felt when my hand made heavy contact with the ground was excruciating and I knew then something was seriously wrong.

When we got back to our ground in Leeds (it had been an away game in Doncaster) I'd planned to jump straight in the car and go to St. James' Hospital for an X-ray, but to my horror I found my car had been stolen! What a day it was turning out to be but, as I said at the start, at least the pleasure of the 7-1 demolition of Swindon was keeping me smiling. It seemed prudent to go to the local Police Station to report the theft before going to hospital, and upon eventually arriving at St. James' the diagnosis proved to be a triple fracture of the hand resulting in a plaster cast being put on my arm. Worse still it would take four/six weeks to heal which effectively put an end to my season. The car was recovered by the police 48 hours later which was pleasing, but as I couldn't drive it didn't seem to matter that much. One little footnote on the return of the car concerns the cassette tapes that were in the car at the time of the theft. There were six tapes in total, five of which were musical, with the sixth being the BBC Radio Newcastle production of the 1992/93 season in sound. The five musical tapes were taken, the Newcastle tape was left untouched (as was my little black and white mascot hanging on the back window) – doesn't that say something about the taste, or lack of it, of the thieves!

There was of course one major bright spot in respect of the injury which was that I'd be able to watch the Toon in virtually every game before the end of the season rather than playing commitments proving to be restrictive.

29/03/94 – NEWCASTLE v NORWICH CITY (3-0)

A slight change in style for this match in the shape of a 'guest' reporter. Thanks to work colleague and Elland Road season ticket holder Phil Crotty for the following:

"This was to be a crucial week for the major contest of the season – is there to be a redistribution of wealth between the North East and Yorkshire? – otherwise known as a bet of £10 between myself and the author, on whose team would finish higher in the table. Leeds United were wallowing in fifth place and looking like a bunch of overpaid professionals going through the motions, whilst making noises in the media about attempting to qualify for Europe. Newcastle on the other hand had just won their last five matches by playing fine football and were looking very secure in third place in the table with a five point advantage over Leeds.

"The wager was made during December when I started work at The English Basketball Association. I declared my allegiance to the club who produced one of the greatest sides ever. The allegiance was acknowledged, but the genuine interest in football was greeted with delight by someone who had clearly spent many Monday mornings bursting to talk about the weekend's football action but had found himself working with those whose lives had not been enriched by the one true religion.

"The week had started badly for Leeds losing at Wimbledon, a club who provide a magnificent example of the power of team spirit, plentiful substance for those who believe dreams can come true, and a fairly horrific example of how thuggery and the criteria of the statistician can succeed in the game.

"Mark had sustained a broken hand whilst playing football, had his arm in plaster and was unable to drive. I had therefore been persuaded to drive up to Tyneside on the Tuesday evening to watch the latest batch of Geordie heroes. The promise of a free seat in the Leazes End and a contribution to expenses helped the decision, as did the opportunity to watch one of the country's most entertaining teams without the distracting influence of partisanship which inevitably results from having your own team involved.

"At this point I feel I should fill in some detail about Mark's professional duties – he has a highly responsible managerial position as Competitions Officer at the Basketball Association, and it is in this context that I would like you to imagine a fully grown man organising a full national, domestic and international basketball programme, whilst frequently jumping out of his seat, with no excuse other than excitement, wandering round the office in his Newcastle United shirt and declaring 'its only 10 hours to kick-off' or 'Andy Cole will have scored a hat-trick in five hours time'.

"I have always found Geordies to be a genuinely friendly breed, something which, in my experience, they share with Scousers (although they may not like the comparison). This may be something to do with each city being a port but this is to my knowledge an untested theory. When this is added to their footballing tradition, and current ascendancy, an entertaining evening was highly likely.

"Mark took me on a route across the Tyne Bridge and I could feel the excitement level in him rise as we did so. We arrived at a pub near the ground, the North Terrace, and met up with the other heroes of this book, those lads who Mark goes to the game with. I was immediately bought a pint and warmly welcomed into the fold. Fortunately I have Geordie ancestry and have made frequent visits to the North East so I am not entirely clueless when the conversation is in full flow. However when the adrenalin of a football match is added to the equation they may as well be talking a language known only to hitherto undiscovered tribes from the Peruvian Andes for all the sense I was able to make of it. For example, 'Its wor hoy in' – It's what? or, 'Ha-way man Peeda, divvent mess aboot'. Some moments later, logical deduction made me realise that this was local hero Peter Beardsley and he was not having his best game of the season.

"We sat in the very impressive new stand at the Leazes End of the ground, and I enjoyed possibly the most enjoyable walk to a ground I can remember (through Leazes Park). Pleasant walks to football grounds in this country are the exception rather than the rule.

"As Mark has already documented, all seater stadia are now mandatory in the top division but unfortunately they present the problem of not being able to move if you are sitting near a complete dickhead – someone who chooses to spend the whole 90 minutes expounding his theories on the game (which are invariably drivel) and trying to be funny to impress his even more intellectually challenged entourage. The law of averages dictates that there will be quite a few in a crowd of 32,000.

"During the opening minutes I realised that the lad behind us had all the potential to reach the upper echelons of the afore-mentioned lamentable breed, he only occasionally paused for breath and did indeed give his theories on the game. Fortunately he was contrary to all my expectations of him, he not only made very funny comments but talked football sense, was fair, and he undoubtedly added to my enjoyment of the evening (Upper Tier, Row D, Seat 73 if you're reading this).

"Newcastle did not play particularly well but they did as much as they were allowed to by a very negative Norwich side. They also did more than was required to enhance the belief that the economy of the North East would receive a modest boost, courtesy of a Leeds fan, before the end of the season. Newcastle cruised to a comfortable 3-0 win and gave the local travel agents who specialise in European excursions good cause for optimism.

"The week concluded with the visit of Newcastle to Elland Road. I was not overly optimistic about my own side's chances and whatever shred of optimism was left was snapped in the third minute. Andy Cole scored a goal which was not only typical of his goal poaching ability, but also of Leeds' inability to be first to a loose ball in their own six yard area. Newcastle spent the next 20 minutes weaving pretty patterns round Leeds' midfield without creating very much. Leeds however re-discovered the spirit which carried them to the title two seasons previously, and started playing with a passion and power that had Newcastle under the cosh for most of the rest of the game. The fact that Leeds only scored the equaliser in the last minute was more to do with Newcastle's good fortune, as a point was the least we deserved.

"At the end of the week the economic situation had not changed but there was still hope."

04/04/94 – NEWCASTLE v CHELSEA (0-0)

A dull uninspiring 0-0 draw which led to chants of 'Boring Boring Chelsea' throughout most of the second half. So much for Glenn Hoddle playing 'pure' football, I seem to remember his Swindon Town team kicked us off the park down at the County Ground towards the end of our promotion season in March 1993.

Before the game I simply had to take the opportunity of walking round the back of the Gallowgate End to take a close look at how far the construction of the new stand had progressed since I'd last seen it. Even though there were only four or five huge steel girders in place it still brought a tremendous amount of excitement and pride to me, particularly when I envisaged what it was going to be like come the start of the 1994/95 season when it would be virtually complete and we would have a ground second to none in Britain – and a team fit to grace it too.

A final word on the match itself concerns the absence of any Chelsea supporters at St. James' Park. It wasn't anything to do with Newcastle United taking revenge over the fact that we were charged the scandalously high price of £25 for a seat at Stamford Bridge earlier in the season, but down to the problem of only being able to accommodate Geordie supporters inside St. James' Park during its re-development. Attendance figures were churned out regularly at 32,216, but the real point is that the lack of any away supporters meant the atmosphere at St. James' Park was becoming a little flat. It even got to a stage of different sections of the crowd chanting at each other trying to stir some life into the proceedings. All I could say was roll on next season when once again away supporters are a regular feature at St. James' Park; football isn't quite the same game without them.

Matches at St. James' Park were also being broadcast live into the Odeon cinema in the city centre for the benefit of youngsters who couldn't get tickets, which certainly was a progressive move by the Commercial Department of the club. In addition Newcastle Breweries showed full recordings of games the following day in hundreds of pubs and clubs throughout the region, but I would guess no one particularly enjoyed the Chelsea match!

I caught the train back to Leeds later in the evening and on taking my seat I noticed a lad across the aisle from me reading a copy of *The Mag.* Naturally I started up a conversation with him by saying 'been to the match then'. Of course he had, but it turned out that he was a Norwegian student, Jon Nilsen, and a Newcastle United fanatic as well. For the duration of the two hour journey we talked football all the time and I was truly amazed at his knowledge of Newcastle United and English football in general, in fact his passion for the club would have put many Geordies to shame. It turned out that he first saw the Toon playing on Norwegian television back in October 1983 when Newcastle beat Charlton Athletic 2-1 which included Kevin Keegan famously scoring a brilliant header in a match played in an absolute downpour. Ever since that day he's followed the fortunes of the club and he told me that had he not had to travel back to Norway the following morning he would have loved to have travelled to Coventry to see the reserves playing. True dedication, and it was a real pleasure to have met him.

09/04/94 – MANCHESTER CITY v NEWCASTLE (2-1)

Another wedding during the football season, really people should know better. This time it was Doc (Mike Ingham) and it meant a long trek for us all down to Chelmsford. As it was also FA Cup semi-final day I don't think any of us would have been in Chelmsford had the Toon been fortunate enough to have progressed to this stage of the competition!

Staying on the FA Cup for a moment and in particular the semi-finals. For the second successive season the Football Association decreed that both semi-finals would be played at Wembley, and I must say I couldn't be more against this. The main reason for this is that it totally takes away the real 'occasion' of reaching the Cup Final. Although the FA say they are trying to cater for all the fans who want to see the game, it appears to me that financial considerations have got in the way of pure football issues. Having said all this, once the decision has been made then of course the supporters have no alternative but to abide by it, and to hear of fans complaining about the expense or inconvenience of having to travel to Wembley (as Sheffield Wednesday's part-timers did in 1993), or even worse being unable to sell their ticket allocation, leaves me gob smacked. Give a Geordie a merest sniff of Wembley and he'll bite your hand off, but there again I guess it's only because we are a unique breed of football supporter. I am pleased to see that 1995 has seen the FA reverting to tradition and the semi-finals are back on club grounds, primarily I suppose because the quality of the stadiums are such that they are entirely adequate for the occasion.

I was still in plaster so Macas kindly gave me a lift down. Obviously a very enjoyable day was had by all, particularly at the reception where the hosts had done a splendid job of putting all the lads (some with wives) on one table so we were able to talk and reminisce about football all evening. Weddings are good in that they bring together all your old friends, many of whom are spread around the country, and although you regularly see them it's not often that we're all together at once. There was one obvious low spot during the celebrations though, when news leaked through that we had lost 2-1 to Manchester City at Maine Road. We'd known it was a 1-1 earlier on, Scott Sellars having put us ahead, but this news was sickening, especially as we had so much still to play for with a European place still very much up for grabs.

I had some work to attend to on Sunday, so rather than stay overnight I caught the train into London and travelled back to Leeds from Victoria on the National Express Coach. It was pretty full when I boarded but immediately saw a lad in a West Ham United shirt. He was sitting alone so it seemed a good idea to join him since it was more than likely we'd be able to talk football during the long trip up the M1. I wasn't wrong. Vince Mott, as I later found out, was an exiled Hammer living in Leeds who travels down to London for every home game, leaving Leeds at 7.00am on Saturday mornings and returning at midnight. Vince was a real football fan and we traded stories with each other all evening making it a very enjoyable journey. We also had something in common with each other apart from the fact that we were exiled football fanatics living in Leeds – we had both recently been dumped out of the FA Cup by Luton! West Ham had lost to a single Tony Cottee strike at Upton Park earlier in the day but Vince, like myself, was still in good spirits. I've always thought of West Ham supporters as being particularly loyal and 'well educated' in footballing matters, and my preconceptions were certainly borne out. The Toon had recently won 4-2 at Upton Park so I had one over on him immediately – his main complaint was that all the visiting fans were being housed in the brand new and impressive Bobby Moore Stand which Vince felt should have been kept for the home fans. I certainly sympathised with him over this point even though the Geordies, including brother John, weren't complaining on the day.

It transpired Vince lived in the same district of Leeds as me so I was fortunate enough to get a lift home from the bus station from his wife which at least saved me the hassle of choosing to walk home or grabbing a taxi. Another good day out where football was the winner.

16/04/94 – LIVERPOOL v NEWCASTLE (0-2)

Wasn't it nice travelling to Anfield knowing that you had a better than even chance of winning. I didn't get a ticket from the club's new 'away ticket allocation scheme' (which for this game went hopelessly wrong when over 2,000 supporters were told they would be getting a ticket, only for them then to be informed that this was in fact not the case due to a computer error), and when John failed to deliver a ticket a friend of his in Liverpool had promised, it simply became a case of driving to Merseyside early in the morning to sort things out across there. Arriving at 9.30 in the morning I wasn't too surprised to already see quite a large number of supporters, mainly Scousers, milling around the stadium. Half an hour later I had a ticket for the Kop in my possession, although the price I paid, £40, didn't please me much despite the fact that I had been prepared to pay £50 (it probably would have cost me a great deal more had this fixture been the last in front of the Kop). I've always respected the Kop, and the fact I was about to stand on it for the first time, coupled with it being the penultimate time it would witness a Liverpool performance as a standing terrace, filled me with anticipation and tremendous excitement.

The Kop was virtually full as early as 1.00pm, a good two hours before the kick off and I even got talking to a couple of friendly Scousers who were just happy to talk football to me. One of them, Matty, had been a Koppite for over 20 years and I could see how visibly upset he was that a huge chunk of his life was soon to be removed – the same of course happened to the Geordies in 1978. Matty told me he rated Keegan higher than Dalglish and also how he could never understand why Beardsley was allowed to leave Anfield. I retorted that he should never have arrived at Anfield in the first place! Terry Mac and Barry Venison were also firm favourites of his although Mike Hooper never rated particularly high in his estimation which says a lot about the rough time he has had on Tyneside. After all the success Matty had enjoyed, by virtue of being a Liverpool supporter throughout the 1970s and 1980s, he also sympathised greatly with the plight of the Geordies in respect of our constant failure over the years – he also rated the Geordie supporters very highly but naturally enough thought the Scousers were still a class above everyone else when it came to passionate support. Of course we begged to differ on this point – come the end of the game he gave me a little wry smile as if to acknowledge the ascendancy of the Geordies, but as we had won 2-0 I suppose we did have more to shout about – I did remind him though of the night back in 1984 when we took over Anfield despite being thumped 4-0.

There was a poignant moment to be witnessed also when a special floral tribute to Liverpool Football Club was made by a Newcastle supporter and his young son. They laid a wreath in front of the Kop End to mark the fifth anniversary of the Hillsborough disaster and it was a gesture much appreciated. A number of black and white scarves were also draped on the Shankly gates which was a tremendous tribute by the Geordies. The atmosphere was possibly the best I have known in my time of following the club, indeed a friend of mine from the basketball world, Ron Harrison, told me that it was his best ever day in 40 years of watching Newcastle United. The whole ground, including my fellow Geordies at the Anfield Road End, joined to pay tribute to those who had died at Hillsborough. It brought tears to my eyes and when the Geordies broke into a deafening rendition of 'The Blaydon Races' soon after it was a treasured moment indeed for me standing on the Kop listening from afar. Proud to be a Geordie?, I've never felt so good.

So to the game itself and when Robert Lee, who deservedly had earned a place in the England training squad earlier in the week, opened the scoring in front of the Kop after only four minutes it was a dream start. There was a degree of Liverpool pressure towards the end of the half but soon after half time, when a flowing move, started by Pavel Srnicek and continued through Sellars and Fox, was finished in typical style by Cole, it was game set and match to Newcastle.

We had achieved a magnificent double over Liverpool, 5-0 on aggregate, and I can rarely remember seeing such celebrations from the travelling Geordie supporters. Was this a sign that we had well and truly established ourselves as one of the major forces in the country and, perhaps in recent years and certainly in my time, the apogee of Newcastle United Football Club?

A final note on the day is that the mutual affinity between the two sets of supporters was truly magnificent. Bearing in mind that the Scousers have never been particularly high on the Geordies Christmas Card list it said even more about the occasion – one that will live with me for ever.

27/04/94 – NEWCASTLE v ASTON VILLA (5-1)

I had no plans to include this match originally but how could I possibly let it pass without comment? Aston Villa arrived on Tyneside with their UEFA Cup spot already assured (by virtue of their victory in the League Cup Final) and with a team short of at least five first team regulars due to injury. They started brightly enough though and took an early lead before Newcastle had got out of first gear. But then things changed, and spectacularly so at that. Paul Bracewell scored a 30 yard screamer, the like of which he could only dream about and, after Beardsley notched the second from the penalty spot, the moment every Geordie had been waiting for happened. In the 41st minute Scott Sellars put a peach of a ball through to Andy Cole who proceeded to calmly round the advancing Spink to slot the ball into the empty net at the Leazes End. It was goal number 40 of the season and gave Cole a place in Newcastle United history as the first player to reach this goal scoring landmark, beating the 39 scored by Hughie Gallacher in the 1926/27 season and George Robledo in the 1951/52 season. I needn't tell you that the ground erupted and for the next five minutes the now famous 'Andy Cole' song reverberated around the whole of St. James' Park – pure unadulterated magic. In the second half two further goals were added and the ethereal form I witnessed; bright, inventive, incisive, thrilling sustained entertaining football, was as good as I can remember seeing – it was that good.

A number of other notable moments stood out during the second half. The first came during a particularly long injury stoppage which resulted in Villa's Shaun Teale regrettably being carried off the field. With the crowd having nothing in particular to sing they spontaneously started chanting the name of every single Newcastle player one by one starting from goalkeeper Pavel Srnicek right through to Scott Sellars. It was made even more special by each player acknowledging the supporters and I'm certain it must have created a unique bond between the two parties. Keegan, Terry McDermott and even Sir John Hall were not missed out and it really showed a great sense of unity within the club – something that would have been unheard of as little as three seasons ago.

It was also the night that record signing Darren Peacock, all £2.7 million of him, showed what a good player he is. After a couple of shaky performances, which included the opening 20 minutes of this game, he turned on the style and I think a lot of the credit for this must go to the inspirational Barry Venison who gave Peacock as much of the ball as possible and put a confident step back into his defensive colleague. Let's just hope that he continues in this vein, I for one think he will. Before Peacock came to the club Keegan had tried to sign the virtually unknown Coventry City defender Phil Babb, also a centre half, but wasn't prepared to meet Coventry's asking price. In view of Babb's magnificent performances throughout USA '94 it is a shame we didn't take a gamble on him. Liverpool did, at an inflated price, but he has yet to really prove himself in the Premier League. Still on the theme of central defenders and there were rumours after the World Cup Finals that Keegan was interested in signing the American cult figure Alexi Lalas. Fortunately, because I didn't rate him at all, he didn't, but he did sign the adventurous Swiss right back Marc Hottiger, and the cultured Belgium central defender, Philippe Albert.

Finally, there was the humorous chanting aimed at Ron Atkinson, particularly with regard to the 'missing' Paul McGrath, 'Ooh, Ah where's McGrath?', and also, 'Are you watching Big Fat Ron' – all in good taste I hasten to add – it was that sort of night.

Next day at the office I found myself £10 richer, a result of course of Leeds United's challenge for third place predictably disappearing.

30/04/94 – SHEFFIELD UNITED v NEWCASTLE (2-0)

Seven thousand Toon Army supporters (to quote Rob Hughes of *The Times*) descended upon Bramall Lane for our last away fixture of the season. I wasn't among them, more of that later, but Hally was, and he took great pleasure in telling me what a fantastic day out it was (Geordies everywhere is I think what he meant) despite our 2-0 defeat. It was one of our less impressive performances, compared to those in recent weeks, however, when news of

Arsenal's defeat at Highbury against West Ham filtered through to the fans in the final few minutes, the Geordies were sent into raptures. The terraces were ignited with a whole series of 'Europe' songs since we were now guaranteed a finishing position of third and, as it would transpire, a place in the UEFA Cup next season.

As for me, it was another trip to London for the end of season basketball finals at Wembley Arena and, in view of my experience last year, I was desperately hoping for another chance to get inside the stadium. I wasn't disappointed. I travelled down on Friday afternoon with Tracey (my colleague in the Competitions Department at the Basketball Association) and, although not really being into football, I convinced her she would enjoy a visit to the stadium. We got into the ground this time through the front entrance, as opposed to up the tunnel, and immediately mingled in with the 20 or so contractors who were getting the stadium in shape for the Leeds-Wigan Rugby League Cup Final the next day. I really was amazed that we got into the stadium without anybody querying our presence but, having said that, there was no chance of any security risk over the two of us.

This time I took the opportunity to walk up the steps to the Royal Box (Tracey stayed on the surrounds of the pitch as she thought I was mad!) and pretended I was Peter Beardsley collecting the FA Cup. After another walk around, which included swinging in an imaginary corner kick from the right flank (I was Scott Sellars this time) we headed off out of the stadium through the players' tunnel. In 1993 I didn't have the bottle to go into the dressing rooms but, as there was no one around, did so this time. The actual changing area simply has a physio's couch in the middle of the room with blue seating (enough for 20 players) going right around the confines of the room. There was a tactics board on the wall and yes, you've guessed it, I was Kevin Keegan giving his final instructions to the players before the game. The shower/bath facilities are in an adjacent room with showers, eight individual baths and a massive communal bath which was at least five feet deep, the biggest I've ever seen.

And so that was it – another fantastic experience for me and I was already looking forward to next year when I fully intended to actually run on the pitch itself. I don't know how I'll manage it but I am sure I will think of something as looking back, it's the one thing I really regret not having attempted – I think I was just too much in awe to have thought about it at the time!

The night finished with a trip to the greyhounds so once again it was an opportunity to go inside the stadium. We won £12 on the first three races, only betting £2/£3 a time, before not surprisingly losing it all on the last race. It was my fault as well. The form guide went out of the window as I chose the dog in trap six to be the winner, but only because it wore a black and white striped coat. It lost!

07/05/94 – NEWCASTLE v ARSENAL (2-0)

Earlier in the season Arsenal had been considerate enough to give the Geordies the refurbished Clock Stand End at Highbury which had just opened. It was a generous act on their part but, perhaps at the same time, they knew the Geordies would fill it and help create a marvellous atmosphere in a ground where the home fans are more often than not a little lifeless. There was of course also the small matter of the additional guaranteed income through the turnstiles for the Gunners.

Three days earlier Arsenal had won the European Cup Winners Cup against the Italian side, Parma, in Copenhagen which was just as well for them as they had gambled somewhat by putting all their eggs in one basket in respect of qualifying for Europe. They had concentrated all their efforts and resources on beating Parma during the final few weeks of the domestic season, as opposed to trying to secure third place in the league. It worked of course, and so before a ball was even kicked on the final day of the season at St. James' Park, both teams were guaranteed finishing positions in the top four; Newcastle third and Arsenal fourth.

In the week leading up to the match there had been a number of major developments at St. James' Park. The most notable was the man himself, Kevin Keegan, committing himself to the club for the next ten years. He was given the title of 'Director of Soccer and Coaching' which elevated his status within the club to a new unparalleled level. Arthur Cox was tempted back to his spiritual home by Keegan to take up a post with the backroom staff and, in view of his previous track record at St. James' Park, this was yet another sign that the club were fully committed to continue making great strides forward.

Andy Cole was on the verge of signing a new four year contract, worth a reported £7,000 per week (chicken feed in comparison to what some of the top players, particularly the foreign stars, were to receive only two seasons later), which was in addition to a footwear contract with Reebok worth £1 million. This was a staggering amount but for the job he was doing, and the pleasure he brought thousands upon thousands of Geordies, he was worth every penny of it in my book. Keegan went on to say that Newcastle United could go on to become 'the biggest club on the planet' – some statement when you step back and consider it but one that is quite possible to contemplate despite having watched Milan destroy Barcelona 4-0 in the 1994 European Cup Final with a performance of such supreme brilliance you could only dream about matching.

Back to the football and it was nice to see the Geordie public giving Arsenal a tremendous round of applause as they took the field for their pre-match warming up exercises. This was followed by the Newcastle players forming a guard of honour to welcome The Londoners on to the pitch at five minutes to three, due recognition for the boost they had given the whole of English football in Copenhagen. But that's as far the hospitality was extended. After a first half where Newcastle were always on top, but only really threatening to score on a couple of occasions, the second half was only two minutes old when a typically mazy run by Beardsley set up Andy Cole for the opening goal – coming against Arsenal made it even more special for him. Beardsley added a second from the penalty spot on the hour and had Lee and Cole not missed gilt edged chances late in the game, a more conclusive victory would have resulted. Arsenal were never in it but, to be fair, it was clear their minds were elsewhere and really who could blame them? Ian Wright got a little bit of good humoured stick from the crowd, who enquired of him as to where his Cup Winners Cup medal was – for the uninitiated he didn't get one because he missed the final through suspension (at least he made up for it 12 months later, albeit with a losers medal after Nayim's spectacular winner in the 120th minute ended Arsenal's dream of back to back wins in the competition). Upon the final whistle Cole and Wright exchanged shirts which illustrated their friendship and mutual respect they have for one another – I thought it was a wonderful way to round off the season for Cole.

The afternoon ended with a lap of honour, which was an inevitable consequence of the fabulous season that had just drawn to a close. Not a single person in the ground left their place and the Geordies accorded their heroes a rapturous reception so much so that it made my hair stand on end such was the feeling of sheer pride the occasion brought.

If I was enjoying myself at St. James' Park, and I certainly was, then I should have taken the time to spare a thought for Everton fans at Goodison Park and Sheffield United supporters at Stamford Bridge. There had been 'pressure' on us in recent weeks to finish in the top three but as we went into the game against Arsenal safe in the knowledge that we had secured third place (barring a 7-0 defeat!) Everton had to beat Wimbledon to stay up and Sheffield United probably had to avoid defeat to do likewise. As it transpired it wasn't until Barry Horne scored an 82nd minute goal that Evertonians could relax whilst the Blades suffered the ultimate agony as Mark Stein's last minute goal for Chelsea condemned them to the drop – how sickening can you get, especially when you consider Stein's goal also left them with an awful looking three sided stadium as the money for redevelopment (which they would have had in the Premier League) ran out.

Almost immediately after the game finished the pitch was dug up in preparation for laying a brand new surface in readiness for the 1994/95 season. It is hoped that the new pitch will provide an immaculate surface for the type of football the team loves to play – regrettably it deteriorated after Christmas which infuriated both Keegan and Sir John Hall. I did hear that the turf for the new pitch had come from Sir John's own land which, if true, was rather ironic. Naturally the old pitch couldn't just be simply disposed of and, inevitably, arrangements were made for supporters to purchase square foot segments of turf (there were 15,000 pieces) the following morning for the sake of posterity. It was nice to see also that the proceeds from the sales went to charity.

And so another season was over and quite simply it was the best I have ever witnessed. Not only was our finishing position of third a truly magnificent feat, but the way it was achieved made you swell with pride. It can be summed up by simply saying I had the privilege to watch a superb team, playing in a magnificent stadium, with the best manager in the business at the helm and with a Chairman, Sir John Hall, who made it all possible by not only giving us Kevin Keegan, but being responsible in the main for putting an incredible £29 million into the club. We were top scorers in the division, two more than League Champions Manchester United, joint winners of the National Fair Play Award, and with Beardsley and Cole picking up accolades from their fellow professionals, and Beardsley also from the football writers, it was all a bit too much to take in.

As for the club itself, whether it can go on to dominate English club football, as Liverpool did in the 1970s and 1980s, and indeed as Manchester United are threatening to do now, is a fascinating question to pose. We shall see, but whatever transpires there is no doubt that the sky is the limit for the Toon which is the very thing Sir John Hall predicted would be the case when he took over as Chairman of the club.

03/07/94 – ARGENTINA v ROMANIA (3-2)

As I have commented on most of the World Cup Tournaments I have watched it seems fitting to turn again to this great festival of football and of course USA '94. No England interest of course but for me this was the best game of the tournament, which included my favourite goal of the competition (Romania's Ilie Dumitrescu) and resulted in Argentina's elimination from the competition. The action flowed from end to end throughout and despite the absence of the disgraced Maradona, I still expected Argentina to make a major impact in the tournament. Turning back to Maradona it was so sad that a player of such immeasurable talent let himself, his country and, perhaps above all, football fans all over the world down. Considering how unfit he was earlier in the year the only way he could have got back into respectable physical shape before Argentina played their first game against Greece was through drug abuse.

The Americans did a splendid job in terms of the organisation and promotion of the tournament despite their naive tendencies over many aspects of the game, their incredibly insular outlook and their irritating habit of referring to football as soccer. Attendance figures reached record levels too (an amazing average of 68,500) with the only negative factor about the tournament, for the players at least, being the midday kick offs which clearly asked too much of the players – I suppose the only benefit of this was that matches were transmitted to Europe at peak time viewing which was a definite plus. On the field their team did as well as one could reasonably expect so much so that Keegan attempted, without joy, to land goalkeeper Brad Friedel. It was a shame he wasn't able to perform on England's greatest stage, St. James' Park, although I'm sure Pavel would have had his say in that. A year later Sunderland also tried to land the American goalkeeper and ran into similar problems with the Employment Department (an organisation I am in constant contact with incidentally in respect of bringing overseas nationals, mainly Americans, into the country to play top level basketball). I actually talked to my 'contact' in the Department at the time we were trying to obtain a permit for Friedel to see if it was likely to come about. He said 'there were difficulties' but obviously couldn't expand on the finer points of the case. The permit was eventually refused but had Friedel ended up at Roker Park he was sure to have looked enviously down the road to St. James' Park and thought to himself what might have been!

I've already mentioned the ineptitude of a number of the referees at the tournament (the Swiss official Kurt Rothlisberger was 'sent home' by FIFA after the Germany/Belgium game in which he failed to award the Belgium's a blatantly obvious penalty at a crucial stage of the game) which leads me to mention the furore that Kevin Keegan caused in some quarters by virtue of his comments during the Brazil/USA match. Keegan was the ITV match summariser and when the Brazilian Leonardo was rightly sent off for elbowing the American defender, Tab Ramos, Keegan commented that perhaps Leonardo should not have been dismissed. Alan Parry vehemently disagreed with him and eventually Kevin changed his mind having watched the replay a few times. The damage had already been done though, *The Sun* took him to task the following day but Keegan was unfortunate in that he didn't quite manage to get across to the viewers exactly what he meant. Of course he didn't condone Leonardo's actions but he understood why it happened and it was a pity that it looked to the average viewer that Keegan was supporting thuggery on the field – which of course he most certainly was not. FIFA subsequently suspended Leonardo for four matches, which was possibly a little harsh, but nevertheless illustrated their desire to rid the game of all such acts of violence – Leonardo obviously missed the rest of the tournament as did the Italian Mauro Tassotti who picked up an eight match ban for his off the ball elbowing of Spain's Luis Enrique. It was noticeable though that both players still collected medals after the final which I thought was rather strange.

The World Cup perhaps raises passions more than any other football occasion in some countries and this was tragically none more evident than in Colombia when, following their shock elimination from the tournament after the first round, their defender Andres Escobar was shot dead shortly after returning to his home country. The incident happened after Escobar left a restaurant in Medellin and all because he was the player who had scored an own goal which had contributed to their defeat against the USA. His killers had been hired by drug barons who had bet heavily on the World Cup matches and, because of Colombia's poor performances, had subsequently lost. Football came to its senses when hundreds of thousands Colombians mourned his death in the proper manner.

Radio 5's coverage of the tournament, with the excellent Jon Champion at the helm, was again second to none (especially with Mark Lawrenson as one of the summarisers) and it was nice also to be able to tune into Eurosport and listen to the lucid commentaries of Archie McPherson who has always struck me as being a true footballing enthusiast whose talents were wasted with BBC Scotland. His commentary on the Bulgaria/Sweden third place match was particularly memorable with one comment, 'Stoichkov's complaining is as long as the Gettysburg Address', being right up in the Sid Waddell class of great sporting 'one-liners'.

A word too on Roberto Baggio, a player you know I admire immensely, who came back to life in the competition with his 89th minute equaliser in the second phase match against Nigeria. If the Italians had been knocked out Baggio would have gone home labelled an under-achiever which would have been a terrible injustice. His subsequent performances against Spain and Bulgaria left me drooling and it was an awful shame that injury prevented him from performing at his best in the final. His penalty miss was just one of those things – just ask Stuart Pearce or Chris Waddle!

Brazil's victory was well deserved in the end as they were clearly the most attractive team in the tournament although both Bulgaria and Romania played as freely as they have ever done. On the final itself three things to comment on. Firstly I was really pleased that Italy's Roberto Donadoni was able to play in the match since it was he who had missed the crucial penalty kick against Argentina in Italia '90 which must have caused him heartache, secondly how nice it was of the BBC to give the game commentary to Barry Davies, and thirdly, the way the final itself was settled. All I need to say is how can the world's most important football match be settled by penalty kicks?

1993/94 – Season's Summary

League	P	W	D	L	F	A	Pts.	Pos.
	42	23	8	11	82	41	77	3rd

Top Scorers

Andy Cole	41
Peter Beardsley	24
Robert Lee	8

1994/95 – EUROPEAN ADVENTURE

What a close season it had been! Kevin Keegan said that the 1983/84 season had been wonderfully exciting but that this, i.e. what was happening at the club now, was something else. Life on Tyneside was on a completely different plane. Jack Charlton, commenting on BBC Radio 5, said the whole of Tyneside had 'gone wild' while Barry Venison compared the quality of the team to that of Liverpool in their heyday, but in terms of achievement, there was no comparison – yet!

It was clear that the level of expectation surrounding the club was so different to any other time I had known. The media, even the London contingent, were forthcoming in their praise of the team. Newcastle United mania had caught on throughout Britain and personally I couldn't get enough of it. Whether I quite liked the idea of little ten year olds in such far flung outposts as diverse as Plymouth and Poole 'adopting' our team as their team also (only because we are in the so called Manchester United bracket of being attractive and successful) I'm not sure, but I suppose it's all part of the inevitable price of success.

Jackie Milburn once said that what was wrong with his beloved club was that the players and the supporters were poles apart. No longer, Kevin Keegan has seen to that, and the affinity is now perfectly cemented.

21/08/94 – LEICESTER CITY v NEWCASTLE (1-3)

Every Geordie remembers the last time we played Leicester City. It was that glorious sunny May afternoon back in 1993, when, in front of an ecstatic Geordie audience, seven goals were put into the back of the Leicester net, six of them before half time. Leicester had reached the Premier League via the Play Offs, due reward for their heartbreaking failures at Wembley over the past two seasons, and like those before them, were considered by the bookmakers as firm favourites for relegation. Notwithstanding this, any newly promoted club playing their first home game in the Premier League, regardless of who they are playing, would almost certainly be on a high and therefore a tough nut to crack (there's always an exception to the rule – ask Crystal Palace).

A limited number of tickets, something in the region of 1200, didn't come remotely close to satisfying the Geordie masses who would have loved to have made the journey down to Leicestershire for the season's opener. For those that missed out, myself included, at least there was the consolation of Sky Television coverage as the 'Entertainers' tag was clearly still very much in evidence. No goals in the first half was just the prelude for a magnificent display in the second 45 minutes. Total dominance brought three goals, including a typically brilliant effort by Peter Beardsley, and the afternoon was only marred by the tragic cheek injury to Beardsley, a hammer blow to everyone connected with the club. It was incredible that the same thing could happen to him in successive years, having had a relatively injury free career, but at least we could console ourselves with the knowledge that the quality and depth of our squad was such that we would pull through without him. The fact that we did speaks volumes about the progress that we have made, but as far as I am concerned Beardsley remains the most influential player at the club, a total inspiration to playing colleagues and supporters alike. His loss, as it was at the end of December, was a crushing blow.

Injuries were also affecting my Fantasy League Team (*Daily Telegraph*). I had Andy Cole and Robert Lee as my two Newcastle players but unfortunately the goals the pair of them banged in at the start of the season didn't count towards my points total as the League rankings didn't get underway until the middle of September. Then, when Cole got injured, I replaced him with Shearer which turned out to be a shrewd move – pity it couldn't happen in real life – or could it!

The other problem I had was that my defence and goalkeepers (I alternated between Coton of Manchester City and Kharine of Chelsea) couldn't keep any clean sheets so I ended up nearer to the bottom end than the top of the table. It was interesting that the Supporters Table, which the Telegraph also compiled, had Newcastle United in 92nd place (rock bottom) which I can only assume was due to the fact that other Newcastle supporters picked similar teams to mine. Clearly we are better off leaving things to the man who knows best – Kevin Keegan.

24/08/94 – NEWCASTLE v COVENTRY CITY (4-0)

An article in *The Times* by their football correspondent Rob Hughes entitled 'Brave new world plays no fanfare for common fans' said a great deal about the way many people were feeling on

Tyneside. The article included such expressions as 'Newcastle's success has come at a high price to some of its most fervent supporters' and 'St. James' Park is a stadium where the place of every spectator is at a premium'.

Sir John Hall had always said that 'there would be a price to pay' and to be honest I'm sure that 99% of the supporters would prefer to see the club where it is today rather than the dark, or should I say pitch black, days of three years ago – remember New Year's Day 1992 and the debacle at Southend – how did you feel then?

St. James' Park, a beacon of the post Hillsborough era, is a monument to the massive social change that has overtaken the national sport. People simply can't stroll along to the stadium on a Saturday afternoon, as we did in the 1970s and 1980s, and this is a tragedy for many young supporters today. The local press, particularly the Saturday evening Football Pink printed long letters of complaint about what the writers call the dictatorship of Newcastle United. Ordinary supporters (what are they?) are dismayed that many lifetime fans cannot afford the so called price of success and, from many, there are bitter recriminations. Bond Holders (supporters paying £500 on top of the cost of their season ticket to ensure their place in the ground) are criticised in some quarters for queue jumping – on the other hand many bond holders are the ordinary fans, those who have virtually from birth grown to love Newcastle United and are the lifeblood of the club – part of the bonding (no pun intended) unique to the Geordie. If there is one concern it has got to be where the next generation of Newcastle United supporters are coming from?

A little aside here is the tale about how the club, fearing a great deal of negative press, took the vast majority of the north-east press corps to Monaco on the day the controversial bond scheme was launched. This was presumably to lessen the impact of the story. The club of course picked up the tab for the whole excursion, quite a substantial one I would imagine, but it does seem a funny way of conducting business – after all, it's not exactly the best way to build bridges of trust and mutual co-operation between two parties who are equally in need of one another.

Over the summer the new Gallowgate End (the club called it the South Stand, later to be renamed the Exhibition Stand) had shot up from the rubble that was once terracing, dank windswept toilets (black painted walls to empty the pre-match beer on) and numerous bushes and trees, a feature I'm sure was unique to any football stadium. It was an exact replica of the Leazes End with the only disappointment being that the two corner sections had yet to be filled in but this was presumably because the grandiose plans for the south west corner, including a restaurant, club shop, more executive boxes and new administration offices, had yet to be finalised.

After the winning start at Filbert Street, Coventry City were there for the taking and they meekly succumbed to a four goal thrashing, their second such reversal at St. James' Park inside six months. Taking their third round FA Cup defeat into account back in January, a combined scoreline of 10-0 in one calendar year was the sorry tale of woe for the Sky Blues. Come 12 months later and this would rise to 13-0, incredible!

Another little intrusion and a quick word on yet another playing season for yours truly. The night before this game I was turning out for Yorkshire Amateurs at Hall Road Rangers (Hull). Midway through the second half, when we were trailing 1-0, we forced a corner and when the ball was cleared I moved up from my full back position and hit the sweetest volley you could ever imagine from all of 40 yards. The ball flew like an exocet missile and thundered against the underside of the bar before bouncing clear. What a shot! Brian Richardson, the Assistant Manager, described the shot as 'the best strike I have ever seen in Non League football' and that was praise indeed. Needless to say the rest of the lads never stopped ribbing me about this comment all the way back to Leeds. The incident reminded me of a very similar comment made by our PE Teacher at Ponteland High School, Peter Lawson, when he described a stunning one handed catch I took at silly mid off as 'the best catch I have ever seen in schoolboy cricket.'

13/09/94 – ROYAL ANTWERP v NEWCASTLE (0-5)

A return to European football after an absence of 17 long years. Johnny Rep's magnificent strike, which sailed into the top corner of the net at the Leazes End, was my last memory of the UEFA Cup on Tyneside and it's not a particularly pleasant one. We couldn't even say that the UEFA ban on English clubs had affected us, like it did many, notably Everton, as we didn't come remotely close to qualifying for Europe in the post Heysel years.

UEFA made us 18th seeds in the competition and, after avoiding the ignominy of having to play in the preliminary round, Royal Antwerp from Belgium, finalists in the European Cup Winners Cup only 15 months earlier, were to be our first round opposition. I wasn't able to go, largely because it coincided with the busiest week of the year at work (registering players, sorting out contractual disputes and masses of media work before the National League Basketball season could begin the following Saturday) so I had to let Hally travel alone. An estimated 5,000 Geordies (4,000 of them travelling independently of the official club tours) descended upon Antwerp and what a time they had. Hally went by coach from London and told me upon his return that he had had the time of his life. Apart from the unbelievable 5-0 scoreline, the Geordies did themselves proud and left Belgium with a reputation second to none in Europe – what a shame Chelsea couldn't do likewise when they visited Brugge later in the season.

I was following the game on Ceefax in the office and was in constant contact with John in London who was entertaining a number of business clients at a London restaurant. His guests must have wondered what was going on when his mobile phone kept ringing in the middle of his meeting as his brother broke the news of yet another Newcastle goal.

18/09/94 – ARSENAL v NEWCASTLE (2-3)

The first real test of the league season after a maximum return from the first five matches. I remember going to Arsenal with Hally back in 1984 when we led the table after three matches and being comprehensively outplayed and lucky to only lose 2-0. This time round things would be different.

London's Ticket Master proved our saviour for tickets and we were able to acquire six seats for the West Stand (Lower Tier). I travelled down with Macas, picking up an Arsenal friend of his, Adan, in Kirkby in Ashfield (Mansfield) en route, and we arrived in the capital just after midday. The plan was to meet John and Hally in the Highbury Tavern but as no such place existed our search round every drinking establishment in the vicinity of the ground proved fruitless. As everywhere was heaving with Geordies we gave them up and settled down to some pre-match refreshment ourselves in the Arsenal Tavern.

It was my first visit to Highbury since the new North Bank (note it has kept its name) had been completed and I have to admit it's an impressive structure even though it's not exactly the noisiest home end I've ever known. The other additions to the ground were two giant video screens located at the two corners of the ground which showed highlights of previous fixtures before the game began and then, during the game, would show replays of the goals and exciting incidents. It didn't show any contentious incidents though which I suppose was entirely understandable. The quality of the picture was first class as well which pleasantly surprised me, especially having witnessed awful picture clarity at large screens at St. James' Park in the past. Technology has advanced in leaps and bounds in recent years though, so perhaps I shouldn't have been surprised and, after all, Arsenal are sponsored by JVC!

Arsenal fans are a pretty friendly bunch and there was never a hint of any trouble as both sets of fans made their way towards the turnstiles. Our seats were at the Clock End of the West Stand and, not surprisingly, there was a fair sprinkling of Geordies in our section, all of whom weren't afraid to voice their support for the lads since the Arsenal support around us didn't seem to mind at all. John had bought a copy of the Arsenal fanzine, *The Gooner*, and it was interesting to read an article in it about home supporters being 'evicted' from their normal seats in the Clock Stand (they were relocated elsewhere in the stadium) when Arsenal had a visit from the likes of Newcastle, Manchester United and Tottenham. The motive for this was that the away supporters would be certain to come in large numbers and fill all the seats (5,000 plus) in the Clock End with the bottom line being a higher attendance at Highbury and, of course, more money into the Arsenal coffers. There were some letters from the Gunners fans complaining about their treatment and the apparent favouring of away supporters. The simple answer is that if they could guarantee filling their stadium with their own supporters the situation presumably wouldn't exist.

The game itself was unusual only for the reason that I was actually watching Newcastle playing at Highbury and expecting us to win, something that would have been inconceivable a couple of years ago. We did win, comfortably as it turned out, even though Arsenal did have a lot of the ball and forced numerous corners only to waste them all as they repeatedly tried to fire them into the near post (a tactic that paid handsome dividends the previous season) where the commanding Peacock or Albert was on hand to clear up. The game also marked the return to first team football for Steve Howey, playing in place of the injured Barry Venison, and all I can say was that he was magnificent.

Come the final whistle and there was the now customary full throated chant of 'Say we are top of the League'. What a pleasure it is to sing this song, it gives you a feeling of real pride knowing that the football team you love more than anything else is, to state the obvious, top of the league (the only shame was that we weren't able to sing this song throughout the whole season). The journey home with Macas at the wheel seemed to take no time at all as I contented myself in the back seat singing the 'Walking in a Keegan wonderland' song all the way up the M1.

Later in the week, after the defeat of Barnsley in the League Cup, Kevin Keegan signed the Derby County forward Paul Kitson (presumably he was influenced to a certain extent by Arthur Cox) who some thought could turn out to be the eventual long term replacement for Peter Beardsley. I wasn't one of them though. Kitson obviously possessed a number of good qualities but a replacement for the incomparable maestro? – no chance. As it transpired it was Andy Cole's shirt he took over after Christmas. His signing wasn't a straight forward one because immediately following the game he had turned down the personal terms offered to him (or perhaps his agent did). It wasn't until 48 hours later, having talked over the move with his wife, that he came back to Tyneside with his tail between his legs to sign on the dotted line. It would have been the biggest mistake of his life had he stayed at Derby. Initially, when I first heard of Keegan's interest in Kitson, I recalled the thoughts I had had when Robert Lee signed two years ago, i.e. what do we need to buy him for? I was so wrong about Lee but Kitson still has to show he can do the business.

At the end of the week, on 25th September, a reunion was organised to commemorate the 25th anniversary of Newcastle United winning the Inter Cities Fairs (UEFA) Cup. All the squad were able to attend and it must have been a tremendous occasion. Talk was rife about a repeat success come May 1995 with the present squad, but this of course was not to be.

27/09/94 – NEWCASTLE v ROYAL ANTWERP (5-2)

After the amazing 5-0 victory in Belgium, St. James' Park was still virtually full despite the tie being over. I suppose that even if all the regular season ticket holders weren't there it at least gave other supporters the opportunity to witness some live action, certainly some of the faces around me were unfamiliar ones. An amazing 10,000 supporters didn't claim their tickets and really they should have their tickets confiscated – were these the so called 'glory hunters'? I cannot fathom the mentality of any supporter who comes up with the line 'Oh it's on television so I'll give the game a miss'. On the other hand the fact that a capacity crowd was not attained meant that many of the criticisms levelled at the club about the ticketing policy were possibly seen as being unjust. Whatever, I cannot understand why so many season ticket holders decided to give this one a miss, in fact if truth be told I find it totally incomprehensible.

Before the game Kevin Keegan said his players had to earn the right to wear the black & white shirt, especially as they had been given away too easily in the past, and this was certainly a heart-warming thing to hear – emphasising that true Geordie pride had been well and truly re-established at the club.

There was also a great deal of controversy over the BBC's decision not to screen the match live. They felt there was more interest in Blackburn's attempt to try and claw back a one goal deficit in Sweden. Given that they had also chosen to screen the first leg from Ewood Park, ignoring Newcastle's romp in Antwerp, it seemed more than a little odd, especially as Newcastle were recognised as the team most neutral fans in Britain wanted to watch. Nevertheless I did understand the rather invidious position the BBC found themselves in. I felt they were wrong to screen the first leg from Blackburn but could understand their desire to cover their second leg match based on the respective results from the two first leg games. Given that they 'messed up' first time round it would have compounded their error to have given in to public pressure and done an about turn so credit to them in the end. The issue of disputed television coverage reared its ugly head again in the second round when, after taking the first leg live from St. James' Park, no agreement could be reached with the Spanish broadcasting company in charge of the game and so fans back in Newcastle were left with radio coverage only, and even that wasn't finally secured until a few hours before kick off. Many supporters who stayed at home were doubly frustrated when they were mistakenly led to believe that they could tune into the game on an obscure Spanish satellite channel when in fact all they got was a Spanish soap drama!

The match, or to be more accurate the tie, was over before a ball was kicked. This was despite Robert Lee making the right noises about having to be careful and warning that Antwerp were capable of doing to Newcastle the same as we had dished out to them in the first leg. As it turned out four first half goals were rattled past the bemused visiting goalkeeper and the final score-line of 5-2 was as easy a victory as you will ever see.

Robert Lee scored four of Newcastle's ten goals in the tie and it was this goal scoring form, as well as his excellent all-round play, that earned him a call up to the England squad for the game against Romania at Wembley on 11th October. Captain David Platt was injured so Lee was an obvious replacement and it was marvellous to see him score the equalising goal on his debut after a typically surging run into the penalty area to clinically steer an Alan Shearer knock down into the net.

Earlier in the season Barry Venison had won a richly deserved first cap against the USA. Venison, like Lee, had replaced an injured 'regular', Manchester United's Paul Ince (a player you don't particularly care for but one whom you are forced to respect for his playing ability), but that shouldn't be allowed to overshadow his call up. Nor should the fact that the USA were appallingly poor opposition distract from the excellent performance given by Venners and it was a tragedy for him that a hamstring injury, suffered against Liverpool, ruled him out not only of the Newcastle United team but also the England squads for the games against Romania and Nigeria. At least Venison could use his enforced lay off to make regular appearances as a pundit on BBC and Sky Television, a role he filled with remarkable success. The outfits he wore also added to his reputation, that is if you like some of the outrageous clothing to be found in the Venison wardrobe. On the theme of England squads it was very unfortunate that the outstanding ability of Scott Sellars wasn't given an International stage too. A knee injury at the end of October, which meant a premature end to his season, was not only a major blow to the player himself but to the team for whom his contribution was far more important than many people thought.

26/10/94 – NEWCASTLE v MANCHESTER UNITED (2-0)

It wasn't really Manchester United we were playing since Mr. Ferguson had decided that his priority this season was not the Coca-Cola League Cup. His policy, which won approval from many quarters including the Football League themselves and Kevin Keegan, was that this particular competition would take too much out of his players whilst his priority remained the European Cup and Premier League Championship, probably in that order. Consequently, the side he fielded on the night included only three first team regulars; Bruce, Pallister and Irwin. Subsequent elimination from the Champions League, after bad defeats in Barcelona and Gothenburg, rather rubbed salt into this particular wound.

Anyway, it didn't stop 34,000 turning up at St. James' Park (including maybe 2,000 from Manchester – they couldn't sell their full 8,000 allocation!) to witness a comprehensive 2-0 victory for Newcastle. Two late goals by Philippe Albert and Paul Kitson, their first for the club, sent us hysterical with joy. It's amazing what a goal can do to you as I found myself jumping, shouting and hugging Ritchie as the two of us went absolutely berserk. Philippe Albert's goal naturally enough led to a deafening rendition of 'Philippe, Philippe Albert, everyone knows his name' sung of course to the tune of Rupert the Bear. Albert has quickly established himself as something of a cult figure since his arrival on Tyneside. He has shown he can operate in the back four, or in midfield, but as far as I am concerned centre of defence is by far his best position, witness his absolutely immaculate performance at Nottingham Forest in November. The knee injury he suffered in training, on the eve of the match at Norwich on New Year's Eve, which kept him out of the team until the 1995/96 season, was a devastating blow. On the injury and recovery theme, what of Paul Gascoigne? Will he ever return to something like his best at Glasgow Rangers? I certainly hope so but must confess to having my doubts as much of his flair has vanished and he has gone from being the linchpin of the team (which ever one that may be) to a liability. Incidentally, quite what Gascoigne is doing plying his trade in the Scottish Premier League is beyond me. Any English player worth his salt should be in England and that's no disrespect at all to Rangers. To his credit he did win the Scottish Player of the Year award at the end of the 1995/96 season, as his hat-trick against Aberdeen clinched the title for Rangers. The quality of his first two goals even suggested that Gazza may prove many of his doubters wrong, myself included, and show the rest of Europe he is still one of the best. The winning goal in the Final of the European Championships at Wembley would do quite nicely.

As it happened there was a little lad in the seats in front of us, not a regular, but one who had purchased a ticket on the night, well his Dad who was accompanying him had anyway, who was supporting Manchester United. Where did his Dad go wrong? When Manchester United came out for the second half he started clapping them so, purely for a bit of fun, I shouted 'Come on you Reds'. He obviously thought a fellow Manchester supporter was with him in the Gallowgate End but when he turned round to look at 'his friend' all he saw was a big Geordie in a black and white shirt grinning at him. I don't think he appreciated the joke – Ritchie meanwhile was killing himself with laughter. Many supporters thought that had Keegan known about Albert's quality and availability around about the time he was looking for a new centre half at the beginning of 1994 then he might not have bought Darren Peacock. Albert and Howey appeared to be the best defensive pairing but Albert's injury at least made Keegan's selection problems a lot easier and it also possibly served to take the pressure off Peacock after Christmas which I'm sure contributed to his good form.

Credit though to Manchester United, on the field that is. They do have a lot of good youngsters and Butt, Beckham and Gillespie (just as well I rated him as he was later to become part of the Andy Cole deal) in particular stood out as players who look to have an exciting future in the game. Harking back to Manchester United's approach to the game wouldn't it have been sweet if they had failed to qualify for Europe through the other three routes available to them.

The League Cup tie also marked Andy Cole's last appearance in a black and white shirt for a six week period in order that he could rest his troublesome shin splints injury. Cole had carried the injury for most of the season and clearly it was affecting his performances. His lack of training meant that he wasn't at his sharpest in and around the penalty box so eventually the player Kevin Keegan and club physiotherapist Derek Wright between them agreed that it was finally time to pull Cole out of the team and order him to take a complete rest from the game. Earlier in the season Cole's injury had caused a mild dispute when Keegan had told England manager Terry Venables that the player was not fit enough to be selected for England. There was of course a nation-wide clamour for Cole to be picked for the squad but in the end the bottom line was that Keegan was correct in his judgement – Cole's time with England will come. The injury to Cole also led indirectly to a dispute between the *Journal* newspaper (with soccer writer Tim Taylor to be precise) and the club which led to Sir John Hall banning representatives from the newspaper from St. James' Park. It came about after the victory at Aston Villa when the paper carried a story that indicated that Keegan and Terry McDermott weren't on the same wavelength as McDermott had, in Keegan's absence, told the media at the post match press conference that there was no reason for Cole not to be included in the England squad that was to be named 48 hours later. As it transpired Keegan hadn't had an opportunity to discuss the matter with McDermott before dashing away from Villa Park hence it looked as if there was some sort of conflict within the club. Keegan cleared the matter up later in the week to everybody's satisfaction but the damage had been done. Thankfully the dispute between club and newspaper only lasted five weeks (five weeks too long in my opinion) before harmony was restored. The unfortunate consequence for Taylor was that he was 'taken off' Newcastle and relegated to covering Sunderland!

Manchester United may have lost this battle but three days later at Old Trafford they inflicted upon us our first defeat of the season, putting an end to our unbeaten 17 match run. Tickets were at such a premium for this match that some supporters paid in excess of £250 for a seat, an incredible sum to pay but there are times when you simply have to do things like that. All good things had to come to an end I suppose but the disappointing thing was that had we won it would have given us a 10 point lead over the Champions, as it was our lead was cut to four points. Still, as was pointed out to the Mancunians at the end of the afternoon, 'Say we are top of the League'. Enough said.

Doug Rawlinson had been at Old Trafford and when I saw him at the airport before jetting off to Bilbao we talked about the problems watching the Toon play away from home. Quite apart from the inefficiency of the ticket office, who quite often send out 'unsuccessful' letters to supporters so as to arrive on the day of the game, it is the way they decide who can and who cannot obtain tickets that infuriates people. The infamous Travel Club seems to be at the root of the problem – join or you don't stand a chance of travelling away is the message continually drummed out by the club. This represents a clear statement from the club that we are not trustworthy, and to say to us that we cannot buy a ticket and choose our own preferred method of transportation to an away game is unacceptable. Furthermore, the fact that even Platinum Club tickets holders sometimes miss out on away tickets in favour of Travel Club members is an extraordinary state of affairs. The other issue here is that surely the club can develop a system of at least knowing which supporters regularly travel away, i.e. it has got to be right that a supporter who travels to virtually every game should have more chance of obtaining a ticket for the 'end of season big game' rather than any Tom, Dick or Harry who quite fancies the look of this particular glamorous fixture. Thankfully, as the 1995/96 season unfolded, this appeared to be the case as the club recognised loyalty and rewarded it accordingly with a place at the front of the queue for away tickets. The notion of introducing 'away' season tickets was even mooted but I would be surprised if this ever happened.

The other things about the ticket situation that rub supporters up the wrong way are the bureaucratic nature of the ticket office staff and the stipulation that postal applications only are acceptable when applying for tickets, although I understand personal applications were being accepted for the FA Cup ties at the beginning of 1995, and it was nice to see this improved state of affairs continuing into the 1995/96 season. Doug told me that when he was trying to sort out his tickets for Antwerp he had to make four separate journeys to the ticket office because the travel club office staff were unable to transfer passport information on to the correct forms, information that was held by their ticket office colleagues on an adjacent desk – 'I'm sorry but we can't touch their files' was the rather weak response to Doug's exasperated plea for a little bit of assistance to be given.

Regarding the situation over postal applications I happened to be at the ticket office picking up a flyer for the 1996 European Championships when applications were being accepted for Nottingham Forest tickets. I enquired if they could accept my application there and then but no, I couldn't even hand them an envelope over the counter, but had to go into town and find a post office which of course couldn't guarantee next day delivery, the closing date for applications. Are they trying to make it difficult for supporters? I wasn't trying to queue jump or anything, as I fully expected my application to be put on the pile with every other application, but surely a little bit of common sense and flexibility could be the order of the day.

As for me, on the day of our Old Trafford reversal, I suffered another unfortunate footballing injury. Playing at Eccleshill (Bradford) I got carted off to hospital with concussion and a broken nose after an aerial collision minutes before half time. No blame to the offender, it was just one of those things, but it led to an uncomfortable night and worse still I didn't find out the score from Old Trafford until about 9.00 in the evening and also missed the highlights on *Match of the Day*. I was grateful to our diminutive, but very talented, centre forward, Johnny White (a bit of a Tony Cottee if you're looking for a comparison), who drove my car home for me. Fortunately, despite medical advice, I was back playing a week later, but a nose operation was the resulting diagnosis. They weren't able to operate straight away as the doctor had told me it was such a bad break that to operate immediately might cause all the bones inside the nose to fall away – reassuring news indeed! At least it meant not being detained further in hospital which could have seriously jeopardised my plans to travel to Spain three days later – every cloud has a silver lining as they say.

01/11/94 – ATHLETIC BILBAO v NEWCASTLE (1-0)

A nice European outing to Spain for the second round of the UEFA Cup. European Football is really something special, and after sending shock waves around the whole of Europe after the 10-2 demolition of Royal Antwerp in Round One, it was Athletic Club Bilbao who got the draw no other club in Europe wanted – Newcastle United.

The first leg of the second round tie had been played two weeks earlier at St. James' Park and it could hardly have been scripted better; well that's how it looked after the first hour of the match. Two first half goals, followed by a marvellous Andy Cole header, gave us a 3-0 lead and all seemed rosy. Visions of another Antwerp style 5-0 mauling looked on the cards as we continued to make European football look anything but difficult. Then reality hit home. Bilbao were no mugs and their neat football produced two crucial away goals in the last nineteen minutes to leave their travelling supporters in a state of delirious excitement; emotions that had seemed a forlorn hope only a short time ago. Naive defending by Newcastle yes, but let's give the Basques some credit as they had really looked down and out after Cole had struck. Let's remember also that they were missing at least two of their most influential players, Goicoechea (who scored against Germany in USA '94) and the precocious 20 year old Guerrero, so perhaps we did catch them at a good time.

And so to Spain. Travelling to Bilbao for the Geordies was complicated by the strained (and that's a major understatement) relationship between the supporters and the club over both the distribution of tickets and the method of travel. The club insisted once again that tickets would only be available to those supporters who went with the Travel Club which, had it been true, would have meant them completely monopolising the ticketing and travel arrangements and making a fair sized profit as a result of being able to charge whatever they wanted. Fortunately this wasn't the case and the vast majority of the fans, probably at least 1,800 of the 2,500 or so who made their way to Bilbao, travelled independently of the club, many with UF Tours, the Cheshire based travel firm who specialise in football tours abroad and had served the supporters so well in Antwerp.

The important thing here is that the supporter should have an individual choice and his/her freedom is not restricted. Fears that Geordies let loose in Europe would misbehave were totally disproved in Antwerp, and the restrictive practices that were again in force seemed to me to be a little over the top.

Having said all this I decided to book up with the club. Why? Well I suppose it was because I didn't fancy two or three days of heavy drinking sessions in Bilbao which many of the UF Tour travellers opted for which of course was their choice and, harking back to what I said before, if they behave themselves then there's absolutely no problem. Pre-flight information indicated that we would have three to four hours of free time in the city before the game so at least on that front the club had been seen to be a little more flexible and customer friendly, which is the one thing it gets criticised for more than anything else. Numerous people I speak to, from all walks of life and with widely different perspectives of the club, agree that the 'PR' emanating from St. James' Park could be improved. The club have certainly got it right on and off the field in most areas and if the 'PR' follows suit no one will have any cause for complaint.

The 'club tour' departed Newcastle Airport at 11.00am and upon checking in it was nice to see a fair few familiar faces including Dave Pickard (one of my brother's good friends from Ponteland), Martin Howlett (former Ponteland United colleague), David Urwin (from the golf club) and Doug Rawlinson. I was actually travelling alone, mainly because none of the lads could afford the time off work or the money to make the trip, which was disappointing really in more ways than one.

After encountering a number of difficulties on the Antwerp trip the club seemed to have learned their lesson this time and check-in procedures went very smoothly with no undue delays. Many supporters were getting 'tanked up' in the departure lounge which boded well for their health for the rest of the day seeing it was only 9.30 in the morning.

The Geordies were in good humour (what else would you expect?) as we trooped on to the plane, a European Airbus, presumably chartered by the club. I wouldn't say I am a nervous flyer but I always fear the worst. Robert Lee for example doesn't enjoy it at all and so sits next to Kevin Keegan on all their trips on the basis that he thinks Keegan is the Messiah and, should the plane crash, then he would be saved! This particular trip wasn't helped by the fact that as I left home in the morning to drive to the airport news was coming in from America of a plane crash that had claimed over 60 lives. There were some comedians on the plane as well with one lad saying 'there's Buddy Holly's sandwich' as he pointed to one of the seats on the plane as we were boarding. He said it in jest of course and I suppose it was quite funny come to think of it. The plane took off over Ponteland and the clear weather enabled me to get a perfect view of our house. We live next to the school and with its large green playing field standing out like a beacon it made spotting the house a simple task. It also helped having a window seat on the right hand side of the plane. The previous times I've flown from Newcastle it's either been dark or we've taken off the other way over Dinnington. A routine two hour flight followed and touch down in Bilbao was greeted with a great roar – the excitement was building and the anticipation of what lay ahead was there to see on everyone's face.

It was now 2.00pm local time (kick off 7.15pm) and the plan was that we were to be taken directly to the ground, conveniently situated right in the city centre (as all good grounds are), and 'let loose' in the city for the afternoon. Congratulations to the club for this but in all honesty if they couldn't trust us to behave responsibly then you could only despair.

It was no surprise to see plenty of Geordies all round the streets as we made our way into town. I'd joined up with Pickie and his mates (including the hyper-active and effervescent Russ) and we headed towards where most of the noise was coming from. What an amazing sight greeted us. What seemed to be the main street through the town was absolutely packed, especially on the two main cross-roads, and this was a good five hours before kick off. Obviously there were more Basques than Geordies but the camaraderie between the two sets of fans was incredible. Supporters were singing and dancing together, drinks were freely flowing and the atmosphere was unbelievable – in all honesty you had to be there to believe it. Steve Sutton from BBC Newcastle was doing some filming and it was pleasing that these scenes were being conveyed back to the north-east. There wasn't a policeman in sight and, what's more, there was never a need for one. A round of drinks for five of us (Heineken or San Miguel) only cost £2.40 as the warmth of welcome from the Basque people became overwhelming. They were genuinely pleased to welcome us to their city (they had of course received much the same welcome in Newcastle two weeks earlier), and as the hours ticked by so the revelry and noise grew to astounding levels. I've never seen or heard anything like it in all my time of following Newcastle United.

You could see the magnificent San Mames Stadium from the main street and I decided to go up to the ground an hour or so before kick off as I wanted to sample the special Basque atmosphere inside the stadium. I wasn't quite sure what to expect but I certainly wasn't disappointed. The locals call the stadium the 'Cathedral' and it was easy to see why – it was a tremendous sight with row after row of red seating extending upwards. I realise it's only half as big as the Nou Camp or Bernabeu but its architecture was magnificent.

There were two areas of terracing, behind each goal, where the most vociferous of the home supporters congregated and these sections were packed even as I entered the ground. Our seats, fairly high above the corner flag, afforded us a splendid view of the pitch (travelling with the club did have its benefits although it was impossible to escape the inevitable, but good natured, banter between the Travel Club members and the 'unofficial' travellers) and for a while I just sat back and took it all in. A few moments later the Newcastle team, looking resplendent in their club suits, came out to look at the pitch and were given a rapturous round of applause by the home fans – such generosity to their opponents. Even upon leaving the pitch to return to the changing rooms the Basques turned up the volume again to salute United.

As kick off approached so the ground filled to its 47,000 capacity. The Geordies were of course in full voice but were more often than not drowned out by the home fans as the crescendo of noise grew to fill the night air. The Basques were all dressed in their red and white shirts and their ritual of all holding their scarfs above their heads and spinning them round was a terrific sight. The band appeared 15 minutes before the start and were roundly booed but this was just the prelude for the main course. As the teams came out side by side the 'Cathedral' erupted and we were ready for battle.

I thought if we could keep the scoresheet blank for the first 20 minutes or so then we would end up winning the tie. As it turned out we looked very comfortable indeed and Robert Lee could well have sneaked a goal either side of half time. I wasn't as nervous as I thought I'd be, we were playing reasonably well, but if the minutes had kept ticking by without a goal then I suppose it would have got worse. Suddenly, midway through the second half, Bilbao broke away and when Ziganda's shot was deflected by Steve Howey under the body of Pavel Srnicek, my worst fears were realised. Bilbao were leading on the away goals rule and the Basques were in a state of uncontrolled joy. The passion and noise of the home supporters had reached a peak and the stadium shook on its foundations.

In a funny way I was quite hoping that Bilbao would score, only so I could witness the reaction of the home crowd celebrating a goal, but this was obviously on the proviso that we would score also and win the tie overall. It wasn't to be though, despite the valiant efforts of Peter Beardsley as he strove in vain in the final couple of minutes, to snatch the equaliser on the night. This game meant so much to Beardsley and the effort he put in during the closing minutes had to be seen to be believed. Steve Howey was inconsolable as the final whistle blew, as he sat alone near the edge of the penalty box with his head in his hands, but the team were able to leave the field with their heads held high – they had let no one down.

By now the Basques couldn't control their feelings as they clambered over the safety fencing on to the pitch to salute their victory (it later predictably cost them a UEFA fine). This led to the only sour note of the day when one Newcastle supporter disgraced himself, and the whole city of Newcastle, by trying to fight a Bilbao fan on the pitch. Fortunately this was an isolated incident as it quickly led to many more Geordies getting on to pitch and joining in the celebrations with the Bilbao supporters – an amazing sight. Regrettably *The Sun* went overboard on this story and told its readers that violence had erupted after the game – they couldn't have been further from the truth.

Shortly afterwards a huge mass of Bilbao supporters came towards our seated area and started chanting 'Newcastle' (in their unique accent) such was their admiration of us and our football team. We responded in the only way we knew by chanting the Basque's favourite song and it reminded me of the day back in 1976 at Wembley when we joined in support of Manchester City's victory in the League Cup Final.

It took a good half an hour to clear the ground and even as we left the stadium to return to our coaches for the short ride back to the airport the Basques were waiting outside the turnstiles to applaud us. Walking away from the ground, fans from both sides were shaking hands and many exchanged shirts to such an extent that back on the coach there were as many red and white shirts in evidence as black and white ones. At a home game a couple of weeks later it was sad to see Doug Rawlinson's mate, Kevin Steel, being barracked by a fellow Newcastle supporter for wearing his red Bilbao scarf outside St. James' Park. Some people are simply beyond belief.

And that was more or less it, the coaches taking us back to the airport drove straight on to the runway so we were able to board the plane straight away without having to bother to go through all the check in procedures inside the terminal building. It was a very subdued journey home but after another two hours, and a less than smooth touch down in Newcastle at midnight, a memorable day was brought to an end – memorable in terms of the experience but the bottom line was that we had been defeated and were out of Europe.

The biggest disappointment about losing was that we would

have to wait at least another year (depending upon when we qualify again) to get back into Europe and enjoy another trip like this one again. I was really gutted that it had all come to an end and when the draw for the third round was made three days later, Bilbao drew the crack Italian side Parma, it made the disappointment even more heartfelt. Parma went on to knock Bilbao out of the competition, 4-3 on aggregate, but note that Bilbao won their home leg 1-0.

So what did it all prove? Well, above anything else, the fact that European football (especially matches away from home in magnificent stadiums like the San Mames) are on a different plane to anything domestic football can offer. There are many reasons for this but if I was to pick out one that stands out more than any other it would have to be playing matches in 'pressure cooker' atmospheres like the San Mames produced.

A day later Manchester United were on the wrong end of a 4-0 hiding in Barcelona and, if I thought the atmosphere in and around the San Mames was incredible, what must 115,000 inside the Nou Camp have been like? Having said that I'm sure the passion and fervour the Basque supporters have for their football exceeds that of their Catalan rivals, a fact I'm sure the BBC's Alan Green could confirm as he commentated on both matches. I was sorry to hear also of trouble between the Barcelona and Manchester United fans in Spain, clearly the atmosphere that prevailed at both games, particularly outside the confines of the match itself, was poles apart and once again it left you so proud to be a Geordie.

16/11/94 – ENGLAND v NIGERIA (1-0)

Three Newcastle United players in the starting line up for England brought an end to an amazing and quite unprecedented week in football. To see Howey, Lee and Beardsley together in the same England team spoke volumes about the progress Newcastle United had made in such a short space of time. It was a little like watching the England/Germany World Cup semi final back in 1990 when Beardsley, Gascoigne and Waddle all donned the white shirt but of course the difference then was that the three of them were Newcastle exiles at the time.

It was around this time that the morons (apologies to the many thousands of decent fans) who watch England at Wembley stopped booing the National Anthem of the opposition. This practice, executed by more than a small minority judging by the amount of noise they created, made you cringe and quite honestly ashamed to be English. It was the most crass and vile act imaginable and thank goodness it is now virtually a thing of the past.

The night before the Nigeria game a staggering 25,863 supporters turned up at St. James' Park to watch an Under 21 International between England and Ireland (later in the season 11,010 watched an Under 15s Schools International at St. James' Park and this too was a record for such a fixture outside Wembley). Of course it had a lot to do with the fact that Kevin Keegan was managing the England Team but even so it was still a phenomenal turn out especially when you compare it to the paltry 7,500 that went to Anfield for the England 'B' International a few weeks later, and there were five Liverpool players in the England team! Comment has been passed on the somewhat unfavourable reception afforded to Sunderland's Martin Smith when he came on as a second half substitute at St. James' Park. I don't think too much should be read into it, it was largely good humoured and it goes without saying that the same thing would have happened to a Newcastle player had an England match been played at Roker Park. The biggest irony of all would be if Smith is transferred to Newcastle in the future. It's not inconceivable, especially as he's one of their few decent players, but I can imagine the Roker Park hierarchy being lynched if it ever did come about. Eighteen months later, when the England Under 21 team played against Croatia at Roker Park, Newcastle's Chris Holland was in the England team, this after thankfully recovering from a vicious assault outside a Newcastle night-club when ammonia was spayed in to his eyes. Predictably the Mackems got their revenge, even though there were under 5000 in the ground – perhaps the reason that so few came along was that they thought it was a regular season league fixture.

Back on Tyneside and the club were announcing ambitious plans to build a £12 million football academy at Woolsington Hall (near Ponteland) including a sports club, multi purpose sports hall, indoor football facility, practice pitches, swimming pool and golf course. Assuming this comes off, and there's no reason to think otherwise, then it will surely be one of the best facilities in Europe and play an integral part in ensuring the long term future success of the club. It was also announced that Radio Magpie would be taking to the airwaves on 26th November. The decision for the club to have its own match day radio station was clearly a good move and just one of those little things that kept the profile of the club moving on an upward path.

Off the field the good name of the game had taken an awful battering and it made you wonder if we were the laughing stock of Europe. Apart from the routine managerial sackings which you expect anyway, although perhaps not as high profile as Ardiles, Atkinson and Walker in such a short space of time, Bruce Grobbelaar was allegedly involved in a match fixing scandal, later to involve two other Premier League players, Dennis Wise was convicted of assault on a London taxi driver and Arsenal's Paul Merson broke down in tears after it was disclosed he was an alcoholic, compulsive gambler and drug addict. I would have thought having one of these three weaknesses would be bad enough but to have all three at once – well, that's some going. On a more serious note I suppose you should be sympathising with him but in all honestly I didn't, even though his club and the Football Association both did. Merson abused his talent and the vast sums of money he earned so he effectively brought it upon himself – in my book that means a lack of self discipline, and that's a tremendous shame. The fact that he went on to sell his story to a National Newspaper sullied his reputation even further. It didn't do Arsenal much good either and this was exacerbated when revelations of George Graham's alleged 'bung' came to light. Not good in anyone's eyes that particular episode and his subsequent departure from the club was not unexpected.

And then there was Cantona (not to mention Paul Ince and Roy Keane's misdemeanours). What an outstanding player but what a liability. His act of folly at Selhurst Park was totally inexcusable and his punishment just. Manchester United persuaded him to remain in the English game but I am sure there were tens of thousands of supporters up and down the country who would have been delighted to wave him goodbye.

21/12/94 – NEWCASTLE v MANCHESTER CITY (0-2)

Three weeks earlier we had travelled to Maine Road and picked up an excellent 1-1 draw in the fourth round of the Coca-Cola League Cup. I had gone across the Pennines with Louise

Harrison, a friend of Doug Rawlinson, who was studying at Leeds University. The away supporters were situated in the half built new Kippax Stand but the problem was that there was only one small entrance/exit area and so you can imagine the total chaos that ensued when 5,000 Geordies tried to leave as the final whistle sounded. Our seats were half way up the stand over the half way line, ideal really, but when we saw Doug at half time we had to sympathise with him and his regular band of travelling mates as they were stuck on the very front row and could hardly see a thing.

Back to the replay and it was an ideal time to play the game as it marked the first day of my extended Christmas holiday, what a perfect start. Well it was meant to be. The 2-0 defeat that resulted was a dreadful result, especially as the route to Wembley looked pretty free of major obstacles. What made it worse was that Manchester City were a very average team and, believe it or not, we couldn't score against them either in the League game at St. James' Park 12 days later. Revenge was sweet come the Fifth Round of the FA Cup in February.

Our form over the past two months, since our elimination from Europe, had been patchy to say the least. Defeat at a revitalised Francis-inspired Tottenham in the first week of December had been unfortunate but we had lost that early season sparkle. People up and down the country who were saying that our bubble had burst were well wide of the mark though, after all, you can't expect to excel in every match you play. Keegan got it about right, as he tends to do, when he said our best football was better than any other team in the country but that we weren't consistent enough and that was why Blackburn in particular were able to steal a march on us in the period leading up to Christmas. They weren't playing flowing attractive football week in week out but they were playing consistently well each week to keep winning – 11 wins and a draw out of 12 league games until they lost in mid January at Old Trafford was a pretty formidable run of results.

Still, I couldn't help feeling that life on Tyneside was still a darn sight brighter than it had ever been in the past, despite this defeat, and that at least served to console me. It's worth adding that the day before the Manchester City defeat the North East media held a lunch to mark Newcastle United's achievements during 1994. During the various speeches that were made, Doug Weatherall, the highly respected *Daily Mail* journalist, was asked to say a few words about the success of the club and what the hopes and expectations in 1995 were and he simply said 'More, More, More' – and that just about summed things up perfectly.

Over the Christmas period Radio 5's *6.06* football phone-in programme had a guest presenter in the shape of *Q* magazine editor and Tottenham supporter Danny Kelly. Regular presenter David Mellor was on holiday and, although he does a reasonable job, Kelly was like a breath of fresh air and how I wish the BBC would take him on full time. Mellor reached the milestone of 100 programmes on 25th November 1995 but he does at times appear not to be entirely in touch with the game, it's difficult to pinpoint but there's something not quite there in his make up. When *6.06* first hit the airwaves it was hosted by the excellent, but irreverent, Danny Baker, but then it took a step backwards when the ultra boring Bob Beaven took over, thankfully only for a short time. Other presenters have included Duncan McKenzie, whose dry humour added a certain style to the show, Simon Inglis and, more recently, Celtic supporter Dominik Diamond who took over the microphone for two shows over Easter 1995. Although he can be pretty humorous he is, in my opinion, somewhat immature and unknowledgeable for the role. Witness his petty argument with a Glasgow Rangers supporter over the virtues of Brian Laudrup and his admission that he had never heard of the Tottenham legend John White. Other than Danny Kelly I think someone like Rodney Marsh would make the ideal host. Kelly also featured on John Inverdale's *Drive Time* programme on Radio 5 on Friday afternoons and this was a wonderfully interesting and funny show. Sadly, when Radio 5 became Radio 5 Live, the programme was banished from the airwaves (as was Dominik Diamond's *Fantasy Football Show* on Sunday mornings) and this was a tremendous shame. At least during the 1994/95 season a new Sunday evening show, *Jim and the Doc*, was launched by Radio 5 Live. The following season, perhaps the best programme yet, *Baker and Kelly Up Front*, was launched, and together with the football programmes every Monday, Tuesday and Wednesday evenings I suppose I can't really complain about the coverage.

08/01/95 – NEWCASTLE v BLACKBURN ROVERS (1-1)

FA Cup time again and what a cracking game to draw in the Third Round (thanks by the way to Gordon McKeag for the home draws in the first three rounds, pity he didn't do the business in the Sixth

Round). The fact we had never beaten Blackburn since Keegan had returned to the club didn't matter – home advantage would prove decisive. The game was the obvious choice for BBC Television which is always good news as it means you can add to your Newcastle video collection, providing it's a decent game of course. As it turned out a 1-1 draw was the end result, Robert Lee's superb second half strike raising the roof and cancelling out Chris Sutton's first half opener.

The next two fixtures, Manchester United in the League and the Cup replay at Blackburn, were mouth watering titantic clashes, but the news that was to break in 48 hours time was to take everyone's breath away.

10/01/95 – ANDY COLE

On 9th March 1993 Dave Ingham phoned me at work to tell me the hot news that Newcastle had paid Bristol City £1.75m for an up and coming, but as yet unproven, striker called Andy Cole. On 10th January 1995 it was Dave again who called me just after lunch to report that Cole was on his way to Manchester United for £7m.

No more work for the rest of the day, the telephone and fax lines never stopped for the rest of the afternoon as the news filtered through to all the rest of the lads spread around the country. I was numb with shock initially. Use any words you wish but I suppose totally unbelievable just about sums it up. Cole was the biggest cult hero Tyneside had had for years and yet, just when he was reaching his prime, he was being off loaded – and what's worse to one of our Premier League rivals (Leeds United supporters have apparently never forgiven Howard Wilkinson for selling Eric Cantona to Manchester United). Was this a return to the days when Newcastle were branded a selling club, a club that lacked ambition that were content to settle for second best? No.

It took only a few hours, which surprised even myself, but I soon began to realise that I wasn't as disappointed and heartbroken as I imagined I would be. Was it because Cole's goals had recently dried up or the fact that his overall team play was ragged? Had he lost his sparkle or was it simply that I had so much faith in the judgement of Keegan that I had to believe he knew what he was doing. Sure enough he and Sir John Hall made all the right noises about the long term future of the club being top of the agenda at all times as supporters besieged St. James' Park to demand an answer to Cole's departure. The two didn't shirk their responsibilities and all credit to them for standing up and being counted when it really mattered. 'I'm in charge, trust me' Keegan said, and it was typical of the man to be so bold and honest as he put his faith in the long term strategies that the club had developed. I was actually on a train to London in the evening (more of that later) when querulous, even angry fans, descended upon the ground and I can imagine the mood was hardly festive – extremely hostile and vitriolic would be a more accurate description. Supporters' emotions ranged from the resigned to the hysterical, from the embittered to the stunned, and from the heartbroken to the suicidal. Surely no one could have been pleased to have seen him go.

Cole hadn't scored since the Ipswich fixture as far back as 26th November and indeed hadn't even looked like doing so in the majority of the games he had played, a missed penalty at Coventry contributing to this sorry run. Was he disturbed by the racial abuse from a sick minority, the death of a close member of the family, or was it that his shin injury was still troubling him to such an extent that it was limiting his effectiveness? It was rumoured (and who believes rumours on Tyneside) that he couldn't find a specialist in the North East to give his shin the all clear which could just be a telling factor for the remainder of his career. I heard also that he wasn't comfortable with his Reebok boots (which he was paid a considerable sum to wear) and if that was true it can't have helped.

Perhaps his attitude was a little suspect too. The incident at Wimbledon in November 1993, when he briefly went missing, is well documented and talk of him mixing with the wrong company in Tyneside night clubs, even allegedly getting involved in the drug scene, which are hopefully wide of the mark, may have been contributing factors in Keegan's eventual decision to sell. It was said the deal came pretty much out of the blue but I would be surprised if this was the case. Keegan clearly saw the money on the table, and Keith Gillespie, as being the best move to take the club forward, and in that respect I back him whole heartedly. Of course I'll miss singing the famous 'Andy Cole scores a goal' song, we all will, but as the days unfolded and the fixture with Manchester United loomed large it was becoming more and more evident that virtually the whole of Tyneside were turning to back Keegan – his immortality, threatened briefly, had been restored and we were ready to get on with the business of playing football once again.

Having said all this about Cole the bottom line as far as I am concerned is that he brought so much joy to the supporters of Newcastle United during his 22 months with the club (68 goals in 84 appearances) that I can only wish him well in his future career with Manchester United and England. Funnily enough I just have a sneaky feeling that he may well be back to grace St. James' Park again, in a black and white shirt of course, before the year 2000.

Back to my train journey to London, which if nothing else gave me time to reflect on the events of the afternoon. I anticipated a quiet ride down but ended up sitting next to a Chelsea fan, Tony Lee, and we were both content to talk football for the entire two hour trip. It's nice to meet acquaintances like this on trains and I was even able to sort him out with some tickets for a forthcoming basketball match in Doncaster when he found out what I did for a living. The purpose of the visit to London was actually for a job interview which, believe it or not, was at the Football Association Headquarters at Lancaster Gate. I was delighted to have made the short list for this particular post, in the Competitions & Regulations Department, but although I felt the interview went very well I was ultimately unsuccessful. A move to London into the football industry would have been a dream come true for me, further away from my beloved Newcastle I know, but this would have been a marvellous opportunity for me. I had also applied for a job at the Welsh Football Association but decided not to pursue that particular avenue when the internal difficulties they were suffering came to light.

15/01/95 – NEWCASTLE v MANCHESTER UNITED (1-1)

As much as I would like to I can't tell you much about this match, I'll have to leave it to Dad who was using my ticket, as I was simultaneously jetting off, ironically from Manchester, to Bulgaria for a skiing holiday (apologies to Steve Taylor). We had carefully planned the trip to take the football fixtures into account, that is flying off the day after the Manchester United game. Needless to say when Sky Television moved the game back 24 hours we were well and truly snookered. I even tried to sell my holiday on the cheap to a few of the lads a day or so before departure such was my desperation to see the game, I even asked Ritchie to phone the travel agent to see whether we could postpone the trip for a week but neither of these plans ever stood a chance of coming off. As it was the skiing week was absolutely fantastic but that's not really the point.

Meanwhile back at St. James Park Dad had taken his seat and found the atmosphere to be phenomenal. In the *Evening Chronicle* the following day Alan Oliver described it as the best he could remember for years and that only made me wince even more over that fact that I hadn't been a part of it. In view of the transfer activity earlier in the week it had been decided by both managers that neither Cole or Gillespie should play and indeed Cole wasn't even in Newcastle which I felt was an unnecessary step to have taken but apparently the Police (interfering in football again?) had the final say in this matter. After a pretty even first half, despite a Mark Hughes goal for the visitors, Newcastle set up camp in the Manchester United half in the second 45 minutes and the equaliser was the least we deserved – if Keane or Cantona had snatched victory at the death for the visitors it would have been the most cruel of blows.

The skiing holiday had been in Borovets which was a new destination for us, primarily because it was cheap – the rest of the lads weren't exactly flush with money so I went along with their choice of destination. I had of course made contingency plans for getting full match details, indeed as we weren't taking off until 4.30pm I was able to hear Mark Hughes put Manchester United ahead on my Sony Walkman as I lingered as long as possible in the departure lounge. Upon boarding I asked the stewardess if she could ask the pilot to radio home and keep us up to date with score flashes but unfortunately this wasn't possible. So, we were left to fly over Europe not knowing what was going on back in Newcastle – an awful feeling. It goes without saying I had my Newcastle shirt on and it was a coincidence that the lad I was sitting next to on the plane was a fellow Geordie and Toon fanatic – Milburn Stand season ticket holder Kevin Mitchell from Chester-le-Street. We struck up a good rapport and as it turned out we were staying in the same hotel in Borovets so saw plenty of each other during the week. Before leaving England I had found out from the travel company the phone number of our hotel so I was able to telephone and obtain their fax number in order that Dad could fax me a match report as soon as he got back from the match. This he did of course and upon arrival at the hotel around midnight the sight of the fax with news of Kitson's equaliser made my day. Three days later and the fax that arrived telling us of the win at Blackburn left us all euphoric. When I watched the video of this game after getting back to England it was marvellous to see the pride on the faces of the players and supporters and of course Keegan getting the better of Dalglish.

Lee Clark had scored a rare goal at Ewood Park but his undisguised joy at scoring the winner must have been tinged with a little sadness because he was desperately disappointed not to be a first team regular. The situation reached crisis point a few weeks later when he requested a transfer and for him to have done such a thing must have been a truly heart wrenching decision. A few clubs, Middlesbrough and Norwich to name but two, were said to be interested but nothing materialised. If he had gone could you imagine how he would feel if he ever had the chance to score a goal against his beloved Newcastle United? – I wouldn't be surprised if he would miss on purpose. I certainly would!

At the weekend in Borovets we managed to tune into World Service and Paddy Feeney for reports on the Sheffield Wednesday game at Hillsborough. Bulgaria is two hours ahead of England so we were able to finish our day's skiing before settling down to the match. I was desperately hoping that the commentator on Radio 5's live match (Ron Jones at Nottingham Forest) would interrupt coverage of his game and say 'And now off to Hillsborough where we've got news of a goal' but alas it was not to be and another 0-0 draw was the final analysis. During our times bombing down the slopes we met a lad called Andy Stewart (holidaying with his wife Kim) who was a die hard Coventry fan. I found it incredible that we had so much in common in terms of our views on football, and sport generally, and Ritchie and I even enrolled him into membership of the 'Rumble Club' (skiing downhill as fast as you can without any regard for your own safety or indeed anyone else's) and that's a pretty exclusive club I can tell you.

25/02/95 – NEWCASTLE v ASTON VILLA (3-1)

A routine win which preserved our unbeaten home record in the league but notable for four exceptional goals. Barry Venison smashed in a 25 yard drive that Bosnich could only watch hit the back of the net, Andy Townsend replied for Villa in similar style, but the *coup de grace* was still to come.

Peter Beardsley, who else, took centre stage in the second half.

His first goal was typical Beardsley, a quick shimmy before drilling the ball into the net. His second was something else. Steve Howey won the ball in midfield and when he gave it to the maestro he waltzed past McGrath and Ehiogu with such quick feet and incredible ball control that it truly mesmerised you. Bosnich was once again left helpless as Beardsley drove the ball into the corner of the net.

It was a season of brilliant finishing by Beardsley. Goals later in the season against Arsenal and Norwich were classical strikes in their own right but his second against Villa stood out for me. The Football Pink even ran a Beardsley all time greatest goal feature which Beardsley himself helped to judge. In the end his brilliant solo goal against Portsmouth during the 1983/84 promotion season came out on top but really you could have chosen any of his classics. Quite honestly there cannot have been another player in the history of the game, and I include Pele, Cruyff and Baggio in this statement, who could possibly have scored as many outstanding individual goals in their career as Beardsley.

The kit theme came to the fore once again when it was confirmed that Adidas were to become the new kit sponsors from the start of the 1995/96 season. Rumours of such a deal had been circulating for months and, despite Freddie Fletcher continually denying them, the end for Asics came as no surprise to anyone. Nearly every supporter I know liked the Asics strips, home and away, so in a way it was sad to see them go. Having said that, Adidas are probably the biggest name in the sports manufacturing world and to be associated with them is clearly a good move. It would obviously mean more money into the club coffers and the quality and design of the new strip would be of the highest order.

Being in basketball I've been very fortunate to deal with many kit manufacturers over the past few years, Champion, Converse, Reebok etc., but I can honestly say that when we have been under contract with Adidas they have produced all the best gear. Ever since schooldays I've always been an Adidas fan so this particular deal went down particularly well with me. As chance would have it I was finalising a new kit deal for the England Men's Team at this time so when I went across to the Adidas Centre in Hazel Grove, Stockport to meet Marketing Manager, Jon Tuck, he gave me a sneak preview of the Newcastle home and away kits. The traditional black & white stripes were of course retained with the main difference being a redesigned collar and the Newcastle

Brown logo replacing the Blue Star/McEwans Lager motif on the front of the shirt. The away strip was also very fashionable, a pale blue and maroon design, but it is on its way out as the 1996/97 season will see a new away strip being produced, purely for commercial reasons of course. At least you never accuse Newcastle United of exploiting their fans to the extent that Manchester United have done in the past, and continue to do so. I have lost count of the number of different shirt designs they have had in recent seasons, and the issue took on ludicrous proportions when, after conceding three first half goals at Southampton towards the end of the 1995/96 season, they took the decision to banish their grey strip to the history books.

12/03/95 – EVERTON v NEWCASTLE (1-0)

After comfortably disposing of Swansea City and Manchester City, a trip to Goodison Park was the reward for reaching the Sixth Round of the FA Cup for the first time in 19 years – an unbelievable record of failure. Obviously a home draw would have been better but it was good to have avoided the likes of Liverpool, Manchester United and Tottenham.

A word or two on the defeat of Manchester City. Firstly the contribution of Keith Gillespie. For a supposed lightweight in the Andy Cole deal Gillespie was certainly producing the goods. I did hear that Manchester United's 'books' actually showed Cole cost the club £6.75m so if that was the case Gillespie only cost Newcastle £250,000, surely the transfer bargain of the season. Secondly, I thought Manchester City were a 'big' club but clearly I was wrong. Any club that returns tickets for a Fifth Round FA Cup tie cannot possibly be so.

Earlier in the year Everton had visited St. James' Park and disgraced themselves with a display of foul play and blatant time wasting. Even Tracey, who was attending her first match with me, thought the team in blue weren't playing very fairly. Everton finished with nine men and had another seven booked. FIFA Referee David Elleray was criticised by Joe Royle for being over zealous but if truth be told he was only doing his job.

The feeling before the game was similar to that experienced before the Fifth Round tie against Wimbledon in 1988 when Cup Fever was rife on Tyneside. It was the 'Year of the Geordie' and Wembley was waiting to welcome the Toon Army. Tickets were scarce and there were never going to be enough to satisfy the Geordie hordes who wanted to descend upon Merseyside. What made it worse was that thousands of supporters, including bond holders and fanatics who had been to every away game during the season, missed out and that cannot be right. I was one of the unlucky ones but fortunately managed to obtain tickets for the Everton main stand through Hally and Andy Conway.

As for the match it can be summed up by simply mentioning two players, Peter Beardsley and Duncan Ferguson. Beardsley absence was devastating; Ferguson's presence crucial. The 1-0 loss was a bitter pill to swallow and as far as I was concerned after the game they might as well have cancelled the FA Cup competition. Seeing Manchester United and Everton contest the Final was soul destroying.

Five weeks later I returned to Goodison Park with Phil Crotty for the Good Friday Premier League fixture which not surprisingly resulted in another defeat. I say not surprising because for some reason I just didn't have a good feeling about this match before kick off and indeed told *The Mag* Fanzine Editor Mark Jensen as much outside the ground. Perhaps it was a sign of our fading fortunes that brought on this mood of depression but whatever it was I hoped it would only be temporary.

As I did for the Norwich fixture at St. James' Park in March 1994 here is Phil's account of his first experience on tour with the Toon Army.

"At roughly this point last season Mark allowed me to contribute to this wonderful diary of football (and particularly Geordie) obsession. The wager that Mark and I had on our respective teams' fortunes last season had been extended this season to £10 for each domestic competition. Blind faith in your chosen team can leave you poor. The hurt is compounded when you bet against your better judgement – I seriously did not believe that Leeds would fare better than Newcastle in any of the competitions.

"The first £10 disappeared in a very embarrassing fashion. Leeds had been dumped out of the Coca-Cola Cup earlier in the season by Third Division Mansfield – unfortunately these embarrassments are becoming part of being a Leeds fan, as they were to Newcastle a few years ago. In 1973 the Mackems pierced the heart of every Leeds fan with a sword of Excalibur proportions. This remains in place and is twisted every time the BBC gleefully replay the grinning clocks of Messrs Porterfield, Montgomery and

Stokoe. I can imagine that this hurt is equally bad for the Geordies every time they witness Ronnie Radford reeling away with his arms aloft seemingly glued to the sides of his head.

"The second £10 was especially disappointing. In the FA Cup Third Round Leeds had taken Walsall back to Elland Road for a replay (this was an achievement given our penchant for not having the imagination to beat lower division teams) while Newcastle had to go to Blackburn for a replay. I was very optimistic. As it turned out Newcastle achieved a tremendous result at Ewood Park and eventually progressed to the Sixth Round. Leeds on the other hand came to grief in the Fifth Round at Old Trafford conceding two goals in the first two minutes. To my knowledge this tactic has never appeared in the coaching manuals when they offer advice on how to win away at the best side in the country.

"This defeat was even more difficult to stomach given Leeds' deep hatred of Manchester United. This hatred appears to be spreading to fans of other clubs who recognise that the club is unspeakably arrogant and feel they should be governed by different rules to the rest of the football community. This can be contrasted with Liverpool when they were winning everything in sight. They were admired and respected and would never be caught shouting about their obvious dominance.

"The third £10 seemed to be destined for the same direction earlier in the season. However, the sale of Andy Cole, and a renewed determination from Leeds, had made it a more even contest by May. Leeds' restored vigour was due in part to the aquisition of Tony Yeboah, the possibility of qualifying for Europe by finishing in the top five and the threat of having to do so through some crazy tournament known as the Intertoto Cup which had been dreamed up by UEFA – some of the other European countries had declined to enter, their belief in allowing players to achieve excellence overriding the short term desire for money. As it transpired Brian Deane's late equaliser at Tottenham on the final day of the season earned us a draw which put us one point ahead of the Geordies and I was chuffed to bits.

"Had we finished sixth there would have been a nightmare scenario. With Blackburn winning the Championship an extra UEFA Cup place would open up if Manchester United won the FA Cup. The dilemma presented by watching the Cup Final, and willing Manchester United to win, is the type of thing which keeps psychiatrists in their lucrative profession. As it turned out this was

Mark's 'pleasure' and I didn't envy him at all. If it had been me a weekend out of the country would have been the best solution.

"To the game in question, and I was now to experience the Toon Army on tour descending upon Merseyside. Everton were rejuvenated having just got through to the FA Cup Final and seemingly confident of kicking their way out of trouble at the foot of the Premiership. Naturally I wanted Everton to win so that Leeds could finish above Newcastle, I also wanted to reduce the losses I had incurred by succumbing to every football fan's mindless optimism in his own team's ability. The ability they display is normally inversely proportional to the fans assessment of it when faced with a competitive bet from a friendly rival.

"The Toon Army were in fine voice, even in the queue for the hot pies! I came to the conclusion that those from the North East are somehow born with larger lungs and more resilient vocal chords than the rest of us. The atmosphere was tremendous due to us being close to the Everton fans and a vibrant vocal exchange took place throughout the game. This was exactly the type of atmosphere I had forgotten could exist in a football ground following the introduction of all seater stadia. Ironically we stood on old wooden seats for the whole game.

"On the field Newcastle were flat and bereft of ideas. Kevin Keegan's plan to match Everton's crunchers in midfield curtailed their natural flair and only Peter Beardsley and Steve Howey could claim any credit for their performances. Everton ran out comfortable winners with two goals from their new hero, Daniel Amokachi. The Nigerian had started the season with the hype enjoyed by every big money signing but struggled as the team did. At one time he was christened Amotaxi – big, black and carrying lots of passengers.

"Kevin Keegan's midas touch was being severely tested although his ability to travel from Durham to Northumberland without needing the Tyne Bridge or the Tyne Tunnel remains un-challenged."

Well it seems Phil had a pretty good time didn't he? One notable point he didn't mention was that we had arrived in Liverpool soon after 5.00pm and, after parking in the huge Stanley Park Car Park (twice as expensive as it had been for the FA Cup game), we took the opportunity to walk up to Anfield and look at the Hillsborough Memorial, partially adorned incidentally by a Newcastle United scarf. It proved to be a really moving occasion, particularly standing there all by ourselves just looking at the names and ages of all those who tragically lost their lives at a football match. It could so easily have been me or you.

The Wednesday prior to the Everton match I had been playing for Yorkshire Amateurs in a Leeds Senior Cup semi-final. The prize for the winners was to play the Final at Elland Road which was obviously a tremendous target to aim for, even more so for the Leeds United supporters in the team as opposed to a humble Geordie! Alas it proved to be a nightmare for us all as we crashed to a surprise 2-1 defeat against rank outsiders Matthew Murray. At least they enjoyed their big day.

Easter was completed with defeat at home to Leeds United which wrecked our unbeaten home record in the Premier League. You can imagine how much stick I got about the result the following day back in Leeds, particularly at football training in the evening. A trivia question that is bound to come out of this match is 'Who was shown the red card in the first half but still took part in the match in the second half?' And the answer? – Steve Watson, whom referee Paul Danson mistook for Steve Howey (who had already been booked), and so gave a yellow and then a red card to for a second bookable offence. Fortunately he realised the error of his ways and corrected his decision, but sadly his performance for the remainder of the game showed no improvement (amazingly John Beresford suffered an identical fate at Old Trafford in December 1995). Danson, you may recall, was also the official who showed a red card to West Ham's Alvin Martin earlier in the season before reconsidering at a later date and changing it to a yellow.

April ended with the annual visit to Wembley for the end of season basketball finals. Arriving outside Wembley Stadium is still one of the biggest thrills imaginable. The whole place is just so awe inspiring even though I'm becoming something of a regular. Newcastle gained a point in a drab draw at Maine Road, Manchester, but for me it was the opportunity I had been waiting for – getting on the Wembley pitch – since my last visit 12 months ago.

Alas it was not to be. The bottom line was that as Dave Watson had shattered Newcastle's Wembley dream, an officious Wembley Steward shattered mine. I walked up the tunnel and out into the sunshine, all set I thought, but then, right out of the blue, I was turfed out of the stadium – heart-breaking.

The other thing that really depressed me over the weekend was seeing all the Leeds and Wigan Rugby League supporters milling around the Stadium and surrounding area. All I could think about was what it would be like if the Geordies had been in town? Unbelievable is the only answer. I realise I am one of the fortunate ones to have followed Newcastle United to Wembley but I was only 14 at the time. I, like every other Geordie, long for the day we return.

Staying with Rugby League, all the talk around the place was to do with the recently announced plans for the super league. Interestingly, Sir John Hall was pitching for Newcastle United to join the super league which was something I totally opposed as I hate the sport. I cannot understand why the BBC (television and radio) give so much coverage to Rugby League since, it's a parochial (and violent) sport, primarily for those people living in Yorkshire and Lancashire.

I must admit to having reservations about his plans of developing a sporting club, on the lines of Barcelona or Real Madrid. The subsequent appointment later in the year of Rob Andrew as Director of Rugby Union at Newcastle Rugby Union Football Club did little to allay those fears, especially as quite a lot of money seemed to be heading down that particular avenue. Many fans wondered why there was any need for Newcastle United to keep diversifying, as the Durham Wasps Ice Hockey, and Newcastle Comets Basketball teams, were also brought into the fold. Surely 100 per cent of all income generated should be used solely for the benefit of the football club? Non footballing ventures are of little or no interest to the Toon Army and lets hope the day never comes when one of the conditions of buying a season ticket is that you have to support the other sports too.

08/05/95 – BLACKBURN ROVERS v NEWCASTLE (1-0)

After missing the FA Cup win at Ewood Park there was no way I was going to miss this game. It was a fascinating scenario. Manchester United had closed the gap on Rovers to only two points but more importantly Leeds had drawn level with us on points with the race for the last guaranteed UEFA Cup spot still up for grabs. Our recent form had been patchy to say the least, despite a magnificently entertaining 3-3 draw with Tottenham at the beginning of the month, whilst Leeds had been gathering points almost unnoticed with Carlton Palmer's injury time winning goals in successive matches proving crucial, not to say infuriating.

Alan Shearer's single strike condemned us to defeat at Ewood Park but it was the goalkeeping of Tim Flowers that really won the points for Rovers. His save from Peter Beardsley's pile driver, at our end, just before half time was probably as good a save as I have ever had the privilege to see – absolutely stupendous. Funnily enough, to have equalised would have been a bad result, because it could have meant helping Manchester United to win the Premiership which was not what we wanted if we were to slip to sixth place in the League. As it transpired all the 'ifs and buts' didn't really matter as we would have finished fifth come the end of the season had we taken a point on the night. I suppose you could go on forever with the 'what if scenario' and all the permutations that accompany such thinking. Like it was at the end of the 1991/92 season, if you do the business yourselves then there's no need to worry about what other teams do. As it happens I think the two most significant things that contributed to our failure to qualify for Europe were Paul Kitson's glaring miss against Leeds United at St. James' Park which would have deprived Leeds of their win, and perhaps more surprisingly, Mark Bosnich's sending off against for Aston Villa at Leeds in virtually the final minute. Had he not lost his temper in a moment of madness Leeds' winning goal would never have come about.

The last game of the season against Crystal Palace was particularly sweet as it condemned the Noades brothers (Chairman Ron and Director Colin), to the Endsleigh League. I felt sorry for Manager Alan Smith but had no sympathy for the club hierarchy. Ron Noades, it had seemed to me, had badly treated his Manager as the season drew to its climax while Colin Noades had incensed me with his ludicrous outburst before the FA Cup semi-final reply against Manchester United at Villa Park. Palace's subsequent defeat in the replay, infront of only 3,000 of their own supporters, was an appropriate outcome. As the joke went they finished the season in the last four of every competition they entered.

The disappointing thing about the match itself was that with only 20 minutes remaining we were in Europe – news of Brian Deane's goal at White Hart Lane put an end to that dream, for a week anyway, and we were left to sweat it out hoping desperately for Manchester United to overcome Everton at Wembley in the FA

Cup Final. 'Come on you Reds' I sung, (I didn't really!), an unimaginable thing to have to contemplate, but there you go.

So, was the 1994/95 season an anti-climax after so much had been expected of the team? A platform had been built during the 1993/94 campaign and the marvellous start to the season raised everybody's expectations. Things were never quite the same after the exit from the UEFA Cup and the league defeat at Old Trafford but why? Obviously the injuries didn't help but perhaps the bottom line was that we weren't quite as good as we all thought we were. The champagne was to stay on ice.

I could only hope that the 1995/96 season would produce even better football than I witnessed throughout the 1993/94 and 1994/95 seasons – I wasn't to be disappointed. The pre-season signings of Les Ferdinand, Warren Barton, David Ginola and Shaka Hislop, for a combined total in excess of £14 million, saw to that. Kevin Keegan, still close to deity amongst the Geordie public, kept reminding us that it's all very well to receive praise for the football the team has played but nothing had been won yet. Having said that, what makes a football club is its supporters, in this case the Geordies – a unique breed and quite simply the best in the world.

1994/95 – Season's Summary

League	P	W	D	L	F	A	Pts.	Pos.
	42	20	12	10	67	47	72	6th

Top Scorers		
	Peter Beardsley	14
	Robert Lee	14
	Ruel Fox	12

1995/96 - SO NEAR, BUT YET SO FAR

So the trophy cabinet was still bare. Of course it was disappointing, especially after the rip roaring start to the 1994/95 season which brought six straight wins in the League, but once again a new season was upon us and that was all that mattered to every Geordie fanatic.

Newcastle United were privileged to have the most creative and genuinely enthusiastic and infectious manager in the country. Kevin Keegan is revered by one and all in Newcastle, adored even, and in encapsulating the spirit of Tyneside through his every breath, has delineated the zest and fervour of the club providing the perfect icon for all Geordies to follow. The city is the heart and soul of the club, and indeed, the intense feelings of pride and passion engendered at St. James' Park, overflowing into every-day life, owe much to the inspiration provided by the manager.

Before diving into the new season, a few more little bits and pieces on the summer. BBC Television produced an enthralling series called *Match of the Seventies* and, having been brought up, football wise, in that particular decade, it was marvellous to see many of the old faces and goal action that helped capture my imagination and develop my love affair with the game. Much of the action centred upon Leeds United, and then Liverpool, as they were the top sides of the era. At least Newcastle merited the occasional mention, and wasn't it lovely to see those goals going in to the Leazes End net, with the obligatory toilet rolls streaming down on to the pitch from behind the goal! Who knows, when Newcastle go on to dominate football in the mid to late 1990s, a series will be made in 20 years time illustrating our supremacy with numerous League Championship and FA Cup wins as the highlights. Wishful thinking? We shall see.

Television also brought home how far we had come in recent years when Sky Television's Classic Sport series on UK Gold featured a re-run of a *Match of the Day* programme from October 1980. The main game came from Stamford Bridge where Chelsea took a young and naive Newcastle United team apart to the tune of 6-0. What horrendous viewing it made, as it did all those years ago, and how thankful I was that such embarrassing defeats are well and truly banished to the memory banks.

And still you had to pinch yourself to see whether it was all a dream. The enormous changes that had come about in the past three to four years are well documented and Sir John Hall's words, after the dismissal of Ossie Ardiles, that the appointment of Kevin Keegan would enable the club to survive in the second division thus enabling its business plan to be put together in order to go on to future greatness, were indeed prophetic. Sir John Hall had put his judgement and reputation on the line and succeeded where many had failed before.

The final piece of the St. James' Park jigsaw, the south west corner, had been completed over the summer months, and what a sight it was. From the rubble of the old, but treasured, West Stand, the pitiful sight of the decaying Leazes and Gallowgate terraces, to the majesty of what we are privileged to have before us now. The false dawns were well and truly behind us. It may seem petty, but the only tinge of sadness I have about the old ground concerns the journey into Newcastle from Ponteland. It's only a little thing, but I always used to love looking down towards the stadium, from about a mile up Barrack Road, and picking out the floodlight pylons, dominating the skyline. You can't do this now of course, and as a result that little extra buzz of excitement is but a distant and treasured memory.

19/08/95 – NEWCASTLE v COVENTRY CITY (3-0)

A new season and a new team. Kevin Keegan had suffered a degree of criticism from a minority of 'uneducated' supporters earlier in the year over his failure to replace key players or add to his squad. He knew who he wanted, but the simple fact was that those players did not become available until the summer; to have bought second rate players before the end of the season would surely have been a crass error. Typically Keegan held firm and the way he re-shaped the team during the close season was mind blowing.

Paul Bracewell and Barry Venison, two players instrumental in establishing the club in the Premier League, were shown the door and are now enjoying pastures new. Speculation that Alan Shearer was coming home to Tyneside was rife, as it was again in November when Blackburn visited St. James' Park, and a bid of £10 million was supposed to have been made for his services. Even I started to believe it when really we all should have known better. Still, the disappointment of this particular dream not coming true was soon to fade when Sir John's cheque book went nap and £10 million was spent in 48 hours as Les Ferdinand and Warren Barton came north from London. Another London based player, Crystal Palace's John Salako turned down a move to Newcastle and quite honestly he must have been out of his mind. Coventry City is probably the best place for him. Going back to Ferdinand, it was an open secret that Keegan had been after him for the better part of a year. Personally I wasn't his biggest fan (I was soon to change my opinion!), and it is worth citing the story of the time Keegan took Andy Cole, when he was in his prime at Newcastle, to watch Ferdinand in action on the basis that he was the complete centre forward and there was much he could learn from watching him. The signing of Ferdinand also reminded me of the last time a London centre forward arrived at St James' Park, 24 years earlier. Malcolm Macdonald was his name, remember him, and if Ferdinand can make the same impact as the legendary Supermac then he will certainly find a place in Geordie folklore.

The fact that John Salako didn't sign meant Keegan could go back again for the idol of Paris St Germain, David Ginola, who was proving a difficult fish to land. Keegan had fancied him for a long time and it appeared more than once that it wouldn't be possible to strike a deal. However, circumstances changed and fate dealt Keegan a kind hand when Ginola, after turning down Celtic and undertaking a modelling assignment in Paris, eventually put pen to paper. I had seen him playing against Arsenal in the European Cup Winners Cup back in 1994, and occasionally in highlights of French National Team games so I was aware of him as a player. What we got though was something none of us could ever have dreamt of – a player possessing the most exceptional talent I have ever seen in all my years of watching football at St. James' Park.

Completing the summer spending spree was goalkeeper Shaka Hislop signed from Reading. This was an interesting signing, but no surprise, as it was well known that Keegan still harboured doubts about Pavel's consistency (not his ability) and was looking to land a top notch goalkeeper to either keep Pavel out of the side, or conceivably to push him to greater heights – all in all a very astute signing. Who knows, if Bolton hadn't staged such a marvellous comeback to defeat Reading at Wembley in the Division One Play Off Final in May 1995, Hislop may have remained a Reading player. It is on such things that footballing careers are shaped.

The town was buzzing long before kick-off time, incredible

really, and the number of new Adidas black and white shirts on display, with the Newcastle Brown logo adorning the front, was mind boggling. An amazing 500,000 home and away kits had been sold inside two months, and the revenue from kit and other club merchandise was helping to swell the rapidly bulging St. James' Park coffers, so much so that the annual turnover at the club had now reached the £40 million mark. By the end of the season, a population survey in Newcastle showed 87 per cent of the city dwellers possessed a Newcastle United replica shirt – the highest proportion of any team in Britain (maybe even the world), no surprise really. The norm in these days of all seater stadia is to roll in through the turnstiles five or ten minutes before kick-off but today was a case of turning back the years as the majority of fans were inside the stadium well before 2.30pm. Why? Well, not only was there that first day feeling of great anticipation and the desire to see the new signings limbering up, more importantly today, for me, and I'm sure thousands of others, was the opportunity to witness and drool over St. James' Park. What a sight, I can't find the words to describe it so you will just have to go and have a look for yourself. Prepare yourself to see the eighth wonder of the world! I must add though that, despite the unsurpassed splendour of the new stadium, there is, and probably always will be, a tinge of sorrow about the demise of the terrace. Thinking back for example to our visit to Peterborough's London Road ground back in September 1992, and the unrivalled atmosphere of following the Toon away from home. It may sound odd, but the terrace was absolutely heaving, steaming (body sweat), and even though the crush at times was overwhelming, it was a mind blowing experience encapsulating unsurpassed feelings of communality. A great sadness when you reminisce about it but the mid 1990s has brought change, and a 'new' game. Life goes on.

To the game, and surely Coventry City must have feared the worst as they rolled into St. James' Park on a wonderfully hot summer's afternoon. With their 1994 aggregate standing at 10-0, the fact that it had been raised to 13-0 come 4.45pm was no surprise – a classic case of lambs to the slaughter despite Ron Atkinson's pre-match protestations that they had nothing to fear. Remember it was he who said the Geordie fans were the most passionate in the country, whilst he was commentating for ITV at St. James Park back in November 1986, as West Ham were being dismantled 4-0. Former Sheffield Wednesday manager Trevor

Francis echoed an identical opinion when his side were defeated at Gallowgate in September 1993. Say no more.

Paul Robertson, Sports Editor of the *Journal*, writing in the newspaper on the morning of the game made a fascinating comparison between the differing emotions and levels of anticipation we had had on 24th August 1991, when Watford opened the new season at St. James Park (put your hand up if you can remember it ended as a 2-2 draw), and 19th August 1995. Talk about chalk and cheese, more like comparing the intellect of a new born baby to Albert Einstein.

Amazingly, with Manchester United suffering a surprising 3-1 defeat at Villa Park, we were suddenly installed as 3-1 title favourites by the bookmakers. Astonishing but true. The pundits were lavish with their praise from all round the country and once again the pleasure of being a Geordie was second to none.

I do have one little moan to make at this stage, not about the football of course, but the fact that Premier League matches, with their 15 minute half times, mean that the era of 4.40pm finishes is now a thing of the past. Indeed the 4.50pm final whistle, once the inevitable injury time is added on, is now the norm these days, but why you might ask does this matter. Simple, it means getting back to the car to hear the start of *Sports Report* on Radio 5, the most traditional of all post match rituals, becomes a difficult task with a quick sprint often being the only answer.

The *Guardian's* David Lacey, and Gary Lineker, both tipped Newcastle to lift the Premier League Championship, the sort of thing which is always very pleasing to hear. As for me, I shared their optimism, but until the day it actually happens, and after all we have been waiting since 1927, I won't be caught shouting the odds.

Victory at Bolton Wanderers the following Tuesday night consolidated our position at the top of the League. It was marvellous to saviour the joys of a standing terrace again even though the ground was terribly run down. Worse still, from Bolton's point of view, was the supermarket behind our terrace which was an absurd state of affairs. How can you possibly have a ground (and any credibility as a football club) when you have a 'supermarket' end. Turning back to football matters and I couldn't help thinking back to August 1980 when we suffered an early season loss at Burnden Park which condemned us to bottom place in the second division. Quite how I was able to stomach those times I simply don't know. Getting back home, just before midnight, the first thing I did was put the teletext on, read the match report, and then quickly turn to the league tables and the thrill of seeing Newcastle United proudly sitting in first place. This is usually followed by flicking over the page to look, and smile at, Sunderland's perilous position in Division One, as it was at the start of the season.

The winning run continued at Hillsborough where we were housed in the embarrassingly named 'Presto' Stand. Before the game I bumped into Andrew Coghill outside the ground and we both managed to get ourselves interviewed by the roving Sky Television reporter who asked us our opinions on the game itself and Newcastle's start to the season. Naturally we eulogised over the new signings and how we were going to collect another three points but regretfully we were both edited out of the programme itself when I watched the recording later in the evening. On the field Ginola and Beardsley scored a goal apiece, both spectacular in their own right, but it was an outstanding save from Shaka on the stroke of half time, from a point blank header from Mark Pembridge, that created the foundation for the win. Just before Shaka's stroke of brilliance many supporters had already vacated their seats in a rush to join the pie and Bovril queues. Amazing, why miss the action just for the sake of a bit of queue jumping. Of course large numbers of supporters, primarily young to middle aged males, often are forced to miss parts of every game as they have to leave their seats to make a toilet stop in order to get rid of the mass quantities of brown liquid consumed before the game. Lowesy, on the occasions he comes to games, has to make two or three trips out each match such is his inability to hold his drink! Another thing that struck me at the match was the number of women and very young children in the Newcastle section of the ground. Was this a sign that the game was attracting a new 'middle class' audience – moving away from the traditional working class roots of the game? Season tickets at the two ends of St. James' Park cost £278 (half that for a child), which was the same cost as the previous season, a nice move by the club – except there were two less matches to watch for your money! In 1996/97 the cost rose to £320, a 15 per cent increase. Affordable? Only just.

Talking of the different type of spectator being attracted to the game, and to St. James' Park in particular, gave cause for concern in other areas too. The club were being a little staid in their attitude towards the more rumbustious fans with standing up, singing and shouting, being frowned upon in certain quarters. One supporter was even warned as to his future conduct for the 'crime' of standing up and blocking an advertising hoarding – whatever next, supporters not being able to come dressed in their black and white tops!. Come on Newcastle, if you want to keep the noisiest most passionate football stadium in Britain, leave the supporters alone. And one more thing, let us have our giant flag back as well.

30/08/95 – NEWCASTLE v MIDDLESBROUGH (1-0)

Middlesbrough were hit by the David Ginola show. The Teessiders, having made an unbeaten start to the season, and talking positively about gaining a place in Europe at the end of the season, made the short journey north up the A19 ready to put a spoke in Newcastle's freewheeling start to the campaign. Could they, would they? No chance. From the outset the black and whites swarmed all over their red shirted visitors who were hardly given a kick. Middlesbrough were given a lesson on life in the top flight, and the fact that it was only a single Les Ferdinand header that divided the teams at the end of the night could not disguise Newcastle's dominance and deserved victory.

The match will be remembered most of all for the display that David Ginola turned on. On his debut against Coventry City he showed flashes of brilliance, the games at Bolton Wanderers and Sheffield Wednesday underlined the fact that we had signed someone special, but tonight at St James' Park we witnessed a display of football that had to be seen to be believed. His ability to beat an opponent on either side was a joy to watch and even the skills of Beardsley and Gascoigne pale into insignificance when Ginola is on the ball (Peter's still my favourite player though!). His direct opponent on the night was Neil Cox who must have finished the 90 minutes in a total daze after being completely outwitted all evening. It was a display of exceptional skill that had the Geordie hordes drooling over the exquisite touches on view with the *coup de grace* being the time midway through the first half, down at the Gallowgate End, when Ginola was trapped next to the corner flag in a defensive position. Most players would have tried to win their side a goal kick or throw in, but not Ginola. He teased, tormented and mesmerised poor Cox with a shimmy, a shuffle and total football skill in weaving his way out of the corner, past two more bewildered and statuesque red shirts, to effect his clearance. Fortunately I had a perfect view of it all and it is a moment I will always treasure. That moment alone, and the rapturous applause from the adoring onlookers, said it all. *Absolument Magnifique.*

Ginola had said that, when he was living in France, the Parisians had many interests more important than football. In Newcastle football is a way of life, and to many people it was all that mattered. I was one of them. National recognition came Ginola's way too as the plaudits and prizes kept piling up on Tyneside. Ginola won the Carling Player of the Month award for August while Keegan scooped the Manager of the Month award, a feat he was to deservedly repeat in September.

Away from the game itself and the Middlesbrough/Sunderland debate came to the fore again. Basically this involves an argument over which of the two other north east sides is the 'bigger' club. The Wearside Mackems or the Teesside Smogmonsters. A year or so ago there would have been absolutely no question about it with Sunderland undoubtedly streets ahead despite their parlous financial plight and paltry playing resources. Now, with the new Riverside Stadium dominating the ICI skyline on Teesside, and close on £10 million having been spent on players (Barmby and Juninho being two fabulous signings which those at Roker could only dream of, and indeed us at Newcastle grit our teeth in admiration), Middlesbrough are aiming to become a real force in the Premier League. Having said that, would either get into Newcastle United's starting eleven at the moment? Maybe not at the present time, but I'm sure one of them would be a perfect long term replacement for Peter Beardsley – watch out Bryan Robson! Ian Murtagh, the *Evening Chronicle* journalist working the Roker Park beat, wrote an article on the subject and concluded that, despite the Middlesbrough revival, Sunderland were still a bigger club and Newcastle's greatest rivals. Their promotion to the Premier League at the end of the 1995/96 season came in the nick of time, otherwise who knows what may have become of them. Middlesbrough will forever remain the poor relations of the north-east.

01/10/95 – EVERTON v NEWCASTLE (1-3)

You would hardly have thought this game mattered as the day was all about the return of the capricious Eric Cantona. Dear me, this hugely talented, but erratic and temperamental Frenchman, who kicked the game in the teeth, is welcomed back into the Premier League like a king. Excuse me but didn't he bring disgrace upon himself and English football on a dark January night at Selhurst Park. He hasn't even had the good grace to publicly apologise to 'the world' for his action which is nothing short of a disgrace. To compound it all, the fact that all the Mancunians at Old Trafford, together with his advertising company Nike, were treating him like a hero, despite his 'crime', left a sour taste. Liverpool, visitors to Old Trafford on the day, at least managed not to be fazed by the occasion and proceeded to play Manchester United off the park to earn a richly merited 2-2 draw. The atmosphere incidentally, bar the hype that greeted Cantona's arrival on the pitch and the two home goals, was a dead as a dodo. Manchester's United's policy, foolishly supported by the Premier League, of not allowing any away supporters into Old Trafford whilst building work on their new stand continued, clearly contributed to this, but Old Trafford isn't exactly the noisiest place at the best of times anyway. To their credit they saw the error of their ways, and decided to re-admit visiting supporters at the end of November. I would be interested to know whether it was outside criticism or their own internal decision that contributed to their change of policy. Back to Cantona and I wonder how I would have felt if a Newcastle player had committed a similar act of folly. A hypothetical question I hope because I'm sure Kevin Keegan would never allow such a thing to happen.

It was my third visit to Goodison Park inside seven months and with the previous two being nightmare experiences, there was obviously a little bit of apprehension in the air. I need not have worried. Everton were never at the races and the 3-1 victory was the result of an outstanding team display capped by a marvellous Les Ferdinand goal and a masterful midfield performance by Robert Lee, thankfully back to his best after an indifferent end to the 1994/95 season. The superlatives were running out as the headline writers racked their brains for inspiration as they compiled their Monday morning reports.

Mention of Cantona stealing the limelight of course leads to the mention of another such character, Duncan Ferguson, the Scottish centre forward idolised by the blue half of Merseyside. I remember seeing his remarkable overhead kick for Scotland against Germany back in 1993 which probably helped bring him to the public eye, certainly as far as English supporters were concerned. Anyone who had that type of skill was surely something special, but possessing all the talent in the world is no use if you behave in such a foolhardy manner. When an assault charge on Raith's John McStay stuck, his fourth such indiscretion, a jail sentence was both deserved and inevitable. The pathetic bleatings of the Everton hierarchy in defence of their star attraction were beyond belief, and did them absolutely no credit at all. Let the man serve his just punishment.

Les Ferdinand, or should it be 'Sir Les' as he was affectionately dubbed, is worthy of a special word of praise, not only for wiping away the ghost of Andy Cole, but for being a superb ambassador for the sport. Apart from sharing a catwalk with David Ginola, Ferdinand has grabbed the number nine shirt with a vengeance and shown the Geordie fans that he can really play. Perhaps a more all round player than Cole ever was, Ferdinand has taken to the Tyneside lifestyle like a fish to water and has met, indeed exceeded, all the expectation and hype that surrounded his move north. On reflection, ask any Newcastle United supporter these days if they would prefer Andy Cole, or Les Ferdinand and Keith Gillespie, and the answer would be the latter every time. Having said that, it has to be said that the joy Andy Cole brought to the supporters of Newcastle United, when he was at his peak during the 1993/94 season, was something that will be treasured forever.

The visit of Chelsea to St. James' Park the previous weekend merits a brief word with three issues standing out. Firstly the entirely predictable approach of Chelsea, negative in the extreme (as Glenn Hoddle is very sadly inclined to be at times), secondly the play of Ruud Gullit whose world class ability shone through like a beacon, and thirdly, the last appearance of Ruel Fox in a black and white shirt. Fox played in place of the injured Peter Beardsley and it was his first start of the season after losing his place to Keith Gillespie. You could see why on this performance. Fox never quite cracked it on Tyneside and, despite a number of pretty good performances, he flattered to deceive more often than not. The £4.2m Tottenham paid for his services was a tremendous bit of business by Kevin Keegan. One place Fox will be missed though is the training ground. On the occasions I have been down to Maiden Castle in Durham to watch training sessions Fox, along with Lee Clark, was always one of the more jovial characters, laughing and joking a lot, but nevertheless still putting in 100% effort.

Progress in the Coca-Cola League Cup was also being made. Unlike previous seasons we now expect to progress beyond the second round and predictably Bristol City proved to be a no contest over two legs. Taking a 5-0 lead into the second leg at St. James' Park you might have expected the attendance to drop slightly below the statutory 36,500 full house. In today's climate there was never any chance of that happening. With many season ticket holders not taking up their option for a ticket it was especially pleasing that the thousands locked out each week, desperate to see their heroes in the flesh, could do so. The only problem was that many spectators, in the ground for the first time, didn't know where they were supposed to be sitting. The confusion resulted in an unusual situation of seeing hundreds of people standing up, looking totally lost as they frantically searched for their seats, as the match kicked off.

Incidentally, having a capacity of only 36,500 is a trifle disappointing to say the least. When the Leazes and Gallowgate stands were being constructed we were all told that the new stadium would hold 40,000, similar to the capacities at Anfield, Elland Road, Goodison Park and Highbury. Somehow 36,500 just doesn't have the same ring to it. Apart from the fact that not everybody who wants to come and watch the lads play is able to, the obvious potential revenue that is being lost is huge. Talks are currently going on about plans to increase the capacity of either the East or Milburn Stand, similar to the reconstruction at Old Trafford, which now holds nigh on 55,000, but sadly this is probably a good few years on the horizon yet. There is also the distinct possibility of having to relocate, away from St. James' Park, if that is the only way the capacity can be increased to over 50,000. If that happens it will be a truly sad day, but as long as the location is suitable, and the quality of the new stadium is second to none, then so be it. One thing though, any new stadium would still have to be called St. James' Park.

On the theme of reduced capacities, I understand that at Middlesbrough's new Riverside Stadium, people are even prevented from getting access to the environs of the ground if they haven't got a ticket. Surely that is taking things too far, and I suppose it's just another nail in the coffin for the game of football, or rather watching it at the top level, being accessible to all the different sections of our society, particularly under-privileged youngsters. At the Newcastle versus Wimbledon game on 21st

October, I was just about to go through the turnstiles when a little lad of no more than eight or nine enquired of me whether he could sneak into the ground alongside me. Compared to 20 years ago this is a much more difficult stunt to pull off, especially as turnstile entry is much more stringently controlled in all seater stadia and there are no longer walls, albeit protected with barbed wire or broken glass, which could be scaled if you were desperate enough. I didn't say no, but on the other hand didn't say yes either, and just left him to his own devices to shuffle through infront of me hoping to get in undetected. Unfortunately the turnstile clicked once, and whilst he got through I was left standing in limbo having handed over my ticket. Not wanting to be seen as the guilty party in this hapless affair, I had to immediately say that the lad was not with me and had sneaked in unlawfully. The stewards then pursued him but failed to track him down. Good for him I suppose, I was then let in myself and in a way I was glad that I had inadvertently aided a soccer mad youngster (or was he simply a little tearaway!) to see his heroes in the flesh. I don't know where he watched the game from though as you would have thought every seat would have been occupied, but no doubt he found a suitable vantage point. Fortunately he was able to witness a goal bonanza as Les Ferdinand helped himself to three more goals as six of the best rattled into the Wimbledon net, three of which were conceded by Vinnie Jones. The Wimbledon hard man, villain turned hero, had taken over the goalkeeping jersey from Paul Heald who was sent off shortly after half time. Jones, to his credit, lapped up the atmosphere and the Gallowgate End in particular accorded him a first class reception as he warmed to his impossible task with remarkable aplomb.

25/10/95 – STOKE CITY v NEWCASTLE (0-4)

This was my first visit to the Potteries, and one I was looking forward to. It turned out to be rather less memorable then anticipated.

I've never for one moment thought that the bad old days of mindless acts of violence had passed by, far from it, but tonight was a sad night indeed. But first the good points. If I thought Ginola had been 'out of this world' against Middlesbrough, then this performance was incredibly on a higher plane still. Maybe the opposition wasn't as good but don't let that detract from what we saw tonight. World class full backs like Ray Wilson and Bertie Vogts wouldn't have held Ginola in this sort of form – and he kept it going for virtually the whole 90 minutes. At times there were three defenders marking him, yes three, and still he continually waltzed past them with skill the like of which you need to see to believe. His game is all about tempting and tormenting opponents – more often than not he will receive the ball, slow to walking pace with the ball teasingly just in his reach, before exploding into life and leaving his markers for dead. One such instance saw him cut inside and unleash a dipping 25 yard thunderbolt which was destined for the top corner before Stoke goalkeeper Mark Prudhoe somehow managed to fingertip it away for a corner. A remarkable save from an even more remarkable strike. Prudhoe couldn't keep the Geordie attacking tides at bay forever though and by close of play, to use a cricketing expression, four goals had been rattled past him to signal as emphatic a team performance as you could wish to see. One feature of the game I particularly liked was to see the fantastic camaraderie between the Newcastle players. For example, midway through the first half, when Ginola tricked his way to the bye-line and won a corner, Peter Beardsley gave him an affectionate and genuine handshake, in total cognizance of his efforts, as he went across to take the corner. I guess this also demonstrates how humble Beardsley is, a world class player himself, and that's no exaggeration, showing due appreciation for his French colleague. The 6,250 Geordie supporters, an exceptional, but not at all surprising, away support for a relatively low key midweek contest, sang themselves hoarse and even the home supporters (the decent ones) applauded the victors from the field of play. One unpleasant note arising from the post match comments saw Stoke manager Lou Macari accusing Ginola of 'diving' and getting the home full-back, Ian Clarkson, sent off – pure sour grapes as television evidence later proved. In the weeks that followed Ginola took a bit of a battering from fellow players, the media and other supporters over his alleged tendency to end up on the ground after being challenged. Kevin Keegan provided the perfect answer when he said that when you're fouled it's quite natural to fall over. Enough said.

And so to the bad. I travelled down to the game in Ritchie's car with Dave and Jim and having eventually located the ground, not the easiest of tasks, we parked next to the station, a good half mile or from the ground. It was around 5.30pm and the idea was to find a pub relatively close to the ground for a good pre-match drink, as is the norm. This didn't prove an easy task. Walking through the side streets we found most pubs either closed or unwelcoming, furthermore the general atmosphere felt a little uneasy as stories of violence earlier in the afternoon permeated through the night air. Eventually we found a place called the Garden Retreat, thankfully heaving with Geordies, where we settled for the habitual pre-match drinks.

After the match, returning to the car was when the trouble started, although apparently there had been isolated incidents just before kick off time of which we were unaware at the time. Fortunately the four of us escaped the worst of it but only just. We were threatened by a group of Stoke fans outside one of the pubs we walked past, but just ignored them, and then, just before the station, a mob of Stoke hooligans charged towards a group of Newcastle supporters in the car park just as we were arriving on the scene. Luckily a small police presence averted a major flare-up. Others were not so fortunate. I later heard that we had got off lightly as the violence in other parts of the city had been much worse, primarily due to the conspicuous absence of any police. I've witnessed much worse incidents over the years, but nevertheless it's still somewhat unnerving. Having said that, I still maintain that nine times out of ten you can avoid getting caught up in trouble if you keep your wits about you – as we did in Stoke.

The whole question of violence raises the question of what you would do if you saw a fellow supporter being mercilessly beaten up? Walk the other way or go and help them? The latter has to be the answer even if the consequence might be to become tarnished with the brush of being a football hooligan, thug even, yourself. A small price to pay for helping an innocent bystander in my book.

So why did it all happen? Violence has all but disappeared at Premier League matches but it seems this trend hasn't yet reached outposts such as Stoke. The home supporters, knowing that in excess of 6,000 Geordies were coming down to their patch, clearly took offence and, having been away from the big time for such a long time, welcomed the opportunity to provoke and cause trouble. The following weekend a number of supporters phoned David Mellor's *6.06* programme to voice their concern at the trouble they had encountered. Mellor was genuinely shocked to hear the tales of horror from respectable supporters, and callers even rang into Sky Television's *Soccer Extra* programme the next morning to reinforce their concern. Mark Jensen from *The Mag* fanzine, whom I had bumped into a week or so earlier, was on the programme, and he had actually forewarned me that Stoke supporters were a little on the 'loony' side and to watch my step. His warning proved regretfully spot on. It was interesting to hear reports at the end of the season that a number of Stoke supporters had been arrested, after a raid by Staffordshire police targeting fans who had allegedly been perpetrating organised violence at matches involving their club.

Ten days later and there were reports of trouble at St. Andrews, the home of Birmingham City, where Millwall were the visitors. A potentially explosive fixture if ever there was one, and it turned out to be the Londoners who were on the wrong end of the violence. Some may say they got what they deserved, given the notorious behaviour a small minority of their followers inflict on visiting supporters at Millwall. Not me though; acts of violence are despicable, and if football is in danger of heading back to the bad days of the 1970s, where gang violence was prevalent, then it will be a very sad day for football and a terrible reflection on our society today.

Despite a very late night, actually it was the early hours of the morning before arriving home from Stoke, I still made the effort to wake up at 7.15am to watch the fourth round draw live on ITV. Anyone at home would do; Liverpool away was what we got! Still, it was better than say having to travel to Southampton and, of course, the undisputed tie of the round would mean a Geordie invasion of Anfield.

It was nice to see Ginola making his debut on *A Question of Sport* at the end of October. His inclusion on the programme was a tribute to the impact he had made in the Premier League, his English being of a sufficiently high standard to feel comfortable in such surroundings, and also perhaps the most pertinent fact that he is a modern day superstar. No doubt Peter Beardsley, a regular on the programme and affectionately known as 'Ceefax' because of his tremendous sporting knowledge, gave him some tips as he certainly acquitted himself very well. I know all the Geordie lads idolise him for his football ability; the Geordie lasses do so too but also love him for his Gallic charm and undoubted good looks. The 5,000 strong audience that attended the Newcastle United Fashion Show, featuring incidentally the four summer signings, and staged primarily to promote the new range of Newcastle United leisure-wear, confirmed that view.

Keith Mollard, a good friend of mine from Plymouth, provided me with a pleasant surprise when a personalised signed photograph of Ginola arrived in my morning post. It turned out that his son, Ian, works for Proserv, who are acting as Ginola's agents, and knowing my passion very kindly organised the memento for me.

Four days later the main talking point at Tottenham was Les Ferdinand's failure to score for the ninth successive game, and in the process equal a 100 year old Newcastle United goalscoring record, held by the illustrious Willie Wardrope. I'm sure he wasn't too disappointed, despite missing a golden opportunity to win the game deep into injury time. The draw was disappointing, only because expectations were so high, but I do feel Keegan made two minor errors of judgement before the game. First there was Lee Clark's injury which meant a tactical re-shuffle resulting in Beardsley and Ginola playing out of position. The result, a poor first half display which was turned round in the second half when the 'regular' pattern of play was re-established. Secondly, I felt strongly that Robbie Elliott, who performed magnificently at Stoke in midweek, deserved to keep his place in the team ahead of the fit again John Beresford. Don't get me wrong, I think Beresford is a quality player, but if you come into the side, and turn in an immaculate display, you deserve better. Anyway, having had my say, and all supporters are entitled to their opinion, I wouldn't dream of criticising Keegan further.

08/11/95 – NEWCASTLE v BLACKBURN ROVERS (1-0)

The pundits had said Newcastle hadn't played any quality teams so far, hence our lofty position in the table was a false one – well inside four days we had defeated many people's favourites for the Championship, Liverpool, and the reigning champions, Blackburn Rovers. An eight point lead at the top of the table was a fantastic achievement for early November; after all you can only beat the teams the fixture computer puts in front of you. One thing we can do without is the playing of that awful tune 'Simply the Best' the moment the final whistle goes to signal yet another home win. It's so cheap and does us no credit at all – surely 'The Blaydon Races' would be far more suitable.

Alan Green, the revered Radio 5 broadcaster, mentioned in his commentary that the Newcastle supporters were booing David Batty, particularly in the second half after his altercation with

David Ginola. He then proceeded to say that perhaps the booing was a sign that he was respected by the Geordie public. Fortunately he had his tongue firmly in his cheek. Some players are heckled because they are class players; Batty's booing was purely and simply because he was putting himself about and not necessarily within the rules – a modern day Billy Bremner perhaps? Batty by name; Batty by nature? We shall see. It's interesting actually that players such as Batty and Paul Ince are despised when they are in the opposition line up, but when they actually sign for your own team your opinion invariably changes! Significantly, his performances in the last two months of the season were nothing short of outstanding.

The previous Saturday the battle of the Titans, Newcastle and Liverpool, had produced a classic encounter at an emotionally charged St. James Park – who cared about Juninho's debut 30 miles down the road. Apparently over 75,000 supporters had wanted to go to the game but of course just under half that number actually had access to a ticket. Newcastle took the three points, thanks to a last minute Steve Watson goal, but it was Liverpool who played the better football on the day and they left Tyneside ruing their misfortune. On the other hand, it is often said that if you can win without producing your best form, as Liverpool in their halcyon days, it is the sign of a good team – one destined to win the Championship perhaps.

Mention of Blackburn Rovers leads me to comment on the appalling record of the British representatives in the European club competitions over recent seasons. Who knows how Newcastle might have fared in the UEFA Cup this season, very well I hope, but that is a purely hypothetical question as we didn't make the starting line. Newcastle didn't get past the Second Round in the 1994/95 UEFA Cup, and this season only Nottingham Forest, of the four English UEFA Cup entrants, managed to clear the obstacles that the first two rounds presented. The Champions Cup and European Cup Winners Cup proved equally bleak in terms of tangible success. So why is this. Many people blame the enforced absence of our clubs from the European scene after the Heysel disaster, which meant, so they said, falling behind our European neighbours technically. Others say we play too many games or that the style of English football is simply not suited to the European style of play, whatever that may be. There was also the 'three foreigners rule', which prevented some of our clubs from fielding their strongest teams on occasions, however a certain Jean-Marc Bosman appears to have put an end to that. I think all these factors are contributory, but still feel we are not so far behind (excluding Blackburn's inept showing in the 1995/96 Champions League where they were simply not good enough) and that the wheel will revolve once more with English clubs prominent again in the latter stages of the three competitions. The English Premiership can hold its own with any League in Europe and 1996/97 will I am sure prove that assertion to be correct. Our football is full of thrills and excitement, even absorbing, with no little amounts of skill. Perhaps the bottom line though is that English football is right for the English public and that does not necessarily add up to success in Europe. To conclude this subject I must say that as much as I admire the views of Gary Lineker, he is far too critical of our game even though his film report on the training ways of Ajax Amsterdam, which has produced the likes of Patrick Kluivert, was very revealing. Their training facilities are far superior to those English clubs can offer and the techniques being instilled in the youngsters can only aid their development into highly skilled, adroit individuals, and subsequently, integrated team players. Perhaps if we can get it right in the kindergartens then England's national sport might just start flourishing once more – a spot of afternoon training might also be a good thing, something common place in Europe but strangely foreign to many of our English clubs. At the moment perhaps the saddest thing about the English game is that the majority of the best players (those you would gladly pay to go and watch) are foreign. The likes of Ginola, Cantona, Gullit and Asprilla spring to mind immediately with only the likes of Giggs and Beardsley being able to be talked about in the same manner in respect of technical ability and pure skill. Even sadder is the fact that these players, Gullit excepted for some reason, are the target for the boo boys in the 'cheap seats' – an indictment of their mentality if you ask me. Sure I boo the dirty players, the likes of Norman Whiteside, but never the quality ones.

29/11/95 – LIVERPOOL v NEWCASTLE (0-1)

Another marvellous night at Anfield capped by a tremendous winning goal from Steve Watson. Was it a better night than the last time I had witnessed a Newcastle win at Anfield? Probably not, but all the same an evening to treasure. Similarly, as was the case after the euphoria of the win at Stoke in Round Three, the draw for the next round the following morning earned us the unenviable task of an away tie at Arsenal. No easy matches in this season's League Cup Competition.

Speaking of cup draws and a word on the revamped FA Cup Third Round draw which the BBC broadcasted live from Lancaster Gate on the Monday evening following the completion of the Round Two matches. Gone were the old Football Association hierarchy, the likes of Bert Millichip and Gordon McKeag; in came the jovial Terry Venables and Denis Law. It wasn't all change though as there had to be some semblance of order given to the proceedings and so Graham Kelly retained his traditional role of introducing the draw and putting the names to the numbered balls, drawn incidentally from a perspex box rather than the customary velvet bag. The other addition to the draw was the presence of players and supporters in the audience which although understandable, didn't really add any extra spice to the occasion. All in all though a welcome change to things and congratulations to those responsible for it but it still didn't have the excitement of the old days (pre 1980s). The radio coverage, with Byron Butler interrupting the Jimmy Young show on Radio 2 at 12.30pm on Monday lunchtimes, was far more exciting with a unique air of suspense prevalent.

22/12/95

A very, very sad day in my life, in fact probably the worst day of my life as it was the day my mother died after a long illness. So many happy memories over the years to enrich my life, some of them chronicled previously, but it's the simple things that can never be replaced. Coming home from the match and seeing her smiling face as you walked through the door, happy as Larry after a win, and greeting you with a suitable comment on the performance. I always had the feeling she was genuinely happy for me, and she was. Her interest in the fortunes of the team in recent seasons, despite her illness, was tremendous; and everything I always asked her to do for me, posting match reports, taping all sorts of odds and ends and keeping me in touch with all the news, was always conscientiously done. She never let me down and I couldn't have asked for a better Mum. She played an enormous part in my footballing life, and needless to say in all my life, and her memories will live with me forever.

02/01/96 – NEWCASTLE v ARSENAL (2-0)

The first game of 1996 and, just for the record, our eleventh home win in succesion in the Premier League this season. It was Dad's birthday and I managed to obtain one of the tickets from the lads for him as a present; what a good job I did. It finished 2-0, but in all honesty could have been five or six. I was surprised, although I'm not really sure why, because I had never seen Dad clapping so much in all the games I had been to with him. The 'new' Newcastle had obviously made a great impression on him, and, as a connoisseur of good football, he was quite rightly showing his appreciation. Indeed, if there was one game throughout the season that convinced me we would be Champions, it was this one. Sadly, come May, my confidence would turn out to be misplaced. On the field the Londoners were very disappointing, not that I was complaining too much. Only Ian Wright looked anything like on form, while David Platt and Dennis Bergkamp in particular were surprisingly very subdued. Before the kick off it was nice to see Arsenal walk out to the centre circle and wave to the crowd, a measure of their respect for the Geordie public which had been built up in recent seasons. Regrettably, the feelings the Geordie public had for Arsenal disappeared eight days later after the League Cup tie at Highbury. One little side issue about this match was that it pitted Warren Barton against his boyhood favourites. Not surprisingly, practically all his family and friends were followers of the Gunners, and indeed season ticket holders at Highbury, but what I found incomprehensible was the fact that they would be wanting Newcastle to be victorious because of their allegiance to Warren – or so the newspapers reported. I could draw an analogy on this scenario. Let's assume my brother John had become a professional footballer, played for another club in the Premier League, and found himself up against Newcastle at St. James' Park. Would I support his team and wish Newcastle to lose? Of course not, the very thought is absolutely absurd. You can draw your own conclusions about my thoughts on the real loyalty of Barton's relations!

Driving home after the game with Dad, we tuned in to Metro Radio and listened to former player Mick Martin's views on the game. Obviously he was waxing lyrical about some of the players, and he went on to say that should Newcastle go on to lift the Premier League Championship, as he believed they would, the celebrations on Tyneside would not be bettered anywhere else in the world, and he meant the whole world. I couldn't help but agree.

The previous week Manchester United had beaten us 2-0 at Old Trafford, and there was no doubt we had been comprehensively outplayed. Andy Cole, after struggling for much of the early part of the season, scored an excellent goal, typical of many of those he had notched during his time at St. James' Park. I must say though it really bugs me when Manchester United supporters sing the 'Andy Cole song'; after all it is our song. Mind you, it certainly surprised the home fans when the Newcastle travelling supporters started singing the Cole song themselves, and properly too. Turning back to the defeat, what was annoying was the reaction of many of the pundits, speculating on our demise, who said that the wheels had come off the Newcastle bandwaggon again and our Championship hopes were in tatters. What nonsense. To write a team off based on one very poor display is scandalously irresponsible. In the same manner also, it was incredible that the praise Manchester United received for their defeat of Newcastle was in stark contrast to the pummelling they received after being defeated at Elland Road only three days previously. A fickle media perhaps? Just a bit.

Incidentally Hally had been at Old Trafford, one of the lucky few from Tyneside to be at the game, even though his ticket source had been through Andy Conway in Bolton who had called in a few markers on his Manchester based business associates. Nice to have the right contacts when you need them the most. Anyway, Hally's report back to me was that the Manchester United crowd turned out to be the most arrogant, and indeed ignorant, supporters he had ever encountered. Of course his view may have been slightly coloured, but, even so, the comments they were coming out with, and their general demeanour, left him shaking his head in amazement. Thank goodness we are not tarred with that particular brush. Hally spent a fair time on Merseyside in his early twenties and didn't care too much for the Scousers; in comparison he said the Scousers and Mancunians were worlds apart. A week or so later I was listening to *Jim and the Doc* on BBC Radio 5 and, interestingly, Jim White, one of their regular contributors, made almost exactly the same point. He was present on that same night at Old Trafford as a neutral football fan and commented that one Manchester United supporter a couple of rows behind him constantly moaned at the deficiencies of the home players, with Giggs and Cantona getting their fair share too, and that this continued unabated throughout the 90 minutes. This is actually one of the problems with all seater stadia in that on the terraces you could usually move away from earshot of any loud mouth or bigot you didn't want to hear droning on; in a seated area, especially where it is all season tickets, if you're unfortunate to be stuck next to an imbecile you have my sympathy. Fortunately, our area of seating in the Gallowgate End is free of such individuals

My view on the Newcastle team, in comparison to other teams such as Manchester United and Liverpool, was that having improved enormously from the 1994/95 season, experience and the influx of more quality players being the major contributory factors, the reason we were now up with the best was that as well as being 'solid' throughout all areas of the team, we had a number of players that I would class as inspirational. Aston Villa and Tottenham had maybe one each, Liverpool two, and the two United's three – Schmeichel; Cantona and Giggs in the red corner; Beardsley, Ginola and Ferdinand in black and white.

Furthermore, what we must not become are 'one season wonders', as Leeds and Blackburn did – two teams who won the Championship in the 1990s and haven't been the same since. Our success must be sustained and built upon. I am certain it will be.

17/01/96 – NEWCASTLE v CHELSEA (2-2)

I really wanted to go to Wembley, or rather 'Wem-ber-ley' as we would sing (understatement of the season) but, within the space of seven days, two London clubs, Arsenal in the Football League Cup and Chelsea in the FA Cup, put paid once again to my dream, one shared by thousands upon thousands of Geordies also. The pundits immediately jumped on the 'they can concentrate on the League' bandwagon, possibly carrying an element of truth, especially as the January and February snow began to create a fixture backlog for those teams at the top of the League also chasing Cup glory; but it is an argument that has never washed with me. Kevin Keegan I am sure thought likewise. Success in all competitions is the best way to enjoy a season. The great Liverpool side of the late 1970s and early 1980s proved that beyond any doubt.

The first Wembley blow was administered at Highbury on a night when the Arsenal team, two or three individuals in particular (and the Manager for implementing such tactics), were a disgrace to their profession. After Ginola had torn the Arsenal defence to shreds at St. James' Park in the previous weeks' league encounter, Bruce Rioch had clearly told his full backs, Lee Dixon and Nigel Winterburn, to kick, niggle and generally adopt spoiling tactics to stop Ginola playing his normal game. From the outset Ginola's treatment was disgraceful, and even more deplorable was referee Gerald Ashby's inability, or was it a reluctance, to protect Ginola from such tactics. Worse still he proceeded to book Ginola for diving when Winterburn had clearly bundled him over as he surged towards the Arsenal penalty area. The Frenchman was clearly livid and, regrettably, his usually calm temperament snapped midway through the second half when he elbowed Lee Dixon after the full back had yet again illegally impeded his movement. Obviously an action that cannot be condoned but, given the provocation, even I might have snapped! Perhaps it would have been prudent for Keegan to have substituted him at half time, indeed John Beresford later commented that 'his head had gone'. His subsequent three match ban was a blow, but as it transpired, not a devastating one in terms of any failure to pick up points in his absence. As far as the match itself was concerned, who knows what might have happened if a few early yellow or red cards had been brandished in the early part of the game; as it turned out Arsenal did deserve their two goal victory on the night as Newcastle all but gave David Seaman the night off.

It was revealing that at football training the following night, Ginola's shabby treatment was the talking point with the Yorkshire Amateur lads. I normally get a load of stick (the regular dressing room banter) for my allegiances, in good taste I hasten to add, but tonight there was more of a sympathetic air to the usual overtones. So much so that during the end of night game, one of the lads, Tony Palmer, when being aggressively challenged, shouted out in jocular manner 'Dixon's all over me Referee' as if making an appeal to those around him that he was being fouled. An interesting and very significant moment.

Apart from FA Cup football January also equals skiing holiday, and this year the Italian resort of Livigno was the destination for the Ingham brothers, Dave and Ritchie, and myself. The skiing holidays we have had over the years have been remarkable in that on each occasion we have gone the snow conditions have always been perfect and the weather has delivered a full week of cloudless blue sky and warm sunshine. It goes without saying that we had a magnificent time with the only minor downside being a high speed crash I suffered which resulted in a broken thumb. It happened on the fifth morning (out of six days) but didn't prevent me continuing my desire to hurtle down the mountain at breakneck speed. I didn't get the injury treated until a week later, as I hadn't appreciated the seriousness of it, but when the plaster went on for a four week period, it meant the disappointment of not being able to participate in active sport for a month was tempered by the anticipation of being able to watch more matches – things weren't too bad after all. At least I didn't break a leg as one of the unfortunate lads in our hotel did. It wasn't even his fault either, as some lunatic had crashed into him as he was stationary midway down the piste. If you haven't tried skiing I'd certainly recommend it – it's one of the most exhilarating sports you can do and the scenery; well it's breathtaking.

En route to Livigno, from the northern Italian airport of Bergamo (near to Milan), we drove past the picturesque Lake Como. The significance being that it's where Paul Ince had set up home and it occurred to us that we could do Kevin Keegan a favour by stopping off at the Ince residence and agreeing personal terms with him, on behalf of the club, for his transfer to Tyneside. I know he's not the most popular player with many English fans, including those at Newcastle when he was at Manchester United, but what an acquisition he would be. Let's see what the summer brings.

Anyway, being in Italy regrettably meant missing the third round replay against Chelsea at St. James' Park. In the first game at Stamford Bridge we were virtually out of the competition at the first hurdle. Mark Hughes had scored in the first half to give Chelsea a deserved lead but Newcastle's never say die fighting spirit was rewarded deep into injury time when Sir Les struck the equaliser – no one could have anticipated the denouement and it was surely an unmistakable sign that our name was on the Cup. Alas, after sharing four goals back on Tyneside, the dreaded spectre of the penalty shoot-out came to the fore once more, and following on the footsteps of Pecsi Dozsa, Sunderland and Bournemouth, we predictably disappeared once again from a major cup competition through our inability to put the ball in the net enough times from a distance of only 12 yards. I don't know if the record books will show a team worse than Newcastle United at this particular art over the past 25 years – I would be amazed if they did. We got the score from Newcastle that evening through the usual manner, Dad faxing through all the details from home direct to the hotel. When it arrived my attention was drawn first to the top of the page which listed the score as 2-2. Penalties I immediately thought, and it seemed like an eternity before my eyes moved down to the bottom of the sheet and read the words Dad had concluded his report with 'so Chelsea won 4-2 on penalties'. I couldn't believe what I was reading and felt almost numbed by the shock.

Whilst we were in Livigno the Mackems were given nation-wide exposure for a change when Sky Television covered their FA Cup 3rd Round replay against Manchester United at Roker Park the day before the Chelsea game (I suspect the Sky technicians must have had a culture shock when they arrived at the spartan ramshackle debris that purports to be a football stadium). Predictably the Galli Sport bar in Livigno was full of glory seekers and the reaction when Scholes and Cole scored Manchester United's two late goals to take them in to the next round was predictably sickening. I am certain that one girl in particular, celebrating at the final whistle, wouldn't even know where Old Trafford was given that she wasn't paying any attention to the screen at all during the match – a trait sadly typical of many of their followers and the reason genuine football supporters all round the country despise the Reds.

Staying with the Mackems for a moment, and a sad, even funny, story that came out of Wearside in the early part of 1996 which illustrated their paranoia towards the Geordies. Kevin Keegan had been enlisted by the makers of Sugarpuffs to do a commercial for them involving the Honey Monster. It was all a bit of fun to advertise the product, and Keegan was presumably selected because of his charisma and general good guy image. Sunderland people didn't share that view though, and they began a ridiculous and concerted campaign for the people of Wearside to boycott the Sugarpuffs product purely because of the link with their foes along the road. It could only happen in Sunderland!

10/02/96 – MIDDLESBROUGH v NEWCASTLE (1-2)

Back in August it was the inspiration of David Ginola that had condemned Middlesbrough to their first defeat of the season. At the Riverside it was another foreign superstar, Faustino Asprilla, who was the key to another three points. A goal down at the interval, it was the introduction of Asprilla midway through the second half which turned the game on its head. Taking a pass from Peter Beardsley he totally bamboozled Steve Vickers with a Cruyff style turn before planting a perfect cross on to Steve Watson's head. Four minutes later the other £6m man, Les Ferdinand, knocked in the winner and it was just a shame than so few Geordies were able to obtain tickets to see the game and savour such a magical occasion. Asprilla was in the thick of the action for barely 23 minutes, yet the repertoire of skills he displayed, including possibly the best nutmeg you will ever see, served only to whet the appetite for the remainder of the season – and Ginola wasn't even playing!

Incidentally I thought it was hilarious that a Middlesbrough supporter rang David Mellor on *6.06* and asked him to shed some light on their poor run of form. He then went on to say he was asking Mellor's opinion because of his experience and knowledge of the game – Mellor!, who is he tying to kid. Okay, he's a high profile Chelsea supporter (formerly a Fulham fan before realising Chelsea suited his political ambitions better) but a real football fan – I don't think so.

The Asprilla transfer saga had become a very long and drawn out affair once news that Newcastle's £6.7m bid had been accepted by his Italian club Parma. Firstly there were doubts about his fitness, more specifically an old knee injury which a scan had shown up during his medical at the Royal Victoria Infirmary in Newcastle, then over the method of payment of the transfer fee, and finally whether a work permit would be granted given a chequered past history in his native Colombia which included a firearms offence. Needless to say the tabloid press grossly exaggerated all these matters and ended up making Asprilla look like a criminal. To be fair to John Hall, he needed to be sure of every little detail before finally closing the deal, but surely a little more information being given to the supporters wouldn't have gone amiss.

The win also clocked up our sixth away win of the season, incidentally the best away record in the Premier League at the time, which gave no credence to those who were quick to suggest that the only thing keeping us at the top of the league was our home form and that our away record would keep the Championship from coming to Tyneside. Alan Hansen, who I have to admit is my favourite television football pundit (despite the criticism that came his way from Tyneside after the FA Cup draw at Chelsea), keeps harping on about the fact that teams win the League away from home, but to be fair to him, and Gary Lineker, they consistently said all season that Newcastle would lift the Championship – unlike Trevor 'I mean' Brooking who I am sure would rather wish any London side, and preferably West Ham United, to win all the major honours. Incidentally I cannot see the point in having two guests on *Match of the Day* when all we need is Alan Hansen doing the analysis on all the games – he's so good at it and I'd rather listen to his views on everything rather than him being forced to keep quiet whilst Trevor or Gary answer Des's questions. At least that's what we get on the midweek *Sportsnight* programmes. The BBC should employ less people, i.e. the better ones, to do more jobs, rather than many people and spreading them out. Having said that, to be fair to the BBC, the vast majority of their sports presenters, both on television and radio, are first rate performers. A final word of Hansen is that as he has such an astute football brain, Kevin Keegan should employ him as one of his coaches, with particular responsibility for defensive tactics.

Asprilla only flew in to the country four hours before kick off, having left Milan at 5.30 in the morning, so his contribution was even more remarkable. I suppose you always have to ask the question, whenever a top class player on huge wages arrives at your club, do they really care about and understand exactly what it means to wear a black and white shirt? I'm not doubting for one moment that any of Keegan's big money buys lack any commitment to the cause, in fact I'm sure it's something Keegan makes sure of before they put pen to paper.

A combination of factors, including an 89th minute goal by Swindon's Martin Ling, giving his side a 1-0 win over Oldham in a re-arranged FA Cup Fourth Round tie, meant that Southampton's visit to St. James's Park the following weekend was put on ice. It also meant Tino's home debut would be delayed until Monday 4th March when there was another run of the mill game coming up on Tyneside. How the Mackems must have looked on enviously!

Not surprisingly I couldn't keep my eyes off the league tables, and on one particular studious reading session (in the bath needless to say), it crossed my mind that if we only won another seven games, and drew four, out of the remaining 13 matches, it would mean Manchester United needing to win 11 of their last 12 games to overhaul us. Surely we could do that, and what a sobering thought too. Had I known at the time we would fall by the wayside, I might have drowned myself! No, of course I wouldn't, it was only a football competition we were playing in.

Incidentally, whilst we were losing 2-0 to West Ham on 21st February, my local team (!), Leeds United, were entertaining Port Vale in a fifth round FA Cup tie. When I saw the attendance the following morning I thought it was a misprint – 18,000, surely not. As the visitors must have brought in the region of 3,000 with them, that makes their embarrassment even greater. Even if you are struggling in the League, as Leeds were, a crowd as low as that for a fifth round tie is pathetic. Four days later against Birmingham in the League Cup Semi Final, Elland Road was still 5,000 short of capacity. In a nutshell that's the simple difference between the Geordies and the Yorkshiremen, and if you want further conclusive proof here it is. Back in 1981 when Newcastle were going through a rough time in the league (13th in Division Two), an FA Cup fifth round tie with mighty Exeter at St. James' Park predictably filled the ground to its 37,000 capacity. Case closed.

Around this time the local papers on Tyneside were posing a question about where the missing fans were at Roker Park, since their surge towards the top of the Endsleigh League Division One had not brought the full house signs out at Roker. The comments seemed quite justified to me, but obviously the Mackems took offence and they were quick to say that thousands were staying away because the club still lacked real ambition and that nothing had really changed, unlike the situation at Newcastle four seasons ago when Sir John Hall had just taken over at the helm. A fair point maybe, but not a decisive one. If you can't pack in 22,000 each week for a team at the 'top' of the league then Sunderland's days as a big club are surely numbered.

24/02/96 – MANCHESTER CITY v NEWCASTLE (3-3)

Quite a number of talking points to come out of this game, a number of which involved Faustino Asprilla whom I was seeing in the flesh for the first time.

The match itself was a very exciting game, and although we equalised on three separate occasions, it still felt like two points dropped – City after all were in the bottom three. Prince Albert was the undoubted man of the match, despite the fact we leaked three goals, and it's a delight to see him restored to full fitness. The man quite simply oozes class.

Maine Road's new Kippax Stand is pretty impressive too. Last season we were housed in the front section of the Kippax, which was still a building site, but now fully completed, it contained home supporters only (except those in black and white in the Executive Boxes, including Hally who appears to have more contacts these days than Eric Hall). Consequently we were moved into the Claremont Road end behind the goal which turned out to be a pretty reasonable substitute.

The first incident involving Asprilla, an elbow thrust in the direction of Keith Curle's face, took place in the vicinity of the corner flag, away to the right from where I was seated. As a result all I saw was the aftermath which was simply Curle lying on the turf holding his face in apparent pain. Referee Martin Bodenham (criticised earlier in the season for letting the Chelsea/Arsenal fixture at Stamford Bridge turn into a 'kicking affair') appeared to be close enough to the incident to make the appropriate decision but took no action. The second altercation occurred after the final whistle due to the fact that both Asprilla and Curle hadn't heard the whistle and so continued battling away for possession. It looked almost like a wrestling match at one stage before Asprilla made what appeared to be a movement of his head towards Curle. Was it a head butt? Possibly, but I wasn't convinced. Driving back to Leeds after the match, David Mellor's *6.06* was flooded with calls about the incident, some defending the Colombian and others pillorying him. My own judgement would be deferred until a few hours later.

When I saw the highlights later in the evening on *Match of the Day* it was, quite frankly, embarrassing. The worst thing, from a pure footballing point of view, was that the two Asprilla incidents took the shine off what was a marvellous encounter. Manchester City's Georgian midfielder, Georgi Kinkladze, had looked a good player during the afternoon; on television he was even better (if that's possible), and I can now understand why so many City fans have been raving about him all season. But back to Asprilla and I'm still trying to think of a way of defending him, but, like my friend Alan Hansen said, the head butt was maybe blown a little out of proportion but the elbowing of Curle was inexcusable. This is despite the fact that Curle had been niggling away at Asprilla all afternoon (not picked up by the television cameras), in the same manner that he had undermined Andy Cole's 'game' the previous season. Like the Ginola sending off at Highbury the previous month, provocation simply is no excuse for violent retaliation. I was confident however that Kevin Keegan would stamp it out right throughout the club without delay – indeed I am sure he read Asprilla the riot act. Regretfully I fear many Geordies may be blind to Asprilla's misdemeanours, and this is unfortunate to say the least.

Closing the book on the Asprilla incident, wasn't it amazing that it took more than two months for the charge of misconduct, levied against the Colombian by the Football Association, to be heard. The outcome was a one game ban, and a £10,000 fine, which being honest appeared to me as being rather lenient. Curle for his part was cleared of the misconduct charge against him and escaped punishment.

04/03/96 – NEWCASTLE v MANCHESTER UNITED (0-1)

A big game or what, especially as there was an estimated £56 million worth of talent on show, and that was in player purchases only hence didn't include the market value of the likes of Ryan Giggs or Steve Howey. Was this the richest game ever between two British sides? And I could so easily have missed it. It was clear months ago that Sky Television would move the date for this match to either the following Sunday or Monday for live transmission. I was dreading the announcement that it would be the Sunday as that 3rd March date clashed directly with the National Basketball Cup Finals at Sheffield Arena, an event I was promoting myself and in charge of its organisation on the day. The relief was immense when I heard that Sky had chosen Aston Villa's visit to Liverpool for their Sunday game, with the Newcastle match being on the Monday evening. Thank you Vic Wakeling.

Manchester United's win at Bolton the previous weekend, by the small margin of six goals, had cut our lead to four points, although we did still have one game in hand. Similarly, Liverpool's impressive demolition of Aston Villa the previous afternoon, had pushed the Merseyside club into the title equation. Not surprisingly, the media, particularly the southern based pundits, were, not for the first time, beginning to doubt the credentials of Newcastle United being able to sustain the momentum that had lifted the club to the top of the Premiership. Tonight was the perfect opportunity to prove them wrong.

I was in the town before 6.00pm and already it was clear there was something special brewing. I had been looking forward to this game for weeks and I wasn't disappointed. The city centre pubs were heaving and the atmosphere was marvellous. I was in the Strawberry, a stone throw from the back of the Gallowgate End, 45 minutes before kick off, and the noise was incredible. I'm sure such feelings could only exist on Tyneside, and quite simply you had to be there to know what I am talking about.

I had arranged to meet Steve Wraith, Editor of *The Number 9* fanzine in the Strawberry. He's actually nicknamed Vinny (when you see him you'll appreciate why) and I'd describe him as a real salt of the earth lad and as typical a Geordie football follower you could wish to know. His fanzine, run by himself, family, and close friends, may not be as colourful and glossy as some of the others on the market, but the fact that the number of Newcastle fanzines has dropped from eight to four in the past twelve months, and his is one of the four, is testimony to him. From the outset it was never intended to be a money making exercise and has survived as a service to his fellow Geordies for the simple return of a little bit of beer money for him and his mates.

Once inside the ground, as kick off approached, the noise was already immense, something regretfully uncommon in all seater stadiums, even St. James' Park. It was as if we had all been transported back to the terrace culture prevalent only a few years ago, and I for one was loving every moment of it. The players were completing their warm-up, and it was fascinating to watch Asprilla as he went through his own particular stretching routines with a few exceptional ball juggling skills thrown in. As he left the field, he balanced the ball on his head, as if it was stuck on with glue, and I was left mesmerised, shaking my head in amazement at the man's talent. For once, even the more reserved supporters were alive with adrenaline, and the reception that greeted the entry of the teams on to the pitch was truly magnificent. I'm sure the players, from both sides, could not have failed to have been moved by the occasion. Looking around, all parts of the stadium were doing their bit and it felt wonderful. All we needed now was for the players to do the business. An early goal and Vesuvius's greatest moment would have paled into insignificance beside the Gallowgate roar, a mere pop gun in comparison.

From the kick off the black and whites tore into their red shirted opponents and laid siege to Peter Schmeichel's goal. Alas, the big Dane was in inspired form, and a combination of great goalkeeping, and misfortune in front of goal, meant half time arriving with the scoresheet blank. I feared the worst, you have to make your advantage tell when you're on top and the second half turned into a bitterly disappointing spectacle, punctuated by a single goal from Eric Cantona. Andy Cole, who received a favourable reception from the Newcastle supporters, missed a golden opportunity to sew the game up late in the second half, and looked to have lost the penalty box sharpness that helped him make his name on Tyneside. I thought also he could have endeared himself to the crowd a little more on the night. He barely acknowledged us, and it's sad that he seems to fail to appreciate how much he was once loved by the Geordies.

And so the night ended in defeat, the end of our unbeaten, indeed 100% home record, and our lead at the top of the table, 12 points only a few weeks ago, was down to a solitary point.

The lads couldn't be faulted. Batty on his debut was outstanding (doing all the simple things without fuss), Ginola and Asprilla tried everything they knew, and Pavel hardly had a touch all night. Beardsley tried his best as ever, but even he couldn't find that inspirational piece of magic when it was needed most as I struggle to find a reason for the temporary absence of his unique touch and goals. Interestingly enough, an article in the Newcastle *Evening Chronicle*, shortly after Asprilla's signing, carried a story of Beardsley fearing for his place in the team. He'll come through though, I have no doubt of that.

Upon the final whistle I was heartbroken, and for the first time in years simply sat in my seat silent, almost like a zombie, until a good ten minutes after the game had finished. The Manchester United supporters at the Leazes End of the ground managed one chorus of 'We shall not be moved' and that was about it. Pathetic.

The walk back to the North Terrace was a lonely one, despite being surrounded by hundreds of grieving Magpies, the after match drink forsaken, and the drive back to Ponteland with the lads completed in virtual silence.

The following morning I watched the first half on tape, but

couldn't bring myself to watch the second 45 minutes, indeed I doubt if I ever will. I did later see highlights, which included the cameras scanning the ground at the end of the game, picking out supporters in various states of depression, some with their heads held in their hands. It reminded me so much of the occasion Hearts lost the Premier League title in Scotland to Celtic on the last day of the 1985/86 season. On that afternoon Hearts were a mere 10 minutes away from being crowned Champions, and the utter helplessness of their supporters upon the final whistle was a really pitiful sight. You can accept losing matches but losing the most important match of the season at St. James' Park to Manchester United, well that was just too much. Even more annoying was the reaction of people who neither cared or appreciated how we felt. But surely it's only a game of football. I wish!

One thing that surprised me a little about the Sky Sports coverage was that the 'big two', Martin Tyler and Andy Gray, weren't at St. James' Park. Even though they don't generally cover the Monday matches themselves, I thought they would make an exception to the rule. As a result we were left with the regular duo of Rob Hawthorne and Trevor Francis who did a thoroughly competent job other than Hawthorne seriously blotting his copybook with his comment that the atmosphere rivalled that at Murrayfield for the Calcutta Cup match 48 hours earlier. What planet is he living on!

So, one point clear with a game in hand, but a tough run in to come, things were still in our own hands. The doom and gloom merchants were out in force but I wasn't among them. I was convinced the League Championship was still destined for Tyneside, its rightful place, purely because we, the fans, deserve it more than anyone else.

The next two nights I watched the Quarter Final action in the UEFA and European Cups, and the thought of rubbing shoulders with the likes of Real Madrid and Juventus in the Champions League next season was a mouth watering prospect. Nottingham Forest meanwhile suffered a 2-1 reverse in their UEFA Cup Quarter Final tie in Munich and I couldn't believe it when Radio 5 presenter Marcus Buckland described it as a 'great' result. An acceptable result yes, but great, not even close. If Frank Clark had heard him I'm sure he would have put him straight. The second leg was certainly a great result, for Bayern Munich that is! I can't leave Forest without mention of one thing that really made me cringe – the sound of their supporters singing 'Swing Low' (the England Rugby song) in Munich. Honestly, if any Geordie sang that, I'd disown my roots.

As the following weekend was scheduled for the FA Cup Quarter Finals (Leeds packed them into Elland Road again!), we didn't have a game once again so interest turned to the Mackems who demolished Derby at Roker Park. Macas was in the crowd, and he reported to me that although the ground was virtually full to its capacity (about time too), there was 'still space to put deckchairs out on the terraces' such were the vagaries of the Taylor Report in respect of reducing terrace capacities to ridiculously low levels. I spoke to Hally later in the weekend, and his predictable comments were that even if they were promoted to the Premier League, they would come straight back down as they had no ground, no money and no players! Furthermore we would have the pleasure of beating (sorry hammering) them twice during the season.

Back to the FA Cup, and it was interesting to hear that Chelsea were 'flying' their huge flag before the start of their game against Wimbledon at Stamford Bridge. If their flag isn't a safety or fire hazard then why can't we have our flag proudly back on display at St. James' Park again? One rule for one maybe. I also read that fog horn canisters (air horns) were to be banned inside the ground because they were potentially explosive/fire missiles. Whatever next!

18/03/96 – NEWCASTLE v WEST HAM UNITED (3-0)

An important win for a number of reasons, not least the fact that it had been a full two weeks after the Manchester United defeat that we were able to take to the field again. West Ham bore the brunt of our frustration, and the only disappointment was that from an amazing 40 attempts at goal (27 on target), only three ended up in the back of the net. Some supporters were heard to complain we were playing too much football. Ridiculous and ungrateful sentiments towards the sort of football we have craved for in seasons past. Well done by the way to Julian Dicks and Iain Dowie for the acknowledgement they gave their travelling supporters at the end of the match – the Peter Beardsley and Lee Clark of Newcastle if you like, and I'm talking about affinity with their supporters rather than appearances – that's purely a coincidence.

The West Ham fixture, played on a Monday evening, gave me

an opportunity to spend a couple of days at home and enjoy the simple things in life like reading the Newcastle *Journal* and *Evening Chronicle*. One article in the *Journal* saw a ludicrous claim by the Mackem midfielder, Steve Agnew, that Sunderland would, in a couple of years, be a 'bigger' club than Newcastle United, and he was deadly serious! Talking of Sunderland, I watched their match at Birmingham on the *Tyne Tees Match*, the first time I had seen them on television this season as Yorkshire Television give them absolutely no coverage at all (tough luck for any Mackems in Yorkshire). Although they won comfortably, the quality of the match was dire, with the commentary from Roger Tames, and his sidekick David Mills, as riveting as ever. I also took the opportunity of going on a ground tour (at St. James' Park naturally) and many thanks to Eric Jobson for looking after us. It's great value at £3 (£2 for children) and you get to see all the backstage rooms, trophy cabinet (not that it's particularly full), and then walk out of the tunnel onto the pitch – what a thrill. Needless to say a selection of choice photographs were taken for posterity. The pitch incidentally isn't in what I would call top condition. Parts of it near the touchline are more like clay, and it even looks as if it's been painted green, presumably for the benefit of the television cameras. I'm no horticulturist, but it seems to me that it could do with a bit more growth, when I understand it apparently is cut virtually every day. Maybe the groundsman should contact his opposite number at Ewood Park to learn his secret, as they have an absolutely beautiful playing surface, except for Tim Flowers' little hump on the six yard line!

Defeat at Highbury the following Saturday allowed Manchester United to reclaim top spot on goal difference, a lead they stretched to three points by defeating Tottenham the next day, and it was the furthest behind we had ever been in the championship race all season – a nightmare. After the Arsenal game a number of pessimists rang into *6.06* complaining about our 'decline', one mentioned Keegan's supposed lack of tactical awareness, another the poor attitude of the players; but hang on, constructive criticism is always welcome, but this was of the paranoid variety. Perhaps the callers were related to former Liverpool player, Phil Thompson, who said on Sky's *Footballers Football Show*, that Newcastle had defensive problems (when in fact we had conceded only 26 league goals all season at the time the programme was broadcast, the joint best record in the League) and that Liverpool may just tear Newcastle apart when the two teams meet at Anfield. I thought television pundits were supposed to give balanced objective opinions, but this was as biased a viewpoint as I had ever heard.

The main debate was whether the signing of Faustino Asprilla had unbalanced the team, especially as it had meant Keith Gillespie not being in the starting line up. Critics were saying that our early season football, based on Ginola and Gillespie on either wing supplying the bullets for Ferdinand, and Beardsley playing in the 'hole', was our most effective formation. My view? I could understand the arguments, but would always have Asprilla, rather than Gillespie, in the team every time.

At least Les Ferdinand had a good weekend in London. After the Arsenal match many of the players remained in the capital for the annual Professional Footballers Association awards. Sir Les was honoured with the Player of the Year award, and when you win an award voted for by your fellow professionals, it really is the ultimate accolade. David Ginola came third, and Peter Beardsley was also in the top six – a marvellous achievement for the club. A few weeks later, the laconic Eric Cantona, following in the footsteps of Jurgen Klinsmann, picked up the Football Writers Player of the Year award, ahead of Chelsea's Ruud Gullit, and I suppose it confirmed his full integration back into the football world. It's interesting that the players tend to vote for their fellow countrymen, whereas the writers maybe take a broader prospective and plump for the outstanding foreign talent. Cantona's performance in the FA Cup Final, spoilt incidentally by the ridiculous and unnecessary pre-match entertainment, which clinched the 'double' for his team, atoned for his previous unacceptable behaviour. What a shame that a Liverpool 'supporter' saw fit to spit at him when he was making his way up the steps to receive the trophy. As for the match itself, Manchester's victory crucially opened the door for the Football Association to invite Newcastle to take part in the 1996 Charity Shield. The previous week I had sent a fax to Graham Kelly of the Football Association detailing the reasons why Newcastle should be playing in the Charity Shield, should Manchester do the 'double'. I stressed the quality of the team, the fact that the Geordies would sell out Wembley by themselves (hence helping the various charities), but perhaps more importantly, the fact that Newcastle supporters, more than any other supporters in the country, deserved a day trip (it may last more than that for some supporters) to Wembley, even if it was through the 'back door' and not for one of the two major Cup Finals. He obviously listened as our wish was granted!

03/04/96 – LIVERPOOL v NEWCASTLE (4-3)

No points gained in our Championship pursuit, but at least I was privileged to be present to witness a truly memorable footballing occasion. All sorts of superlatives were banded about after the game, no doubt some of them a little over the top, but it really was a special night.

Steve Wraith had got me a ticket for the Centenary Stand (Liverpool's equivalent to the Milburn Stand) and we had arranged to meet at 6.30pm outside the Arkles Pub, a stone throw from the ground. I had arrived in Liverpool at 5.00pm and, as usual, parked up in the Stanley Park Car Park (£2.20 this season talk about spiralling inflation). Anyway, it allowed me plenty of time to wander round the ground and enjoy the atmosphere that was already building up. I started in the main club car park and noticed the Sky TV technicians putting the finishing touches to the setting up of their equipment. Alongside the production trucks was a clapped out old single deck bus which, amazingly, had been converted into a canteen for the Sky presenters, and yes, inside munching away were Richard Keys, Martin Tyler, Andy Gray and Nick Collins. How the mighty live!

A short while later I saw Radio 5 commentator Alan Green outside the main entrance and took the opportunity to have a brief word with him. He may be labelled as a controversial and outspoken commentator, but he genuinely is a nice chap and the best in the business at his job. He was with his wife and son who incidentally was kitted out in a Liverpool shirt.

I met up with Steve and friend Bobby (goalkeeper in Steve's Sunday football team, the Ship Inn) and we managed a couple of pre-match drinks. The atmosphere was very friendly between the two sets of fans which was exactly as I had expected it to be – regrettably you couldn't say the same about everywhere you go in the country. Just before we left for the ground a Scouser came up to us and said 'Just two words to say to you lads, Robbie Fowler.' It only took 97 seconds for his prophetic words to hit home.

The three of us went in through the turnstiles in our black and white gear but once inside were stopped by the police and stewards who insisted that we didn't display our colours inside the stadium, a bit provocative perhaps. Naturally we followed 'orders' and made our way to our seats where despite our hidden colours we still stood out clearly as three fanatical Geordies. The Scousers around us were sociable enough, except for a couple of nutters a few rows back who constantly threatened our welfare, especially when we celebrated our goals in typically exuberant fashion. Indeed, when Bobby ventured to the toilet at half time, the Scouse nutter followed him down to try and pick a fight. Bobby sensibly ignored his taunts and told him where to stick his infantile behaviour. We were here to watch and enjoy a football match, not to indulge in gang warfare. Bobby was also confronted by another Scouser on his half time sojourn, but this time he was congratulated for proudly wearing his colours.

Our seats were in the lower tier of the stand, in line with the penalty spot at the Kop end of the ground, and afforded us a pretty good view. The only complaint was that the seats were so closely packed, both with the people on either side, and those infront and behind, it made life a trifle uncomfortable. A stark comparison to the comforts of the Gallowgate End, and, the obvious reason why Anfield holds 40,000 spectators compared to St. James' 36,500 – packing them in with no consideration for comfort. The Kop will never be the same as it was in days gone by, but it was still a pretty impressive sight, especially when the occupants were waving their flags and banners – something that's a thing of the past at St. James' Park. Perhaps the club could consider doing the same as Manchester United did for their game against Coventry on Easter Monday, and have a 'flag day', or better still a flag season!

Five minutes before kick off, as the announcer finished reading out the teams, the tannoy started playing the Liverpool anthem 'You'll never walk alone'. Even as a Geordie I was moved to watch the reaction of the Kop as they all joined in – a really poignant moment. Generally I am against clubs having to blast out music on the tannoy in order to encourage fan participation, but this was different, and probably the only song and only place in Britain it would work – when they tried it at Wembley before the 1996 FA Cup Final, it was an unmitigated disaster (as was Liverpool's performance against Manchester United, but that was probably something to do with those outrageously distasteful Giorgio Armani cream suits they wore on the day, not to mention John Barnes' white boots).

With the score at 3-3, and only a few minutes remaining, I mentioned to Steve, light-heartedly, that the game was drifting to a draw but perhaps there was still a sting in the tail. Little was I to know that Stan Collymore would seal a famous victory for Liverpool which was perhaps the sort of result the game deserved. As far as we were concerned we upped and left our seats as soon as Collymore's strike hit the back of the net. I was running down towards Stanley Park as the final whistle went and the roar of the crowd, followed by the Liverpool anthem blaring out from 37,000 Scouse throats once again, told its own story.

I mentioned previously the respect I have for the Kop, and in many respects this still holds, for example the marvellous reception they gave Pavel Srnicek at the start of the second half. However, they let themselves down by their moronic booing, and foul mouthed racist abuse, of David Ginola throughout the game. I am sure Eric Cantona was the catalyst for this as Ginola himself has never done anything to earn such disrespect. Thankfully, on the night, he let his football do the talking. On one occasion, at our near side touch line, he nutmegged Jason McAteer with a most delightful piece of skill before being blatantly obstructed by the Liverpool full back and then, much to his consternation, watched in amazement as the referee waved play on. A similar incident, when Faustino Asprilla outwitted Rob Jones on the same touchline in the second half, to keep the ball in play with one of the most outrageous pieces of skill I have ever seen, sadly went unrewarded as the linesman, beaten by the speed and dexterity of Tino, raised his flag to signify the ball had gone out of play when quite clearly it had not. I'm sure he won't be the only official to be 'caught out' by the Colombian.

Was it the game of the decade as many observers wrote? Maybe, football was the real winner on the night and to be honest, that softened the blow of defeat. A couple of days later, Sepp Blatter, FIFA's General Secretary, faxed Kevin Keegan at St. James' Park to commend him on the philosophy he has for the game. I suppose when the governing body of the world game gives you an official stamp of approval you must be doing something right.

The following weekend two Peter Beardsley specials snatched victory from the jaws of defeat against Queen's Park Rangers at St. James' Park. Manchester United beat their near neighbours City for the umpteenth time, despite the fact that rumours (predictable really) were spreading throughout the Gallowgate end, as

Beardsley hammered in his second, that they were losing – if only. With Liverpool, the outsiders in the title race, losing at Coventry, their victory over us at Anfield seemed meaningless.

08/04/96 – BLACKBURN ROVERS v NEWCASTLE (2-1)

Heartache, torture, and, all in all, a footballing tragedy. David Batty's goal 14 minutes from time had sent the Geordie hordes into ecstasy, but then our whole world came tumbling down as two goals (awful goals from a defensive point of view) from Tynesider Graham Fenton broke our hearts. The only people smiling on the night were those at Old Trafford and the sad Mackems who have nothing better to do than look on enviously at a prosperous and successful football club 10 miles up the road.

It was interesting to read an article in the *Daily Telegraph* a couple of days after the game which said that Manchester United's lead (six points at the time of writing) was effectively the result of their two victories over Newcastle. Furthermore, the way both games were settled presented the most significant snapshots of the season. Three times the ball was played into the area allegedly patrolled by Newcastle's left back, and thank you very much said Andy Cole, Roy Keane and then Eric Cantona. Graham Fenton continued in the same theme tonight. The one constant in this equation is of course John Beresford. As a member of the 'full back union' I appreciate the difficulties he found himself in and really would certainly not heap all the blame on his shoulders – defending is a team effort.

Blackburn is only a 45 minute drive from Leeds, and I arrived at the Fernhurst (pub adjacent to the ground which is always commandeered every time the Geordies descend upon Ewood Park) shortly after 5.00pm. Manchester United's game with Coventry had just ended, and their single goal victory had opened up a six point gap at the top of the table – taking three points back to Tyneside was therefore a must. I ventured into the main car park to watch the Newcastle Team Coach arrive and was disappointed to see so few of the staff sign autographs; Steve Watson, Lee Clark and Kevin Keegan being the notable exceptions. I know it may seem a bind to do this as you're trying to get off the bus and into the stadium, but a few minutes isn't too much to ask. I realise all the players sign hundreds of autographs at the training ground, and on the various PR jaunts they undertake, but I still think more effort should be made on match days – as I have already mentioned, visiting teams at St. James' Park are no better.

The team line-up was once again the talking point with most supporters, and it came as no surprise to me that an unchanged eleven was announced. I've already made my feelings clear on this matter, but I must say tonight that Asprilla was a big disappointment, and congratulations to Keegan for bringing him off in the second half – it was just a shame he ran straight down the tunnel after leaving the pitch rather than joining his team-mates on the bench. Gillespie, to his credit, did ever so well again and was heavily involved in Batty's goal. The rest is history. Had we hung on the celebrations would have been sensational. A word also for the fans who made up the chant to counter Sunderland's song about Peter Reid, sang to the tune of 'Day Dream Believer'. I can't repeat the new words that were used in place of the 'Cheer up Peter Reid' line, and indeed other lyrics also, but they went down a treat.

I was home shortly before 11.00pm and watched the last 15 minutes on Sky (no staff canteen tonight for Rob Hawthorne and Trevor Francis) before tuning into *Match of the Day* for the full highlights. After the 'enjoyment' of the highlights it was tremendous to listen to the interviews that Kevin Keegan gave – he really is a credit to his profession, and despite the bitter disappointment he must have been feeling, his magnanimity shone through like a beacon.

17/04/96 – NEWCASTLE v SOUTHAMPTON (1-0)

As the Championship race continued, and with Kevin Keegan having said that he wasn't interested in second place, this was the second of two rather nervy 1-0 home victories – against the team that had done us a massive favour by thumping an off colour Manchester United four days earlier at The Dell. Andy Cole was still receiving a very critical press from much of the country's media, but I'd still welcome him back to St. James' Park with open arms. I saw Kev Fletcher, editor of the fanzine *Talk of the Tyne*, before the game and he told me he had been up at Ibrox the previous Saturday to see Rangers knock five goals past Partick Thistle to all but secure their eighth successive Scottish Premier League Championship. Can you imagine Newcastle doing likewise? No I can't either, and I suppose it is a sad reflection on the overall poor quality of Scottish football. The interesting thing was that when the tannoy announced the result from the Dell, the Rangers supporters cheered loudly clearly demonstrating their hate for Manchester United (who have tenuous links with Celtic) and maybe also their support for Newcastle in their quest to be Champions of their country also.

Aston Villa were first up, and as usual there was a lot of talk about Villa's Geordie connections (Brian Little and Tommy Johnson) putting a spoke in our title hopes, as Graham Fenton had done the previous week. As it turned out, Villa rarely threatened and Tommy Johnson did us all a favour by striking all but one of his shots at least 10 yards wide of the target.

When Johnson had last played on Tyneside, in his Derby County days, he had gone out in the 'Toon' after the game and ended up getting 'nutted'. I heard stories of a similar occurrence on the Sunday night after the Villa game although this time, it was a Newcastle player who was allegedly hit. Apparently a few of the Villa players were down the Bigg Market, and so too was Keith Gillespie. In a moment of madness, Gillespie, it was said, made some derogatory comments to Dwight Yorke and Ugo Ehiogu, and the big Villa defender laid one on him – serves him right is all I can say.

Incidentally, I heard from a very reliable source after the Villa game, that Keith Gillespie, aside from being injured and mildly out of favour with the management, was in hot water with Keegan once again. Earlier in the season the local newspapers had revealed a unfortunate tendency for the Irish winger to bet large amounts of money, mainly on the horses. Indeed it was reported he had run up losses of around £60,000. However, Keegan's wrath was due to the fact that Gillespie had also placed a £10,000 wager on his former club, Manchester United, winning the Premiership back in January when their odds had lengthened considerably after Newcastle had opened up a 12 point lead in the title chase. Foolish or what! It reminded me of the time the two Australian cricketers, Rod Marsh and Dennis Lillee, had bet on an English win at the Headingley Test in 1981, at odds of 500-1, before Botham went to work. A 'no loss' bet I suppose in many ways, but the amount, well that's something else.

During the Villa game, one chap who sits behind me in the Gallowgate End (6'2", all of 18 stone, with tattoos all over his arms, and of course the obligatory black and white shirt) made a comment that one of the players was off side when he took possession of a throw in by the Gallowgate End touch line. Of course any self respecting football fan knows that you cannot be off side from a throw in, so I turned round and told him. He looked at me rather blankly, and then said 'even if he's on the goal line'. Anyway, at the Southampton game an almost identical situation arose when Ginola received the ball right next to the corner quadrant. 'He's off side', came the voice from behind me – I gave up in despair whilst smiling at the lads around me.

The usual rumours were rife around the ground once again. Barton's off to Spurs or Arsenal, Les is going back to London, and Shearer is coming to Newcastle in the summer. How many times have we heard that one. Probably only the first one has any truth to it as Barton has lost his place to the excellent Steve Watson who hopefully has found his best position and will make it his own for years to come. Speaking of full backs, what about John Beresford? Early on in the Villa game he had been given some touchline instructions by Keegan, and amazingly responded by telling Keegan he was talking f****** s***. Needless to say Keegan substituted him almost immediately and brought on Robbie Elliott in his place. Elliott slotted in perfectly, kept his place for the Southampton game, and it may just be the biggest mistake Beresford ever makes in his career.

The following weekend I was back in Leeds and with England playing at Wembley on Wednesday, it meant the Premiership programme was suspended once again to allow Terry Venables the sort of preparation required to get the team into shape for the European Championships. It also led to the slightly absurd situation of their being 15 days of the season left, but Newcastle having to cram their last three games into the final 7 days.

Not being in the north-east also enabled me to miss Tyne Tees Television's presentation of the Sunderland versus Stoke City match (not that I would have watched in anyway) and their promotion celebrations. *The Great Escape*, screened by Yorkshire Television, offered a much more enjoyable alternative. If I didn't know better I might have thought I was tuning in to watch Sunderland's miraculous escape from the Endsleigh League, rather than a World War II film! On the night Sunderland clinched promotion, without kicking a ball incidentally, it is worth noting three of the callers who rang in to speak to David Mellor on *6.06*. The first was a Mackem who quite naturally was in good spirits. The interesting, even commendable, point was that he wished Newcastle all the best in their quest to lift the Premiership title so that the two 'big' north-east teams (note there is no mention of Middlesbrough) could proudly display their Championship trophies together. The second caller was a Geordie who forecast Sunderland's relegation at the end of the 1996/97 season with them struggling to reach 20 points! The last call to mention highlighted the ignorance of David Mellor on even the most simple of football matters, not to mention the caller himself. He questioned the fact that the Mackems were celebrating automatic promotion, when in his opinion, both Derby and Crystal Palace could still catch them. David Mellor began blabbering on about goals scored and similar rubbish, and even tried to change the subject, as he obviously was totally confused, embarrassed, and didn't know what to say next. Fortunately his producer came to the rescue, as he clearly had placed a note on Mellor's desk advising him that as Derby and Crystal Palace had still to play each other, Sunderland's promotion was after all confirmed. Mellor tried to portray the fact that he had known this all along but no, it was patently obvious that he had been given a helping hand. The caller ate humble pie.

I had to smile also at the irate Everton supporter who rang in later in the show. Upset at the deficiencies of his own team, and sick of all the hype surrounding Newcastle, he angrily asked Mellor who the Toon Army were and what that stood for. What was this mystic word 'Toon' which was causing him so much anxiety. Alas the poor Evertonian will never know as Mellor certainly didn't enlighten him.

Sunderland's promotion party consisted of two wonderfully exciting goalless draws against Stoke City and West Bromwich Albion, stark contrast to our 7-1 demolition of Leicester City in identical circumstances back in 1993. The shirt sponsorship, Newcastle's in comparison to Sunderland's, sums it all up nicely. Their Vaux Samson sponsorship equals a second rate beer and consequently a second rate team – across the great divide Newcastle Brown Ale and Newcastle United are light years ahead.

29/04/96 – LEEDS UNITED v NEWCASTLE (0-1)

Yet another Sky game. It was remarkable that out of our 38 Premier League games, 15 were covered live by Sky, 17 were afforded full highlights by the BBC on either *Match of the Day* or *Sportsnight*, leaving only six which were goal highlights only. What a change from years gone by when it used to be a real thrill to be featured on *Match of the Day*, a treat that didn't come our way too often. Throw in the matches in the two Cup competitions that were televised, and it was like being in heaven for all the armchair football fans. Sadly I have to report the worrying attitude of some supporters, and I won't embarrass them by naming them, but they know who they are, who commented to me when I asked them if they had applied for their tickets for Leeds, 'What's the point? It's on Sky.'

The dislike, even hatred, that Leeds United's supporters have for Manchester United is well documented. Paul Lowrey, one of my football colleagues at Yorkshire Amateurs, said to me at training before the game that he hoped Newcastle would stuff Leeds 10-0, and he was being deadly serious too. There's no love lost between the Geordies and Yorkshiremen, but when Manchester United enter the equation, then it's a whole new ball game. Alex Ferguson had already stirred up a hornets nest by suggesting, after his side had defeated Leeds by a solitary goal at Old Trafford on the same night we had beaten Southampton, that the Leeds players had been 'cheating' their manager earlier in the season by producing below par performances. He also insinuated that Leeds would be putting less effort into their game with Newcastle than they had against his side. Interesting to say the least.

As it turned out these comments rose to the surface once again after the game at Elland Road when Kevin Keegan, in as angry and emotional state as I had ever seen him, lambasted Alex Ferguson to the amazement of the watching Sky viewers. Keegan was on the point of completely losing his self control as he said his Manchester United counterpart had gone down in his estimation as a result of his accusations, the title was still there to be fought for, and perhaps even more significantly, said he would 'love it' if Newcastle beat them to the Championship. I don't know if it's relevant here, but I immediately thought of the comment Joe Mercer made, when Peter Swales appointed Malcolm Allison as Manchester City's manager in 1972, rather than himself, that you should never feel animosity, because if you do, you're the one who hurts the most.

And what about the match itself. Nottingham Forest's capitulation at Old Trafford the previous afternoon had done us no favours at all. It meant a win, with a few goals thrown in for good measure, was now imperative. Incidentally I had been working in Coventry on the day of this game, and listened to it on Radio 5 whilst driving up the M1. As I did, a Manchester United fan (!) drove past and gave me a vulgar insult as he passed. One had to wonder why he wasn't at Old Trafford, but there again, that's what supporting Manchester United is all about.

This was like a home game for me, in that the journey to Elland Road was a mere four miles, which certainly was a welcome change. Outside the ground, Geordies were everywhere, but I still managed to bump into Hally who had managed somehow to wangle a business trip north from his Berkshire base to see the match – one suspects it wasn't entirely legitimate business. Like many of the grounds I had been to in recent weeks, Elland Road was no different in that the seats were packed in so closely, a sardine in a tin with his friends could have claimed a breach of the trade descriptions act. Before kick off, I sensed the atmosphere was just a tiny bit deflated, due entirely to Manchester's result 24 hours earlier, and it could have got even worse if Leeds had scored in the first few minutes as Shaka's woodwork was struck twice. Fortunately that was the end of Leeds as an attacking force, and after Keith Gillespie headed us ahead on 17 minutes, the goal that would ultimately win the game, it really was a case of how many we would score. Regretfully no more goals arrived; disappointing, but it was the points that mattered. After Gillespie's goal a dozen or so Newcastle supporters were escorted out of the Main Stand as feelings intensified, probably for their own safety. I reflected back to my own experiences at Anfield at the beginning of the month and could only conclude that Leeds was one of a handful of grounds where such mingling of supporters would be a recipe for violence. At least there were a couple of 'shared' moments when the two sets of supporters sang in unison of their hatred towards Manchester United – 'Who are Manchester United', or words to that effect!. One last word on the match itself concerns the occasion when Asprilla and Gillespie found themselves on different wavelengths, Asprilla passed the ball inside the full back early on in the second half expecting Gillespie to run on to it, Gillespie didn't move forward, but instead pointed to his feet saying that was where he wanted the ball playing. What annoyed me was Asprilla's dissent, maybe it was frustration, towards Gillespie, which does nothing to engender team spirit and quite frankly is unacceptable.

On the way home, all of a ten minute drive, two vans full of joyous Geordies raced past me (and I'm no slouch) with fans in both vehicles hanging out of the windows, virtually on the roof, waving and singing. With the inevitable can of beer in one hand, risking life and limb by their actions seemed to be of no concern at all to them – still, that's not an untypical sight in my experience.

02/05/96 – NOTTINGHAM FOREST v NEWCASTLE (1-1)

Three days later and the Championship chasing juggernaut rolled down to Nottingham. Talk was still rife amongst the travelling supporters about Keegan's attack on Alex Ferguson. Aside from the Leeds matter, the integrity of the Forest captain, Stuart Pearce, was also called into question by Keegan's favourite Scotsman, who questioned the commitment the England defender would show in the league match against Newcastle because the same team would be providing the opposition for his testimonial a week later. Did he really have to stoop so low in the 'game' of psychological warfare he felt it necessary to play? Surely not.

I was down at Trent Bridge at 4.00pm, actually I was hoping to see a bit of cricket, but the rainy weather put paid to that. The Trent Bridge pub, a haven for many an away day in seasons past, was regretfully not allowing away supporters in. The landlord must have been a well off chap as his takings would have gone through the roof had he had the sense to let the Geordies in. Perhaps he feared trouble. If so he was well wide of the mark, and it was left to the Larwood and Voce pub around the other side of the cricket ground to accommodate the hundreds of Geordies who had arrived well in advance of kick off time. I would be interested to know how many of the Tyneside drinkers appreciated the signifi-cance of the name of the pub they were using. If you don't, tough, I'm not going to explain it to you now.

It's nice to see the same old familiar faces on away trips, and as I made my way to the ground, the Sky cameras were doing their usual job of filming the antics of the away supporters as they put on a show for their family and friends at home. The away end at the City Ground is peculiar in that the roof above the top tier doesn't go right along the whole end of the pitch. Apparently it's because a number of local residents objected to it and so consequently the club are left with something of at best an eyesore, and at worst a white elephant. I really do wonder about the mentality of people who object to the grand plans of building majestic looking football stadiums. This situation is in stark contrast to Swansea's Vetch Field ground which has a stand behind one goal which is still incomplete due to a lack of money – a result of their freefall from Division One to Division Four during the early 1980s.

Unlike the feelings I sensed at Elland Road, the atmosphere amongst the supporters was markedly more upbeat; it was as if belief had been restored once more. Inside the ground no one was sitting down, and this remained so for the whole evening – it was simply a case of no one even giving consideration to sitting. I saw Pickie a couple of rows behind me, so as it didn't matter where you were in relation to your numbered seat, I went and stood next to him. A number of fans had brought flags into the ground with them and it was unfortunate that the police saw fit to confiscate the flag poles from two young girls in front of me. What did they think they were going to do with them – use them as spears? No, wave their flags joyously above their heads that's all. If this was to be police policy then why didn't they prevent people outside the ground from selling them in the first place? Anyway, it didn't prevent the raucous atmosphere building up to near hysterical levels as kick off approached as we targeted another crucial three points.

After Peter Beardsley scored a typically superb solo goal to give us a first half lead, it was frustrating beyond belief as numerous other chances went begging. The tension in the away end was unbearable, and I can't recall feeling as nervous and tense at a football match in a long long while. Perhaps inevitably, Ian Woan rocketed a rasping drive past Shaka and a single point was all we picked up. Philippe Albert could have snatched all three points in the dying minutes but agonisingly, in front of the baying Geordies behind the goal, trying to suck the ball in to the net, he didn't strike his shot with sufficient power or accuracy, and Mark Crossley made a routine save. Crossley of course had let in five at Old Trafford the previous weekend, against the team he supported as a boy, not that I'm implying anything, and when he came out for the second half, he joked with the fans behind the goal by holding up four and five fingers – as if to indicate how many goals he might concede in the second half – some chance!

So, two points behind, with an inferior goal difference, and just one game left. It was still anybody's title.

05/05/96 – NEWCASTLE v TOTTENHAM HOTSPUR (1-1)

D-Day in the FA Carling Premiership, but more importantly at St. James' Park and down the road at the Riverside Stadium in Middlesbrough. Relegation battles at Maine Road and Highfield Road were mere bit parts in the overall plot.

Manchester United were most people's favourites, and rightly so, but 35,000 Geordies rolling up to St. James' Park thought otherwise, and the pre-match atmosphere reminded me of the occasion, almost three years to the day, when Leicester arrived on Tyneside as sacrificial lambs to the slaughter. Tottenham though still had a European place on their minds, and would certainly prove a tough nut to crack. I tried to get in to the Strawberry an hour or so before kick off but the queue was 50 deep. Standing outside, the noise inside was incredible, and I watched as a few Tottenham supporters wandered by, their faces expressing amazement at the passion being generated from within the pub. One Londoner I had spoken to earlier in the afternoon in the North Terrace told me he wouldn't mind losing heavily if it meant Manchester United being denied the title, on the assumption of course that their North London rivals were going to beat Bolton and pip them to that last European place. It just shows how the whole country was behind us, including the Manchester public, since it seems only City fans who live in Manchester itself!

The teams emerged to a tumultuous reception and the stage was set – 90 minutes away from glory. But then, not long into the game, news of a Manchester United goal at Middlesbrough permeated through the air and it was like a dagger through the heart of the players (who surely must have heard), and of course the supporters. The first half finished with the scoresheet blank. Into the second half and it was all over, a Tottenham goal and another one for Manchester United, from Andy Cole of all people, ended all hope of the Championship coming to Tyneside. Les Ferdinand did grab an equaliser, and it was lovely that the fans, released from all their nervous tension, could still rise to the team and back them to the hilt in the final 15 minutes. Truly wonderful support.

There was no bitterness as the final whistle sounded, simply a fulsome appreciation to the players who had given their all in the past nine months. A lap of honour ended proceedings and barely a soul left their seats (bar one person who I will come back to in a moment) as we were given a final opportunity to express our love for the one thing more important than virtually anything else in the world – Newcastle United Football Club.

Two more things I must mention before closing, one good, one bad. First the good. Gary Mabbutt. Aside from an outstanding defensive display on the day, his appreciation for the Newcastle supporters as he left the field, the last Tottenham player to so incidentally, was the mark of the ultimate and consummate professional. Remember he did select Newcastle as the opposition for his testimonial at the start of the 1995/96 season.

And now sadly the bad. Remember the big 18 stone chap who sits behind us in the Gallowgate End, the one who doesn't know the offside law, well it turns out he's an ignorant, racist bigot. Shaka made a mess of a clearance, and the racist called him a 'black ****'. The bloke who sits next to us immediately turned round and told him in no uncertain terms to shut his mouth or get out of the ground. The racist took umbrage, forcibly re-emphasised his opinion, and blows were close to being exchanged. Fortunately nothing came of it as everyone else around our section looked on in admiration at the brave stance our friend had taken – not easy when a 18 stone thug is threatening to dismember you. You will recall I said virtually all the supporters stayed for the lap of honour – the racist was nowhere to be seen and that said everything about the type of supporter he is, or hopefully was, as we don't want to see him back at St. James' Park again.

And so to the final analysis. We lost the crunch matches, the ones that really mattered. Manchester United at home, where Cantona scored the most crucial goal of the season, and Blackburn away to name but two. I don't subscribe to the Asprilla theory, the one that blames him for unsettling a winning combination. We just didn't do the business in the last few weeks of the season, dropping out of top gear whilst Manchester United went in to overdrive. The players gave their best shot, but in the end it wasn't good enough – all you can do is pay tribute to the team that finished the season with the most points.

On that evening's *Match of the Day*, Keegan completely scotched the absurd rumours that he might leave the club, as many of the 'cheap' tabloid Sunday newspapers had speculated with headlines like 'Keegan on the Brink' and 'Kev Quit Fear'. Do these journalists really know what they are talking about, or is their sole aim to write utter drivel week after week. Newcastle, along with the other teams at the top of the league, produced a superbly entertaining and memorable Premiership season.

We will never lose our sense of humour and perspective though, and one joke to finish on is that I heard Newcastle Brown Ale will only be available in cans in the New Year – to stop the Geordies losing their bottle after Christmas.

Newcastle United, King Kevin, the Toon Army and all, will be back next season.

1995/96 – Season's Summary

League	P	W	D	L	F	A	Pts.	Pos.
	38	24	6	8	66	37	78	2nd

Top Scorers		
Les Ferdinand	29	
Peter Beardsley	11	
Robert Lee	9	

THE FINAL ACT

It seems appropriate to round things off with a few personal memories and in particular those things I've been able to savour most during my lifetime love of Newcastle United. I have included 20 in each of the five categories and, as befits such listings, they are all in rank order (except for my all time best team which is listed in playing positions) with number one being the best (or worst) memory.

MY BEST NEWCASTLE UNITED TEAM (1969-1996)

An impossible task really, but at the same time it would be a manager's dream to pick a team from all the players who have pulled on the black and white shirt down the years – and even more of a thrill to put your dream eleven out on to the park. I doubt any two supporters would come up with the same team, but that's what football is all about – opinions.

1.	Pavel Srnicek	'Pavel is a Geordie' and now one of the best in the Premier League.
2.	Irving Nattrass	Cultured full back, desperately unfortunate not to win an England cap.
3.	Alan Kennedy	Adventurous, strong and entertaining defender.
4.	Tony Green	Tragically had his career ended by injury but still left an indelible mark.
5.	Bobby Moncur	Captain of Scotland and solid as a rock at the heart of the defence.
6.	Steve Howey	Class personified, capable of becoming a permanent fixture for England.
7.	Kevin Keegan	Genuine superstar, Special 'K' and The Messiah all in one.
8.	Paul Gascoigne	Gazza, irresistible, irresponsible but oozes a unique talent.
9.	Malcolm Macdonald	Supermac, a goalscorer supreme and an adopted Geordie hero.
10.	Peter Beardsley	My favourite all time player – simply irrepressibly brilliant.
11.	David Ginola	The French artist, a magical talent on the ball and a true entertainer.

Substitutes (nine listed, to complete the squad of 20)

12. Mick Mahoney	'Mick Mahoney – Super Goalie' we sang and that said it all.
13. Ray Hudson	Could have achieved great things had he stayed at St. James' Park.
14. Tommy Craig	Possessed a marvellous left foot, highly skilled and competitive too.
15. Andy Cole	Well, he had to be in there didn't he.
16. Robert Lee	Has come of age as a truly quality player.
17. Les Ferdinand	Near enough the all round centre forward, Sir Les to the Geordies.
18. Chris Waddle	A wonderful ball player, a true artist.
19. Jimmy Smith	'Jinky', a throw back to the great Scottish ball players.
20. Philippe Albert	The Prince, quite simply a quality defender.

TOP 20 LOWS

Football wouldn't be football without causing a great deal of heartache. Supporters of teams up and down the country can claim their fair share of disappointments over the years – it just seems to me that the Geordies have had more than most. Although they are not listed, the disasters at Bradford, Heysel and Hillsborough, all three of which I witnessed on television, outweigh any of those occasions listed below.

1. Losing the FA Premiership title to Manchester United at the end of the 1995/96 season.
2. Selling Supermac, Waddle, Beardsley and Gascoigne.
3. Losing to Sunderland in the 1989/90 Play Offs.
4. The 1980/81 season with Shinton/Rafferty et al.
5. The closing down of the Leazes End in March 1978.
6. Jim Pearson missing that penalty against Sunderland on 5th September 1979.
7. Last minute defeats at Liverpool and Blackburn in April 1996.
8. Missing out on going to the 1974 FA Cup Final.
9. Humiliation by Exeter City in the FA Cup on 18th February 1981.

10. Defeat by Hereford United on 5th February 1972.
11. Tony Cottee scoring at Goodison Park after 34 seconds on 27th August 1988.
12. Losing to Everton in the FA Cup on 12th March 1995.
13. St. James'Park *only* having a capacity of 36,500 in 1996.
14. Losing to Wimbledon in the FA Cup on 20th February 1988.
15. Peter Beardsley being injured, at any time, and not being able to play for Newcastle.
16. Losing to Manchester United on 4th March 1996.
17. Defeat in Bilbao in the UEFA Cup on 1st November 1994.
18. West Ham United putting eight goals past us on 21st April 1986.
19. Missing out on playing at St. James' Park with Ponteland United.
20. Penalty shoot out defeats in the FA Cup in 1992 and 1996.

TOP 20 GOALS

It would be possible to actually fill this section with 20 Peter Beardsley goals, such is the quality of his finishing. As it is only five are listed, and these do not include some of the memorable goals he scored during his time on Merseyside.

1. Malcolm Macdonald's second versus Burnley on 30th March 1974.
2. Peter Beardsley versus Brighton on 12th May 1984.
3. Peter Beardsley's second against Aston Villa on 25th February 1995.
4. Malcolm Macdonald versus Leicester on 23rd August 1975.
5. Peter Beardsley's second against Sunderland on 1st January 1985.
6. Alex Mathie versus Sheffield Wednesday on 13th September 1993.
7. Liam O'Brien versus Sunderland on 18th October 1992.
8. Peter Beardsley versus Nottingham Forest on 2nd May 1996.
9. Paul Gascoigne versus Swindon on 30th January 1988.
10. Peter Beardsley versus Portsmouth on 4th February 1984.
11. Malcolm Macdonald's second versus Bolton on 14th February 1976.
12. Andy Cole versus Oldham on 8th November 1993.
13. Les Ferdinand versus Everton on 1st October 1995.

14. Andy Cole versus Aston Villa on 27th April 1994.
15. Malcolm Macdonald versus Leeds United on 23rd September 1972.
16. David Kelly's third versus Leicester on 9th May 1993.
17. Kevin Keegan versus Queen's Park Rangers on 28th August 1982.
18. Faustino Asprilla versus Liverpool on 3rd April 1996.
19. Alan Gowling versus Tottenham Hotspur on 21st January 1976.
20. Tommy Cassidy versus Sunderland on 1st January 1980.

TOP 20 GAMES

There are many games over the years that can be classed as memorable. Some are truly outstanding due to the importance of the occasion or the opposition, and certainly no other sport can take you through so many emotions during 90 minutes.

1. Newcastle v Sunderland on 1st January 1985.
2. Liverpool v Newcastle on 16th April 1994.
3. Liverpool v Newcastle on 3rd April 1996.
4. Grimsby v Newcastle on 4th May 1993.
5. Newcastle v Manchester City in the League Cup Final on 28th February 1976.
6. Athletic Bilbao v Newcastle on 1st November 1994
7. Newcastle v Leicester City on 9th May 1993.
8. Newcastle v Carlisle United on 23rd April 1984.
9. Newcastle v Liverpool on 21st November 1993.
10. Derby County v Newcastle on 20th April 1992.
11. Newcastle v Tottenham in the League Cup semi-final on 21st January 1976.
12. Newcastle v Manchester United on 4th March 1996.
13. Middlesbrough v Newcastle on 7th October 1992.
14. Newcastle v Leeds United on 19th August 1989.
15. Newcastle v Tottenham on 3rd May 1995.
16. Tottenham Hotspur v Newcastle on 18th August 1971.
17. Newcastle v Queen's Park Rangers on 28th August 1982.
18. Newcastle v Aston Villa on 27th April 1994.
19. Newcastle v Sunderland on 27th December 1976.
20. Newcastle v Liverpool on 12th February 1975.

TOP 20 MAGIC MOMENTS

These are the moments in your life when the joy brought about by a simple moment on a football field surpasses virtually any other moment in your life. Life every other Geordie, I long for the day when another goal at Wembley can be re-lived again, only this time in a winning performance.

1. Sharing in the excitement of any Newcastle goal with the lads.
2. Alan Gowling scoring at Wembley on 28th February 1976.
3. Standing on Liverpool's Kop on 16th April 1994.
4. The Andy Cole song during the Leicester promotion celebration on 9th May 1993.
5. Seeing the new St. James' Park in its full glory on 19th August 1995.
6. Beating nine men Sunderland 3-1 on 1st January 1985.
7. Staying up after beating Leicester on 2nd May 1992.
8. David Ginola mesmerising Middlesbrough's Neil Cox on 30th August 1995.
9. Kenny Wharton sitting on the ball against Luton on 24th April 1988.
10. Mirandinha's debut at Norwich City on 1st September 1987.
11. Andy Cole scoring at Grimsby on 4th May 1993.
12. Listening to the whole ground reverberate to the sound of 'The Blaydon Races'.
13. Being in the Anfield Road End during the FA Cup tie against Liverpool on 6th January 1984.
14. The unrivalled atmosphere on the packed terrace at Peterborough on 26th September 1992.
15. Supermac rampaging through Norwich City's defence on 18th October 1975.
16. Andy Cole scoring his record breaking 40th goal against Aston Villa on 27th April 1994.
17. Walking up the Wembley tunnel by myself and then out on to the pitch.
18. Re-signing Peter Beardsley from Everton in the summer of 1993.
19. Surging forward in a mass of heaving bodies in the Leazes End in the 1970s.
20. Faustino Asprilla's touchline 'drag-back' to beat Rob Jones at Liverpool on 3rd April 1996.

OTHER TITLES AVAILABLE FROM KEEPDATE PUBLISHING

NORTHUMBRIA: KINGDOM BY THE SEA
David Bell & M. W. Marshall
ISBN 1-899506-05-5 £19.95

**CLASSIC SALMON FISHINGS OF
THE RIVER TYNE**
Bill Bewick
ISBN 1-899506-15-2 £13.50

THE LIFE CYCLE OF THE ATLANTIC SALMON (poster)
Ginty
£4.95

ON THE RIGS: IMAGES OF A LIFE OFFSHORE
Allan Wright & George Gunn
ISBN 1-899506-00-4 £19.95

**THE ART & SCIENCE OF RACEHORSE
TRAINING: THE 'BILL' MARSHALL GUIDE**
M. W. Marshall
ISBN 0-9520494-9-X £14.95

TALL SHIPS TWO RIVERS
A. Osler & A. Barrow
ISBN 0-9520494-2-2 £18.00

WALKING THE WALL – Tony Hopkins
ISBN 0-9520494-0-6 £12.00

WRECKS & RESCUES – Alison Gale
ISBN 0-9520494-4-9 £4.00

THE TYNE OARSMEN – Peter Dillon
ISBN 0-9520494-3-0 £4.00

CUSHY BUTTERFIELD – Jorge Lulić
ISBN 0-9520494-5-7 £3.50

BLAYDON RACES – Jorge Lulić
ISBN 0-9520494-6-5 £3.50

THE LAMBTON WORM – Jorge Lulić
ISBN 0-9520494-7-3 £3.50

THE BAMBURGH SERPENT – Jorge Lulić
ISBN 0-9520494-8-1 £3.50

To order any of the above, or to obtain further details, contact:

Keepdate Publishing Ltd
21 Portland Terrace
Newcastle upon Tyne
NE2 1QQ
Telephone: (0191) 281 9444
Fax: (0191) 281 3105